A Practitioner's Guide to
THE FSA HANDBOOK

A Practitioner's Guide to
THE FSA HANDBOOK

Consultant Editor
**Andrew Winckler
Ernst & Young LLP**

2001 Edition

City & Financial Publishing

City & Financial Publishing
8 Westminster Court, Hipley Street
Old Woking
Surrey GU22 9LG
United Kingdom
Tel: 01483 720707 Fax: 01483 727928
Web: www.cityandfinancial.com

This book has been compiled from the contributions of the named authors. The views expressed herein do not necessarily reflect the views of their respective firms. Further, since this book is intended as a general guide only, its application to specific situations will depend upon the particular circumstances involved and it should not be relied upon as a substitute for obtaining appropriate professional advice.

This book is current as at 31 August 2001. Whilst all reasonable care has been taken in the preparation of this book, City & Financial Publishing and the authors do not accept responsibility for any errors it may contain or for any loss sustained by any person placing reliance on its contents.

ISBN 1 898830 43 6
© 2001 City & Financial Publishing.

Material from the Handbook of Rules and Guidance or other FSA publications is reproduced with the permission of the FSA and remains the copyright of the FSA.

British Library Cataloguing-in-Publication Data. A catalogue record for this book is available from the British Library.

Printed and bound in Great Britain by Biddles Limited
Guildford and King's Lynn

BIOGRAPHIES

Simon Morris is a Partner with CMS Cameron McKenna. He is experienced in advising and representing institutions in their dealings with the FSA regulators, including over 50 investigations and disciplinary cases. He became a Partner in 1988 and is author of *Financial Services: Regulating Investment Business*. He has since become an advisor to HM Opposition on the FSM Bill.

Andrew Winckler is Chairman of Ernst & Young LLP's Regulatory Practice. He is also the Senior Independent Director of Crestco Ltd and a former Chief Executive of the SIB/FSA, he was also previously Deputy Chairman of the SFA and chaired its enforcement committee. Andrew began his career in HM Treasury and moved to the City in the early 1980s. He joined Lloyds Bank International before becoming a founder Director and Deputy Chairman of European Capital.

George Elwes is a Senior Manager with Ernst & Young LLP dealing with UK Regulatory Practice. He is a regulatory and compliance specialist primarily concerned with the review and development of compliance arrangements within banks arising from new authorisations, mergers, acquisitions or business development. Previously he was Head of Finance and Compliance at the Industrial Bank of Japan Limited London Branch and Financial Controller for the Abu Dhabi Investment Authority.

Guy Morton is Head of the Financial Services Group at Freshfields Bruckhaus Deringer. Specialising in banking and securities regulation, payment systems and trading law, he became a Partner in Freshfields in 1986. He is Chairman of the City of London Law Society Regulatory Sub-Committee, which has been reviewing and commenting on the Financial Services and Markets Bill and the associated regulatory reforms in the UK.

Simon Gleeson joined Allen & Overy in 1998 as a member of the Financial Services Regulatory Team. He is a former stockbroker who has particular expertise in market regulation. He was on secondment to the FSA last year, assisting with preparation of the new market abuse regime in the UK. Among his many publications is *Financial Services Regulation: the New Regime*.

Richard Stones is a member of the City of London Law Society Regulatory Working Party, and of the Securities Institute. Having joined Lovells in 1977 he went on to qualify in 1980, becoming a Partner in 1987. He has also contributed to the *CCH Financial Services Reporter*.

Tamasin Little is a Partner at SJ Berwin. Having become a Legal Associate, seconded to the Bank of England's Legal Risk Review Committee in 1991/2 she went on to become a Partner at Stephenson Harwood from 1992 to 1996. Specialising in financial markets and regulatory matters, in 1999 she was editor of *Bond Markets Law and Regulation*.

Charles Abrams is Head of the Financial Services Group at SJ Berwin. His practice covers all non-retail securities regulation, including EU Directives and other cross-border issues, the marketing of securities and investment funds, the disclosure of interests in shares, insider dealing and market abuse.

Charles is named in *Legal Experts 2001* as a leading lawyer in financial services and in both the *Chambers Guide to the Legal Profession 2000-2001* and the *European Counsel Industry Report on Banking and Finance* (1999) as one of the top five regulatory lawyers in the UK.

Ruth Fox has spent her entire career with Slaughter and May, becoming a Partner in 1986. Her practice has covered a wide range of commercial work, but has focused principally on banking, building society and capital markets transactions. In 1998, she became head of the firm's then newly-established financial regulation group.

John Tattersall is a Partner at PricewaterhouseCoopers and Chairman of its Financial Services Regulatory Consulting Group and also of its Banking and Capital Markets Technical Forum. He is responsible for the firm's relationship with a number of major banks and capital markets institutions and has specialised in that sector since becoming a Partner in 1985. He is a member of the Capital Committee of the Securities and Futures Authority, the Prudential Sourcebook Advisory Group of the Financial Services Authority and also of the Institute of Chartered Accountants in England and Wales Banking Sub-Committee. He was responsible for the firm's publication on the regulation of e-commerce in the financial services sector, *Protect & Survive*; he writes and lectures frequently on regulation.

Alistair Graham qualified at Freshfields 1987, was admitted to the Supreme Court of Hong Kong in 1990, joined Travers Smith Braithwaite in 1991, and was made a Partner 1994. He specialises in heavyweight commercial litigation, and has advised on the *Maxwell*, *BCCI* and *Barings* cases. He is presently on secondment to the Financial Services Authority.

Margaret Chamberlain is a Partner in the City law firm Travers Smith Braithwaite where she is the lead Partner in the firm's Financial Services and Markets group. She is a member of the Counsel of the British Venture Capital Association and Chairman of its Regulatory Committee. She is a contributor to Tolley's Company Law, Chairman of the International Bar Association Sub-Committee Q-4: Regulation of Capital Markets and Securities Exchanges, and is a member of the City of London Law Society Regulatory Sub-Committee.

Philip Mackay is a Partner in the Retail Financial Services Team within the Banking & Finance Group in Dundas & Wilson CS which is a member of the Andersen Legal network. Philip has been with the firm since 1979 and has been a Partner since 1986. Philip specialises in work for insurance and asset management companies, banks and building societies and other financial services institutions (as well as dealing with the legal aspects of all types of retail financial products). Philip is the Head of the Retail Financial Services Team in the Firm and is a member of Andersen's UK Financial Services Leadership Team which is responsible for the strategy and direction of all the professional services provided by Andersens to the financial services industry.

FOREWORD

Howard Davies
Chairman
Financial Services Authority

Building Britain's single new regulatory system has turned out to be something of a marathon, but we have now got the finishing line of N2 well in sight. As we contemplate the finishing line, it is worth reflecting for a moment on why it was necessary to undergo the long foot slog in the first place.

Essentially it was because London's financial markets had moved on and the old sector-based regulatory system was no longer fit for purpose. The divisions between the regulation of banks, insurance companies, securities firms, investment managers etc. no longer reflected the way the UK's financial sector was organised, with mergers and integration creating ever more multi-purpose conglomerates. Under the old regime these financial supermarkets had to seek authorisation from sometimes half a dozen different regulators, each with different requirements and rulebooks. Furthermore, none of the regulatory bodies was able to look at a complex financial group as a whole, and the interactions between the different types of risk it took on.

So the Chancellor's announcement in May 1997 of a new single regulator was widely welcomed in the financial services industry. Consumer groups were enthusiastic too. They saw the prospect of better protection for savers and investors. The creation of a single Handbook of rules and guidance, applying to all authorised firms and individuals and replacing the dozen or so rulebooks operated by the predecessor regulators, is one of the major gains of the whole process. The Handbook is now in final form for N2, thanks in part to the firms, trade associations and consumer groups who have put considerable time and effort into the consultation process. This has been vital in creating a Handbook which sets out in a coherent and sensible way a set of requirements that the industry largely accepts and is already familiar with through consultation.

The Handbook is available on CD-ROM, although we are also making it available in paper format. It is accessible from the FSA website (www.fsa.gov.uk) and regular updates and bulletins will be posted there. User-friendly navigation tools will allow people to identify those parts that are important to them. Once the Handbook is up and running we will keep the dialogue going with practitioners about how to make it even more useable. And we will, of course, continue to consult widely on future changes to the Handbook's content as it evolves in response to developments in the financial services market place.

The creation of a single regulator has also given us a unique opportunity to develop a radical new risk-based approach to regulation which will enable us over time to regulate in a sharper more effective and economical way to the benefit of both firms and their consumers. We explained how we intend to achieve this in January 2000 in a grandly-entitled paper *A New Regulator for the New Millennium*. The new regime is founded on a clear statement of the realistic aims and limits of regulation, and will recognise both the proper responsibilities of consumers themselves and of firms' own management, and the impossibility and undesirability of removing all risk and failure from the financial system.

The starting point in determining our new strategy is the statutory objectives we have been given by the Financial Services and Markets Act 2000: market confidence, consumer protection, consumer understanding and reducing financial crime. For us the basic question is; what developments, events or issues pose a significant risk to these objectives? And how should we allocate our resources to focus on the risks that matter most?

Over the last year, we have increased our understanding of the risks to our objectives and their source; developed an integrated risk-assessment framework and prioritised risks according to their potential impact if they materialised and the probability of this happening; drawn up risks profiles of all firms and allocated firms accordingly to a range of regulatory categories which will determine the future nature and intensity of our relationship with them; and categorised the wide range of regulatory tools at our disposal. These are diagnostic tools (designed to identify, assess and measure risks), monitoring tools (designed to track the development of identified risks), preventative tools (to limit or reduce identified risks) and remedial tools (to respond to risks when they have crystallised).

The reaction to our new regulatory approach from the industry has been positive. In particular, firms have welcomed our undertaking that the nature and intensity of the relationship between the FSA and an institution will be related to the degree of risk that it might pose to our statutory objectives. But although low-risk institutions may have a less intense relationship with us than they had with their regulators in the past, this does not, of course, absolve them from the need to meet the rules and requirements set out in the Handbook. So it is important that firms remain familiar with its contents. This Practitioner's Guide should help them to do so.

I welcome its publication.

CONTENTS

Chapter 1
THE ROLE AND STATUTORY POWERS OF THE FINANCIAL SERVICES AUTHORITY **1**
Simon Morris
Partner
CMS Cameron McKenna

Chapter 2
THE FSA'S HIGH LEVEL PRINCIPLES . . .39

Andrew Winckler
Chairman, Regulatory Practice, Financial Services
George Elwes
Senior Manager, Regulatory Practice
Ernst & Young LLP

Chapter 3
THE APPROVED PERSONS REGIME, TRAINING AND COMPETENCE 71
Guy Morton
Partner
Freshfields Bruckhaus Deringer

Chapter 4
PRUDENTIAL REGULATION UNDER THE FINANCIAL SERVICES AND MARKETS ACT 2000 . . . .**119**
Simon Gleeson
Partner
Allen & Overy

Chapter 5
CONDUCT OF BUSINESS 155
Richard Stones
Partner and Head of the Financial Services Group
Lovells

Chapter 6
THE INTER-PROFESSIONAL CONDUCT 229

Tamasin Little
Partner, Financial Services Group
SJ Berwin

Chapter 7
MARKET CONDUCT AND THE MARKET ABUSE REGIME 279

Tamasin Little
Partner, Financial Services Group
Charles Abrams
Partner
SJ Berwin

Chapter 8
MONEY LAUNDERING 333
Ruth Fox
Partner
Slaughter and May

Chapter 9
AUTHORISATION AND SUPERVISION
PROCESSES 359

John Tattersall
Partner
PricewaterhouseCoopers

Chapter 10
DISCIPLINE AND ENFORCEMENT 409
Alistair Graham
Partner
Margaret Chamberlain
Partner
Travers Smith Braithwaite

Chapter 11
CONSUMER RELATIONS: COMPLAINTS AND COMPENSATION 469

Philip Mackay
Partner
Dundas & Wilson CS

Chapter 1

THE ROLE AND STATUTORY POWERS OF THE FINANCIAL SERVICES AUTHORITY

Simon Morris
Partner
CMS Cameron McKenna

1.1   Introduction

This Chapter reviews the role and powers of the Financial Services Authority (the "FSA"). The FSA will not assume its main powers under the Financial Services and Markets Act 2000 (the "FSMA") until 1 December 2001, so while the scope of its powers may be deduced from the FSMA, the manner of their performance must be surmised from the FSA's extensive consultative papers and other statements of policy rather than from practical experience. Nonetheless, the likely tenor of the FSA's regulation is clear enough from this voluminous material, and a number of features are apparent:

(a) the FSA possesses extensive powers;

(b) the FSA is placed under express duties as to how these powers are to be exercised;

(c) the FSA has consulted extensively on the formulation of its rules and procedures;

(d) the FSA is held accountable by a number of means to Parliament, the industry, investors and to the Courts.

Taken together, it appears that while the FSA may be a powerful leviathan, it is in fact required to operate within clear constraints. Furthermore, the extensive consultation exercise undertaken to determine its rules, and the detailed explanations of its intended operating procedures which the FSA has published, together indicate that the FSA should operate in a clear and transparent manner.

This Chapter examines in turn:

(a) the constitution of the FSA (*see* Section 1.2 below);

(b) the duties of the FSA (*see* Section 1.3 below);

(c) the powers of the FSA (*see* Section 1.4 below);

(d) the accountability of the FSA (*see* Section 1.5 below).

1.2   Constitution of the Financial Services Authority

1.2.1   Name and status

The FSA is the new name for the former Securities and Investments Board, which was renamed thus in October 1997. It is a company limited by guarantee and authorised, for the time being, to omit the word "Limited" from its name (Schedule 1 14, 15). It has functions conferred upon it by the FSMA (Section 1(1)) and Schedule 1 provides for a number of requirements with which its constitution must comply (Section 1(2)).

1.2.2   Exemption from liability in damages

The FSMA provides that the FSA is not acting on behalf of the Crown and its members, officers and staff are not crown servants (Schedule 1 13).

It is therefore necessary to exempt both the FSA and its members, officers and servants from liability in damages (Schedule 1 19), although this does not extend to protecting the FSA from an action for injunction or judicial review. This exemption from liability extends to damages for anything done or omitted in discharging or purported discharge of the FSA's functions, subject to two qualifications:

(a) if the act or omission is in "bad faith" (Schedule 1 19 (3)(a)). Bad faith is used here in a "Wednesbury" sense (*Associated Provincial Picture Houses Ltd v. Wednesbury Corp* [1948] 1 KB 233) and means an act or omission which no reasonable regulator would make. This therefore imposes a high requirement upon a claimant to demonstrate that the FSA's action is outside the spectrum of action that competent regulator would take;

(b) if the act or omission is unlawful under Section 6(1) Human Rights Act 1998 (Schedule 1 19(3)(b)). This provides that it is unlawful for a public authority to act in a way which is incompatible with a Convention Right. In this context, relevant Convention Rights are likely to be those contained in Article 6 – a fair hearing which includes the right to an impartial and independent tribunal; Article 8 – right to privacy; and Article 10 – freedom of expression subject to restrictions as prescribed by law. Article 10 extends to individual expression and commercial speech and advertising.

1.2.3   *Governing body – appointment*

The FSA's constitution is required to provide for a chairman and a governing body who are appointed, and liable to removal from office, by the Treasury (Schedule 1(2)(3)).

1.2.4   *Chairman*

The chairman of the FSA is an executive appointment; in other words, he is currently employed as chief executive as well as appointed to act as chairman of the governing body, although the two roles do not necessarily go together. An arrangement of this kind is no longer considered good practice in listed companies – *see* the Greenbury Committee Report 17 July 1995 – and drew adverse comment during the Parliamentary passage of the Bill; for example:

> "Many of those in the financial services industry are worried about the authority's overriding powers, and they will be even more worried if those powers are seen to be largely under the control of a single person,

> however good he or she may be at the job. Accountability is not helped by concentrating so much power in the hands of one individual." [Standing Committee A 8 July 1999 col 24 Mr Loughton].

> "The reason for the Government's reluctance to contemplate splitting the roles of chairman and chief executive at the top of FSA and what is so puzzling to practitioners in the industry is that the FSA is the body which supervises the very companies which themselves are obliged to supervise the application of the combined code to their clients. So reasonable people are mystified as to why the rules of governance that they are expected to apply to their clients should not be applied to the body that regulates them." [HL Hansard 13 April 2000 col 298 Lord Saatchi].

However, the response was clear:

> "The case for maintaining authority in one person is based on the fact that the authority will have to make rapid and important decisions. When it does, it is vital that people know who has the authority to take them. Splitting the authority at the top will allow infinite scope for lobbying two separate people, and those two people may be in two different places when a crises arises." [Standing Committee A 8 July 1999 col 29 Mr Nigel Beard].

The combined role is contrary to general principles of good corporate governance (*see* Section 1.2.6 below) but the last minute concession permitting the FSA to apply only those principles which are "reasonble", enabled the FSA to proceed as planned with the combined role.

1.2.5 Governing body

The FSA is required to secure that the majority of the members of its governing body are non-executive (Schedule 3 (1)(a)). Non-executive members serve in their personal capacity and currently include:

(a) the Deputy Governor (Financial Stability, Bank of England);

(b) the Vice Chairman, National Consumer Council;

(c) the Chief Executive, Bradford & Bingley Building Society;

(d) the Reader in Government, Queen Mary & Westfield College, London;

(e) the Chairman, West Midlands Region NHS Executive;

(f) the Group Chief Executive, HSBC Holdings plc.

Membership of the governing body also includes three Executive Directors who currently are:

(a) Managing Director, Consumer, Investment and Insurance Directorate;

(b) Managing Director, Deposit Takers and Markets Directorate; and

(c) Managing Director, Regulatory Processes and Risk Directorate.

1.2.6   *Non-executive committee*

The FSA must also secure that a committee comprising solely non-executive members of the governing body, chaired by one of their number appointed by the Treasury, is maintained to discharge prescribed functions (Schedule 1 3(1)(b), (3)). They are (in summary) to review:

(a) whether the FSA is acting in the most efficient and economical way in using its resources in discharging its functions in accordance with the decisions of the governing body (Schedule 1 4 (3)(a));

(b) whether the FSA's internal financial controls secure the proper conduct of its financial affairs (Schedule 1 4 (3)(b)); and

(c) to determine the remuneration of the governing body's chairman and executive members (Schedule 1 4 (3)(c)).

These three non-executive functions are described as functions of the FSA (Schedule 1 4(2)). The functions relating to financial controls ((b)) and remuneration ((c)) are analogous to those performed by a commercial company's audit and remuneration committees and may, indeed, be performed by subcommittees of the non-executive committee (Schedule 1 4 (4)). Any such subcommittee must be chaired by the chairman of the committee, but may include non-members (Schedule 1 4(5)).

The non-executive committee must include in the FSA's annual report to the Treasury a report on the discharge of its functions, covering the same period as the FSA's own report (Schedule 1 4(6), (7)).

The non-executive committee is thus empowered to act as a scrutineer of the FSA's efficiency, and as the basis of an audit and remuneration committee function. These are not stated to be its exclusive functions, and no constraint is imposed upon the role of the non-executive committee. Nonetheless, it is interesting to note that the stated remit of the committee does not extend to any of the customary functions of persons in the position of non-executive directors, such as:

(a) holding the chief executive to account;

(b) examining the activities of senior officers;

(c) scrutinising the formation of policy and its implementation.

The FSA is, however, required to have regard to "such generally accepted principles of good corporate governance as it is reasonable to regard as applicable to it" in managing its affairs (Section 7), presumably in order to command respect in the industry which it regulates. However the FSA's particular circumstances as a statutory regulator without shareholders necessarily limit the application of these principles, although the following are likely to be relevant to the FSA managing its affairs, and to which the FSA should therefore have regard. The "generally accepted principles of good corporate governance" are likely, for the present, to include *The Combined Code Principles of Good Corporate Governance and Code of Best Practice* which are, in summary, as follows:

(a) *Board of directors* – the board should meet regularly, and retain full and effective control over the company and monitor the executive management. There should be a clearly accepted division of responsibilities at the head of a company, which will ensure a balance of power and authority, such that no one individual has unfettered powers of decision. A decision to combine the posts of chairman and chief executive in one person should be publicly justified. The board should include non-executive directors of sufficient calibre and number for their views to carry significant weight in the board's decisions. There should be an agreed procedure for directors in the furtherance of their duties to take independent professional advice if necessary, at the company's expense.

(b) *Non-executive directors* – non-executive directors should bring an independent judgement to bear on issues of strategy, performance, resources, including key appointments, and standards of conduct. The majority should be independent of management and free from any business or other relationship which could materially interfere with the exercise of their independent judgement apart from their fees and shareholding. Their fees should reflect the time which they commit to the company. Non-executive directors should be selected through a formal process and both this process and their appointment should be a matter for the board as a whole.

(c) *Executive directors* – there should be full and clear disclosure of directors' total emoluments and those of the chairman and highest paid UK director, including pension contributions and stock options. Separate figures should be given for salary and performance-related elements and the basis on which performance is measured should be explained.

(d) *Reporting and controls* – the directors should review and report on the effectiveness of the company's system of internal control.

1.2.7   Functions of the governing body

The FSA must act through its governing body when exercising its legislative functions (Schedule 1 5(2)). These functions include the implementation of key policy areas whereby the FSA defines, in the form of rules, the standards which firms must observe on a day-to-day basis, and establishes its criteria for bringing disciplinary action where they are infringed. The concept of acting "through" its governing body is not defined, but it is clear that when making the first rules (or equivalent), or making amendments to them, the draft should be laid before, and approved by, the governing body.

The legislative functions are defined by Schedule 1(2):

(a) making rules, which includes conduct of business and other rules;

(b) issuing codes of practice in relation to statements of principle for approved persons (Section 64(2)) and in relation to whether behaviour amounts to market abuse (Section 119(1)). These are particularly significant because they may be relied upon as tending to establish conformity with the principle (Section 64(7)), or that certain behaviour is not market abuse (Section 122);

(c) issuing:

    (i) statements of principle in respect of conduct of approved persons (Section 64), breach of which renders an individual liable to disciplinary action (Section 66);

    (ii) a statement of policy on the imposition and amount of penalties under Section 66 (FSA's disciplinary powers against approved persons) (*see*), and under Section 124 (FSA's disciplinary powers in respect of market abuse) and Section 210 (general disciplinary powers);

(d) making directions to extend the FSMA to the activity of Lloyd's underwriting (Section 316); to the Council of Lloyd's or Lloyd's in relation to the exercise of their powers (Section 318). The FSA may also give directions to disapply the exemption from the general prohibition otherwise applicable to members of a profession (Section 328);

(e) issuing general guidance under Section 157, which is guidance given by the FSA to persons, or class of persons generally, in legible form and which is intended to have continuing effect.

1.2.8 Delegation

The FSA may make arrangements for any of its functions which are not legislative functions (as discussed above) or non-executive functions (Schedule 1 5(3)) to be discharged by any committee, subcommittee, officer or member of staff (Schedule 1 5(1)). Examples of such functions will include:

(a) grant of authorisation, to be performed by an appropriate officer;

(b) proposals to take disciplinary action, or to refuse authorisation, to be performed by the Regulatory Decisions Committee.

1.2.9 Monitoring and enforcement

The FSA is expressly required to maintain arrangements for:

(a) determining whether persons are complying with the FSMA's requirements (Schedule 1 6 (1));

(b) enforcing the FSMA's provisions (Schedule 1 6 (3)).

The FSA is permitted to delegate its monitoring functions to anyone whom it considers competent to perform them (Schedule 1 6 (2)).

The FSA has described in detail how it intends to perform its monitoring functions in the Supervision Manual.

1.2.10 Records

The FSA must make arrangements for:

(a) recording decisions made in the exercise of its functions, for example of the governing body, or in admitting firms;

(b) safekeeping of those records which it considers ought to be preserved (Schedule 1 9).

This contrasts with the strict record-keeping obligations imposed on firms.

1.2.11   Penalties

The FSA may not take into account expenses which it incurs in discharging its functions in determining its policy on penalties. Instead, it must ensure that incomes which it receives from penalties is applied for the benefit of authorised persons. The FSA must consult on such arrangements. However, while the FSA may not take account of penalty income in fixing any particular fee (Schedule 1 16, 17(2)), the FSA's proposal is to use penalty income to reduce its fees generally (CP79 December 2000).

1.2.12   Fees

The FSA may make rules for charging fees in connection with the performance of its functions (Schedule 1(17)) other than in relation to:

(a) applications for passporting in and out under Schedule 3;

(b) successful applications for individual approval under Section 59 (Schedule 1 18).

The FSA may charge such fees in order to meet its expenses, repay loans and maintain adequate reserves (Schedule 1 17). The FSA may recover fees owed as a debt (Schedule 1 17(4)).

1.3   Duties of the Financial Services Authority

1.3.1   Introduction

The duties of the FSA, and the standard to which they should be performed, are contained in Sections 2 – 6 FSMA which are headed *The Authority's general duties*, although the words "general duties" do not appear other than in Section 8.

The duties of the FSA are expressed in a somewhat convoluted fashion, but can be summarised thus:

(a) the FSA has four general functions (Section 2(4)(a) – (d));

(b) in discharging these general functions, the FSA must act compatibly with the regulatory objectives (Section 2(1));

(c) there are four regulatory objectives, listed at Section 2(2) and then each elaborated upon in an individual Section (Sections 3 – 6);

(d) the FSA must also, in discharging the general functions, have regard to seven additional requirements (Section 2(3)(a) – (g)).

We now consider each of these elements in turn.

1.3.2   *Financial Services Authority's general functions*

The FSA is stated to have four general functions:

(a) *making rules* (Section 2(4)(a)). These powers (which includes issuing standards of principle and codes of practice (Section 64(11)) are contained in Part X (Sections 138 – 156).

(b) *preparing and issuing codes* (Section 2(4)(b)). This power is contained in Sections 64 (code for approved persons' conduct) and 119 (code giving guidance on market abuse) which are discussed in Chapter 3 and 7 of this Guide respectively;

(c) *giving general guidance* (Section 2(4)(C)). "General guidance" is defined as above. This power is contained in Sections 157 – 8;

(d) *determining the general policy and principles by relation to which it performs its particular functions* (Section 2(4)(d)). These presumably include both policies expressly referred to in the FSMA, such as on penalties against approved persons in Section 69, and its other general policies.

It will be noted that the general functions are only concerned with establishing policy and making rules, codes and guidance. Furthermore the first three general functions, of making rules, preparing and issuing codes and giving general guidance, are stated to be "considered as a whole".

When discharging the general functions, the FSA is required to act compatibly with the regulatory objectives and to have regard to the seven additional factors. However, it is clear from the wording of Section 2(4) that this duty does not extend to:

(a) the making of any particular rule or provision within a Code or Guidance, since they are to be considered "as a whole";

(b) any operational matter, such as refusal to authorise a firm or an individual, or the performance of monitoring or taking of disciplinary action, since the application of the general functions are restricted to determining general policy and making rules, codes and guidance.

By way of example, the FSA could refuse to authorise a firm planning to revolutionise banking because of its failure to meet threshold conditions, even though authorisation of the firm might act to promote additional innovation and competition in the banking sector.

1.3.3 *Duty to act compatibly with the regulatory objectives*

Section 2(1) provides as follows:

> "In discharging its general functions the Authority must, so far as is reasonably possible, act in a way –

(a) which is compatible with the regulatory objectives; and

(b) which the Authority considers most appropriate for the purpose of meeting those objectives."

The general functions are, as noted in the previous section, of restricted application, and this Section falls short of imposing strict compliance with the regulatory objectives upon the FSA in three particulars:

(a) the FSA need only, *so far as reasonably possible,* act in accordance with the regulatory objectives;

(b) the FSA should act in a way *compatible* with the regulatory objectives;

(c) the FSA should act in a way *which it considers most appropriate* for the purpose of meeting these objectives.

In other words, it is for the FSA to determine the most appropriate way of acting compatibly with the regulatory objectives and then, so far as reasonably possible, to act in that way.

1.3.4   *The regulatory objectives*

There are four regulatory objectives, and we consider each in turn. The following descriptions of how the FSA views the four regulatory objectives, and the steps which it has taken to implement them, are taken from the documents entitled *A New Regulator for the New Millennium* (January 2000) and *A Short Guide to our Preparations* for *the New Regulatory Regime* (January 2000). Taken together, and including more recent developments, they form a clear statement of the FSA's stance.

1.3.5   *The market confidence objective*

The market confidence objective is to maintain confidence in the financial system (Section 3). The "financial system" is stated to mean that operating in the UK and is defined to include:

(a) financial markets and exchanges;

(b) regulated activities – a regulated activity is defined by Section 22 to mean, in effect, an activity specified in the FSMA (Regulated Activities) Order 2001 carried on by way of business, as determined by a Treasury Order (Section 419);

(c) other activities connected with financial markets and exchanges.

The FSA views market confidence as fundamental to a successful financial system in order to ensure participants and users are willing to trade on financial markets and to use the services of financial institutions. The FSA will seek to maintain market confidence by preserving actual stability, and reasonable expectations that the system will remain stable. It will do this through preventing material damage to the soundness of the UK financial system caused by conduct of, or collapse of, firms, markets or financial infrastructures.

The FSA's purpose is to maintain a regime which ensures as low an incidence of failure of regulated firms and markets as is consistent with maintaining market competitiveness and innovation. Under its public awareness objective (*see* below) the FSA will seek to explain what a regulator can and cannot achieve in preventing market failures. The FSA recognises that a zero failure regime is impracticable in the light of inherently volatile financial markets, and would in any case be unduly burdensome and stifling of innovation. It would also detract from the responsibility of firm's management and customers' responsibility for their own actions.

Action which the FSA states that it has taken so far in order to achieve the market confidence objective include the following, listed in the FSA's Annual Report for 1999/2000 as achievements towards market confidence:

(a) "a number of projects relating to the pensions review, encompassing work on improving some of the materials used to help consumers understand and gain access to the review, and an evaluation of the effectiveness of the FSA's national advertising campaign;

(b) a series of studies supporting the development of "decision-trees" – step by step flowcharts – that will be used to help consumers determine whether or not a stakeholder pension will be appropriate for them;

(c) diagnostic work to enable us to improve the effectiveness of consumer literature;

(d) other projects ranging from purchasing of high-yield investment bonds to consumer awareness of compensation arrangements and consumer experience of complaint-handling processes."

1.3.6 *The public awareness objective*

The public awareness objective is to promote public understanding of the financial system (Section 4). "Financial system" has the same meaning as in Section 3. The public awareness objective is stated to include:

(a) promoting awareness of the benefits and risks associated with different kinds of investment or other financial dealing;

(b) the provision of appropriate information and advice.

The FSA states that the reason for the public awareness objective is that many consumers to not understand the financial system, its products or services and how they relate to their financial needs. The FSA therefore intends to improve general financial literacy by promoting financial education and by other means, and to improve generic information and advice available so that the public has a better understanding of the risks and opportunities involved in investment markets. Steps which the FSA states that it has taken so far include the following, set out in the FSA's Annual Report 1999/2000 as initiatives towards raising public awareness:

(a) "issuing 12 new consumer guides and factsheets, and four updated titles;

(b) including a consumer help website;

(c) further developing the consumer helpline service;

(d) successfully influencing the development of the National Curriculum to ensure that personal finance education is delivered in schools;

(e) continuing its consumer research and consumer policy work, particularly in retail markets, and undertaking analysis for a number of high profile projects such as stakeholder pensions, endowments and mortgages;

(f) progressing with the establishment of the new Financial Ombudsman Service and the Financial Services Compensation Scheme."

1.3.7 *The protection of consumers objective*

The protection of consumers objective is to secure the appropriate degree of protection for consumers (Section 5).

"Consumers" is given a wide definition. It comprises persons who are consumers under Section 138 (7)-(9), which is:

(7) "persons –

(a) who use, have used, or are or may be contemplating using, any of the services provided by –

> (i) authorised persons in carrying on regulated activities; or
>
> (ii) persons acting as appointed representatives;
>
> (b) who have rights or interests which may be adversely affected by the use of any such services by persons acting on their behalf of in a fiduciary capacity in relation to them.

(8) If an authorised person is carrying on a regulated activity in his capacity as a trustee, the persons who are, have been or may be beneficiaries of the trust are to be treated as persons who use, have used or are or may be contemplating using services provided by the authorised person in his carrying on of that activity.

(9) For the purposes of Subsection (7) a person who deals with an authorised person in the course of the authorised person's carrying on of a regulated activity is to be treated as using services provided by the authorised person in carrying on these activities."

and also, under Section 5(3)(b) persons:

> "who, in relation to regulated activities carried on otherwise than by authorised persons, would be consumers for those purposes if the activities were carried on by authorised persons."

The objective is to secure the *appropriate* degree of protection for consumers and, in considering what degree of protection may be appropriate, the FSA is required to have regard to four specific factors which are:

> "5(2)   ...

(a) the differing degrees of risk involved in different kinds of investment or other transaction;

(b) the differing degrees of experience and expertise that different consumers may have in relation to different kinds of regulated activity;

(c) the needs that consumers may have for advice and accurate information; and

(d) the general principle that consumers should take responsibility for their decisions."

Taken together, these factors highlight the key issues in achieving investor protection. The first is that neither investments nor investors are homogenous. In recognising that different investments involve differing degrees of risk, and that consumers have different degrees of experience, the FSA acknowledges that there can be no single approach.

Secondly, that the provision of advice and information is the key tool in achieving investor protection; indeed, the FSA attaches great importance to the training and control of advisers and to the disclosure of information to retail customers at point of sale.

Thirdly, that investors should in general take responsibility for their own decisions; the FSA recognises that its duty is to help to provide a clean market for risk investment and not to eliminate the risk itself. The implementation of this principle is, though, dependent upon fulfilment of the proceeding criteria: all investors, whether professional or private, require adequate information, while others may seek advice on the merits of their entering into a transaction. The extent of the advice and information they require will in turn depend upon the risk involved in the particular investment, and their own experience.

The FSA views the protection of consumers objective as to provide an appropriate degree of protection for consumers in respect of risk. Significantly, the FSA must have regard to the general principle that consumers should take responsibility for their own decisions. The FSA sees its role as reducing prudential risk – that a firm may collapse; bad faith risk – that the features of a product or service may be misrepresented, or an unsuitable one sold; and complexity (or unsuitability) risk – that customers do not understand the product or service they have bought. The FSA is not responsible to protect consumers from performance risk, which is risk that an investment does not deliver hoped for returns, subject to the important proviso that the firm has accurately described the product or service and attendant risk.

Steps which the FSA states that it has so far taken to implement this regulatory objective include the following, listed in the FSA's Annual Report 1999/2000 as actions taken with regard to satisfying this regulatory objective:

(a) "In excess of 750,000 consumer factsheets and booklets were distributed either free or by paid-for distribution through the industry.

(b) Around six million endowment policyholders in the UK received an FSA factsheet with a letter from their endowment company explaining that they would be receiving a re-projection of their policy.

(c) A new section of the FSA website written specifically for consumers has been launched. It explains consumer rights and responsibilities, suggests how consumers can protect themselves against scams and swindles and provides updates for consumers on market and regulatory developments.

(d) FSA has continued to work to encourage the effective teaching of personal finance in schools throughout the UK, with the support of the Personal Finance Education Group.

(e) Nearly two hundred primary school teachers and educationists attended the first FSA annual education conference in February 2000.

(f) The FSA is developing a financial services learning programme for adults."

1.3.8   *The reduction of financial crime objective*

This objective is to reduce the extent to which it is possible for certain businesses to be used for a purpose connected with financial crime (Section 6). These businesses are those carried out by a regulated person (which means an authorised person, recognised investment exchange or recognised clearing house (Section 6(5)), or in contravention of the general prohibition in Section 19. "Financial crime" is given a wide definition in Section 6(3). It includes any offence (including any act or omission which would be an offence if it had taken place in the UK (4)) involving:

(a) fraud or dishonesty;

(b) misconduct in a financial market;

(c) misuse of information relating to a financial market;

(d) handling the proceeds of crime.

Financial crime may therefore include any act or omission in the UK or overseas, and extends far beyond the previous regulatory concerns of misleading markets and money laundering in relation to the proceeds of drug trafficking or terrorism.

The objective is to reduce financial crime and it is the FSA's duty to act compatibly with this regulatory objective when discharging its general functions. However, this particular objective recognises the role which a regulated person may have in facilitating financial crime, and the FSMA therefore places the onus on regulated persons, rather than just the FSA itself, to counter financial crime. Subsection 6(2) provides that, in performing this objective, the FSA must, in particular, have regard to the desirability of:

(a) "regulated persons being aware of the risk of their businesses being used in connection with the commission of financial crime;

(b) regulated persons taking appropriate measures (in relation to their administration and employment practices, the conduct of transactions by them and otherwise) to prevent financial crime, facilitate its detection and monitor its incidence;

(c) regulated persons devoting adequate resources to the matters mentioned in paragraph (b)."

In other words, the FSA is in effect charged with ensuring that firms and exchanges are made aware of the risk of being involved in financial crime and devote adequate resources to monitoring for, detecting and preventing it.

The FSA explains that confidence in the financial system and consumer protection will be seriously undermined if the financial system and individual institutions are abused for criminal purposes. The FSA's particular concerns are to combat:

(a) money laundering, placing the emphasis on the effectiveness of individual firms' own procedures;

(b) fraud and dishonesty;

(c) criminal market misconduct.

As drafted, this along with the other three, is an objective imposed by Parliament upon the FSA, and the FSA has explained that it has sought to implement it in relation to firms and exchanges by taking the following steps:

(a) "The key approach the FSA will be taking is to concentrate on where the regulatory regime can make the most difference and to recognise that the fight against money laundering calls for active partnership between the financial services industry, the police and other criminal law enforcement and intelligence bodies and the FSA and other bodies with regulatory responsibilities. They pursue through their Financial Crime Liaison Unit, a programme of organised liaison with the Joint Money Laundering Steering Group and with the National Criminal Intelligence Service.

(b) In combating financial fraud the FSA continues to organise and financially underwrite the central secretariat for the Financial Fraud Information Network. This network now links all relevant UK bodies (police, government, professional bodies, FSA, customs, the exchanges and so on) to share information and suspicions of possible cases of major financial fraud and other serious criminal activity which pass through and make use of the financial system. The FSA also sponsors the Shared Intelligence Service which provides direct electronic access for regulatory bodies to an index of intelligence data about individuals and firms." (Annual Report 1999/2000)

1.3.9 Financial Services Authority's further criteria

The final set of requirements to which the FSA is subject are the seven items to which it must have regard in discharging its general functions (Section 2(3)). They may therefore be viewed as means to that end.

They are as follows:

> "2(3) In discharging its general functions the Authority must have regard to –
>
> (a) the need to use its resources in the most efficient and economic way;
>
> (b) the responsibilities of those who manage the affairs of authorised persons;"

This is of particular significance, as it underlines the FSA's commitment to hold a firm's management personally responsible for achieving compliance within the firm and, specifically, within that part of the firm for which each particular executive is responsible. The FSA's requirements are contained in the FSA's Senior Management Arrangements, Systems & Controls Sourcebook ("SYSC"), and are discussed in detail at Chater 2.

> (c) "the principle that a burden or restriction which is imposed on a person, or on the carrying on of an activity, should be proportionate to the benefits, considered in general terms which are expected to result from the imposition of that burden or restriction;"

The concept of proportionality is an important one in the field of administrative law. It requires consideration of the balance between the interests of the regulator, the firm and the wider public. It also calls for an appropriate and proportionate relationship between the exercise of the regulator's powers and its intended objective. A burden is likely to be disproportionate if it imposes an excessive burden on the firm or individual in question.

By requiring the FSA to have regard to ensuring that the burden of its policy and rules are commensurate with their expected benefits, it is made clear that the FSA is not required to create a regulatory system of suffocating perfection. If the requirement to observe the FSA's rules should be proportionate to the resulting benefit, it is explicitly recognised that there is an inevitable margin of consumer disadvantage, which is where the burden of imposing rules to prevent such occurrence would outweigh the likely benefit.

(d) "the desirability of facilitating innovation in connection with regulated activities;"

The FSA should seek to ensure that its policies and rules facilitate innovation, and do not stifle it. In light of the increase in transborder provision of financial services – as discussed in Chapter 5 – it is considered important that the FSMA does not have the effect of fossilising those financial services subject to FSA's regulation.

(e) "the international character of financial services and markets and the desirability of maintaining the competitive position of the United Kingdom;"

While it is not the job of the FSA to promote the competitiveness of the UK financial services industry, this criterion requires the FSA to have regard to maintaining its competitive position. Together with the proceeding and two following criteria, it enjoins the FSA to be alert to the costs and consequences of its regulation.

(f) "the need to minimise the adverse effects on competition that may arise from anything done in the discharge of those functions;

(g) the desirability of facilitating competition between those who are subject to any form of regulation by the Authority."

1.4   Powers of the Financial Services Authority

This Section identifies the principal powers conferred upon the FSA by the FSMA. The purpose of listing them is to illustrate the range of the FSA's powers.

Certain powers under the FSMA are reserved to the Treasury including:

(a) making financial promotion rules (Section 21);

(b) specifying regulated activities (Section 22);

(c) defining persons exempt from the general prohibition (Section 38);

(d) making regulations for authorised open-ended investment companies (Section 262);

(e) designating professional bodies (Section 326).

Principal powers granted to the FSA are as follows:

(a) to grant, vary and cancel **permissions**. A person holding permission is an authorised person under the FSMA (Section 31) (Sections 42, 44 and 49);

(b) to **approving individuals** to perform controlled functions (Section 59); to issue principles and codes for their conduct (Section 64) and to take action against them for misconduct (Section 66). The FSA may also withdraw approval (Section 63) and make a prohibition order against an individual (Section 56);

(c) the right to be heard in court on a **banking or insurance transfer** (Section 110);

(d) to impose a penalty or public statement for **market abuse** (Section 123) together with additional enforcement powers (Section 381, 383 – 386). Seeking injunctions and restitution orders for market abuse (Section 380, 382) is a power shared with the Treasury;

(e) to **make rules** (Section 138 – 147). This is a particularly significant power which enables the FSA to make rules for the conduct of wide range of activities, including:

　(i)　conduct of business rules;

　(ii)　client money rules;

　(iii)　financial promotion rules;

　(iv)　money laundering rules;

(f) to require an authorised person to **provide information**, documents or an expert's report (Section 165, 166). These are powers commonly exercised by the FSA as part of its routine monitoring activities;

(g) to perform **investigations** (Section 167, 168). This is a power shared with the Treasury;

(h) to regulate the acquisition, increase and continuation in **control** over UK authorised persons (Section 178 – 192);

(i) to take **disciplinary action** against an authorised person by issue of a decision notice (Section 208). The authorised person may refer the subject matter of the disciplinary notice to the Financial Services & Markets Tribunal (Section 133);

(j) to establish a **compensation** scheme (Section 213);

(k) to make or approve rules for the **Financial Ombudsman Scheme** (Sections 225 to 234);

(l) to authorise **unit trust schemes** (Section 242); the FSA may make rules for the regulation of authorised unit trust schemes (Section 247, 248), must approve certain alterations (Section 251), and may revoke authorisation and intervene (Section 257, 258);

(m) to **recognise overseas Collective Investment Schemes** (Section 264), schemes from designated territories (Section 270) and individual schemes (Section 272);

(n) to **recognise investment exchanges** and clearing houses (Section 290) in accordance with regulations made by the Treasury (Section 286);

(o) to keep under review the desirability of regulating **Lloyd's** in accordance with Part XIX of the FSMA (Sections 314 – 324);

(p) to keep under review the desirability of exercising its powers over the **designated professional bodies** in accordance with part XX of the FSMA (Sections 325 – 333);

(q) to maintain a **public record** of authorised persons, schemes, prohibited individuals and approved persons (Section 347(1));

(r) to initiate or participate in **insolvency** proceedings in accordance with Part XIV of the FSMA (Sections 355 to 379);

(s) to **cooperate with other regulators** and other persons concerned with preventing or detecting financial crime (Section 354);

(t) to institute **criminal proceedings** under the FSMA, subject to restrictions imposed by the Treasury (Section 401). This power is shared with the Treasury and can also be exercised by or with consent of the DPP (Section 401). The FSA may also institute proceedings, subject to restrictions imposed by the Treasury, for insider dealing and money laundering (Section 402);

(u) finally, there is a curious power under Section 404 whereby if the Treasury considers there is evidence that there has been **widespread or regular failure** to comply with rules, and private persons may suffer compensatable loss, the Treasury may authorise the FSA to establish and operate a scheme for investigating the situation and compensating investors. This provision is curious for three reasons:

    (i) it does not form part of the original scheme for the FSMA, but was added by virtue of a minority opposition amendment shortly before the third reading;

    (ii) it does not empower the FSA to do anything that it could not do already;

    (iii) it requires a positive statutory instrument in order to be implemented (Section 429) and is therefore very unlikely ever to be used.

1.5   The accountability of the Financial Services Authority

The FSA is accountable, or at least liable to give an explanation of its conduct, in 11 separate ways, which we now summarise.

1.5.1   *Governing body*

The FSA must have regard to applicable principles of good corporate governance, and the rules and responsibilities of the governing body and its directors are discussed above.

1.5.2   *Non-executive committee*

The limited remit of this committee is also discussed above.

1.5.3   To Parliament

The FSA will be answerable to Parliament through submission of an annual report (*see* 1.5.4.1 below), and also through the Treasury ministers.

1.5.4   Public accountability

1.5.4.1   Annual report

The FSA must make a report to the Treasury at least once each year on matters including the discharge of its functions, the extent to which it considers the regulatory objectives (as above) have been met, and its consideration of the seven matters to which it is required to "have regard" (*see* above) (Schedule 1 10). The Treasury may require the FSA to comply with the provisions of the Companies Act 1985 with regard to the FSA's accounts and their audit, with such modifications as it may require. The Treasury must lay this report before Parliament (10(3)).

1.5.4.2   Public meeting

The FSA must hold an annual public meeting within three months of making the report for it to be considered (11(1)). This is a public meeting and not just for the investment community, and must be brought to the notice of the public ((5)(e)). The FSA may organise and conduct the meeting as it sees fit ((3)) save that it must allow:

(a) a general discussion of the report;

(b) a reasonable opportunity for those attending the meeting to question the FSA about the discharge of its functions during the period of the report ((2)).

The FSA must give reasonable notice of the meeting ((4)) which notice must contain certain particulars ((5)). The FSA must publish a report of the proceedings within one month of the meeting ((12)).

1.5.5   To the courts

As stated above, the FSA is exempted from liability in damages, but is not protected against either an injunction or an action for judicial review. Furthermore, it appears that the FSA may not be liable in negligence or breach of statutory duty to the customers of a firm which it regulates (*Yuen Kun Yeu v. Attorney General of Hong Kong* [1988] 1 AC 175; *Three Rivers District Council and Others v. Governor and Company of the Bank of England* [2000] 3 All ER 1; a similar approach has been taken in British Columbia in *Cooper v. British Columbia (Registrar of Mortgage Brokers)* 2000 BCCA 151).

1.5.6   To HM Treasury

The Treasury may appoint a person (the "Reviewer") to review the FSA's use of its resources (Section 12(1)). The review must relate to the "economy, efficiency and effectiveness" with which the FSA has used its resources and discharged its functions, and is not to be concerned with either of:

(a) the merits of the FSA's general policy or principles in pursuing regulatory objectives;

(b) the FSA's exercise of its listing functions (Section 12(3)).

The Reviewer has a right to obtain documents and information (Section 13). On completion of the review, the Reviewer must make a written report to the Treasury setting out the results of his review, and making any recommendations (Section 12 (4)). A copy must be laid before Parliament and published as the Treasury considers appropriate ((5)).

The Treasury may arrange for an independent enquiry to be held where there has been a serious failure in the regulatory system or its operation. The circumstances are as follows:

"14(2) The first is where it appears to the Treasury that:

(a) events have occurred in relation to:

(i) a collective investment scheme; or

(ii) a person who is, or was at the time of the events, carrying on a regulated activity (whether or not as authorised person), which posed or could have posed a grave risk to the financial system or caused or risked causing significant damage to the interests of consumers; and

(b) those events might not have occurred, or the risk of damage might have been reduced, but for a serious failure in:

    (i) the system established by this Act for the regulation of such schemes or of such persons and their activities; or

    (ii) the operation of that system.

"14(3) The second is where it appears to the Treasury that:

(a) events have occurred in relation to listed securities or an issuer of listed securities which caused or could have caused significant damage to holders of listed securities; and

(b) those events might not have occurred but for a serious failure in the regulatory system established by Part VI or in its operation."

There are three defined terms:

"14(5) "Consumers" means persons:

(a) who are consumers for the purpose of Section 138; or

(b) who, in relation to regulated activities carried on otherwise than by persons, would be consumers for those purposes if the activities were carried on by authorised persons.

14(6) "The financial system" has the same meaning as in Section 3.

14(7) "Listed securities" means anything which has been admitted to the official list under Part VI."

These powers focus on individual schemes, firms and companies. They could therefore be used in relation to matters similar to the Barings, Morgan Grenfell or Maxwell affairs, although not perhaps the personal pensions misselling review because the events related to firms generally rather than any one particular firm.

The Treasury is not obliged to arrange for a public enquiry, but may do so if it considers that it is in the public interest that one should be held into the events and circumstances surrounding them (4). If the Treasury so decides, then:

(a) the Treasury may appoint such a person as it considers appropriate to hold the enquiry (Section 15(1));

(b) the Treasury may control the scope, period and conduct of the enquiry and making of any reports ((2),(3));

(c) the person appointed to hold the enquiry is empowered to obtain information and documents (Section 16) with obstruction or contempt punishable by the court (Section 18);

(d) on completion of the enquiry, he must make a written report to the Treasury, which it may publish (Section 17).

1.5.7   *To practitioners and consumer*

Section 8 provides as follows:

> "The Authority must make and maintain effective arrangements for consulting practitioners and consumers on the extent to which its general policies and practices are consistent with its general duties under Section 2."

"General policies and practices" is undefined; it is however wider than the FSA's general functions at Section 2(4) as "practice" will include the *operation* of the FSA's rules and policy, whereas the general functions are only concerned with the *making* of policy and rules. Use of the word "general" to qualify procedures and practices connotes generalised oversight rather than specific investigation, and corresponds to the expression "considered as a whole" appended to the first three general functions.

The FSA is therefore required to consult practitioners and consumers, in the manner specified below, about whether its general policies and practices, and their implementation, are consistent with the four regulatory objectives and seven criteria to which the FSA must have regard. The arrangements which the FSA must make and institute are stated to include the establishment of a Practitioner Panel (Section 9) and a Consumer Panel (Section 10).

The Practitioner Panel, which is to represent the interest of practitioners, is to be appointed by the FSA from individuals who are authorised persons and individuals representing authorised persons, recognised investment exchanges and recognised clearing houses (Section 9(1),(5)).

The Consumer Panel, representing interests of consumers, is to comprise individuals appointed by the FSA who are consumers or persons representing their interests (Section 10(1)). The FSA must ensure that membership of the Consumer Panel gives a fair degree of representation to those who use services for non-business purposes (Section 10(6)). Consumers is given the same wide meaning as under Section 5(3) (Section 10(7)).

In the case of both panels:

(a) the FSA appoints a member of that panel to be its chairman;

(b) Treasury approval is required for the appointment or dismissal of the chairman;

(c) the FSA must consider any representation made by the Panel in accordance with the statutory requirements in Section 8 (Section 11(1),(2));

(d) if the FSA disagrees with the view expressed or proposal made by the Panel, it must give the Panel a written statement of its reasons for disagreeing (3).

1.5.8 To the Complaints Commissioner

A key element of the investor protection regime remains the requirement that authorised firms must investigate and resolve complaints made against them by investors. The FSA is placed under a corresponding requirement in relation to complaints made against it, and is required to appoint an independent investigator to conduct investigations against it in accordance with a complaints scheme (Schedule 1 7). The following description is taken from the FSMA, and includes the FSA's proposed procedures set out in CP73 *Investigation of Complaints Against the FSA* (November 2000) and CP93 (*Investigation of Complaints Against the FSA – Feedback on CP73* (May 2001)). Together, these contain the draft Complaints Against the FSA ("COAF") Rules.

The FSA states its policy as follows:

> "FSA will seek to maintain high standards in all its dealings with consumers, regulated firms and others. If it fails to meet these standards, those directly and adversely affected should be entitled to seek a thorough and impartial enquiry into what went wrong, and to be told what the FSA will do to put things right" (CP73, paragraph 2.2).

In particular, it is clear from the following provisions that the FSA will seek to handle complaints made against it to the same standard as it requires regulated firms to handle the complaints which they receive.

The complaints scheme will have the following features:

(a) it will provide for the investigation of complaints "arising in connection with" the exercise or non-exercise of any of FSA's non-legislative functions (Schedule 1,7,(1)(a)). This encompasses maladministration in the shape of negligence, unreasonable delay, unprofessional behaviour, and lack of integrity. A person cannot complain about the FSA's legislative functions, such as the making of a rule, or failure to issue guidance, although he could complain about the exercise of enforcement or disciplinary powers, or refusal to admit a firm;

(b) implicitly, a complaint can be made by an investor, a firm or a person otherwise affected by the FSA's action or inactivity;

(c) complaints should be investigated quickly (2);

(d) the FSA must publicly consult on the proposed scheme and, once made, on any alterations or replacements of it; must take any representations into account and must publish them together with its response ((5) to (9), (14)). The FSA's initial consultation is contained in CP73, and CP93;

(e) the FSA must publish details of the scheme (10), (11).

The Complaints Commissioner:

(a) must be independent of the FSA (7 (1)(b)). In appointing the Commissioner, who will hold office for three years, the FSA will be advised by an independent panel (COAF 1.3);

(b) must conduct investigations into complaints falling within the remit of the complaints scheme (7(1)(a));

(c) requires Treasury approval for his appointment or dismissal ((3));

(d) must be appointed under terms which the FSA considers are reasonably designed to secure that he acts independently of the FSA, and that his investigations will not favour the FSA (Schedule 1,7(4));

(e) together with his agent under (8(8)), is not liable in damages in respect of these functions (19(2)).

Procedure for handling complaints against the FSA will be as follows (Schedule 1 8):

(a) a complaint is made against the FSA, which will seek to acknowledge it within five working days (COAF 1.5.1);

(b) the FSA will investigate the complaint (Schedule 1,8(10). This will be carried out by a senior and independent (in the sense of not previously involved) member of the FSA's staff who will seek to resolve the matter within eight weeks by, if appropriate, recommending rectification or an ex-gratia payment;

(c) the FSA is not obliged to investigate the complaint in accordance with the complaints scheme:

(i) if it relates to its legislative functions. COAF 1.4.3 gives the examples of complaints expressing dissatisfaction with the FSA's policies or proper exercise of discretion;

(ii) if the FSA reasonably considers it will be more appropriately dealt with in another way, such as a reference to the Financial Services and Markets Tribunal or by instituting legal proceedings (8(1)). The FSA is therefore given wide discretion initially to exclude from the Investigator's remit complaints:

    i. which arise out of warning notice/disciplinary notice/supervision notice procedures (*see* Chapter 10), for which the appropriate remedy may be to refer the matter to the Tribunal. This will principally affect applicants for authorisation or approval and disciplinary issues relating to firms and approved individuals;

    ii. which could be dealt with by legal proceedings, for example judicial review of administrative action against the FSA, or an intermediate customer's or market counterparty's action against a firm in default. Again, this is likely to affect firms and individually approved persons;

In consequence, the Commissioner's remit may in practice be restricted to complaints from individuals directly against the FSA.

(d) a complaint relating to ongoing FSA action – for instance, disciplinary or admission proceedings – will not usually be investigated until the complainant has exhausted relevant remedies (COAF 1.4.4);

(e) if dissatisfied, the complainant may refer the matter to the Investigator (8(2)(a)). The Commissioner will investigate personally or by his agent (8(8)) who may not be an officer or employee of the FSA (8(9)). However, reference to the Commissioner will not normally stop the FSA taking or continuing with the action which is the subject of the complaint (COAF 1.5.10 –14);

(f) also, if the FSA decides not to investigate a complaint, it must notify the Commissioner who may nonetheless proceed to investigate it (8(3), 8(4));

(g) when investigating a complaint, the Commissioner:

  (i) must have the means to conduct a full investigation;

  (ii) must report the result of the investigation to the FSA and the complainant;

  (iii) may publish all or any part of his report which he considers ought to be brought to the attention of the public (8(2)(b));

(h) the Commissioner may recommend that the FSA does either or both of:

  (i) compensate the complainant;

  (ii) remedy the matter complained of (8(5));

(i) if the Commissioner reports that a complaint is well founded or has criticised the FSA, then the FSA must inform both him and the complainant of steps which it proposes to take in response (8(6)). The Commissioner may require the FSA to publish all or part of that response (8(7)).

Before the Commissioner recommends a compensatory payment, the draft Scheme (COAF 1.5.23) requires him to have regard to the FSA's statutory objectives and general duties. If, having done so, he still recommends compensation, then the FSA will give proper consideration to the recommendation and, in deciding whether to make such payment, will have regard to:

(a) its statutory objectives and general duties;

(b) the gravity of the maladministration;

(c) whether the matter complained of was an operational or administrative matter or a policy issue, with the latter being less deserving of compensation;

(d) the impact of the cost of the proposed compensatory payment on firms and, ultimately, consumers.

In other words, the FSA may accept the Commissioner's recommendation in the case of serious maladministration in the operational sphere where a limited class of persons, or a single person, has suffered significant direct loss. The FSA gives the following examples (CP73 paragraph 3.25). The FSA may choose to compensate in the following two cases:

(a) a firm suffers loss because the FSA wrongly deletes it from the public register of authorised firms;

(b) a customer suffers loss because, on the basis of information received from the FSA, he entrusts funds to an unauthorised firm in circumstances where it should have been clear to the FSA that those funds would be at risk;

but not in the case of customers (or other firms) suffering loss because of the failure of a firm.

1.5.9   The Financial Services and Markets Tribunal

Certain decisions of the FSA can be referred to the Tribunal for review.

An authorised person or individual is entitled to refer a number of matters to the Tribunal, of which the principal ones are as follows. The ability of a firm or individual to require that certain key decisions of the FSA be determined by an independent tribunal will, in principle, constitute an important check to ensure that the FSA is properly exercising its powers in those particular circumstances.

(a) refusal to consent to passport out (Schedule 3 paragraph 19);

(b) imposition of requirements on permission (Section 52);

(c) cancellation of requirements on permission (Section 54);

(d) prohibition order (Section 57 and 58);

(e) withdrawal of approval (Section 63);

(f) disciplinary action (Section 67);

(g) penalty for market abuse (Section 123);

(h) change of control (Sections 183, 185 – 187);

(i) refusal of application to vary requirement on authorisation (Section 200);

(j) disciplinary action (Section 207, 208);

(k) refusal to authorise unit trust scheme (Section 245);

(l) revocation of authorisation of unit trust scheme (Sections 255 to 257);

(m) recognition of overseas schemes (Sections 265 and 269);

(n) recognition of other schemes (Sections 271, 280);

(o) reapplying general prohibition to individual professional firms (Section 331);

(p) disqualification of auditor or actuary (Section 345);

(q) restitution for market abuse (Section 385, 386).

1.5.10   *Obligation to consult*

The FSA is required to consult in relation to a number of areas.

The FSA's approach to consultation is both thorough and transparent. By N2 the FSA will have issued well over 100 Consultation Papers which:

(a) explained the FSA's policy in that area;

(b) set out, where applicable, draft rules, codes and guidance;

(c) contained, again where applicable, a detailed analysis of how the proposals were compatible with the FSA's statutory objectives and the seven matters to which it must have regard, and why the proposals were the most appropriate way for the FSA to meet its objectives;

(d) where so required under Section 155, include a cost benefit analysis;

(e) invited comments.

The FSA has in each case considered the comments and generally published a detailed response to them, sometimes inviting further comments on revised proposals prior to determining the final rule or policy.

Areas where the FSA is required to consult include the following:

(a) codes for individuals (Section 65);

(b) penalties for individuals (Section 70);

(c) market abuse penalty policy (Section 125);

(d) issuing new or varied rules (Section 155);

(e) FSMA penalties (Section 211);

(f) extension of FSMA to Lloyd's underwriting (Section 319);

(g) reapplication of general prohibition to professional firms (Section 330);

(h) procedures for the issue of warning notices, decision notices and supervisory notices (Section 396);

(i) scheme for investigating complaints against the FSA (Schedule 1 paragraph 7);

(j) application of penalties for the benefit of authorised persons (Schedule 1 paragraph 16).

1.5.11   Competition scrutiny

Finally, the FSA's rules, guidance and practice are subject to competition scrutiny under Sections 159 to 164. In summary:

(a) the FSA's regulations and practices are subject to review by the Director General of Fair Trading. If at any time the Director considers that either a regulation or practice standing alone or together with one or more other regulation or practice has an anti-competitive effect, he must make a report to that effect. The reports must be submitted to the Treasury, the Competition Commission and the FSA. If the consideration is that the regulation is anti-competitive, such a report must be published in the best way to bring it to the attention of the public;

(b) if the Director makes a report regarding the anti-competitiveness of a regulation or practice, the Commission must investigate the matter;

(c) if the Commission concludes that the regulation or practice or a combination of them does have a significantly adverse effect on competition, it must state whether it considers that the effect is justified and, if not, state its conclusion as to what action, if any ought to be taken by the FSA. If the Commission makes a report under this Section it must send a copy to the Treasury, the FSA and the Director;

(d) if the Commission makes a report stating the effect is not justified, the Treasury must give a direction to the FSA requiring it to take such action as may be specified in the direction.

The author would like to thank his colleague Lisa Savio for her assistance with this Chapter.

Chapter 2

THE FSA'S HIGH LEVEL PRINCIPLES

Andrew Winckler
Chairman, Regulatory Practice, Financial Services
George Elwes
Senior Manager, Regulatory Practice
Ernst & Young LLP

2.1 Introduction

The foundations of the Financial Services Authority's (the "FSA") regulatory system are set out as High Level Principles in Block 1 of the Handbook and they cover the following topics:

(a) Principles for business;

(b) threshold conditions for authorisation;

(c) Principles and Code of Practice for approved persons;

(d) senior management arrangements, systems and controls.

The Principles formulate succinct high level precepts which define the fundamental obligations of regulated businesses and persons. The FSA's Principles rely heavily on the Securities and Investments Board's (the "SIB") Principles arising out of the Financial Services Act 1986 and the minimum criteria in Schedule 3 of the Banking Act 1987. The Principles are also intended to be in harmony with international standards as set out in the *Core Principles of Effective Banking Supervision*, published by the Basel Committee on banking supervision in September 1997 and the IOSCO Consultation Draft on the Objectives and Principles of Securities Regulation published in 1998.

The Principles are clearly a continuation of a regulatory tradition which can be traced back to the General Principles of the UK Takeover Code. The SIB effectively followed this model of broad principles which sit over and seek to express the spirit of, or the standard embedded in, more detailed rules. However, there are two striking differences from the Takeover Code environment. First, the community to whom the Takeover Code applied was relatively small and professionally homogeneous. The FSA's Principles will apply, with a few exceptions, to the entire spectrum of financial service businesses. Second, the FSA's Principles can provide the basis for more formal, statute based, disciplinary proceedings potentially resulting in a much wider range of sanctions. Perhaps for these reasons, the FSA's approach even at this high level introduces new elements of prescriptive detail particularly in the area of senior management arrangements and the Code of Practice for Approved Persons. Some may find the detail useful in designing management arrangements and guiding personal conduct. Others may find the requirements difficult to apply in practice. The FSA's motive in introducing this level of detail may be to facilitate the use of its disciplinary powers rather than to assist firms to establish effective systems of management. Since regulators are paid to regulate and managements to manage, it will be unsurprising if there is some tension between the detail of the rules and the practice of management. As with the current position, the Principles can be used by the FSA for enforcement including the FSA making orders for restitution but the Principles cannot be used by third parties to claim compensation from firms nor can they give rise to civil litigation.

2.2   FSA's rationale for establishing High Level Principles

The FSA believes that sound management, individual competence and a culture of good business ethics as set out in the High Level Principles are the most effective means of delivering its regulatory objectives. Such an approach builds on past regulatory practice. The implication for regulated businesses is that if they can demonstrate sound management arrangements, high individual competence and a good ethical culture, then the amount of routine monitoring and direct intrusion into the business by regulators will be minimised.

The FSA's aspiration is not in doubt: nevertheless, the growing size and scope of the Handbook with its proliferation of Principles, Rules, Codes and Guidance rather belies the rhetoric.

2.2.1   Scope and applicability

The High Level Principles are defined in general terms and they will be applied proportionately to different classes of business. Small firms will not be required to establish management structures and controls to the same degree as larger organisations. It will be open to each regulated firm to apply the Principles in a way that is appropriate to its circumstances so long as the firm can convince the regulator that its procedures are effective in their context.

Issues of proportionality may be particularly important to the authorisation of start up firms. These are likely to be small, financially constrained and may have a management team strong on ideas and ambition but lacking in proven managerial competence. These factors all raise regulatory risk but if the FSA does not apply its High Level Principles proportionately to new firms it will stifle competition and innovation.

The FSA has emphasised that a breach of the Principles, even if it does not involve a breach of any specific rule set out in the Handbook will still be a basis for disciplinary action. This approach is justified on the grounds that in a fast developing and complex financial environment detailed rules can never cover all eventualities. Others argue that hindsight prevails when a regulatory failure occurs and that discipline based on anything other than specific rules is likely to be less fair and more unpredictable. To mitigate the risks inherent in the direct application of the Principles to discipline, the FSA has undertaken to provide informal, prompt and substantive guidance to firms and individuals on the application of the Principles to specific circumstances although it will expect applicants for such guidance to make a "bona fide effort to analyse the issue" for themselves.

2.2.2   The Principles for business

The FSA has established 11 Principles and provides high level guidance as to their meaning.

Principle 1 states that a firm must conduct its business with integrity. The FSA has described "integrity" as a moral concept. Few have difficulty defining fraud, deception, misrepresentation and breach of trust as being failures of integrity perhaps not only because they are failures of morality but also because they give rise to remedies under general law and are therefore well defined and understood. Integrity in other less traumatic situations is less easy to define. In particular, the moral conventions which govern the relationships between market professionals may well be different from those required when a professional deals with an inexpert private customer. It is to be hoped that the FSA will have due regard to context and market custom and that decisions will not be unduly influenced by media attention.

The FSA has stressed that breaches of Principle 1 are the most likely to give rise to disciplinary action so that, whatever the difficulties , the precise definition of integrity does matter.

Principle 2 requires a firm to conduct its affairs with due skill, care and diligence. The concept of care is primarily directed to a firm's obligations to its customers. Neglect of shareholders' or employees' interests will not normally be regarded as a breach of this Principle. The standard of diligence and skill required will depend on the business carried on by the firm and the reasonable expectations of its customers.

Principle 3 requires a firm to organise and control its affairs effectively. This Principle introduces FSA's precepts for management arrangements and controls. The Principle itself contains greater detail than the other Principles and separate rules and guidance on this Principle are included later on in Block 1 of the Handbook. This detail emphasises the importance the FSA places on systems and controls and indicates the extent to which the Principle may be deployed in disciplinary proceedings against a firm and its management.

Principle 3 requires a firm to have adequate procedures to ensure that its senior personnel are fit and proper. This requirement extends to agents of the firm and outsource suppliers who provide administrative services. A firm must also have in place procedures to apportion responsibilities to individual directors in such a manner that all risks are adequately monitored and controlled. There must also be appropriate supervision by a Board of Directors or other governing body. Principle 3 also requires a firm to have in place robust arrangements to ensure compliance with the regulatory system and to prevent the financial system from being used to facilitate financial crime.

A major new requirement arising under Principle 3, is for firms to maintain adequate and orderly records of its business and internal organisation. This requirement extends far beyond accounting records to include records of senior managers' assigned responsibilities. The FSA acknowledges that the documentation that firms have traditionally maintained to record senior management responsibilities (both organisation charts and job descriptions are mentioned) should be sufficient to meet the new requirements of Principle 3. In practice, these documents rarely disclose the whole picture nor are they kept current or "real time". Senior management relationships and responsibilities are usually subtle and complex reflecting individual personalities, competences and rivalries and can change quite rapidly in response to the pressures of the business. Chief executives may need to realign the responsibilities of their team to reinforce areas of weakness or to remove responsibility from an officer who has failed to perform a particular task and it is difficult to see how these important realities can always be promptly set out in orderly records as required by Principle 3. Equally, however, the requirements should restrain the extent to which top management responsibilities are left ill-defined or subject to architectural ambiguities as a result of chief executive officers or Boards being unwilling or unable to avoid fudges.

Principle 4 requires firms to conduct and organise their affairs with prudence. Prudence includes foresight and circumspection but not risk aversion. Speculation is not excluded. Prudence will be evidenced by the maintenance of adequate capital, liquidity and risk management systems. The prudence principle will be extended beyond the regulated business particularly to the financial affairs of other group companies including their unregulated business. In these cases the focus will be on the adequacy of the group's capital resources and liquidity.

Prudence will apply particularly to qualitative assessments of capital adequacy which may lead to the FSA requiring capital in excess of international norms. However, firms are likely to find that in re-assessing the adequacy of their capital and liquidity they will need to pay more attention to the complexities of the FSA's financial resources rules rather than abstract principles of prudence. It is generally acknowledged that the relationship between current financial resources requirements and to economic risks is not straightforward or obvious. So there must be a risk of the regulator interpreting "prudence" with the benefit of hindsight when a firm experiences financial difficulty.

Principle 5 requires firms to maintain proper standards of market conduct. This Principle will underpin the FSA's own Code of Market Conduct and its regime for inter-professional dealings. Of greater complexity will be defining the relationship between Principle 5 and the Takeover Code and the rules of exchanges and clearing houses. Issues may arise as to the detailed supervision of these overlapping rules and codes and how regulatory responsibilities will be apportioned.

Principle 6 requires a firm to have regard to the interests of its customers and treat them fairly. General law relating to agency or trusts may impose obligations on a firm in excess of the requirements of the Principle 6 and Principle 6 does not reduce these. However, Principle 6 will not generally be applied to banking or general insurance where statutory conduct of business regulation is not applied at present.

Principle 7 requires a firm to provide its customers with clear and fair communication. The use of the word "clear" is intended to mean understandable so that it will be important for a firm to have regard to the level of understanding of its particular customers. The FSA justifies the emphasis on clear communication because of its statutory obligation to promote public understanding of financial products.

Principle 8 requires firms to manage conflicts of interest fairly. Conflicts can arise between the interests of the firms and its customer or between one customer and another. There is no guidance as to how firms should manage risk. There is no guidance in the Principle as to how conflicts should be managed although disclosure, internal rules of confidentiality and declining to act may all be applicable.

Principle 9 requires a firm to take reasonable care to ensure the suitability of its advice and discretionary decisions for any customer who is entitled to rely on its judgement. Where advice is given to customers or discretion exercised on their behalf, firms must take reasonable care to ensure that advice given or discretionary decisions made are suitable with regard to the customers' needs and situation. However even where advice is suitable or discretion suitably exercised, this does not detract from the need to provide "best advice" where this is applicable.

Principle 10 requires a firm to make adequate arrangements for its customers' assets when it has responsibility for them.

Principle 11 requires a firm to deal with its regulators in an open and co-operative way. This apparently extends to overseas regulators and it applies to matters of relevance to the regulators even if these arise in unregulated parts of the business or unregulated group companies. This Principle will only apply during the routine processes of authorisation, supervision and enforcement. If tribunal processes are resorted to, the nature and extent of communications will be determined by the tribunal.

2.2.3 *The general application of the Principles*

A casual reader might have expected "Principles for businesses" to have been self-evident and universal in their application. In practice, the Principles will be subject to a range of important limitations.

The Principles will not generally apply to the unregulated business of regulated firms but will only apply to regulated and, if a firm is authorised to carry on designated investment business, ancillary, activities.

The Principles will only apply to companies directly authorised by the FSA but not to other group companies.

The Principles relating to conduct of business and the care of customers (primarily Principles 6 and 9) will not apply to banking business and general insurance.

The prudential implications of the Principles will be applied to the worldwide operations of FSA authorised firms but the conduct of business principles will only be applied in the UK.

For inwardly passporting European Economic Area ("EEA") firms, the Principles relating to conduct of business will only be applied to their activities in the UK.

The Principles will apply to inter-professional dealings but will be "conditioned" by the conventions of those markets.

2.2.4   *Specific applications*

The FSA has indicated that it will use the Principles in these specific situations:

(a) they will be relevant to judgements of fitness and propriety but not exclusively so;

(b) they will be relevant in determining when the FSA will exercise its powers of investigation and intervention;

(c) they will be used as a basis for obtaining injunctions;

(d) they will be used as a basis for disciplinary proceedings; and

(e) they will be a basis for requiring restitution.

2.3   Authorisation under Financial Services and Market Act 2000 and the threshold conditions

Section 19 Part II of the Financial Services and Markets Act 2000 (the "FSMA") imposes a general prohibition on the carrying on of a regulated activity unless the person carrying on that activity is either:

(a) an authorised person; or

(b) an exempt person.

However, a person becomes authorised not by seeking authorisation generally but by seeking permission to carry on one or more regulated activity. Once a firm has been granted permission by the FSA to carry out one regulated activity, it automatically becomes an authorised person and the general prohibition contained in Section

19 is disapplied. Where a firm carries on a regulated activity, which is outside the scope of the permission granted, this is a breach of the FSA's rules but would not give rise to a criminal offence under Section 19.

2.3.1 Part IV permission

To become an authorised person, an applicant must seek a "Part IV permission" from the FSA. Part IV of the FSMA, Section 41, requires the FSA only to grant a permission if the applicant satisfies "threshold conditions" which are set out in Schedule 6 of the Act. Permission granted under this procedure will cover one or more regulated activity and permissions may be subject to conditions or restrictions as the FSA sees fit. The FSA has provided high level guidance on how it will apply the threshold conditions to the granting of permission, the varying of permission and the withdrawal of permission. High level guidance is contained in Block 1 of the Handbook but greater detail will be given in the Authorisation, Supervision and Enforcement Manuals.

2.3.2 The threshold conditions

These are set out in Schedule 6 FSMA 2000. There are five conditions:

(a) legal status;

(b) location of offices;

(c) close links;

(d) adequate resources;

(e) suitability.

The first two impose finite requirements. The last three will involve the FSA exercising a large measure of judgement and discretion. The FSA has provided considerable guidance on how it will form its judgements and how it will utilise its discretion.

2.3.2.1 *Qualifying condition (a) – legal status*

If an applicant seeks permission to carry out insurance business then the applicant must be a body corporate, a registered friendly society or a member of Lloyds.

If an applicant seeks permission to carry on deposit taking business then the applicant must be a body corporate or a partnership.

These restrictions are required to comply with European Directives. Apart from these restrictions Section 40 FSMA provides that an application to the FSA for permissions may be made by: (a) an individual; (b) a body corporate; (c) a partnership; or (d) an unincorporated association.

2.3.2.2 *Qualifying condition (b) – location of offices*

If the applicant is incorporated in the UK, its head office and its registered office must be in the UK.

If the applicant is a person but not a body corporate, its head office must be in the UK and it must carry on business in the UK.

The major difficulty with this requirement is how to determine the nature of activities constituting a head office and the location at which these activities are carried out. The FSA provides guidance on this issue in its Authorisation Manual.

2.3.2.3 *Qualifying condition (c) – close links*

If an applicant has close links with another person, then the FSA must be satisfied that these links are not likely to prevent it exercising effective supervision. Secondly if it appears to the FSA that the closely linked person is subject to foreign laws and regulations, the FSA must be satisfied that these laws and regulations will not prevent the FSA exercising effective supervision.

Closely linked entities are defined as parent organisations, subsidiaries, fellow subsidiaries or relationships with a 20 per cent shareholding or any other form of relationship through which control is exercised.

The FSA provides guidance in the Authorisation Manual of examples where it would regard an organisation, structure or relationship as unsupervisable.

2.3.2.4   *Qualifying condition (d) – adequate resources*

An applicant must have resources which, in the opinion of the FSA, are adequate in relation to the regulated activities to be carried on. In forming this opinion the FSMA permits the FSA to have regard to the effect that membership of a group may have and to take into account the level of provisions made and the procedures in place to manage the risk.

The FSA's high level guidance on this requirement cross refers to the Integrated Prudential Sourcebook which will set out a range of detailed provisions. Resources are not limited to financial resources but include information systems, risk management procedures, human resource management procedures and the high level systems and controls requirements set out in Block 1 of the Handbook.

In assessing the impact of group activities on the resources of the applicant, the FSA will require detailed financial information on group capital adequacy and large exposures and will require qualitative information on the activities and managements of material group companies. The FSA requirements relating to group activities under the new regime are unlikely to be more onerous than under the preceding regimes.

The FSA will examine whether the applicant's resources are not merely sufficient to meet present requirements but whether the business has sufficient resources to meet the future requirements identified in the firm's strategic plans (including possible stress scenarios) and are clearly sufficient to continue to comply with prudential standards as the business grows.

If an applicant or anyone close to it has been adjudged bankrupt or has gone into liquidation (voluntary or involuntary) the FSA will want to consider whether this is relevant to the question of resources, though some might regard this as an issue relating to a particular officer's suitability rather than to the resources of the firm.

The FSA in assessing the adequacy of resources will examine the extent to which the applicant has identified the risks inherent in its business plan and designed risk management procedures to control these risks. The FSA will seek to establish that the applicant has identified the interests of consumers in his business case, has tested the business plan and that the firm's finance and other resources are commensurate with the risks.

The FSA will expect the applicant to have carried out market research in its economic sector to ensure that, as far as is reasonably possible, that its business will be viable and competitive. The FSA will examine viability and competitiveness only to the extent that they are required to protect consumers (one of its statutory objectives) but not to the extent that it stifles innovation. This is likely to be a difficult balancing act.

2.3.2.5   *Qualifying condition (e) – suitability*

The FSMA requires the applicant to satisfy the FSA that it is fit and proper "having regard to all the circumstances including:

(a) connections with any person;

(b) the nature of the regulated activity it seeks to carry out; and

(c) the need to ensure that its affairs are conducted soundly and prudently".

The suitability condition applies primarily to the applicant firm. The suitability of directors and senior employees will be assessed separately under the approved persons regime. But in assessing the suitability of the applicant the collective suitability of the management team may be called in to question even where individual managers would qualify under the approved persons regime.

The FSA high level guidance on suitability places emphasis on the following matters:

(a) any previous convictions for fraud, dishonesty or tax offences applicable to the firm or relevant individuals. Particular emphasis will be placed on offences in relation to financial services, banking, company law, insurance services and consumer protection;

(b) any involvement by the applicant or persons closely connected with it in any previous regulatory investigations or disciplinary proceedings even if these did not give rise to adverse findings. The requirement extends to proceedings of overseas regulations and proceedings before clearing houses, exchanges, professional bodies and other government agencies;

(c) whether the applicant or any person closely connected to it has breached any of the FSA's regulatory requirements or any of the rules, guidance, codes of practice and statements of principle of other regulators, clearing houses, exchanges, professional bodies and government bodies. The FSA will apply a materiality standard in assessing the importance of such breaches but will seek a high level of disclosure from applicants so that the FSA remains the judge of what is material;

(d) whether the applicant has put in place adequate procedures to ensure as far as is reasonably possible that all staff are aware of regulatory requirements applicable to their duties and there are adequate procedures to monitor ongoing compliance. This requirement applies particularly to the training and monitoring of approved persons sponsored by the applicant;

(e) whether the applicant or anyone closely connected to it has been refused registration, authorisation, membership or licence to carry out a trade, business or profession or had such permission terminated;

(f) whether the applicant or persons connected to it have become insolvent;

(g) whether an applicant or person connected to it has been dismissed from an employment or has been disqualified as a director; and

(h) whether the applicant or a person connected with it has been truthful and candid with the regulator in past dealings and has demonstrated a willingness to comply with regulatory requirements.

In assessing suitability, the FSA will also have regard to what procedures the applicant has established to ensure competent and prudent management. The FSA will have regard to these factors in particular:

(a) that the Board of Directors or governing body has an appropriate range of skills and experience;

(b) that the Board is organised in such a way to allow it to control the activities of the business and supervise the activities of senior personnel;

(c) that there are procedures to ensure compliance with the FSA training and competence regime;

(d) whether those persons that the applicant proposes to carry out controlled functions are or will be capable of meeting the requirements of the FSA's approved persons regime;

(e) whether personnel policies are in place to ensure that the applicant only employs individuals who are honest and committed to high standards of integrity;

(f) whether sound financial and risk management policies, including robust information and reporting systems have been properly developed, tested and installed;

(g) whether a sound business plan and strategy has been established which demonstrates as far as it is reasonable to do so that the business proposal is viable;

(h) that the anti-money laundering procedures (training, verification of identity, record-keeping and reporting) are properly established;

(i) that suitably qualified auditors have been appointed; and

(j) that all other factors are satisfactory including:

(i) assurances by overseas regulators;

(ii) position in the group; and

(iii) the firm's plans to seek variations or extension to its permission.

2.4   The Statement of Principles and Code of Practice for approved persons

The Principles for business are to be supplemented by Principles for approved persons supported by a Code of Practice. The Code of Practice will not be mandatory. It is designed to assist approved persons to determine what conduct does not comply with the Statement of Principles for approved persons.

For persons who were formally registered under the self-regulatory organisation regimes, in substance, not a great deal will have changed, although there will be much more explicit detail about what standards will apply and what actions approved persons have to take to avoid their conduct falling below the required standard. But for those individuals who were subject to the old statutory regimes for instance in banks or building societies, they will now be required to seek prior approval before they take up their posts, will be subject to the explicit requirements of the Principles and Code of Practice and will be subject to disciplinary proceedings if things go wrong. The Principles and Code will also apply to approved persons at the Society of Lloyd's, approved persons employed by recognised professional bodies whose investment business is deemed not to be incidental, mortgage lenders and mortgage administrators.

The justification for the enhancement of the FSA's powers directed at the behaviour of individuals is the perception that under the unreformed regulatory procedures firms had considerable incentives to align their commercial policies and compliance procedures with good practice and regulatory requirements but that this was not so at the individual level, for instance, the rogue trader or the commission hungry salesman. The emphasis on personal standards and a Code of Practice directly applicable to individuals is an attempt to provide incentives to individuals to align their activities more closely to good practice and regulatory requirements.

2.4.1 Application and scope

Section 64(1) FSMA gives the FSA powers to establish Statements of Principles. Section 64(2) requires the FSA to publish a Code of Practice if it publishes Statements of Principles applicable to approved persons. The intention of this legislation is undoubtedly to ensure that the FSA's requirements are made as explicit as possible to assist approved persons to fulfil their obligations.

Section 64(3) FSMA allows the FSA to apply different provisions according to circumstances, for example in relation to a person's conduct. The primary example of this is the application of Principle 1 to 4 to all approved persons and Principles 5, 6 and 7 only to those who perform significant influence functions.

The Principles will only apply to an approved person when he is carrying on a controlled function in relation to a regulated activity. Where a person's functions extend to activities which are not controlled, then the Principles will not be applied to these activities.

2.5 The Statement of Principles for approved persons

The Statement contains seven succinct provisions. Principles 1 to 4 apply to all approved persons.

Principle 1: an approved person must act with integrity in carrying out his controlled function.

Principle 2: an approved person must act with due skill, care and diligence in carrying out his controlled function.

Principle 3: an approved person must observe proper standards of market conduct in carrying out his controlled function.

Principle 4: an approved person must deal with the FSA and other regulators in an open and co-operative way and must disclose appropriately any information of which the FSA would reasonably expect notice.

Principle 5: an approved person performing a significant influence function must take reasonable steps to ensure that the business of the firm for which he is responsible is organised so that it can be controlled effectively.

Principle 6: an approved person performing a significant influence function must exercise due skill, care and diligence in managing the business of the firm for which he is responsible in his controlled function.

Principle 7: an approved person performing a significant influence function must take reasonable steps to ensure that the business of the firm for which he is responsible in his controlled function complies with regulatory requirements imposed on that business.

2.5.1 *The Code of Practice*

The Code of Practice sets out examples of behaviour which in the FSA's opinion tends to show that an approved person has breached a Principle. In consequence, the Code has a predominantly negative tone. In a more positive vein the FSA has undertaken to assess any breach of the Code after all the circumstances of the case have been examined, in particular the context in which a course of conduct was undertaken, the precise circumstances of the case, the characteristics of a particular controlled function and the behaviour expected in that function. Nor will there be a breach of a Principle unless an approved person has been personally culpable. Personal culpability arises:

(a) where a person acts knowing it to be wrong; or

(b) where a person's standard of conduct falls below what is reasonable in all the circumstances.

It is not clear whether this is reasonable from the point of view of a responsible trader at the time he undertakes the behaviour or reasonable from the point of view of a regulator reviewing the behaviour after the event with hindsight.

Strict compliance with the Code will not provide a safe harbour. The prescribed behaviours set out in the Code are not exhaustive. The FSA expects to amend the Code from time-to-time to deal with new mischief before it can become prevalent.

In assessing whether an approved person has complied with the Principles, the FSA will take into account whether the person's behaviour is consistent with the detailed requirements set out in the rest of the Handbook and whether the approved person's conduct is consistent with the compliance requirements applicable to his firm.

For those who perform significant influence functions the FSA will consider whether the person exercised reasonable care when considering the information available to him, whether he reached a reasonable conclusion and acted on it. These judgements will be made in the context of the:

(a) size and complexity of the business;

(b) the role and responsibility of the person; and

(c) the knowledge he had of regulatory concerns.

2.5.2   *Principle 1 – act with integrity*

An approved person who, in the FSA's opinion, deliberately misleads a customer, his firm or the FSA, will be in breach of Principle 1. The catalogue of behaviour regarded as "misleading" is long, varied and obviously drawn from the regulator's past experience and includes:

(a) falsifying documents;

(b) misleading a customer about risk, charges, performance or cost of investment products;

(c) mismarking the value of investments or positions;

(d) misleading the firm about a customer's creditworthiness;

(e) providing inaccurate information about training, qualifications and past employment;

(f) providing false and inaccurate information to the FSA;

(g) destroying documents, etc. relevant to questionable behaviour; and

(h) failing to disclose personal account dealings.

An approved person who deliberately recommends an investment to a customer or undertakes a discretionary transaction on behalf of a customer where he is unable to justify its suitability will be regarded as having breached Principle 1.

Where an approved person is aware that a customer, his firm or the FSA are misunderstands a material issue, he will be in breach of Principle 1 if he does not clarify the issue.

The deliberate preparation of false or inappropriate records such as inaccurate performance reports, inaccurate training records and inaccurate trading confirmations, relating to a controlled function will be regarded as a breach of Principle 1.

The deliberate misuse of confidential information or customer assets will be regarded as a breach of Principle 1. Such behaviour includes:

(a) front running customer orders;

(b) churning customer accounts by unjustified trading;

(c) misappropriating customer assets;

(d) using one customer's funds to settle calls on another customer's account;

(e) using a customer's funds for a purpose other than for which they were provided.

Deliberately disguising breaches of regulatory rules and deliberately failing to disclose conflicts of interests in dealings with customers will also be regarded as breaches of Principle 1.

2.5.3   *Principle 2 – due skill, care and diligence*

Many of the failings listed as breaches of Principle 2 are similar to those listed under Principle 1 except that under Principle 1 the failing must be deliberate whereas under Principle 2 the failings arise because of a lack of skill, care or diligence.

Failure to provide material information to a customer or firm where the person knew or ought to have known of his duty to provide it, is a breach of Principle 2. Such a failure could include:

(a) failing to explain risks to a customer;

(b) failure to disclosure details of charges;

(c) mismarking trading positions;

(d) providing inadequate or inaccurate information to auditors; or

(e) failure to disclose personal account dealings.

An approved person who advises a private customer to acquire an investment without reasonable grounds for believing it is suitable or without a reasonable understanding of the risks will be in breach of Principle 2.

An approved person who deals on behalf of his firm without sufficient understanding of the risks, will be in breach of Principle 2.

Failure to segregate customers' assets or to process customer payments promptly will be regarded as a breach of Principle 2.

Continuing to undertake a controlled function despite failing to meet the standards of knowledge and skill required will be a breach of Principle 2.

2.5.4   *Principle 3 – proper standards of market conduct*

Where an approved person's functions require him to participate in an organised or over-the-counter market he will be required to observe proper standards. Compliance with the FSA's Inter-professional Conduct, the FSA's Code of Market Conduct, with the rules of exchanges and other market codes will tend to show compliance with Principle 3.

2.5.5   *Principle 4 – dealing with regulators in an open and co-operative way*

In this context a regulator includes the FSA, an exchange or an overseas regulator.

The FSA would regard a failure to report a matter in accordance with a firm's internal procedures (or if none exist, to the FSA) as a breach of this Principle. This makes it clear that approved persons should not bypass the internal reporting processes of their firm and should in normal circumstances use the established routes for reporting between the firm and the regulator. In determining whether a matter should have been reported the FSA will have regard to:

(a) the significance of the information to the FSA;

(b) whether the information related to the individual or the firm; and

(c) whether the decision not to report was taken after reasonable inquiry and analysis.

Where an approved person's duties require him to report directly to the FSA, any failure to report a significant matter to the FSA will be regarded as a breach of Principle 4.

Failure to provide information in respect of a regulator's question, failure to attend an interview or answer questions and failure to supply the regulator with relevant documents will be regarded as breaches of Principle 4.

2.5.6   *Principles 5 to 7*

Principles 5 to 7 apply only to those approved persons whose functions exert significant influence over the conduct of a firm's business.

2.5.6.1   *Principle 5 – senior manager must ensure that the business is organised so that it can be controlled effectively*

An approved person whose responsibilities give him control of an area of the business will have breached Principle 5 if he does not apportion clearly all areas of responsibility. Similarly, failure to apportion responsibilities clearly among staff to whom responsibility has been delegated will also be a breach of Principle 5. Evidence of failure to apportion effectively will be:

(a) confusing or uncertain reporting lines;

(b) confusing or uncertain authorisation levels; and

(c) confusing or uncertain job descriptions.

An approved person who is required to apportion directors' and senior managers' responsibilities in accordance with the FSA requirements for senior management arrangements (SYSC 21.1.R and SYSC 2.1.3R) will be in breach of Principle 5 if he fails to take reasonable care to maintain clear and appropriate apportionment of all significant responsibilities. Evidence tending to show failure to apportion high level responsibilities will include failure to perform a regular review or failure to act where the review shows that responsibilities have not been clearly apportioned. The frequency and depth of this review should be based on the inherent risks of the business.

Where the rules speak of apportionment of responsibility this should normally be taken as meaning apportioned to an individual, presumably in preference to a committee or to a number of individuals jointly.

Reporting lines should be clear and properly communicated. Where there are dual or matrix reporting lines it is important that responsibilities and accountabilities are clear and understood.

Authorisation levels, where they are relevant, should be set out in writing usually in job descriptions.

An approved person who is required to apportion responsibility to individuals must ensure that the individuals are, and continue to remain, suitable. This review is particularly important if there are concerns relating to an individual's compliance with regulations or internal controls and this review must be undertaken, however great the person's commercial contribution is to the firm. Persons who are found to be unsuitable must be removed from positions of responsibility.

Where there are temporary vacancies an approved person must ensure that suitable cover is arranged either by temporary staff or an outside consultant. If the vacancy relates to a controlled function, the temporary member of staff or consultant will need to be an approved person. If no cover can be provided the activity should be suspended.

2.5.6.2   *Principle 6 – senior managers must carry out their duties with skill, care and diligence*

The key requirement is for a senior manager to keep himself informed about the business for which he is responsible. Failings in this area could include:

(a) permitting transactions he does not understand;

(b) permitting the over expansion of the business without assessing risk;

(c) inadequate monitoring of excessively profitable or unusual transactions;

(d) accepting unsatisfactory explanations without testing their veracity; and

(e) failing to obtain independent and expert advice where appropriate.

A senior manager may delegate responsibility but will be in breach of Principle 6 if he:

(a) does not have reasonable grounds for believing that the delegate has the necessary capacity and competence; or

(b) fails to review the conduct of this delegated business.

Such a failure could arise from:

(a) failure to require adequate reports;

(b) accepting inadequate explanations;

(c) failing to exercise adequate supervision; or

(d) failing to take action when progress is unreasonably slow.

However, the FSA will not always expect the approved person who is carrying out a significant influence function to be in daily contact. The extent of his involvement will be determined by the nature of the business being conducted and the competence and seniority of the delegates. Nor is the approved person to be an expert in all aspects of the business but where his understanding is limited or the business is particularly complex he should seek advice from within the firm or firm outside.

2.5.6.3 *Principle 7 – senior managers must ensure business is compliant*

Principle 7 requires all approved persons who have a significant influence function to ensure that the business for which he is responsible complies with regulatory requirements imposed on the business. Failure would arise if adequate compliance procedures are not established or compliance with procedures is not monitored. A failure of Principle 7 would arise if a breach of a compliance requirement was identified but not rectified. Failure to review compliance procedures regularly would be a breach of Principle 7. As regards the Money Laundering Reporting Officer (the "MLRO") failure to discharge his responsibilities under the rules would be a breach of Principle 7.

2.6 Senior management arrangements, systems and controls ("SYSC")

High Level Principle 3 requires a firm to take reasonable care to organise and control its affairs responsibly, effectively and with adequate risk management systems. Block 1 of the Handbook sets out a number of important rules as to steps firms must take to comply with Principle 3. There is also some important guidance.

2.6.1 *The purpose of SYSC*

The FSA justifies the creation of rules and guidance in this area on the following grounds:

(a) to encourage firms' directors and senior management to take practical steps to manage their firms effectively;

(b) to amplify the FSA's expectations underlying Principal 3 and to provide certainty as to interpretation; and

(c) to encourage firms to allocate responsibilities to specific directors and senior managers.

2.6.2   *The apportionment of responsibilities*

SYSC 2.1.1R requires a firm to take reasonable care to maintain clear and appropriate apportionment of significant responsibilities among its directors so that:

(a) it is clear who is responsible for what; and

(b) the business of the firm can be controlled by directors, relevant senior managers and the governing body of the firm. There are a number of clear components in SYSC Rule 2.1.1R some of which are quite wide-ranging. Firstly, responsibilities for all areas of business have to be allocated to specific directors or senior management. This will require great care where responsibilities meet and overlap or where responsibilities are shared. Secondly, all areas of responsibility have to be assigned so that underlying the assignment of responsibilities to individuals there has to be an assessment of all areas of risk affecting the business. There is no requirement that this risk assessment should be formalised (it could be left to the judgement of the chief executive) but it may be easier to demonstrate reasonable care has been taken in accordance with Principle 3 if a formal and objective risk assessment process is adopted.

SYSC 2.1.3R requires a firm to allocate to one or more individuals the responsibility to:

(a) allocate to other directors and senior managers their responsibilities required by SYSC 2.1.1R; and

(b) oversee the establishment of systems and controls within the firm.

The FSA's expectation is that the responsibility to assign responsibilities to other directors and senior managers will be allocated to the chief executive. However, to provide flexibility SYSC 2.1.4R sets out a number of permissible variations. The permissible variations relate to:

(a) the type of firm, that is, a body corporate which is part of a group, an EEA incoming firm or any other firm;

(b) whom the function of allocating responsibilities may be given, that is, the firm's chief executive (or jointly if there is more than one), a director or senior manager with overall responsibility for the firm, the group or a division within the group; and

(c) whom the chief executive may assign responsibilities to, that is, the firm's (or its group's) directors or senior managers.

A chief executive need not allocate all responsibilities to other directors or senior managers. He may reserve some of these responsibilities for himself. The chief executive need not be involved in the discharge of all responsibilities. He has a responsibility to oversee the execution of these responsibilities which he could do by direct monitoring or with the assistance of internal audit or the risk management department. He need play no part at all in those areas of corporate governance such as the audit committee where it would be contrary to good practice for him to be involved.

The "apportionment and oversight function" carried out by the chief executive is an arrangement under Section 59 FSMA and before a chief executive can take up his role he will be required to obtain the prior approval of the FSA.

If the firm is managed by a management committee the apportionment and oversight function can be assigned to the committee so that each member of the committee is jointly responsible. If the firm has a chief executive who is not a member of the management committee, joint responsibility must also be assigned to him.

2.6.3   *Non EEA branches*

Firms which are non EEA branches must apportion responsibilities for systems and controls applicable to the activities carried on in the UK establishment. Such a branch must allocate responsibility to a chief executive who can either be the person resident in the UK responsible for the operations in the UK or can be the chief executive of the firm as a whole.

2.6.4   *Incoming EEA branches*

A firm which is an incoming EEA branch is not required to allocate the apportionment role to the chief executive. However, it must assign the oversight role but only in respect of oversight of systems and controls, the supervision of which is reserved for the host state supervisor; this relates primarily to the systems and controls over the conduct of business carried on from the UK branch. These activities may be summarised as matters covered by

(a) the Conduct of Business Sourcebook excluding COB 9 relating to client assets;

(b) the Money Laundering Sourcebook in respect of activities carried on from the branch in the UK; and

(c) the Inter-Professional Conduct.

2.6.5   *Recording the apportionment*

A firm must make a suitable record of arrangements it has made to:

(a) apportion responsibility for particular risks to individual directors and senior managers under SYSC 2.1.1R; and

(b) the allocation to the chief executive of the responsibility to apportion responsibility to other directors and to exercise oversight over systems and controls under SYSC 2.1.3R.

Such records must be kept for at least six years after they have been superseded by new rules. Firms will have to set up procedures to review these records on a regular basis so that they can demonstrate reasonable care although the records should be updated as soon as is practicable for all material changes.

The records required to be kept need not be prepared specially. They can include records that are kept for other purposes. The types of records envisaged are:

(a) organisation charts;

(b) project management documents;

(c) job descriptions; and

(d) committee terms of reference.

2.6.6   *Systems and controls*

Apart from the rules relating to the allocation and apportionment of senior management responsibilities SYSC 3.1.1R requires firms to monitor systems and controls over other aspects of their business. The required systems and controls must be commensurate with the :

(a) nature, scale and complexity of the business;

(b) diversity of operations;

(c) volume and size of transactions; and

(d) degree of risk associated with operations.

The high level guidance on systems and controls provided relates to typical organisational structures but these are not exclusive. Different classes of firm will require different approaches to systems and controls. Where a firm is subject to the Combined Code prepared by the Committee on Corporate Governance, the FSA will grant credit for compliance with the provisions of the Code.

The FSA will expect the firm to have in place procedures to ensure that its systems and controls are kept under regular review. This review should be designed to ensure that systems and controls have kept pace with developments in the market place and within the business. The firm should also obtain regular confirmation that systems and controls are being operated effectively. This assurance can be gained by:

(a) departmental self assessment;

(b) internal and external audit;

(c) compliance review; and

(d) risk management processes.

Key exceptions from these processes should be reported to senior management and the executive committee and remedial actions monitored to see that they are implemented effectively.

The FSA Handbook provides general guidance as to the areas it would normally expect to see covered by its policies on systems and controls. Apart from Rules relating to compliance, FSA's expectations are covered by guidance. The guidance does not require systems and controls to be in writing, to be communicated or reviewed in any particular way but the nature of the guidance implies for many firms that there should be substantial formality surrounding these matters:

(a) **Organisation**: reporting lines and responsibilities should be clearly defined and communicated within the firm. Where responsibility is delegated to employees or appointed representatives the firm should assess whether the recipient is suitable to carry out the delegated responsibility. Limits to delegated authority should be set. There should be procedures in place to supervise and monitor the delegation of responsibility and follow up action should take place where there is a cause for concern.

Similar processes should apply to delegation to an outsource supplier. Where appropriate, delegated responsibilities should be properly segregated. For instance, no one individual should be responsible for initiating, processing and controlling a transaction.

(b) **Compliance**: it is a rule that the firm must monitor procedures to ensure compliance with regulatory requirements and to ensure that the facilities of the firm are not used to facilitate financial crime.

It may be appropriate for the firm to have a compliance department but this is not required. If a firm does have a compliance function it should be staffed by a sufficient number of competent individuals, should be independent, should have access to relevant records and ultimate recourse to the firm's governing body.

FSA rules relating to the fight against financial crime are set out in the Money Laundering Sourcebook which includes a requirement to appoint a MLRO. This individual is often the same person as the compliance officer but this is not a requirement.

It is an FSA rule that a firm which carries out designated investment business must allocate to a director or senior manager the duty to oversee the firm's compliance procedures. This person must report directly to the firm's governing body. In respect of this rule "compliance" means the Conduct of Business Rules and the rules relating to collective investment schemes. The controlled function described in the supervision function as the "compliance oversight function" relates to the activities covered by this Rule.

(c) **Risk assessment**: where appropriate a firm should have a risk management function. The organisation and responsibilities should be documented, should be adequately resourced and independent of operational areas.

(d) **Management information**: this should be relevant, timely and delivered to the firm's governing body or to those whom the firm considers should receive it. The FSA's reporting requirements will focus on information which relates to its regulatory objectives, that is, fair treatment of customers, protection of consumer confidence in the financial system and the fight against financial crime.

(e) **Employees and agents**: firms should have in place personnel procedures to ensure as far as is practical that employees are competent and honest. Honesty should be assessed at the commencement of employment; competence at the outset and subsequently. The FSA has established particular requirements for approved persons in its training and competence arrangements. These requirements will apply to persons who exercise significant influence, those dealing with customers substantially connected to carrying on a regulated function and those who deal with customers' assets.

(f) **Audit committee**: it will be for management to decide whether to have an audit committee though for larger businesses it is likely that an audit committee will be established. It should have clear terms of reference and a non executive element.

(g) **Business strategy**: all firms are required to plan their business effectively.   Planning means the process of identifying, measuring and controlling risks. For larger firms these plans should be documented and updated regularly.

(h) **Remuneration policy**: this should not create a tension between personal gain and compliance with the regulatory systems. For instance, strong controls should be in place to supervise traders or salesmen who are highly incentivised.

(i) **Business continuity**: firms should have plans to enable it to continue to meet its regulatory obligations. These plans should be reviewed and tested regularly.

(j) **Records**: the FSA's Handbook requires firms to maintain a wide variety of records. A consolidated list of these requirements will be included. At the high level the FSA requires these records to be:

   (i) kept in English, unless they relate to business carried on overseas;

   (ii) accessible;

   (iii) retained for an appropriate period of time; and

   (iv) held securely.

Chapter 3

THE APPROVED PERSONS REGIME, TRAINING AND COMPETENCE

Guy Morton
Partner
Freshfields Bruckhaus Deringer

3.1 Introduction

The basic focus of regulation is on firms: it is the firm carrying on a regulated activity which is required to obtain authorisation. However, regulatory regimes have long recognised that a regulated firm's ability to meet and maintain proper standards depends crucially on the quality of its individuals, especially those in key positions. The UK is no exception, and the regulatory arrangements in force prior to the implementation of the Financial Services and Markets Act 2000 (the "FSMA")[1] include various requirements applicable to individuals. In particular, certain directors and executives of banks and insurance companies must be approved as controllers and individuals performing various functions within investment firms must be registered under schemes laid down by the Self-Regulatory Organisation ("SRO") under the Financial Services Act 1986 (the "FS Act").

Under the FSMA the Financial Services Authority (the "FSA") will be responsible for operating a single regime for approving persons who are to perform certain functions (known as "controlled functions") for authorised firms.[2] The new regime will apply to employees of, and contractors used by, authorised firms and all approved persons

---

[1]   In this Chapter all references to Sections, schedules or paragraphs of schedules are, without further designation, to the FSMA.

[2]   In this Chapter references to a "firm" are to an authorised person.

will be required to comply with a set of high-level principles, which will be supported by a code of conduct and backed by disciplinary sanctions. Although the FSMA provides the framework for the new approved persons regime, the detail will be contained in the FSA's new single Handbook of Rules and Guidance[3] (the "FSA Handbook").

Ensuring satisfactory levels of competence in the financial services industry is also a prerequisite for achieving the FSA's statutory objectives, particularly consumer protection. The FSA's new approach to training and competence is to encourage firms to take responsibility for deciding how their business should best comply with the regulatory requirements contained in the FSA's Training and Competence Sourcebook, which will also form part of the FSA Handbook.

3.2   Approved persons regime

3.2.1   *Scope of the regime*

The approved persons regime will affect a large number of people and will cover not only employees of authorised persons but also directors, sole traders, partners, representatives (including certain persons employed by appointed representatives) and contractors of an authorised person. The term "approved person" covers not only individuals, but also companies that perform certain functions for an authorised person. In addition "matrix managers" carrying on certain functions may also be subject to the new regime, irrespective of whether or not their direct employer is an authorised person.

3.2.2   *Territorial scope*

The new regime does not apply in circumstances where the question of whether a particular individual is "fit and proper" to perform a function is, under any of the single market directives, a matter for the regulators in another European Economic Area ("EEA") Member

---

[3]   The Handbook will contain all the FSA's rules and guidance under the FSMA.

State.[4] It is also clear that the only controlled functions (*see* Section 3.2.4 below) which will apply to senior managers and staff of UK branches of EEA firms are in respect of money laundering and designated investment business[5] which is carried on in the UK and is subject to UK conduct of business requirements. So, where the activities of senior managers of a UK branch fall within a controlled function covering UK designated investment business, they will need to be approved (even if the person responsible for the function is outside the UK), but only in respect of those aspects of their controlled function activities for which the FSA has responsibility, namely the conduct of business requirements.

3.2.2.1   *Inwardly passporting institutions and EEA branches*

As prudential regulation is broadly a matter for home state regulation, much of the approved persons regime will not apply to non-UK companies which take advantage of the EEA "passport". The FSA has, however, specified a particular controlled function, the EEA investment business oversight function, which will apply to EEA branches. This function covers the individual responsible for the oversight of designated investment business in the UK. The FSA expects that the person carrying out this function will normally be in the UK. Where an overseas senior manager has not delegated this function to a senior manager in the UK, he is likely to be performing the controlled function in the UK and will require approval.

The only other controlled functions[6] which will apply to such firms are:

(a) the compliance oversight function;

(b) the money laundering reporting officer (the "MLRO") function;

---

[4]   *See* Section 59(8).

[5]   Designated investment business is carrying on any of the regulated activities in relation to a designated investment. Designated investments are broadly those which correspond to the categories of investment covered by the FS Act; these include shares, debentures, warrants, units in a collective investment scheme and various derivative instruments.

[6]   *See* 3.2.4 below for an explanation of the controlled functions.

(c) the significant management (designated investment business) function;

(d) the significant management (settlements) function (if the activities relate to designated investment business); and

(e) the customer functions.

3.2.2.2   Non-EEA branches

For branches of non-EEA firms, the only applicable controlled functions are:

(a) the chief executive function;

(b) the required functions;

(c) the significant management (designated investment business) function;

(d) the significant management (settlements) function (if the activities relate to designated investment business); and

(e) the customer functions.

Overseas managers of EEA and non-EEA firms with a UK establishment which are concerned with the firm's strategy will not generally fall within the approved persons regime unless they are responsible for implementing strategy in the UK in accordance with UK conduct of business requirements and there has been no delegation to a senior manager in the UK. Where there has been delegation, the senior manager in the UK must be an approved person.

3.2.2.3   Regulation of individuals in overseas branches of UK firms

Managers in charge of the overseas branches of a UK firm will not normally fall within the regime unless they require approval under the significant management functions.[7]

---

7   *See* Section 3.2.4.1 below.

Although individuals in an overseas branch office are likely to be dealing with residents of the country where the branch is established, some individuals who deal with customers may fall within the scope of the new regime to the extent that they deal with customers or the property of customers where UK regulatory conduct of business requirements apply.

3.2.3 The statutory framework

Part V of the FSMA[8] contains the provisions which deal with the regulation of approved persons. It outlines the process for obtaining approval, the standards of conduct expected of approved persons and the FSA's disciplinary powers in relation to approved persons. Section 59(1) of the FSMA provides that persons:

(a) who carry on particular functions (i.e. "controlled functions") for an authorised person;

(b) pursuant to an arrangement[9] entered into by the authorised person (or a contractor of the authorised person, such as an appointed representative);[10]

(c) in connection with the performance by the authorised person of a regulated activity;

will need to be approved by the FSA.

The FSA is required to maintain a record of all persons approved by it. This record must specify the name of the approved individual, the name of the relevant authorised person and, if the approved person is performing a controlled function under an arrangement with a contractor, the name of that contractor.[11] This record will be open to

---

8   *See* Sections 56 to 71.

9   Arrangement is defined in Section 59(10) of the FSMA as "any kind of an arrangement for the performance of a function" and includes the appointment of a person to an office, his becoming a partner or his employment.

10   *See* Section 59(2).

11   *See* Sections 347(1)(h) and 347(2)(g).

inspection by the public at such times and in such forms as the FSA may direct. It will be possible to obtain a copy of the record (or part of it), but the FSA is entitled to charge for this service.

3.2.4   Controlled functions

The approved persons regime only applies to persons performing "controlled functions". The concept of a controlled function is defined in the FSMA as "a function of a description specified in the rules"[12] but the FSA may only specify a function as a controlled function if the individual who is performing the function:

(a) is likely to be able to exert significant influence over the conduct of the firm's affairs in so far as they relate to a regulated activity; or

(b) will be involved in dealing directly with the firm's customers in a manner substantially connected with the carrying on of a regulated activity; or

(c) will be involved in dealing with the property of the firm's customers in a manner substantially connected with the carrying on of a regulated activity.[13]

Controlled functions are therefore designated by the FSA and can be amended by it from time to time. The FSA published its list of controlled functions in February 2001;[14] the final list is set out in the FSA's Supervision Manual.[15] The FSA has specified 27 controlled functions, of which 20 fall into the first category listed above ("significant influence functions") and seven into the second and third categories ("customers functions"). This list of 27 controlled functions sets the parameters of the approved persons regime and any person wishing to perform one of these functions must be approved by the FSA before being allowed to do so.

---

[12]   *See* Section 59(3).

[13]   *See* Sections 59(4) to (7).

[14]   *See* FSA policy statement *The Regulation of Approved Persons: Controlled Functions – feedback on CP53 and 'final' text*, February 2001.

[15]   *See* the "final" text of the FSA's Supervision Manual ("SUP"), May 2001.

3.2.4.1   Significant influence functions

The significant influence functions are divided into four categories:

(a) *governing functions:* directors, shadow directors, non-executive directors, chief executive officers, partners, directors of an unincorporated association, persons acting jointly or solely in directing the regulated activities of a small friendly society and principals of sole trader firms will be carrying on these functions;

(b) *required functions:* these functions will cover the activities of the director(s) or senior manager(s) who have been allocated responsibility for the apportionment and oversight functions in accordance with the FSA's requirements relating to senior management systems and controls,[16] the individual responsible for overseeing the establishment and maintenance of systems and controls for designated investment business carried on from a branch in the UK of an incoming EEA firm, the firm's compliance officer (where the firm conducts designated investment business),[17] the MLRO and the appointed actuary (in the case of long-term insurers);

(c) *systems and controls functions:* any senior manager who performs finance, risk assessment or internal audit functions will be carrying on a systems and controls function; and

(d) *significant management functions:* any person who does not perform a governing body function but who is given significant responsibility or material managerial or strategic influence over a significant business unit of the firm and any person who effects certain contracts of insurance, or who is authorised to commit the firm's financial resources or to process confirmations, payments, settlements, client money, etc., will be carrying on a significant management function.

---

[16]   *See* further Chapter 2 of this Guide.

[17]   Compliance in this context means compliance with the rules in the FSA Conduct of Business Sourcebook and Collective Investment Schemes Sourcebook (see SUP 10.7.10).

The test for determining significant influence over the conduct of a firm's affairs is one of fact, and whether a person's role amounts to the exercise of significant influence will depend on the circumstances.[18] Members of the governing body of a firm are, for example, included in this category because they set the firm's business strategy, regulatory climate and ethical standards. All the directors of a limited company that is authorised under the FSMA will therefore need to be approved persons.

It is not just those who are able to exercise significant influence who must be approved; those who are *likely* to exercise the necessary significant influence will also require approval. The scope of the approved persons regime is therefore wide enough to cover those with senior management authority.

Any person approved to perform a governing function (other than the non-executive function)[19] will not need to apply for further approval before being able to carry on systems and controls[20] or significant management[21] functions.[22] Such a person will, however, need to seek approval before performing any of the required functions[23] or customer functions.[24]

3.2.4.2 Customer functions

These functions are likely to require the largest number of approvals and will cover the activities of most people who advise customers. They are not, however, intended to apply to persons who effect transactions on an execution-only basis or who merely introduce

---

[18] *See* SUP 10.5.4.

[19] *See* the Table of Controlled Functions set out in SUP 10.4.5: controlled functions 1 to 7.

[20] Op.cit. controlled functions 13 to 15.

[21] Op.cit. controlled functions 16 to 20.

[22] *See* SUP 10.6.2 and 10.6.3.

[23] Op.cit. controlled functions 8 to 12.

[24] Op.cit. controlled functions 21 to 27.

customers to a firm, distribute advertisements etc. The FSA interprets the words "dealing with" to mean "having contact with" customers.[25] The customer functions can be divided into two broad categories:

(a) *advisory functions:* this category will cover those who provide investment advice (including those not yet assessed as competent), advice to clients in connection with corporate finance business, advice on pension transfers or pension opt-outs and advice to underwriting members of the Society of Lloyd's in connection with participation in Lloyd's syndicates.

In determining the functions to be specified under Section 59(6) of the FSMA, the FSA indicated that there were two key factors to be taken into account. These were: the extent to which the customer places reliance on the adviser or the advice received; and the existence of a UK regulatory conduct of business regime in respect of the relevant regulated activities.[26] So, for example, a bank cashier who accepts a deposit from a customer arguably does not satisfy these criteria, whereas a pensions salesman selling door-to-door arguably does.

(b) *customer trading and investment management functions:* the customer trading function covers the activities of persons who effect (either as principal or agent) or arrange deals (other than execution-only deals), in investments for private customers and intermediate customers.[27] The advisory element of such activities will fall within the first category outlined above.

The investment management function essentially covers the discretionary management of customers' investments (and, when ancillary to this function, the customer trading and investment

---

[25]   *See* SUP 10.6.

[26]   *See* paragraph 3.46 of CP53, June 2000.

[27]   To constitute a customer trading function, the dealing and arranging must be governed by Chapter 7 of the FSA's *Conduct of Business Rules (Dealing and Managing). See* FSA Policy Statement *Conduct of Business Sourcebook– Feedback on consultation and 'final text' and consultation on supplementary rules,* February 2001.

adviser function). These functions recognise the fact that fund managers and custodians who both hold and/or manage the property of the firm's customers do not necessarily deal directly with those customers or exercise a significant influence over the firm's regulated activities.

3.2.5   *The approval process*

Those who are subject to the new approved persons regime will need to be approved by the FSA before they can carry on controlled functions. This broadly reflects the regime applied by the SROs under the FS Act but differs from the approach of the banking and insurance regulators, who currently approve individuals after they have taken up their positions, save in a few limited cases.

Applications for approval should be made by the authorised person or, where a firm is awaiting authorisation, the prospective authorised person (i.e. by the employer firm rather than by the individual approved person).[28] Where applications are submitted by a firm which is not yet authorised (e.g. an applicant for a Part IV permission), the FSA has said that approvals will be granted to coincide with the granting of a Part IV permission or automatic authorisation.[29]

Where a firm has outsourced the performance of a controlled function, the details of the outsourcing arrangement will determine where responsibility lies for making the application. The FSA has provided guidance for firms in its Supervision Manual.[30]

The FSA's Authorisation Manual explains the process by which an applicant for a Part IV permission, or a person who will be automatically authorised under the FSMA, obtains approval for persons who will be carrying on controlled functions on its behalf (in the case of a firm which is already authorised, the process of

---

[28]   *See* Section 60(1) and explanatory note 140.

[29]   *See* the "final" text of the FSA's Authorisation Manual ("AUTH"), May 2001 at AUTH6 Annex 1G (frequently asked questions), question 2.

[30]   *See* SUP 10.12.4.

applying for individual approval is set out in the FSA's Supervision Manual).[31] An application for approval must be made on a prescribed form[32] and submitted to the Individual Vetting and Registration Department at the FSA. The form will require:

(a) personal details about the candidate seeking approval, including the candidate's name, address, national insurance number and FSA Individual Reference Number (if the candidate does not have or know the FSA individual reference number, the name of the previous regulator and previous Individual Reference Number should be provided as applicable) (Section 1);

(b) identification of the firm making the application (the FSA firm reference number and a contact name within the firm should be provided) (Section 2);

(c) information about the nature of the arrangement between the candidate and the applicant (e.g. whether the candidate is an employee, working under a contract for services etc.) and the controlled functions for which approval is being sought (Section 3). A firm will also be required to confirm in Section 3 that the candidate meets the required levels of training and competence for the particular controlled function(s) in accordance with the FSA's Training and Competence Sourcebook (*see* Section 3.4 below);

(d) a full 10 year employment history for the candidate (Section 4);

(e) responses to a number of questions, which are designed to establish whether the candidate is fit and proper. For example, the applicant will be asked whether the candidate has ever been convicted of an offence involving fraud or dishonesty or has any judgment debts under a court order outstanding (Section 5);

---

[31]   *See* SUP 10.11 and 10.12.

[32]   *See* "Form A – Application to perform controlled functions under the approved persons regime", which is set out in SUP 10 Ann 40. This form is to be used where the candidate is an individual. Applications for corporate candidates should be made using a modified Form A which will be supplied by the FSA on request.

(f)   a list of all directorships currently held or held in the past ten years by the candidate and any additional information which the candidate or the firm considers relevant to the application (Section 6); and

(g)   declarations to be signed by:

(i)   an appropriate person for the firm (e.g. a person approved to carry on a significant influence function) or the person submitting the application; and

(ii)   the candidate (Section 7).

Before granting an application for approval the FSA must be satisfied that the candidate is fit and proper[33] (*see* Section 3.2.6 below).   The FSA also requires firms to notify it of any significant matter which might affect an assessment of fitness and properness as soon as the firm becomes aware of it.[34]

Although the FSA has if necessary up to three months to process completed applications for approval[35] it expects, in practice, to process applications more quickly and will even grant temporary approval where necessary (*see* further below).   The FSA has outlined proposed standard response times for routine applications and anticipates that a new routine, fully completed application in respect of a significant influence function will be processed within seven business days.[36] If, however, the application is not fully completed the FSA can request further information from the firm.   If it does so, the three-month time limit stops running when the FSA requests the information and only starts running again when that additional information has been received by the FSA.[37]

---

[33]   *See* Section 61(1).

[34]   *See* SUP 10.13.16.

[35]   *See* Section 61(3).

[36]   This period will be reduced to four business days for all customer functions. *See* SUP 10 Annex 1G (question 21).   The FSA has also indicated that it proposes to allow firms to submit applications over the internet.

[37]   *See* Sections 60(3) and 61(4).

At the end of the three-month period the FSA must either grant the application (in which case it will notify all interested parties concerned, i.e. the firm making the application, the person who has been approved and, if applicable, the contractor)[38] or, if it proposes to refuse the application, it must issue a warning notice to all interested parties. The warning notice will inform the parties of the FSA's proposed course of action and of the reasons for its action and will specify the period within which the interested parties may make representations to the FSA.[39] If the FSA subsequently decides to refuse the application it must issue a decision notice to each of the interested parties, setting out its decision and its reasons, and each interested party may refer the matter to the independent Financial Services and Markets Tribunal (the "Tribunal").

A firm can withdraw an application for approval at any time before the FSA has reached a decision provided that notification is given to the FSA[40] and the consent of the candidate and the person by whom the candidate is, or would have been, employed (if this is a person other than the firm e.g. a contractor) has been obtained.[41] Full reasons must be given for the withdrawal and, if the withdrawal is due to the candidate's resignation or dismissal from the firm, an explanation of the reasons for the candidate's dismissal or resignation must be provided.

In certain circumstances the FSA will permit a short-form application for approval to be made; for example, when one authorised person (A) sub-contracts services to another authorised person (B). Strictly speaking, under the FSMA, the persons who will be performing the services (i.e. the controlled functions) will need to be approved by the FSA in respect of both firm A and firm B. However, to avoid

---

[38]   *See* Section 62(5).

[39]   *See* Sections 62 and 63 and Sections 387 and 388.

[40]   The notification must be made to the FSA on a prescribed form (*see Form B – Notice to withdraw an application to perform controlled functions under the approved persons regime*, which is set out in Annex 5R to the FSA's Supervision Manual).

[41]   *See* Section 61(5).

potential duplication, the FSA will allow a short-form application to be made in respect of the approvals sought by firm A (i.e. to allow employees of firm B to also carry on controlled functions for firm A).[42]

In the responses which the FSA received to its first Consultation Paper on the regulation of approved persons,[43] many firms expressed concern about how the approval process would operate in an emergency situation and in relation to approvals for temporary vacancies. The FSA has responded to these concerns by excluding from the definition of "significant influence functions" any activities which are undertaken by a person for less than 12 weeks in a consecutive 12-month period. This will allow firms to obtain cover quickly in emergency situations and to deal with unforeseen staff shortages and staff leave. It will also mean that individuals from overseas offices can occasionally do business in the UK without needing to be approved.[44]

3.2.6 *Fitness and properness*

An application for approval will only be granted by the FSA if it is satisfied that the candidate is a fit and proper person to perform the functions for which approval is sought.[45] Although the FSMA does not define fitness and properness in this context,[46] the FSA proposes to apply the following criteria when considering whether an individual is fit and proper to perform a controlled function:

---

[42]   *See* SUP 10.13.4 and 10.13.5.

[43]   *See* FSA CP26 *The Regulation of Approved Persons*, July 1999.

[44]   *See* SUP 10.5.5 and 10.5.6.

[45]   *See* Section 61(1). *See also* the *Fitness and Propriety* Section of the FSA's Handbook of Rules and Guidance ("FIT") which forms part of the High Level Standards block.

[46]   The only express provision in the FSMA is that, in deciding whether a person is fit and proper, the FSA may have regard, *iter alia*, to whether the person has obtained the required qualifications, undergone the required training or possesses the required level of competence (Section 61(2)).

(a) honesty, integrity and reputation (the FSA must be satisfied that the individual intends to be open and honest in his dealings and is able and willing to comply with the requirements imposed on him);

(b) competence and capability (the individual must have the necessary skills to carry on the function which he is to perform); and

(c) financial soundness.[47]

The burden is on the firm supporting the application to prove that the person is fit and proper to perform the functions for which approval is sought.[48]

When determining fitness and properness, the FSA will take into account the particular controlled function or functions which the individual is to perform (or is performing) and the activities or intended activities of the firm. For example, the skills and experience needed by a chief executive in a small firm that carries on few regulated activities will be very different from the skills and experience needed in a large multinational firm. When considering a candidate's fitness and properness the FSA may consider all relevant matters and it may refer to current, past and future matters when determining whether to grant approval. It is for the FSA to decide which matters are relevant and it can, for example, have regard to the cumulative effect of a number of small and, in isolation, insignificant factors to show that a person is not a fit and proper person to perform a controlled function.

It is important to bear in mind that, although a person may be considered fit and proper by the FSA for a particular role within a firm, that person will not necessarily be judged fit and proper for any other role that he may wish to carry on at a later stage, either with the same or with a new employer.

---

[47]   *See* FIT 1.3.1.

[48]   *See* SUP 10.12.9.

3.2.6.1   *Honesty, integrity and reputation*

In assessing honesty, integrity and reputation,[49] the matters that the FSA will take into account include whether the person:

(a) has been convicted of any criminal offences, particularly those involving dishonesty, fraud or financial crime;

(b) has been the subject of any adverse finding or settlement in civil proceedings (particularly in connection with investment or other financial services business, misconduct, fraud or the formation or management of a company);

(c) has been involved in any existing or previous investigation or disciplinary proceedings by the FSA, other regulators or government bodies;

(d) has been or is the subject of any pending proceedings of a disciplinary or criminal nature or been notified of any potential proceedings or investigations which might lead to such proceedings;

(e) has contravened any FSA rules or the rules of other regulators or government bodies;

(f) has been involved with businesses which have been refused authorisations or licences or had them revoked;

(g) has been (or whether any business with which he has been involved has been) investigated, disciplined, censured or suspended or criticised by a regulatory or professional body or a court or tribunal, whether publicly or privately; and

(h) has been dismissed or asked to resign from employment or positions of trust or from a fiduciary or other similar appointment.

This list of matters is extensive; in effect, any matter which impacts on the honesty, integrity or reputation of a person will be relevant to the question of whether he is fit and proper. In considering each of

---

49   *See* FIT 2.1.3.

the matters listed above, the FSA will also have regard to whether the person's reputation might have an adverse impact on the firm and the person's responsibilities.[50]

3.2.6.2   Competence and capability

In determining a person's competence and capability the FSA will consider whether the person satisfies the requirements of the FSA's Training and Competence Sourcebook and whether he has demonstrated by experience and training that he is able to perform the particular controlled function.[51]

Convictions or dismissals or suspensions from employment for drug or alcohol abuse (or other "abusive acts") will also be relevant to assessing capability and a person's continuing ability to perform the particular function.

3.2.6.3   Financial soundness

Financial soundness[52] in this context does not relate to a person's financial resources, but to whether he has:

(a) been the subject of any judgment debt or award that remains outstanding or which was not satisfied within a reasonable period of time; or

(b) made an arrangement with creditors, been bankrupt or had assets sequestered;

either in the UK or elsewhere.

If the FSA is not satisfied that the criteria relating to fitness and properness have been met then it can refuse to approve an individual. After approval is given, the criteria will have to be met on a continuing basis; if not, the FSA may withdraw its approval.

---

50   *See* FIT 2.1.2.

51   *See* FIT 2.2.1.

52   *See* FIT 2.3.

3.2.7 *Withdrawal of approval*

Where the FSA decides that a person is no longer fit and proper to carry on the functions for which he has been approved, the FSA has the power to withdraw approval.[53] A decision to withdraw approval is based on the same factors as a decision to grant approval and the withdrawal may be, for example, because additional information has been obtained by the FSA which casts doubt over its initial decision to grant approval.[54]

When deciding whether to withdraw approval the FSA will take into account all relevant factors including the following:[55]

(a) the matters set out in the FSMA, including the person's qualifications, training and level of competence as required by the FSA's rules;

(b) the criteria for assessing the fitness and properness of approved persons (i.e. the honesty, integrity and reputation, competence and capability and financial soundness of the approved person);

(c) whether and to what extent the approved person has:

  (i) failed to comply with the Principles for approved persons (*see* Section 3.2.9.2 below); or

  (ii) been knowingly concerned in a contravention by the firm of a requirement imposed on it by, or under, the FSMA;

(d) the relevance, materiality and length of time since any matters indicating unfitness occurred; and

(e) the severity of risk which the person poses to consumers and confidence in the financial system.

---

[53] *See* Section 63.

[54] *See* paragraph 143 of the explanatory notes.

[55] *See* paragraph 7.5.2 of the "final" text of the FSA's Enforcement Manual ("ENF") May 2001.

Where the information available to the FSA casts doubt on an approved person's fitness and properness to be involved in a regulated activity generally, the FSA may also consider making a prohibition order against that person in addition to withdrawing approval (*see* Section 3.2.11.4 below).   As with the granting of approval, interested parties must be notified of the FSA's intention to withdraw approval via the warning and decision notice procedure.[56]

3.2.8   *Obligation on firms to take reasonable care*

Authorised persons are required to take reasonable care to ensure that no person performs a controlled function for them without first being approved by the FSA.   Failure to do so may result in the firm being publicly censured or fined.[57]

The term reasonable care was inserted into Section 59(1) of the FSMA when the Financial Services and Markets Bill was being considered by the House of Lords.[58] Lord McIntosh commented that, without it, an absolute requirement to ensure that no person performed a controlled function without FSA approval would mean that an authorised person could be in breach of a duty (and would be exposed to disciplinary action by the FSA and to a possible action for damages)[59] even when it had taken all reasonable care to ensure that it had complied with the requirement. Although the inclusion of the reasonable care wording in Section 59(1) removes the absolute obligation on firms to identify and obtain approval for every individual carrying on a controlled function, even the reasonable case obligation may prove to be quite onerous, given the range of controlled functions and the complexity of the business of many firms. Firms will need to ensure that their structures and procedures for appointing and promoting staff and defining their

---

[56]   *See* Section 63(3) *et. seq.*

[57]   *See* Sections 205 and 206.

[58]   *See* Lord McIntosh of Haringey, Committee Stage, column 173, 21 March 2000.

[59]   *See* Section 71.

responsibilities address the controlled functions and ensure that sufficient information continues to pass to those responsible for dealing with individual approvals.

Authorised persons must also take reasonable care to ensure that their contractors comply with this requirement.[60] It is difficult to know what the practical effect of this requirement will be on the relationship between firms and their contractors. The FSA has commented that the purpose of the reference to "reasonable care" in Section 59(1) is to provide firms with flexibility in the way in which they comply with this requirement and not to reverse the burden of proof.[61] The FSA has assured firms that there will not be any presumption of failure to take care and that, when considering whether a firm has taken reasonable care, the FSA will have regard to:

(a) what information the firm knew at the time of the behaviour and what information it ought to have known in all the circumstances;

(b) what steps the firm took to comply with the rule and what steps it ought to have taken in all the circumstances; and

(c) the regulatory standards at the time of the behaviour.[62]

As a minimum, firms using contractors may be expected to insist on warranties that all individuals carrying on controlled functions will be approved. They may go further and require the power to inspect and monitor contractors' procedures in this area.

---

[60]   *See* Section 59(2).

[61]   *See* paragraph 2.10 of the FSA's policy statement *High level Standards for Firms and Individuals: Issues Arising Out of CP35 and CP26*, June 2000.

[62]   *See* ENF 11.7.2.

3.2.9   *Consequences of approval*

3.2.9.1   *Standards of conduct expected of approved persons*

The consequences for the relevant person of being approved are potentially far-reaching. The FSMA creates a new system of standards of conduct, backed by statutory disciplinary powers and operating separately from the disciplinary regime applicable to authorised persons. At the core of the new system are Statements of Principle[63] (the "Principles") issued by the FSA, which set out the conduct expected of an individual once approval has been granted. These Principles are supported by a Code of Practice (the "Code") which is issued by the FSA to help to determine whether the conduct of an approved person complies with the Principles. This Code has evidential status; it may contain descriptions of conduct which complies with a Principle, or of conduct which does not comply, or of factors which are to be taken into account in determining compliance (in each case in the opinion of the FSA). In fact most of the material in the draft Code relates to non-compliant conduct or to factors relevant to compliance.

3.2.9.2   *The Principles*

The Principles[64] are high-level standards which apply to all approved persons in the day-to-day performance of their controlled functions. There are seven Principles, of which four apply to all approved persons. The other three only apply to persons who carry out significant influence functions (e.g. senior managers).

---

[63]   *See* Section 64.

[64]   *See* Section 64 and Annex E (APER 2) of the FSA's policy statement *High level standards for firms and individuals*, February 2001.

The first four Principles require all individuals to act with integrity (Principle 1) and with due skill, care and attention (Principle 2), to observe proper standards of market conduct (Principle 3) and to deal with the FSA and other regulators[65] in an open and co-operative way (Principle 4) when carrying on their controlled functions.

The other three Principles (the "Senior Management Principles") require individuals who have been approved by the FSA to perform significant influence functions to:

(a) take reasonable steps to ensure that the regulated business of the firm for which they are responsible is organised so that it can be controlled effectively (Principle 5);

(b) exercise due skill, care and diligence in managing that business (Principle 6); and

(c) take reasonable steps to ensure that the business complies with any relevant regulatory requirements (Principle 7).

Failure to comply with the Principles will constitute an act of misconduct which may give rise to disciplinary or other enforcement consequences for the individual. In determining whether or not an approved person's conduct complies with the Principles the FSA will take into account whether the conduct:

(a) relates to activities that are subject to other provisions of the FSA Handbook; and

(b) is consistent with the requirements imposed on his firm.[66]

However, these are only factors to be taken into account and will not preclude a finding by the FSA that a Principle has been breached on other grounds. The FSA has said that it will not discipline approved

---

[65]   Principle 4 only extends to regulators that have recognised jurisdiction in relation to the regulated activities and have the power to call for information from the approved person in connection with his controlled function (*see* the High Level Standards block of the FSA's Handbook of Rules and Guidance within the Statements of Principle and Code of Practice for Approved Persons ("APER"), 4.4.2).

[66]   *See* APER 3.2.1.

persons on the basis of vicarious liability and that disciplinary action will not be taken against an approved person who performs a significant influence function simply because a regulatory failure has occurred in an area of business for which he is responsible. The FSA will only consider that an approved person has breached Principles 5 to 7 if his conduct falls below the standard which would be reasonable in all the circumstances; an approved person will not be in breach if he has exercised due and reasonable care when assessing information, has reached a reasonable conclusion and has acted on it.

In applying the Senior Management Principles, the nature, scale and complexity of the business under management, the role and responsibility of the individual performing the significant influence function and the knowledge that such person has (or should have had) will also be relevant in assessing whether an approved person's conduct is reasonable. For example, the smaller and less complex the business, the less detailed and extensive the systems of control need to be.

3.2.9.3   *The Code of Practice*

The FSA's Code sets out examples of generic conduct which, in the FSA's opinion, does not comply with the Principles (except in relation to Principle 3 where it contains affirmative guidance) and the factors to be taken into account in deciding whether a person's conduct complies with the Principles. The Code also contains guidance which, while not binding, indicates the type of conduct that the FSA regards as desirable.

Although the Code is not exhaustive and compliance with it does not constitute a safe harbour, it does have evidential status. This means that conduct at odds with the Code will tend to establish non-compliance with the relevant Principle. However, the fact that a person's conduct is not covered by the Code does not necessarily mean that it complies with the Principles.

The FSA may amend the Code if there is a risk that an unacceptable practice may become prevalent, so as to make clear what conduct falls below the standards expected. However, in assessing whether the person complied with the Principle it is the Code in issue at the time when the conduct occurred that is relevant.[67]

Principles 1 and 2: the FSA has specified that behaviour which deliberately misleads or attempts to mislead a client, the approved person's firm or the FSA (e.g. falsifying documents, providing false or inaccurate information to the firm or misleading a client about the risks of an investment) will not comply with Principle 1.

Failure to inform a customer or the firm (or its auditors or appointed actuary) of material information in circumstances where the approved person was aware, or ought to have been aware, of such information and of the fact that he should provide it, is behaviour which the FSA believes will not comply with Principle 2. For example, failure to disclose to a customer details of the charges or surrender penalties applicable to investment products will constitute behaviour which does not comply with Principle 2, as will continuing to undertake a controlled function without meeting the required levels of knowledge and skill specified in the FSA's Training and Competence Sourcebook.[68]

The focus of Principle 2 is on doing something without reasonable grounds or failing to do something which ought to have been done. This reflects the difference between a lack of integrity (in relation to which, according to the guidance provided in relation to Principle 1, the focus is on deliberate misconduct) and a failure to take reasonable care.

Principle 3: this Principle provides that an approved person must observe proper standards of market conduct in carrying out his controlled function and, in assessing compliance with this Principle, the FSA will take into account whether the person, or his firm, has complied with the rules relating to Inter-Professional Conduct, the

---

67   *See* APER 3.1.2.

68   *See* APER 4.2.13.

Code of Market Conduct or other relevant market codes and exchange rules. Compliance with those codes or rules will tend to show compliance with Principle 3.

Principle 4: Principle 4 requires an approved person to deal with the FSA and other regulators in an open and co-operative manner. If, for example, an approved person fails to report promptly (either in accordance with the firm's *internal* procedures or, if none exist, direct to the FSA) any information which it is reasonable to assume would be of material significance to the FSA this will constitute non-compliant behaviour. In practice, most approved persons will be required to report relevant matters internally; only those approved persons who are responsible for reporting matters directly to the FSA will be obliged to do so.[69] This obligation, which corresponds to a similar obligation imposed on firms by the Principles for Businesses, may present individuals with some difficult challenges. In determining whether an approved person's conduct complies with Principle 4 in this context, the FSA will have regard to:

(a) the likely significance of the information which it was reasonable for the individual to assume;

(b) whether the information related to the approved person or to his firm; and

(c) whether any decision not to report the matter internally was taken after reasonable enquiry and analysis of the situation.

Principle 5: Principle 5 requires an approved person who is performing a significant influence function to take reasonable steps to ensure that the regulated business of the firm for which he is responsible is organised so that it can be controlled effectively. The Code provides that failure to:

(a) take reasonable steps to apportion responsibilities for all the areas of business under the approved person's control; or

---

[69] However, the FSA has indicated that if an approved person tries to influence a decision to report (or obstructs reporting) to the FSA then the FSA will consider that person to be someone who has taken responsibility for deciding whether to report the matter to it (APER 4.4.5).

(b) apportion responsibilities clearly (e.g. by implementing confusing or uncertain reporting lines, authorisation levels or job descriptions);

will amount to behaviour which does not comply with Principle 5.

An approved person is also required to take reasonable steps to ensure the suitability of persons who are delegated responsibility for aspects of the business under the control of an individual performing a significant influence function. The competence, knowledge, skills and performance of staff should therefore be reviewed to assess their suitability. Suitable cover should also be arranged for any managerial vacancies which could put a firm's ability to comply with its regulatory obligations at risk.[70]

Principle 6: behaviour which the FSA has indicated will not comply with Principle 6 includes the approved person:

(a) failing to take reasonable steps to inform himself adequately about the affairs of the business for which he is responsible (e.g. permitting transactions without a sufficient understanding of the risks involved or inadequately monitoring highly profitable transactions or unusual transactions or business practices);

(b) delegating the authority for dealing with a particular issue or a part of the business to an individual or individuals without reasonable grounds for believing that the delegate(s) have the necessary capacity, competence, knowledge and/or seniority or skill to deal with the issue or part of the business;[71]

(c) failing to take reasonable steps to maintain an appropriate level of understanding about the issue or part of the business that has been delegated (e.g. disregarding the issue or part of the

---

[70]   *See* APER 4.5.9.

[71]   In determining whether or not the conduct of an approved person complies with Principle 6 the FSA will have regard to the competence and/or knowledge and/or seniority of the delegate and the past performance and record of the delegate.

business once it has been delegated or accepting, without question, implausible or unsatisfactory explanations from delegates);

(d) failing to supervise and adequately monitor the individual or individuals to whom responsibility has been delegated (e.g. failing to take personal action where progress is unreasonably slow or where implausible or unsatisfactory explanations have been provided).

These indications demonstrate that the responsibilities imposed by Principle 6, while not amounting to strict liability,[72] are likely to be burdensome, especially when one takes into account that they will in practice be judged in circumstances when problems have emerged and there is therefore the risk of hindsight.

Principle 7: examples of conduct which will be regarded by the FSA as not complying with Principle 7 will be:

(a) failing to take reasonable steps to monitor (either personally or through a compliance department or other departments) compliance with the regulatory requirements of the firm's business in respect of its regulated activities;

(b) failing to take reasonable steps to find out why significant breaches (whether suspected or actual) of regulatory requirements relating to regulated activities may have occurred (taking account of the systems and procedures in place); and

(c) in the case of the MLRO, failing to discharge the responsibilities set out in Chapter 8 of the Money Laundering Sourcebook.

---

[72] The references to reasonable care in the Principle itself, and to reasonable steps in the examples, reflect criticisms of earlier regimes dealing with senior management responsibilities under the FS Act which some viewed as imposing strict liability.

3.2.9.4   *Notification requirements*

An authorised firm is required to notify the FSA no later than 31 July in each year of the name of each individual who is approved to perform any significant management function,[73] together with a brief description of the job performed.

The FSA's approval is also required for any changes to approved person status. If, for example, an approved person moves job within the same firm and takes on additional controlled functions then an application form must be submitted to the FSA[74] detailing the changes and providing any additional information that the FSA may require.[75] If, however, the approved person will cease to perform controlled functions (in addition to requiring approval in respect of certain new controlled functions) then the firm must notify the FSA using Form E.[76] Similarly, if an approved person is to carry on controlled functions for another firm, that authorised person will have to make a new (albeit short-form) application to the FSA to allow the approved person to perform controlled functions for it.[77]

There is also a requirement to notify the FSA if an approved person ceases to carry on a controlled function. The firm must notify the FSA on a prescribed form[78] no later than seven business days after the person ceases to perform the function. If the reason why the person is ceasing to perform the function is because the firm has dismissed the approved person, the approved person has resigned while under investigation by the FSA or another regulator or the firm has information which may affect the FSA's assessment of the fitness

---

[73]   *See* SUP 10.9.8

[74]   The FSA will, however, accept a short-form application. *See* SUP 10.13.1 and 10.13.2.

[75]   *See* Section 60(2)(b).

[76]   *See* SUP 10.13.3 and *Form E – Internal transfer of an approved person*, which is set out in SUP 10 Annex 8G.

[77]   *See* also Section 3.2.5 above.

[78]   *See Form C – Notice of ceasing to perform controlled functions*, which is set out in SUP 10 Annex 6R.

and propriety of the approved person, the firm must notify the FSA as soon as reasonably practical upon becoming aware of this information, usually by telephone, fax or email within one business day and then submit Form C within seven business days.[79] A person will automatically cease to be an approved person when he no longer carries on any controlled functions.

There is also a prescribed form[80] for notifying the FSA of a change in the personal details of an approved person (e.g. a change of name or National Insurance number), and the firm must notify the FSA within seven business days of becoming aware of the matter. This form should also be used to notify the FSA (as soon as practical) of any significant matter relevant to the fitness and properness of the approved individual.

The FSA has been investigating the use of the internet for receiving applications for approved persons (and for providing approval), withdrawals of approved person status and notification of transfers of approved persons and changes to approved person status. The approved persons forms which have been included in the FSA Supervision Manual are expected to be adapted for use on the internet and it is hoped that this will accelerate the turnaround time for routine applications.

3.2.10   Disciplinary action

The FSA may take disciplinary action against an approved person if two conditions are met: it must appear to the FSA that the approved person is guilty of misconduct; and it must be appropriate in all the circumstances for the FSA to take disciplinary action.[81] Section 66(2) of the FSMA provides that a person will be guilty of misconduct if, while he is approved, he:

---

[79]   *See* SUP 10.13.7 and 10.13.8.

[80]   *See Form D – Notification of changes in personal information or application details*, which is set out in SUP 10 Annex 7R.

[81]   *See* Section 66(1).

(a) fails to comply with one of the Principles (the FSA will consider the extent to which the approved person has complied with the Code); or

(b) has been knowingly concerned in a contravention by the firm of a requirement imposed on it by, or under, the FSMA.

Disciplinary action will, however, only be brought against an approved person where there is personal culpability. According to the FSA, personal culpability will arise where an approved person's behaviour is deliberate or falls below that which would be reasonable in all the circumstances. Where the breach also involves the authorised person the FSA may consider whether it is more appropriate for it to take disciplinary proceedings against the authorised firm,[82] rather than the approved person.

In deciding whether to take disciplinary action, the FSA will consider the full circumstances of each case and may take into account a number of other factors which include:[83]

(a) the nature and seriousness of the breach (the FSA will, for example, consider whether the breach was deliberate or reckless, the duration and frequency of the breach, the amount of any benefit gained or loss avoided as a result of the breach, and whether the breach reveals any serious or systemic weakness of the management systems or internal controls of the firm's business);

(b) the conduct of the approved person after the breach, including how quickly and effectively the approved person brought the breach to the FSA's attention, the degree of co-operation shown during the investigation of the breach and any remedial steps taken since the breach was identified;

(c) the previous regulatory record of the approved person;

(d) any guidance issued by the FSA on the conduct in question and the extent to which the approved person has sought to follow that guidance;

---

[82] *See* paragraph 147 of the explanatory notes.

[83] *See* ENF 11.4.1.

(e) action taken by the FSA in previous similar cases; and

(f) whether any action that is to be taken by other regulatory authorities is adequate to address the FSA's concerns.

The FSA's guidance makes it clear that it regards formal disciplinary action as a serious matter and indicates that for minor breaches it may decide to give a private warning instead.[84]

There is a limitation period of two years from the date on which the FSA knew of the misconduct, after which time the FSA will be prevented from taking action unless proceedings have already been commenced.[85]

3.2.11   Sanctions for misconduct

If the FSA concludes that an approved person has been guilty of misconduct and considers that the case is sufficiently serious to warrant disciplinary action, it may issue a public statement of misconduct or impose a fine.[86] In addition, where an approved person's fitness and properness to carry on regulated activities is called into question, the FSA may withdraw status as an approved person and prohibit the person from performing controlled functions. In either case the FSA must go through the warning and decision notice procedure and the approved person has the right to make representations and to refer the proposed decision to the Tribunal.[87]

3.2.11.1   Public statements of misconduct

In deciding whether to publish a public statement of misconduct, the FSA will consider all the relevant circumstances of the case. It has issued the following broad guidelines:[88]

---

[84]   *See* ENF 12.3.1 and 3.2.11.3 below.

[85]   *See* Sections 66(4) and 66(5).

[86]   *See* Section 66(3).

[87]   *See* Sections 57 and 67.

[88]   *See* ENF 12.3.3.

(a) if the approved person has made a profit or avoided a loss as a result of the misconduct the FSA is more likely to impose a fine;

(b) if the misconduct is serious in nature or degree the FSA is more likely to impose a fine;

(c) if the approved person has admitted the misconduct, co-operated with the FSA and taken steps to ensure that consumers are fully compensated for any losses arising from the contravention, this is more likely to result in a statement of misconduct (rather than a fine), depending upon the nature and seriousness of the conduct;

(d) if the approved person has a poor disciplinary record or compliance history the FSA may take the view that a fine is more appropriate because it may deter future instances of misconduct; and

(e) if the approved person has inadequate means to pay the level of financial penalty which the particular misconduct would usually attract, this may be a factor which will result in either the imposition of a lower level of fine or a public statement.

3.2.11.2   *Financial penalties*

The FSA will consider all the relevant circumstances of a case when deciding on the level of fine which is appropriate. In accordance with Section 69 of the FSMA the FSA must, when determining the amount of a fine to be imposed on an approved person, have regard to:

(a) the seriousness of the misconduct in question in relation to the nature of the Principle or requirement concerned;

(b) the extent to which that misconduct was deliberate or reckless; and

(c) whether the person on whom the penalty is to be imposed is an individual.[89]

Other factors which may be relevant when determining the amount of the fine payable include the disciplinary and compliance history of the approved person and the person's conduct following the contravention.

3.2.11.3   *Private warnings*

Notwithstanding that a contravention has taken place the FSA may, in some cases, consider that it is not appropriate to bring formal disciplinary action against an approved person. This may be the case, for example, where the contravention is only minor or the approved person has taken immediate and full remedial action. In such circumstances, the FSA may decide to issue a private warning.

3.2.11.4   *Prohibition orders*

In addition to being able, through the granting and withdrawal of approvals, to ensure that only appropriate people exercise "controlled functions" in relation to firm's regulated activities, the FSA has a broader power (under Section 56 of the FSMA) to prohibit any individual, including an approved person, from performing particular functions. The individual can be prohibited from performing a specified function, a function within a specified description, or any function at all, and the specified function can relate not only to particular regulated activities or types of regulated activities but also to authorised persons generally. The FSA can therefore prohibit an individual from being involved in any aspect of the business of any regulated firm. When considering whether to make a prohibition order, the FSA will take into account:

---

[89]   *See* ENF 13.3.2. The FSA will consider the financial resources and other circumstances of the approved person and may take into account whether there is evidence of financial hardship if the person was to pay the level of penalty associated with the contravention; the purpose of the penalty is not to render an approved person insolvent.

(a) whether the person is fit and proper to perform functions in relation to regulated activities;

(b) whether the person has been involved in misconduct under the FSMA;

(c) the relevance, materiality and length of time since any matters indicating unfitness occurred;

(d) the controlled function performed by the approved person, the nature of the firm's regulated activities and the markets in which the individual operates;

(e) the risk which the individual poses to consumers and to confidence in the market; and

(f) the previous disciplinary record and general compliance history of the individual.[90]

A person who contravenes a prohibition order by either performing or agreeing to perform a controlled function will be guilty of an offence and authorised persons are required to take reasonable care to ensure that no functions are performed for them by a person who is subject to a prohibition order.[91]

Persons who are the subject of a prohibition order may apply to the FSA for a revocation or variation of the order.[92] In determining whether to vary or revoke an order the FSA will consider:[93]

(a) the seriousness of the misconduct that resulted in the order;

(b) the amount of time which has elapsed since the original order was made;

(c) the steps (if any) which the individual has taken to remedy the misconduct;

---

[90] *See* ENF 8.5.2.

[91] *See* Sections 56(4) and 56(6).

[92] *See* Section 56(7).

[93] *See* ENF 8.9.2.

(d) evidence which (had it been known to the FSA at the time) would have been relevant to the FSA's decision;

(e) all available information relating to the individual's honesty, integrity or competence in the period since the order was made;

(f) where the FSA's finding of unfitness arose as a result of the person's incompetence, whether there is any evidence that this unfitness has been or will be remedied;

(g) the financial soundness of the person concerned; and

(h) whether the person has ceased to pose a risk to consumers or market confidence.

3.2.11.5   *Injunctions and restitution orders*

The FSA also has other remedies available to it under the FSMA to deal with the misconduct of approved persons. It may, for example, apply to the court for an injunction (under Section 380) or a restitution order (under Section 382). Section 380 of the FSMA allows the FSA or the Secretary of State to apply to the court for an injunction restraining a person from contravening a requirement imposed by or under the FSMA, requiring him to take steps to remedy a contravention or restraining him from disposing of, or dealing with, any assets of his.

Section 382 of the FSMA also allows the FSA or the Secretary of State to apply to the court for a "restitution order". Such an order will be granted if the court is satisfied that, as a result of a contravention, profits have accrued to the approved person or that one or more persons have suffered loss or been otherwise adversely affected. The effect of a restitution order is to require the approved person to pay to the FSA a sum of money which the court considers just (having regard to the profit or loss involved).

3.2.12   *Insurance policies for approved persons*

The approved persons regime imposes obligations on a large number of people who work in the financial services industry. Such persons are potentially liable to a wide range of sanctions for breach of the FSA's requirements and many industry associations are developing insurance policies which are designed to cover the legal costs and expenses incurred by approved persons under the new regime. These policies will cover the cost of any examinations required and/or proceedings brought by any regulatory body in relation to the business carried on by approved persons on their employer's behalf.

3.2.13   *Transitional provisions*

The FSMA (Transitional Provisions) (Authorised Persons etc.) Order 2001[94] was made and laid before Parliament on 20 July 2001. Part VI of the order contains the transitional provisions relating to approved persons. It provides that if a person is working for an authorised person before N2 in a position for which they would need to be approved by the FSA (under part V of the FSMA) after commencement, that person will be treated as having been approved by the FSA for the purpose of working in that position post-N2 unless, for example, that person was working in breach of an applicable SRO rule before commencement of the FSMA. The effect of the order is therefore to "grandfather" individuals who are properly registered under the existing regimes, and also individuals who are actually performing functions which do not currently require registration but will be controlled functions under the new regime. Unsurprisingly, individuals who are operating in breach of existing requirements will not be "grandfathered". As a practical matter, the order underlines the importance of firms agreeing with the FSA a list of currently registered individuals and of individuals actually performing functions which will become controlled functions for the first time.

The order also carries forward certain approvals given under the Insurance Companies Act 1982 and the Banking Act 1987 where the person approved has not taken up the appointment before N2.

---

[94]   SI 2001/2636.

3.3 Senior management

3.3.1 Requirements of senior management

The FSA has stated that a firm's senior management will be responsible for the firm's activities and for ensuring that the firm's business is conducted in compliance with relevant regulatory requirements.

The new regime of senior management responsibilities under the FSMA, which is based on a combination of requirements applicable to the firm and requirements applicable to identified individuals under the approved persons regime, is the culmination of a number of initiatives by the FSA (or SIB as it was then) and SROs under the FS Act.

In December 1999 the FSA published a consultation paper[95] clarifying the regulatory obligations of senior managers and directors who will be approved persons under the new regime and amplifying the requirements of Principle 3 of the FSA's Principles for Businesses which provides that, "a firm must take reasonable care to organise and control its affairs responsibly and effectively, with adequate risk management systems".

Firms will have two key obligations under Principle 3. They will be required to:

(a) ensure that each senior manager's sphere of personal responsibility is clearly delineated and understood (firms will need to take reasonable care to establish and maintain a clear and appropriate apportionment of responsibilities among their directors and senior managers to allow them to properly monitor and control the firm's affairs); and

---

[95]   *See* FSA CP35 *Senior management arrangements, systems and controls*, December 1999.

(b) take reasonable care to establish and maintain such systems and controls as are appropriate to their business (having regard to a number of factors including the scale, nature and complexity of the business).[96]

Firms may allocate the jobs of apportioning senior management responsibilities and overseeing the establishment and maintenance of the firm's system of internal controls (the "Functions") to one individual or to a group of individuals, provided that the allocation is appropriate. The FSA has said that it will be common for both functions to be allocated solely to the firm's chief executive. It has, however, included further guidance on the allocation of functions in the form of a table of frequently asked questions. This table addresses issues such as what happens if the firm does not have a chief executive and what is meant by "appropriately allocate" in this context.[97]

There is no limit on the number of individuals to whom the Functions may be allocated, provided that the allocation is "appropriate" (i.e. it can be expected that the function will be successfully discharged). However, all the individuals to whom the Functions have been allocated will need to become approved persons (although there are exceptions – for example, in the case of an incoming EEA firm). These individuals can be selected from the firm and/or the group (where the firm is part of a group), but where there is a chief executive he must be one of the individuals to whom the Functions are allocated unless an appropriate individual of greater seniority from elsewhere in the corporate group can be substituted. Where a firm does not have a chief executive, responsibility for allocation of the Functions will fall on an equivalent individual or group of individuals.[98]

---

[96] *See* FSA policy statement *High level standards for firms and individuals,* February 2001 – *Senior Management Arrangements, Systems and Controls* ("SYSC") 2.1.1 and 3.1.1.

[97] *See* SYSC 2.1.6.

[98] SYSC 2.1.4 and 2.1.6 of the SYSC chapter of the FSA's Handbook of Rules and Guidance provide further guidance on the allocation of Functions to individuals. *See* further Chapter 1 of this Guide.

3.3.2   *Discipline of senior management*

The FSA does not consider that it is appropriate to discipline senior managers who are approved persons simply because a breach of the regulatory requirements has occurred in an area for which they are responsible. There will, for example, only be a breach of a Senior Management Principle where there is personal culpability (i.e. where the breach is deliberate and where the standard of behaviour is below that which the FSA could reasonably expect from an individual managing a particular business or part of the business, taking account of the size and complexity of that business).[99]

3.4   Training and competence

3.4.1   *Introduction*

In December 2000 the FSA published its "final" Training and Competence Sourcebook[100] (the "TC Sourcebook") setting out the standards which it requires authorised persons to meet to ensure future standards of competence within the financial services industry. In developing a single coherent framework applicable to all participants in the industry, the FSA's approach has been to encourage firms to take responsibility for determining how their business can best comply with the requirements.

The FSA believes that the training and competence of staff is an important prerequisite to achieving its statutory objectives, particularly consumer protection and market confidence.

The FSA established the Training Advisory Panel (the "TAP") in August 1999[101] to assist it in the development of its policies on training and competence. The TAP advises the FSA on the

---

[99]   *See* further Section 3.2.9.2 above.

[100]   *See* FSA CP34 *Training and Competence Sourcebook*, November 1999. The FSA published a feedback statement (in the form of CP60) on CP34 in July 2000. This was followed by publication of a policy statement *Feedback Statement to CP60: Training and Competence Sourcebook* ("TC") in December 2000.

[101]   *See* FSA press release 79/1999.

assessment of competence and the promotion of training within authorised firms and on the approval of examinations for regulatory purposes. It is made up of 13 practitioners, one consumer interest representative and four observers from educational and trade union backgrounds.

The TC Sourcebook is divided into two parts. The first part contains an overarching set of industry commitments to training, to which all firms should aspire (the "Commitments") and the second contains detailed rules and guidance applicable to certain investment business activities carried on by firms. The TC Sourcebook also sets out the "approved examinations" which an employee must pass in order to be able to carry on particular activities and the exemptions from the requirement to take approved examinations. The FSA has sought to harmonise the existing examination structures which apply to the different SRO regimes to develop consistent standards throughout the financial services industry.

3.4.2   The Commitments

The Commitments set the general direction for training and competence and apply to all regulated activities carried on by a firm. They are "aspirational" in nature and expand on Principle 3 of the FSA's Principles for Businesses, which provides that a firm must take reasonable care to organise and control its affairs responsibly and effectively with adequate risk management systems.[102]

Directors and senior managers must be fit and proper for their roles and firms will be required to put appropriate systems in place to ensure the suitability of all those carrying on functions for them. The FSA believes that competence is a key element of suitability and the Commitments, which apply to all employees carrying on regulated activities within a firm,[103] require firms to ensure that:

---

[102]   *See* FSA CP13 *The FSA Principles for Businesses*, October 1998, the *Response to CP13: The FSA Principles for Businesses*, October 1999 and FSA policy statement *High level standards for firms and individuals*, February 2001 at Annex A ("PRIN").

[103]   *See* TC 1.2.1.

(a) their employees are competent;

(b) their employees remain competent for the work they do;

(c) their employees are appropriately supervised;

(d) their employees' competence is regularly reviewed; and

(e) the level of competence is appropriate to the nature of their business.

The FSA believes that firms with high standards of training and competence are much more likely to achieve consumer protection and therefore to help to prevent the mis-selling scandals of the past.

3.4.3   Detailed rules and guidance

Chapter 2 of the TC Sourcebook sets out rules and guidance on:

(a) the recruitment of employees;

(b) assessment of employees to identify their training needs;

(c) supervision of employees;

(d) monitoring of employees to ensure that they attain and maintain competence for the activities which they carry on;

(e) approved examinations; and

(f) record-keeping requirements.

However, the rules and guidance do not apply to all employees. Rule 2.1.4 specifies that they only apply to employees engaged in:

(a) dealing as an agent or principal for customers in securities or derivatives (e.g. sales and trading staff);

(b) managing designated investments (e.g. fund managers and discretionary portfolio managers);

(c) giving investment advice on designated investments (e.g. independent financial advisers and unit trust operators); and

(d) giving advice on syndicate participation in Lloyd's.

In addition, employees engaged in overseeing any of the following activities on a day-to-day basis are also covered:

(a) operating a regulated collective investment scheme;

(b) providing safekeeping and administration of investments;

(c) administrative functions[104] in relation to managing designated investments;

(d) administrative functions[105] in relation to effecting or carrying out contracts of long-term insurance;

(e) taking private customers through decision trees in connection with stakeholder pensions; and

(f) administrative functions[106] in relation to the management of a stakeholder pension scheme.

The rules do therefore cover employees whose functions cover only banking activities not related to securities or derivatives, or general insurance, or who carry out certain back office functions.

Firms are required to retain records which demonstrate compliance with the requirements of the TC Sourcebook and, broadly speaking, these records must be kept for at least three years after the employee ceases to be employed by the firm.   Records relating to pension transfers and opt-outs should, however, be kept indefinitely.[107]

3.4.3.1   Recruitment and training

Although the rules relating to recruitment and training only apply to business carried on by the firm with, or for, private customers, it may be difficult in practice for firms to differentiate between their employees on this basis.

---

[104]   Administrative functions include arranging settlement and ISA or PEP administration.

[105]   Administrative functions in this context include new business administration, processing claims, fund switching and preparing projections.

[106]   Administrative function in this context include fund allocation and switching and receipt of (or alteration to) contributions.

[107]   *See* TC 2.7.1.

When hiring staff to be involved in such business, firms will be required to ensure that appropriate checks are made to identify and verify the recruit's previous activities and training.[108] The onus is on the firm to ensure that an appropriate level of competence is, or can be, obtained by the new recruit and the recruitment process must take into account the actual skills and knowledge of the recruit in the light of the skills needed for the job.

Firms are also required to identify the training needs of all relevant employees from time to time and to ensure that their training is appropriate, up-to-date and properly structured having regard to changes in the market, products, legislation and regulation.[109] The FSA believes that employees should be able to have access to suitable learning opportunities so that the required level of competence can be achieved as quickly as possible.

3.4.3.2   Attaining competence

Rule 2.3.1 of the TC Sourcebook provides that an employee will not be allowed to undertake or oversee an activity for which he has not been assessed as competent without supervision. If an employee is to undertake an activity directly with, or for, private customers under supervision then he must not only possess the appropriate level of knowledge and skill but he must also have passed the regulatory module of an approved examination before being allowed to do so. On the job training is not enough.[110] The FSA has also specified that employees who are to engage in certain activities,[111] even under supervision, must have passed all modules of the appropriate approved examination.

---

[108]   *See* TC 2.2.1.

[109]   *See* TC 2.2.3 to 2.2.5.

[110]   *See* TC 2.3.2.

[111]   These specified activities are: dealing as principal or agent for customers in securities or derivatives; giving advice on syndicate participation at Lloyd's; and acting as a broker fund adviser or pension transfer specialist.

To be assessed as competent, the FSA has specified that the employee must have passed each module of the appropriate approved examination (or have been exempted from doing so) and must be able to apply the knowledge and skills necessary to engage in the relevant activity without supervision.[112] This not only ensures that the firm's customers are protected but also that all firms are in the same position and that none are put at a competitive disadvantage by the Rule. Any assessment of an employee's knowledge and skills will include consideration of the employee's knowledge of the firm's systems, procedures, investment business and the products provided by the firm and its marketing group.[113] Any assessment of competence must also take into account changes in the market with regard to products, legislation and regulation. Employees should therefore ensure that they possess up-to-date knowledge and skills if they want to attain and maintain competence.

The TC Sourcebook requires firms to make and keep records of the criteria applied in assessing competence and how and when a decision of competency is reached.[114]

3.4.3.3 *Maintaining competence*

The FSA views attaining competence as only the first step in an on-going process and requires competence to be maintained to ensure that market confidence is sustained, customers are protected and financial crime is reduced. A firm must therefore ensure that an employee who is competent in a certain activity remains so and must put in place (and maintain) systems to monitor the competence of its employees on an on-going basis.[115]

If an employee changes roles or takes on additional responsibilities the standard of competence required will need to be reassessed, as will the employee's training and examination requirements.

---

112   *See* TC 2.3.5.

113   *See* TC 2.3.4.

114   *See* TC 2.3.8.

115   *See* TC 2.5.

3.4.3.4   Supervising competence

This requirement only applies to business which a firm carries on with, or for, private customers, although there is a Commitment applicable to all regulated activities. Supervision plays an important role in the quality control of an employee's work and, where an employee has not been assessed as competent (or is to engage in additional activities for which he has not been assessed as competent), the firm must ensure that he is adequately supervised until such time as he has been assessed as competent to perform those activities.

Firms whose employees give investment advice to private customers on packaged products[116] must also ensure that their supervisors have passed the appropriate approved examination(s) and possess the appropriate technical knowledge, assessment skills and coaching skills to act as supervisors.[117]

3.4.4   Approved examinations

Where an employee under supervision has not passed an appropriate approved examination, a firm must require the employee to do so[118] (generally either before starting the activity or within two years of the date on which he commenced that activity).[119] Where an employee fails to do so, the firm must ensure that the employee stops carrying on that activity and passes the examination before resuming the activity.[120] An employee who deals

---

116   Packaged products include a life policy, a unit in a regulated collective investment scheme and a stakeholder pension scheme.

117   *See* TC 2.6.5.

118   *See* TC 2.4.1.

119   In calculating the time spent by an employee under supervision the firm can aggregate periods of time spent engaging in, or overseeing, the activity during different periods of employment and can disregard any period of 60 business days or more in which the employee is continuously absent from engaging in or overseeing the activity.

120   *See* TC 2.4.1(3).

as principal or agent for clients in securities or derivatives is prohibited from carrying on these activities if two years have elapsed since the date he passed an appropriate approved examination, unless the firm can show that he has sufficient experience (i.e. at least three years' relevant experience in the past five years) and up-to-date knowledge.

There are, however, exemptions from the requirement to pass approved examinations. If an employee has:

(a) at least three years' up-to-date relevant experience in the activity in which he is engaged (while employed other than in the UK);

(b) has not previously been required to comply with examination requirements; and

(c) has passed a relevant regulatory module of an approved examination;

   he will not be required to pass other modules of an approved examination.[121]

This approach is designed to facilitate the international transfer of employees while ensuring that they have up-to-date knowledge. The exemption does not, however, apply to employees who are pension transfer specialists or broker fund advisers, or to those who give advice on syndicate participation at Lloyd's or give investment advice to private customers on packaged products.

By having set examinations and time limits the FSA's aim is to ensure that all firms in a sector are on a competitive par. Although the TC Sourcebook contains a schedule of approved examinations, the review and identification of industry examinations is a long-term exercise that may take several years. The FSA is working with national training organisations, the TAP and various qualifications and curriculum authorities to develop the criteria for approval of examinations.

---

[121]   *See* TC 2.4.5.

3.4.5   *Transitional provisions*

The FSA's approach is that individuals who are competent on "N2" (the day on which the FSMA comes into force) will be "grandfathered" and will continue to be considered competent if competency is maintained and the individual is carrying on substantially the same activity before and after the day on which the FSMA comes into force.[122] This will be the case for employees who are currently regulated by SRO schemes. However, where an employee is not yet competent but is undergoing training, the employee will fall under the ambit of the FSA's new training and competence regime as from the specified day.

The FSA has, however, proposed that where the "overseers" of certain administrative functions have not previously been subject to a training and competence regime, there will be a 12-month period during which the firm may assess them as competent (without requiring them to pass an approved examination) but only in relation to the activities which they were able to carry on before N2. This provision is aimed at those in discretionary investment business and in the life and pension office who will fall within the scope of training and competence requirements for the first time.[123]

3.4.6   *Industry toolkits*

The FSA recognises that some firms may need help in implementing or developing their training and assessment systems. To assist different sectors of the financial services industry in developing their own training and competence regimes, a number of trade bodies are producing industry-specific toolkits. The FSA has welcomed this approach and has issued a general toolkit template to help trade organisations to develop their sector-specific toolkits. Although these toolkits are intended to assist firms, they are not intended to

---

[122]   The Treasury announced on 12 July 2001 that N2 will be midnight on 30 November 2001 (i.e. 1 December 2001).

[123]   *See* paragraph 9.14 of FSA CP60 *Feedback statement to CP34: Training and Comeptence Sourcebook – supplementary consultation on record-keeping rules and transitional arrangements*, July 2000.

form guidance; their aim is to provide practical support and assistance to help firms to meet their business objectives and regulatory requirements.

The FSA has recommended that toolkits should comprise statements of market norms and accepted market practice (specifically tailored to the business of the firm), together with practical examples and models of procedure and case studies of policies and arrangements. However, the FSA's template makes it clear that it is the responsibility of firms to tailor the toolkits accordingly and that they should be updated as and when required. Toolkits will not be used as a basis for regulatory supervision by the FSA.

Training and competence forms an integral part of the new regime and the FSA hopes that it will be a priority for all firms carrying on regulated activities to ensure that their employees are trained and capable of performing their activities. This should be the case because a firm's training and competence procedures may also impact on its ability to satisfy the threshold conditions for authorisation. For example, the competence of a firm's management and staff is relevant when satisfying the FSA that the firm is a fit and proper person.[124] The FSA's standards relating to training and competence do not appear to be unduly onerous and, with the aid of the toolkits, all firms should be able to implement adequate systems to comply with the Commitments (and where applicable) the rules.

---

[124]   *See* paragraph 5 of Schedule 6 to the FSMA.

Chapter 4

PRUDENTIAL REGULATION UNDER THE FINANCIAL SERVICES AND MARKETS ACT 2000

Simon Gleeson
Partner
Allen & Overy

4.1   Introduction

Businesses fail. This is endemic in the nature of commercial enterprise, and is as true in the financial services sector as any other. Business failure in general is not wholly undesirable – assets freed from one use can be put to another potentially more productive use. It is therefore no part of the Financial Services Authority's (the "FSA") job to preserve regulated firms from failure. However the consequences of failure of a regulated business can have two effects which the FSA is mandated to prevent. One is disruption of the financial markets, which potentially affects that confidence in the UK financial system which the FSA is required to promote, and the other is the suffering of financial loss by consumers, which the FSA is required to minimise by securing an appropriate degree of consumer protection. In the interests of discharging these two functions, the FSA is therefore required to take an intelligent interest in the financial management of authorised firms.[1]

---

[1]   It should be emphasised that the imposition of prudential regulation is not the only (nor even in some cases the main) way in which this interest can be manifested, but the idea of ensuring that a firm operates with a certain minimum of capital available to it meshes so neatly with FSA's obligation to reduce the consequences of failure that the two are usually regarded as synonymous.

It would seem to follow from this argument that firms whose failure would produce neither of these undesirable consequences do not need to be regulated in their financial management. However this is not quite true. Paragraph 4 of Schedule 6 to the Financial Services and Markets Act 2000 (the "FSMA") prevents the FSA from giving a permission to any person who does not have adequate (financial) resources. Further, Principle 3 provides that "a firm must take reasonable care to organise and control its affairs responsibly and effectively with adequate risk management systems" and Principle 4 provides that "a firm must maintain adequate financial resources". It follows that all regulated firms must be required at least to satisfy themselves that they have adequate capital for their business. However, there is no compulsion upon the FSA to prescribe detailed capital requirements for every authorised person, and in some cases the FSA imposes on an authorised person nothing more than an obligation to ensure that it is able to meet its liabilities as they fall due.[2]

4.2   The structure of prudential regulation

There are three primary ingredients to any system of prudential regulation. The first is a mechanism for assessing the value of the risks faced by the regulated firm. This conventionally involves some element of risk weighting, and results in the calculation of a risk exposure amount. The second is a set of rules for calculating the amount of the firm's capital. The third is a set of rules for determining what proportion the firm's risk exposure amount must bear to the firm's capital.

The creation of the Interim Prudential Sourcebook focuses primarily on changes to the first of these elements; the calculation of the risk exposure amount. However, before focussing on these changes it will be helpful to summarise the proposals in respect of the second and third elements:

---

[2]   This is the requirement imposed on, for example, market infrastructure providers.

(a) *available capital* – regulatory capital creates a buffer enabling firms to absorb losses without damaging the interests of creditors (in particular customers and counterparties). In order to achieve this, regulatory capital must have the following characteristics:

  (i) *no fixed costs* – no obligation to pay dividends on equity. The firm must be entitled to defer payments of interest in the case of subordinated capital debt;

  (ii) *fully paid up* – the capital must be readily available and not contingent on anything or in guarantee form;

A firm's capital is divided into tiers depending on the extent to which it has the ability to absorb losses (the technical terms vary from rulebook to rulebook but the concepts are common to all). Tier One (equity and equity-like capital) creates the best form of "buffer" and is known as a firm's "core" capital. It consists mainly of: permanent share capital on which the firm is entitled to pay no dividend; reserves appropriated from retained earnings; share premiums; capital gifts; and retained profit and loss. Certain deductions are made from the total – for example, holdings of other firms' regulatory capital (in order to avoid double-counting on a systemic basis).

Upper Tier Two includes subordinated debt which is perpetual (undated), non-repayable without regulatory consent, and whose interest may be deferred. Lower Tier Two includes subordinated debt with a minimum original maturity of five years and a day. There are detailed conditions which must be complied with before any particular class of debt counts as Tier Two.

Tier Three includes short term (i.e. minimum two years) subordinated debt which otherwise meets the general conditions for Tier Two subordinated debt. The terms of the debt must include a clause "locking in"/suspending payments of interest and principal should the firm's capital position fall outside its target ratio. Tier Three can only be used to support trading book positions, and does not count towards banking book capital. The reason for this is that since trading book exposures should have a run-off time of around 10 days, there is no reason to require five-year minimum term capital to support them.

(b) *percentage capital requirement* – currently, the agreed international minimum is eight per cent, and outside the UK the majority of national regulators require compliance with only the eight per cent basic solvency ratio.

The existing practice in the UK in this area is inconsistent as between different regulators. In investment business capital requirements vary between a basic minimum of required capital (starting at £10,000 for a non-ISD (Investment Services Directive) corporate advisory firm) and an eight per cent risk weighted requirement. In the UK, banks tend to be set a capital requirement which is well above the eight per cent basic solvency ratio. This higher *trigger* ratio is determined according to criteria such as the nature of the bank's business, the markets in which it operates etc. A bank will also be set a target ratio, usually at least two per cent above the trigger ratio. The target ratio is set at a level which, when breached, will indicate that the trigger ratio is in danger of being breached. Because the highest requirements are those imposed on banks, it is likely that it is the bank system which is likely to be rolled out to at least the high-risk high-impact section of the UK market.

4.3 The development of the Interim and Integrated Prudential Sourcebooks

The primary problem for the draftsmen of the new Prudential Sourcebook was the large number of existing regimes in place in the UK. The simplest (and the oldest) is the "banking" regime, which derives from the structure set out in the Basel Accord of 1988, and involves the ascription of risk weightings to counterparty exposures. This was supplemented in the mid-1990s by the "trading" regime, which applies to the trading of securities. This forms the basis of the investment business requirements of The Securities and Futures Authority (the "SFA"), Investment Management Regulatory Organisation ("IMRO") and the Personal Investment Authority (the "PIA"), although each applied the core system with modifications. The Building Societies regime followed the banking regime, but money market participants were subject to a different regime than that which applied to securities market participants. Separately from this, the insurance company regime requires that the assets of an insurance company (calculated according to specific rules) be greater than its liabilities (valued on an actuarial basis) by a specified margin.

Although all of these regimes existed within UK regulatory rulebooks, the power to alter them was seriously circumscribed by international agreements and EU law. For banks, the basic design of the system follows the rules set by the Basel[3] Committee on Banking Supervision of the Bank for International Settlements, known as the "Basel Capital Accord" (the "Accord"). The Accord is followed by internationally active banks in the G10 countries (including the UK) and has been approved by most Organisation for Economic Cooperation and Development ("OECD") countries, although interpretation of the rules differs between countries. In the early 1990s the EU enacted the Basel Accord into EU law with amendments, and the FSA is bound to make rules consonant with these directives. The supervision of investment firms is to some extent covered by the "market risks" amendments to the Basel Accord made in the late 1990s, which prescribe a capital regulatory regime for the securities trading activities of internationally active banks, but this is by no means universally followed outside trading businesses. Insurance business regulation is covered by the EU life and non-life directives, but these follow a distinctly different pattern from the Basel system and are at a different phase of their life cycle, with emphasis currently being placed on the supervision of consolidated groups containing insurance companies rather than on reform of technical calculations.

This global environment, having remained fairly static for most of the decade after the original Accord of 1988, is currently in a state of rapid change. This is being driven in good part by the increasing realisation amongst sophisticated regulators worldwide that the existing international frameworks, originally conceived as a minimum set of requirements designed to ensure unanimity amongst regulators, fall some way short of the requirements of the financial markets of the early 21st century. Important initiatives

---

[3]   The conventional spelling in English and French is Basle, but in German it is Basel. Since Basel is the German-speaking part of Switzerland, the Committee calls itself the Basel Committee.

currently ongoing at the international level include the process for developing a revised consolidated supervisory framework into which insurance, banking and financial groups can all be fitted; the development of the EU financial services action plan for a radical overhaul of the EU's financial market regulatory system and of course the proposals for a completely revised Accord (known as "Basel II"), intended to rewrite the entire prudential supervisory framework for internationally active banks.

All of these processes are, to one degree or another, scheduled to come to fruition shortly after N2. Applying the invariant laws of financial regulation, that deadlines slip and proposals change in consultation, this faced the FSA with the unenviable prospect of either developing a revised prudential rulebook which would require complete revision within a few years of publication, or postponing the prudential regulatory component of the FSMA process to an unspecified date on which it might reasonably be hoped that the concurrent international initiatives might have run their course. Given that FSA, as a regulator, has a realistic appreciation of announced timetables for regulatory reform, it was keenly aware that the latter course of action might have involved the delay of the prudential restructuring for a decade; however the industry which it regulated left it in no doubt that two complete restructurings of capital adequacy requirements within a few years was at least one restructuring more than could be coped with without serious disruption to the very financial management which the rules purported to promote.

The consequence was a compromise. The FSA announced that although it could not defer the construction of its new-look prudential rulebook indefinitely, the rulebook which it would introduce at N2 would be largely a repetition of existing rulebooks in an Interim Prudential Sourcebook. These rules would therefore, with minor amendments, remain in force after N2 until the new Integrated Prudential Sourcebook was implemented (expected to be 2004). This proposal carried the caveat that the industry should not necessarily expect the Integrated Prudential Sourcebook to be merely the implementation of Basel II, and in particular that the development of the Sourcebook would proceed independently of the Basel II process.

The Interim Prudential Sourcebook therefore constitutes little more than extracts from the old self-regulatory organisation ("SRO") rulebooks. The FSA considered a complete stylistic rewrite, in order to ensure that the relevant materials were at least presented in a format which conformed with the remainder of the handbook as to fair and clear communication. However even this proposal was swiftly dropped, since it rapidly became clear that such a rewrite would require a very substantial investment of time and resources, would serve no good purpose since the vast majority of the regulated population had been subject to the rules for many years and did not need a restatement of them. Conversely, the danger of inadvertent change to rules was sufficient to render such a project positively dangerous.

As a result, the clearly-expressed policy of the FSA is to the effect that no regulated firm should face any substantial change to the way in which its regulatory capital position was calculated on N2.

This approach will result in a regime in which banks, investment firms and insurance companies will share a common authorisation, but be subjected to prudential requirements based on their historical characterisation under a repealed enactment. This structure is probably not one which the FSA relishes, but is one which it has had to accept. As a result, capital adequacy treatment under the new regime will commence with allocation to a regulatory classification under the old regime according to the following table.

Prudential categories	Overlap with other categories (Note)	Prudential sub-categories
Bank	*	European Economic Area ("EEA") bank Overseas bank UK bank
Building society	*	
Credit union	*	
Friendly society		Incorporated friendly society Registered friendly society
ICVC	*	
Incoming EEA firm		
Incoming treaty firm		
Insurer		Long-term insurer General insurer
Investment management firm	*	OPS firm Non-OPS life office Non-OPS local authority Individuals admitted to authorisation collectively Individual whose sole investment business is giving investment advice to institutional or corporate investors Other

Prudential categories	Overlap with other categories (Note)	Prudential sub-categories
Lead regulated firm Media firm	*	
Members' adviser		
Personal investment firm	*	Category A firm
		Category A1 firm
		Category A2 firm
		Category A3 firm
		Category B firm
		Category B1 firm
		Category B2 firm
		Category B3 firm
		Low resource firm
		Network
Professional firm	*	
Securities and futures firm	*	IPRU(INV) 3:
		Adviser
		Arranger
		Broad scope firm
		Corporate finance advisory firm
		Dematerialised instruction transmitter
		Derivative fund manager
		Local
		Oil market participant

Prudential categories	Overlap with other categories (Note)	Prudential sub-categories
		Venture capital firm
		Other
		IPRU(INV) 10:
		Category A
		Category B
		Category C
		Category D
		Category D – corporate finance advisory firm
Service company	*	
Society (of Lloyd's)		
UCITS qualifier		
Underwriting agent		Managing agent
		Members' agent
Wholesale marketbroker	*	Foreign exchange broker

Note. It is possible for a *firm* to have more than one prudential category. But those prudential categories marked "*" are mutually exclusive of other categories marked "*".

In order to discuss the changes which will be implemented at N2, it is therefore necessary to analyse the individual rulebooks as they will survive into the new regime.

4.4 Deposit takers

4.4.1 *Risk weights and basic solvency*

In order to calculate capital requirements, the risks associated with a bank's instruments/assets (market risk, interest rate position risk, counterparty risk etc.) are weighted. The total of weighted risks arising from all of the bank's instruments/assets are then multiplied by a basic solvency, trigger or target ratio to calculate a required capital level.

4.4.2 *Credit risk weightings*

Credit (or counterparty) risk is the risk that borrowers may default on their debts. It is traditionally one of the main forms of risk run by banks. Currently, the internationally agreed risk weightings for credit risk used to determine capital ratios provide only very broad categories of relative riskiness (namely, zero per cent, 10 per cent, 20 per cent, 50 per cent and 100 per cent). Indeed, virtually all assets are bucketed into the 100 per cent weighted category without differentiation. Treatment differs depending on whether the assets are on or off-balance sheet.

4.4.2.1 *On-balance sheet treatment*

For on-balance sheet items, the formula for calculating the risk weighted asset is *outstanding principal amount of facility x counterparty risk weighting*. For loans to OECD sovereigns, a zero risk weighting currently applies. This means that a bank need not apply any capital to that loan for regulatory purposes and accordingly, whatever return the bank makes on the loan gives the bank an infinite return on regulatory capital employed (which can then improve its return on capital employed across the entire banking book). However in practice direct loan exposure to sovereigns is fairly rare, since most sovereigns raise debt in the bond markets rather than by bilateral borrowing. A 20 per cent weighting currently applies to OECD government bonds[4] as well as to all exposures (debt or bond) to OECD-incorporated banks. For corporate and non-OECD

---

[4]   10 per cent if the bond is floating-rate or has a term of one year or less.

sovereign/bank obligations, a 100 per cent risk weighting is applicable, save that claims on non-OECD banks benefit from a 20 per cent risk weighting where the residual maturity is less than one year .

4.4.2.2   Off-balance sheet treatment

Off-balance sheet items are obligations, contractual or otherwise, that a bank has entered into to make loans or other payments in the future. Treatment differs between over-the-counter ("OTC") derivatives and other off-balance sheet items.

OTC derivatives include interest rate, foreign exchange rate, equity, precious metals and other commodities contracts which are not traded on an organised exchange. The counterparty risk for OTC derivatives may be recorded in the banking or trading book. Exposure is measured by marking the derivative to market, applying an "add-on" to reflect the outstanding duration of the derivative and the riskiness of the underlying asset, applying the credit risk weighting of the counterparty and then reducing this by 50 per cent. The justification for the 50 per cent reduction is that OTC derivative business is usually conducted between highly creditworthy entities.

Otherwise, the principles which are applied are that the exposure is treated as an on-balance sheet exposure to a borrower of the relevant class and a discount factor is then applied. The discount factor for direct credit substitutes (such as absolute commitments to pay at a future time) is 100 per cent, that is, these exposures are treated as if they were fully drawn. Most other exposures (such as undrawn borrowing facilities) attract a 50 per cent weighting, whilst trade-related exposures (letters of credit backed by trade documentation) receive a 20 per cent weighting.

One perceived loophole in the current system is the zero per cent credit conversion factor accorded to commitments of up to one year (364 day commitments). Many credit facilities have been structured to take advantage of this treatment.

4.4.3   *Banking book and trading book distinction*

Items generating risk are recorded in a bank's banking book or trading book (but not in both). The distinction is that assets held in the banking book are those where the primary risk exposure of the institution is to the creditworthiness of the obligor – for example a bank loan, where the risk of loss is non-payment by the borrower. All assets are held in the banking book apart from those which qualify to be held in the trading book. The trading book contains assets where the primary risk arises from exposure to the market – for example, for the holder of a share in a FTSE company the primary risk is a fall in the share price rather than the credit risk of the company. The test is that investments may only be held in a trading book if they are in tradable form (i.e. are bonds, shares or similar) and are held for resale or with the intention of benefiting from short-term price or interest rate movements. Not all tradable securities are necessarily held in the trading book – any tradable security which is held for long-term investment purposes must be held in the banking book.

Exposures arising from hedging transactions (designed to transfer credit risk to another party) should appear in whichever book the position being hedged (i.e. the underlying asset) appears in. Some risks arise in both books for example, counterparty, foreign exchange, commodity position and large exposure risk.

4.4.4   *Other important risk treatments[5]*

Foreign exchange ("FX") risk: open positions[6] in foreign currencies, including gold, are subject to the risk that movements in the relevant exchange rate(s) will increase or decrease their value. FX risk is

---

[5]   The risks referred to below, excepting large exposure risk, fall within the umbrella of "market risk".

[6]   An open position is where the inflow exposures of a currency are not equal to the outflow exposures of that currency. Open positions may either be short (on a sale of the currency): liabilities exceed assets, or long (on a purchase of a currency): assets exceed liabilities. Banks with short open positions are exposed to the risk that the currency might appreciate. Banks with long open positions are exposed to the risk that the currency might depreciate.

usually calculated by reference to the banking and trading books combined. To calculate the capital requirement, the larger of the total net FX long positions and the total net FX short positions in the reporting currency is taken (this being the overall net open position).

Commodity position risk (arising in banking and trading books): commodities are physical products that may underlie commodities futures contracts. They are subject to the risk of price changes due to shifts in supply and demand. To calculate the capital requirement, each commodity position[7] is given a notional value comprising its spot price and a maturity assigned to it based on its expiry date. Each commodity is then assigned to one of seven maturity bands to reflect its outstanding duration. Long and short positions in the same maturity band are matched and their total multiplied by the spread rate (yield) for the band in question (1.5 per cent). Remaining unmatched positions are carried out to the next time band and used to match unmatched positions in that next time band.[8]

Large exposure risk (arising in banking and trading books): this is the risk to which a bank is exposed when one exposure to a counterparty or group of closely-related counterparties is greater than or equal to 10 per cent of its capital base. Except in exceptional circumstances (so-called "soft limits"), the large exposure must not exceed 25 per cent of its capital base (thus, if its capital base is 16 per cent of its total loan book, no single exposure may exceed four per cent of its loan book – 25 per cent of 16 per cent).

Interest rate position risk (arises in the trading book only – interest rate risk in the banking book is currently ignored): it is the risk of an adverse variation in cost or return caused by a change in the absolute

---

[7] A commodity position is either long or short. A short forward position is where future production is sold at an agreed price at a date in the future. A long forward position is where future production is to be purchased at an agreed price at a future date.

[8] This is the maturity ladder approach. Banks which trade lightly or irregularly may use the simplified approach. Again, the FSA permit banks to use their own internal value-at-risk models.

level of interest rates or the shape of the yield curve.[9] Risk may be specific (where an individual position in a portfolio moves more or less than the general market) or general (relating to the overall market or interest rate movements). To calculate the capital requirement for general risk, long and short positions in debt instruments are netted off against each other. A capital charge is made in respect of each unmatched position and these are then added up to obtain a total charge.[10] Other methods include the maturity band method and the duration method. For specific risk, exposures are graded according to their maturity, and weightings are applied to give a total capital charge.

Equity position risk (arises in the trading book only): specific equity position risk is the risk that the market price of particular securities (shares, depository receipts and derivatives based on them) in individual companies may move against the bank. General equity position risk is the risk that markets as a whole may move against the bank. To calculate the capital requirement for general equity risk, long and short positions in individual equities are netted off. Every individual net equity position is assigned a weighting of either eight per cent or four per cent according to a dual liquidity or diversity test.

Operational risk (not explicitly addressed in the UK banking supervisory policy): this is the risk to an institution arising from a breakdown in internal controls and corporate governance, including the failure of management information systems and other non-financial aspects of management. However, in practice the FSA has explained the fact that it requires a premium from banks over eight per cent as being due to the need to take operational risk into account.

---

9   The yield curve is obtained by plotting the yields (percentage rate of return) of all default-free coupon bonds in a given currency against maturity.

10   This is the simplified method.

4.4.5   Risk mitigation techniques

Collateral and guarantees: the current regime only gives limited recognition to the risk reducing effects of collateral and guarantees. Exposures secured by cash and OECD government (or OECD public sector entity or multilateral development bank) securities attract a zero risk weight, all other exposures are fully weighted regardless of the quantity or quality of collateral available. The position is better for exposures which are guaranteed, since a guaranteed exposure takes the risk weighting of the guarantor.

Netting: the current regime only gives limited recognition to netting and set-off. Recognition of on-balance sheet netting is limited to setting off debit and credit balances of the same customer or to customers in the same group. Some off-balance sheet items may be netted such as OTC derivatives in the banking and trading book, bond and equity forwards, interest rate positions and repos in the trading book (netting against repo exposures in the banking book is not generally possible because the issuer of the securities retains the issuer risk so that counterparty risk is deemed to be zero).

Hedging: a financial instrument, for example, a credit derivative, may be used to hedge an exposure. In the trading book a hedge is treated as a position in the underlying instrument, in the banking book as a guarantee. The effectiveness of the hedge for capital adequacy purposes will only be recognised as long as certain criteria are met. Problems arise with mismatches, where the reference asset (e.g. a security) and the underlying asset are different, the assets are denominated in different currencies or the assets have differing maturities.

4.4.6   *Banks under the Interim Prudential Sourcebook*

Comparing the proposed Interim Prudential Sourcebook for banks with the FSAs Guide to Banking Supervisory Policy reveals that although a significant amount of the material previously contained in the Guide has been redeployed (fitness and properness criteria to the Authorisation Manual, annual reports requirements, EEA institution arrangements and former authorised institutions regimes to the Supervision Manual), the remainder is largely intact.[11]

The one substantive proposal which was made when the Interim Prudential Handbook for banks was originally proposed was the integration of the banking and building societies capital adequacy regimes in relation to defaulted mortgages. The EU bank capital directives (to which building societies are subject) prescribes a 50 per cent weighting for loans secured by a first charge on residential property, but leaves local regulators discretion to apply a higher weighting if they see fit. In reliance on this the Building Societies Commission (the "BSC") had developed a variety of weightings for mortgages in different conditions of default, and in particular had adopted a rule that where a mortgage was in arrears to the extent of more than five per cent of the amount due, the mortgage should attract a 75 per cent weighting rather than 50 per cent. It was initially proposed to extend this treatment to mortgage lending by banks. This proposal produced significant resistance from banks and was eventually dropped in favour of a proposal to eliminate the 75 per cent band entirely for both banks and building societies.

4.4.7   *Building societies under the Interim Prudential Sourcebook*

The rules for building societies are broadly being brought into line with those which apply to banks. However, since the rules for building societies were on balance slightly more stringent than those which applied to banks, the net effect of this change is that building societies will be required to hold slightly less capital than was previously the case under the Prudential Guidance Notes of the BSC.

4.4.7.1   *Mortgage weightings*

As mentioned above the BSC had a 75 per cent weighting for mortgages in arrears to the extent of more than five per cent of the loan value. Some other mortgages also carried a 60 per cent

---

[11]   Apart, of course, from the Chapter relating to representative offices, which has been removed since the status of representative office will no longer exist under the FSMA regime.

weighting. Both of these are removed in the new Sourcebook. The FSA makes clear that it expects building societies to have in place both provisioning policies sufficient to ensure that mortgages in default are provided for in a prudent manner, and also adequate arrears management policies, but the net effect of this change will be to free up a significant amount of capital for building societies.

4.4.7.2   Second charges

The BSC's Prudential Notes permitted building societies to apply a 50 per cent weighting to second and subsequent charges, whereas the FSA required a 100 per cent weighting for any charge other than a first charge. Here again building societies will be required to adhere to the bank treatment. The FSA is convinced that the impact of this change will be minor, since there are currently very few building societies which have any significant exposure to second charges. It is also possible that this provision was drafted with an eye to the proposed regime for the regulation of mortgage lending. For reasons which are not entirely clear this will make the lending of money secured by a first charge a regulated activity but leave the lending of money regulated by a second charge unregulated. It may well be that against this background the FSA wish to discourage banks and others from transferring their business to a second charge basis by imposing a penal weighting on second charge business.

4.4.7.3   Securitisation

The BSC was never entirely comfortable with the issues surrounding the securitisation of mortgage assets by building societies, and at the time of its absorption into the FSA its rules on the subject had not progressed further than a consultative draft. The FSA intends to deal with this issue by imposing the bank rules on securitisation (currently Chapter SE of the Guide) on building societies. This is a sensible decision, since it places building societies and banks on an equal footing *vis-à-vis* this form of capital raising. However, building societies do have one problem which banks do not have, in that because they are mutuals their borrowers are also members of the society. The FSA takes the view that it is incompatible with the "clean break" principle for a borrower to have his mortgage transferred by the society to a special purpose vehicle ("SPV") whilst at the same time retaining full membership of the society. The FSA initially proposed to deal with this issue by requiring building societies to terminate the borrowers membership of the society before his mortgage could be securitised. However, building societies have complained that this treatment was unnecessarily draconian, and the FSA has now amended its policy such that a building society which wishes to securitise a loan portfolio is required only to have a board policy for dealing with issues relating to the membership of such borrowers.

Perhaps more importantly, the BSC imposed a residual charge on any building society that performed the role of loan administrator in respect of a portfolio of mortgages which had been securitised. The logic of this was, presumably, that where a building society transferred a portfolio of mortgages to an SPV but retained the administration function that it continued to retain some moral risk in respect of those assets, and that there was therefore a potential breach of the clean break principle; however it as also applied in situations where the society was simply acting as a third party administrator in respect of loans made by a different entity. This charge will disappear at N2.

4.4.7.4   Buy to let mortgages

Under the old regime building societies were required to weight "buy to let mortgages" at 100 per cent, whereas banks were permitted to weight these at 50 per cent. Here again, post N2 the building society regime is to be brought into line with the banking regime, and societies will be able to weight these assets at 50 per cent.

4.4.7.5   Public universities

Building societies were previously able to apply a 50 per cent weighting to loans to public universities where the loan was secured on residential property. This concession is to be withdrawn except in the case of loans which are secured on property which is either: (a) let in the non-student market; or (b) easily saleable.

4.4.7.6 *Mortgage premiums*

Due to the vogue for payment of mortgage premiums and cash-back offers, the BSC imposed a requirement on building societies that where any such payment was not to be amortised over the course of the loan, 67 per cent of its value was immediately to be deducted from own funds. This requirement is to be withdrawn.

4.4.7.7 *Large exposures*

Building societies had historically faced a more severe large exposures cap than banks – around 300 per cent of own funds, as opposed to the 800 per cent of own funds available for banks. However, in consequence of this a partial exemption was available in respect of loans to local government and exposures of one to three years maturity to other credit institutions. The proposal is that the maximum cap is to be raised to bank levels and these concessions are to be removed.

4.4.7.8 *Issued capital*

Building societies have in the past benefited from a slightly more generous regime in terms of the requirements which must be complied with before subordinated securities issued by them will be counted towards regulatory capital; in particular in that they are permitted slightly greater step-ups than banks. There are also differences of rules in respect of the "taper" which is applied to subordinated debt which is close to maturity. In both cases the building society rules will be brought into line with the bank rules, but in order to avoid any existing issues being affected by the rule change, any issue made prior to N2 in compliance with the rules in force at that time will be grandfathered.

4.4.7.9 *Outsourcing*

Building societies will be required to comply with the outsourcing rules of the FSA. This is a new and potentially a significant burden, but one whose imposition could have been foreseen, since there is no objective justification for not subjecting building societies to the same regime as banks in this regard.

4.4.7.10   Reporting accountants

The FSA intends to create an entirely new regime relating to the use of "skilled persons" in its supervision of authorised persons (*see* CP 91 *Reports by Skilled Persons*). It was originally proposed that the existing banking system, providing for a relationship between the auditor of an authorised institution and the regulator, along with a power for the regulator to commission special reports, should be extended to building societies, but this material has now been withdrawn from both the bank and the building society manuals pending the publication of a unified policy on this issue.

4.5   Investment firms

The investment firms regimes under the old SROs were loosely based on the Basel market risks structure, but differed according to individual requirements. This summary is based on the SFA rulebook.

The European Capital Adequacy Directive (the "CAD") was implemented into UK law on 1 January 1996. Firms which conduct investment business within the scope of the Investment Services Directive (the "ISD") and meet the definition of an investment firm set out in the ISD are required to comply with the capital adequacy regime established by the CAD. If any of a firm's investment activities constitute ISD investment business then the whole of that firm's investment activities (whether ISD investment business or not) are subject to the provisions of the CAD. Some market transactions are not covered by the ISD – for example arranging deals in and dealing in commodities – but the vast majority are.

4.5.1   *The SFA capital adequacy regime*

The SFA transposed the requirements of the CAD (with certain permissible modifications) into Chapter 10 of its rulebook. SFA Rule 10-1 provides that a firm which meets the ISD definition of an investment firm must comply with the capital adequacy regime set down in that Chapter.

4.5.1.1   *Initial capital and own funds*

Capital adequacy for SFA is composed of two requirements, an initial capital requirement and a financial resources requirement.

"Initial capital" is the SFA's term for Tier One capital, and a firm must at all times maintain its initial capital at a level equal to or greater than its initial capital requirement. For firms which have no risk exposure and are not subject to the ISD (such as corporate finance advisory firms), this is set at a very low level – £10,000. Firms which have the same profile but which are caught by the ISD are subject to the minimum requirement laid down in the CAD of €50,000, and the initial capital requirement for a full authorisation €730,000.

"Financial resources" is equivalent to the banking concept of "own funds" and loosely includes Tiers One, Two and Three capital. The "financial resources requirement" is calculated by reference to the risk exposures taken on by the firm, using methodology largely common to trading book measurement in the banking book. Some firms, of course, have no risk exposure, and in these cases there is a backstop requirement that financial resources may not be less than initial capital.

The firm's financial resources requirement is calculated as the sum of its "primary requirement" and its "secondary requirement". The primary requirement will be the higher of:

(a) Position Risk Requirement ("PRR") + Foreign Exchange Requirement ("FER") + Counterparty Risk Requirement ("CRR") + Large Exposures Requirement ("LER") + base requirement (with base requirement being calculated as 1/4 of the firm's relevant annual expenditure multiplied by 1/4 of the firm's relevant annual expenditure divided by PRR+FER+CRR+LER+1/4 of the firm's relevant annual expenditure); and

(b) the initial capital requirement.

The secondary requirement is essentially at SFA's discretion and may be applied to cover an unusual risk profile or to cover the "inadequate management of operational risk to which a firm is exposed". It is possible then to avoid a secondary requirement altogether, and most firms do so. The function of the secondary requirement is to permit SFA to impose variable capital requirements so that, in the same way that the FSA as banking supervisor is able to set trigger and target ratios higher than the eight per cent minimum, SFA should be able to do the same.

4.5.1.2   *General principles of Position Risk Requirement*

The purpose of PRR is to address the risk associated with a change in the value of investments held by the firm. SFA applies PRR in respect of all "trading book" positions (essentially, short-term proprietary positions in financial instruments and related hedges) as well as physical commodities derivatives items.

The ISD rules set out a variety of means by which PRR is calculated in relation to equity, debt, index-based and commodity derivatives. A detailed treatment of those rules is outside the scope of this Chapter. A firm is expected to be able to calculate its PRR on an intra-day basis and to mark its on and off-balance sheet positions to market on a daily basis.

Because it is the net position which is weighted for PRR purposes, long and short positions in the same security are netted off before the PRR calculation is performed. Positions can be either physical or synthetic; a synthetic position being one which is created by entry into an appropriate derivative, such that the terms of the derivative have an economic impact equal to the holding of a long or short position in a physical security. By way of example where a firm enters into an interest rate or currency swap, for the purpose of the PRR rules it must treat each leg of that swap as a notional position in a government security in the currency concerned, which:

(a) must be a long position if the firm is receiving interest and a short position if the firm is paying interest;

(b) has maturity:

    (i) in the case where the firm is paying or receiving fixed rate interest, equal to the length of the swap; and

    (ii) in the case where the firm is paying or receiving floating rate interest, equal to the period remaining to the next interest rate reset date; and

(c) has a coupon equal to the rate of interest payable or receivable on that leg of the swap.

4.5.1.3   *General principles of Counterparty Risk Requirement*

CRR is the SFA regulatory capital requirement which has the effect of guarding against the risk of counterparty failure in respect of trading book activities. A firm which engages in trading business will not be exposed to CRR in respect of securities held on its trading book, but the process of getting them on and off that trading book will give rise to counterparty exposures in respect of unsettled trades, repo agreements and derivative transactions. Again, a detailed treatment of the CRR rules is outside the scope of this Chapter.

Briefly, a firm must be able to calculate its CRR at least once on every business day so as to demonstrate if requested that the firm has financial resources in excess of its financial resources requirement. The amount of the counterparty exposure on which CRR must be calculated may be reduced to the extent that the firm makes a provision for the counterparty balance in its accounts. The level of CRR will vary in accordance with the nature of the counterparty, since counterparties receive the same risk weightings for this purpose as they receive for banking book treatment (e.g. exposures to certain sovereign counterparties are nil-weighted, exposures to UK corporate entities incur a 100 per cent risk weighting etc.).

CRR can be reduced by the use of collateral, adequate credit management policies and the application of netting. By way of example the CRR for any interest rate swap is determined by reference to the replacement cost of the contract, the notional underlying amount, the maturity and the quality of the counterparty.

4.5.1.4   *General principles of Large Exposures Requirement*

Firms are required to provide additional regulatory capital in respect of "large exposures". Large exposure means:

(a) in relation to non-trading book exposures, an exposure or number of exposures to a third party or a group of connected third parties which exceeds or exceed 10 per cent of the firm's own funds; and

(b) in relation to the aggregate of non-trading book and trading book exposures an exposure or number of exposures to a third party or a group of connected third parties which exceeds or exceed 10 per cent of the firm's financial resources.

The method for calculating LER is the same for SFA firms as it is for banks. The applicability of LER is dependent upon the nature of one's counterparty: it may be excluded in respect of exposures to certain counterparties and in respect of certain secured exposures.

4.5.1.5   *General principles of Foreign Exchange Requirement*

Generally, a firm must calculate FER where it has any asset or liability or any off-balance sheet item which is denominated in, or gives rise to an exposure in, any currency other than the currency of its books of account. FER must, where appropriate be calculated in respect of currency futures, forwards and options and cross-currency swap as well as other instruments.

4.5.2   *Investment firms under the Interim Prudential Sourcebook*

The prudential requirements sections of the rulebooks of the different SROs have been copied wholesale into the Interim Prudential Sourcebook with little regard for consistency or order. Even distinctions within SRO rulebooks have been maintained - thus the SFA maintained two different sets of prudential regulations for firms which were subject to the ISD (set out in Chapter 10 of the SFA rulebook) and those which were not (set out in Chapter 3), and this distinction has been carried forward into the Investment Business Prudential Sourcebook, which therefore contains two separate legacy SFA rulebooks.

There is a particular tension which manifests itself in the Investment Business Prudential Sourcebook as between the FSA's intentions of moving a to risk-based supervisory approach and its aim of not disturbing unduly the capital base of UK investment business. To the extent that the different SRO's rulebooks represent the considered view of the SRO concerned as to the most appropriate capital requirements for firms engaged in its regulated businesses, it would seem logical to apply each component to the relevant activity. However, the demarcations in the Financial Services Act 1986 (the

"FS Act") system were never in practice that clear, and it would be difficult to conclude that, for example, the IMRO prudential rules should be applied to all investment management activities where individual institutions had previously been measuring their capital requirements under the SFA or the PIA rules. The result has been that firms will be allocated to a particular chapter of the Investment Business Interim Prudential Sourcebook according to which SRO they were regulated by prior to N2, and until the Integrated Prudential Sourcebook comes into effect, newly authorised firms will be allocated to one or more chapters according to which SRO they would have been regulated by had they applied for authorisation under the FS Act. This is neither an unreasonable nor an unworkable system – at the time of writing new applicants to the PIA are still subjected to rules based upon the test as to which of the PIA's predecessor organisations (LAUTRO or FIMBRA) they would have been regulated by had they applied for authorisation before the creation of the PIA. It does, however, serve to emphasise the extent to which continuity has prevailed over harmonisation in the construction of the Interim Prudential Sourcebooks.

The easiest way to review the rulebook is therefore to consider the individual chapters as they apply to formerly regulated firms.

4.5.3   *The Securities and Futures Authority*

The SFA prudential regime is divided into the ISD rules contained in Chapter 10 of the SFA rulebook and the non-ISD rules contained in Chapter 3. The reason that the SFA remains the only SRO with two entirely separate sets of prudential rules is in part explained by the fact that SFA probably has wider scope of activities amongst its membership than does any other SRO, but in part remains a mystery. This structure is continued into the Interim Prudential Sourcebook.

The division between the Chapter 3 and Chapter 10 provisions of the rulebook will undoubtedly disappear under the new Investment Business Integrated Prudential Sourcebook. However both regimes serve some purpose; Chapter 10 being the CAD-regime loosely analogous to the trading book requirements applied to banks, and Chapter 3 being the residual regime applicable to SFA member firms which, for whatever reason, deal in investments but are not trading businesses. The fact of this distinction is blurred by the inclusion of redundant material in Chapter 3 relating to position risk, and FSA have suggested that this material be deleted from the Chapter 3 content of the Investment Business Interim Prudential Sourcebook and replaced by a flat rate eight per cent requirement in respect of all investment holdings.

The primary issue for investment firms in respect of prudential supervision is the use of risk models. The prudential regulatory structure set out in any rulebook is at bottom a very rough risk model. A modern investment firm of any size will employ a number of mathematical risk models to assess its exposure to a variety of different factors, and since the second capital adequacy directive, regulators have been permitted to allow regulated firms to use these models, rather than the mechanisms set out in the regulatory rulebooks, to assess risk exposure and consequent capital requirements. Risk models are not unitary – a very large firm may operate a single integrated mathematical model which assesses every aspect of its exposures (value-at-risk models), but a firm may model all, some, or none of its exposures on a one-by-one basis (risk assessment models). In both cases the firm may use a variety of modelling techniques in doing so. The SFA has given some guidance in respect of the recognition of such models. However, the use of such models for reporting purposes gives rise to two difficulties for the FSA.

One is that the grant of permission to use the output of a model for reporting purposes is technically a waiver of rules, and must be dealt with under Section 148 of the FSMA rather than in the rulebook. This leads in turn to the problem that the FSA is required to publicise any waiver given under Section 148 unless it is satisfied that it is inappropriate or unnecessary to do so. Since the FSA has not in the past publicised the list of firms which have been given internal model waivers, there is a certain amount of interest as to whether it will do so under Section 148.

The other difficulty is that users of models tend to acquire their regulatory characteristics almost by chance, there being less differentiation amongst sophisticated market participants between banks and investment houses than in other areas of the rulebook. As a result it is undesirable to allow any distinction in respect of the criteria for use of models between the Investment Business Interim

Prudential Sourcebook and the Bank Interim Prudential Sourcebook. This is dealt with by retaining the SFA guidance on use of models in respect of risk assessment models, but the SFA guidance on the use of value-at-risk models will disappear, and the criteria for recognition of value-at-risk models set out in the Bank Interim Prudential Sourcebook will be cross-referred into the Investment Business Interim Prudential Sourcebook.

One of the more unusual aspects of the SFA rulebook is the adequate credit management policy ("ACMP") regime, whereby a firm which could demonstrate an ACMP is permitted to use reduced counterparty risk weightings in respect of certain exposures. In reality the ACMP regime is the mirror image of its apparent presentation, in that the system does not in fact permit firms with an ACMP to use reduced weightings but requires firms without an ACMP to use enhanced weightings. Because of this it is possible to continue with the ACMP regime without requiring each member wishing to use an ACMP to apply for a specific waiver under Section 148.

An interesting issue flagged in earlier discussions for SFA firms is the revision of the deduction of illiquid assets regime. SFA firms are currently subject to a fairly simple liquidity regime by which holdings of designated "illiquid assets" (notably holdings in other companies) are deducted from capital, but the remaining positions are not subject to any further liquidity monitoring. This creates an interesting dilemma for the FSA, in that, on the one hand many former SFA firms are extremely unhappy about the imposition of a liquidity monitoring regime, whereas others would regard such a regime as a small price to pay for the removal of some of the current mandatory deduction requirements. It is probable that this issue will be dealt with in the Liquidity Risk chapter of the Integrated Prudential Sourcebook (due for publication early 2002), by offering former SFA firms an election between the full deduction method and a liquidity monitoring regime.

4.5.4   *The Investment Manager's Regulatory Organisation*

The IMRO prudential rules contained little to differentiate them from those of other SROs. The primary change which has been made to those rules as they appear in the Interim Prudential Sourcebook is that the elements which purported to confer on IMRO an express discretion to waive rules (notably the provisions in Rule 5.2.3(2) relating to waiver of liquid capital requirements and in Rule 5.2.5(1)(c)(ii) relating to treatment of subordinated loans in the last few years of their lives). However, the FSA is at pains to point out that the removal of these provisions does not mean that such waivers will not be available to regulated firms in the future, but merely that since it is now a statutory body the FSA can no longer confer discretion on itself in respect of a statutory obligation through its own rulebook.

A somewhat curious amendment is also made in respect of the occupational pension scheme regime. This regime was initially created for the benefit of those responsible for occupational pension schemes who felt the need to become authorised under the FS Act. It is to some extent a concessionary regime, in that an occupational pension scheme member is subject to significantly lower requirements than an ordinary IMRO member. The scope of this concession has been somewhat limited by the provision that occupational pension scheme members will only enjoy the benefit of the concessionary prudential regime as long as they are formed on a not-for-profit basis. The status of firms whose only activity is the management of occupational pension scheme assets will continue to be available to firms which are incorporated on a for-profit basis, but such firms will be required to comply with the normal prudential requirements applicable to IMRO member firms.

It is also notable that the specimen subordinated loan agreement (IMRO Chapter V Table 2.5(5)) and qualifying undertaking (Table 2.6(2)) will disappear from the rules and appear in a separate compendium of FSA precedent documentation.

4.5.5 *Personal Investment Authority*

The PIA rulebook is retained largely intact into the Interim Prudential sourcebook for investment businesses, and the only area which will be significantly changed is that relating to Professional Indemnity Insurance ("PII"). The PIA required firms to have PII in addition to maintaining regulatory capital, primarily because PIA members are very exposed to mass customer claims. An exception was made in the PIA rulebook for subsidiaries of parent companies where the parent company had given written confirmation to the regulator that it would stand behind the subsidiary financially in respect of investor claims (but not otherwise). This will be replaced by a requirement that an agreement be entered into between the subsidiary and the parent which explicitly confers rights on investor creditors of the subsidiary, using the mechanism set out in the Contracts (Rights of Third Parties) Act 1999.

4.5.6   *Wholesale market firms*

This heading includes those firms who were admitted to the list maintained by the Bank of England under Section 43 of the FS Act and were as a result entirely outside the scope of any of the SRO rulebooks. The prudential regime to which these firms were subject was set out in the Bank of England's criteria for admission to this list (known as the "Grey Paper"), and was distinct from any of the regimes operated by the SROs.

The reasons for the exclusion of the Section 43 regime from the FSA regime are lost in the mists of time, and relate primarily to the Bank of England's concern, at the time the FS Act was passed, to protect its influence over the wholesale money markets. In broad terms the Section 43 regime was created for banks, and the vast majority of Section 43 listed institutions are also authorised banks. However, two classes of money market participants, wholesale market brokers ("WMBs") and non-bank principals ("NBPs"), operated exclusively in the money markets under the Grey Paper regime. Dealing with these entities under the Interim Prudential Sourcebook proved difficult. However, the FSA has come to believe that for a variety of reasons there will be no NBPs left at N2 who have not applied for FSA membership, and the issue that remains relates exclusively to WMBs.

The FSAs response to this has been to propose the abolition of the Grey Paper regime and subject WMBs to the SFA regime which is the closes equivalent to their existing activities (in this case a category D ISD firm). The reason that it is possible to integrate these two regimes at the Interim Prudential Sourcebook stage is twofold; first that the number of Grey Paper firms is relatively small, and second that the regime set out in the Grey Paper was significantly stricter than that set out in the SFA rulebook, such that the change should result in a significant improvement of the position of most former Grey Paper firms.

The significant differences between the Grey Paper and SFA regimes are summarised in the following table:

	Grey Paper regime	SFA regime
Expenditure/ financial resource requirement	Two months	Six weeks
Large exposure rules apply?	No	No
Consolidation rules apply?	No	No
Initial capital requirement	€50,000	€50,000
Deduction for connected counterparty exposures	100 per cent	Eight per cent x counterparty weight
Deduction for aged debtors	100 per cent	Eight per cent x counterparty weight
Netting of intra-group balances permitted?	No	Yes
Interim unaudited profits allowable?	Yes	No
Monthly accrual for tax required?	Optional (to year end)	Yes
Requirement to allow for cash/foreign exchange risk?	No	Yes
Differences deduction?	Yes (100 per cent)	No

As will be seen, the only adverse consequence for WMBs of this change is that they will no longer be able to count unaudited interim profits towards regulatory capital.

4.5.7 *Professional service firms*

Professional services firms are discussed here since the financial business which they undertake is almost invariably investment business. The position of professional service firms under the FS Act was always unsatisfactory. It is probably impossible to practice as a lawyer, chartered accountant or actuary without at some stage doing something which could be construed either as arranging an investment transaction or as giving investment advice; however, it is probable that it was never the Government's intention to include such persons within the scope of the Act. Bad drafting rendered the exemption provided for such firms in the FS Act ineffective, and as a result a very large number of professional firms obtained precautionary authorisation under the Act from their professional body (designated under the FS Act as a Recognised Professional Body ("RPB")). The scale of this problem can be indicated by the fact that of the 15,000 professional firms authorised under the FS Act, the FSA estimate that only 2,000 of them intentionally engage in investment business.

One of the results of this arrangement was that since the vast majority of those regulated by RPBs had no intention of doing investment business, the RPBs rulebooks were in some respects less sophisticated than those of the SROs, and in particular RPBs in general did not provide for any form or capital adequacy requirement to be imposed on member firms.

Part XX of the FSMA corrects the drafting errors made in the FS Act and provides a broadly useable safe harbour for professional firms. As a result of this it is expected that the vast majority of professional firms who are authorised under the FS Act will cease to be so under the FSMA, and that those who elect to retain FSMA authorisation will be engaged in real rather than theoretical investment business. It is not reasonable for such firms to be permitted to do investment business without being subject to the same rules in regard to regulatory capital that other authorised persons are subject to, but the lack of existing sets of regulatory capital rules has created a problem for the draftsmen on the Interim Prudential Sourcebook.

The FSA has taken a two-stage approach to this problem. The first stage is to impose on all professional firms which are authorised to do investment business a basic solvency requirement that they be able to meet their liabilities as they fall due. (It is arguable that every firm in the UK is subject to this requirement in any event by reason of the insolvency legislation.) The second stage involved the imposition of two further requirements, one aimed particularly at firms engaged in discretionary investment management business (who would be required to maintain the same level of capital as equivalent regulated firms) and the other aimed at all professional firms, who would be required at all times to maintain a positive net worth. However the FSA has now taken the view that the imposition of these requirements on professional firms engaged in investment business would be too draconian, since it would involve them in considerable cost. The situation is therefore that as from N2 professional firms will be permitted to engage in investment business whilst being required only to satisfy the basic solvency test. However, this will last only until the implementation of the Integrated Prudential Sourcebook, when requirements in line with other firms engaged in the same business are likely to be imposed on all professional firms.

One aspect of the regulation of professional firms which has been seized upon by the FSA and which looks set to spread to other areas of the system is the requirement of some RPBs (notably the three Institutes of Chartered Accountants) that members must maintain a surety bond with an independent insurance company in respect of assets managed by the firm on a discretionary basis and client money and client assets held by the firm. The FSA intends to extend this requirement to members of the Institute of Actuaries and ACCA (the "Association of Chartered Certified Accountants"). It is notable that the FSA also requires firms to maintain adequate PII, but has not made rules in this direction since it has reviewed the existing PII requirements of the RPBs and has concluded that a firm which caries PII cover in accordance with the requirements of its RPB will be satisfactorily protected for prudential purposes.

Given that this regime represents a significantly weaker regime than is ordinarily applied to investment firms, the FSA notes that it will be necessary to confine the activities of professional firms within narrow bounds. This is to some extent required by EU directives – professional firms are excluded from the scope of the ISD by virtue of Article 2.2 (c) thereof, and a firm which engages in investment business outside the terms of that exclusion is necessarily within the scope of the ordinary prudential regime. However, the FSA also notes that there are certain activities which it regards as being necessarily outside the scope of any professional firm; notably market making in investments, acting as a stabilising manager, acting as a trustee or operator of a collective investment scheme, entering into a broker fund arrangement or acting as a broker fund manager. Any firm which has a permission to engage in any of these activities will therefore be required to comply with the prudential requirements for an ordinary investment firm.

It should be noted that where a professional firm is authorised by the FSA, the prudential rules of the FSA will apply to all of the activity of the firm, including activity which would otherwise be exempt by reason of Part XX of the FSMA. Thus, once a firm becomes authorised it cannot ringfence its investment business activities but must satisfy the prudential requirements as a whole.

4.6   Insurance business

Every UK insurance company is required to maintain a specified excess of assets over its liabilities, referred to as a "margin of solvency". Companies headquartered in the UK and pure re-insurers (i.e. companies whose business in the UK is restricted to insurance), wherever headquartered, must maintain a "global" margin, that is, a specified excess of world-wide assets over world-wide liabilities; a non-EEA insurance company which has made a deposit in the UK (a "UK deposit company") must maintain, in addition to a global margin, an excess of assets attributable to its business in EEA States taken together over the liabilities attributable to that business; and a company headquartered outside the EEA which has made a deposit in an EEA State other than the UK (an "EEA deposit company") must maintain a "UK" margin of solvency, that is, an excess of assets attributable to its business in the UK over the liabilities attributable to that business; and all other insurance companies headquartered outside the EEA must maintain both a global and a UK margin of solvency. In the case of a composite (i.e. a company which carries on both long-term (i.e. life) and general insurance) a separate margin of solvency must be maintained for each activity.

If a company's required margin of solvency ("RMS") is not maintained, the FSA may require the company to submit a plan for the restoration of a sound financial position and may exercise powers of intervention or withdraw the company's authorisation.

The Insurance Prudential Sourcebook for insurers prescribes how the RMS and the guarantee fund are to be calculated. Different methods are prescribed for general and for long-term business. In the case of a company which carries on several classes of long-term business for which different calculations apply, the calculations must be made separately and then added together.

4.6.1   *Long-term insurance requirements*

For life and annuity, marriage and birth and social insurance, the RMS is the sum of two calculations. The "first calculation" is four per cent of the reserves to cover insurance liabilities less a maximum reduction (normally 15 per cent) for reinsurance. The "second calculation" is normally 0.3 per cent of the gross capital at risk less a maximum reduction of 50 per cent for reinsurance. For permanent health and capital redemption the first calculation only applies. For linked long-term business, pension fund management and collective insurance there is potentially no requirement. This is because the first calculation is disapplied so long as the company bears no investment risk itself and profits or losses are passed on to customers, and the second calculation only applies if the company covers a risk under the contract (unusual except in the case of a death benefit provided as part of a linked policy).

4.6.2   *General business requirements*

In the case of general business, the RMS is the higher of two calculations based on the company's premiums and claims, currently known as the Schedule 3 and Schedule 4 calculations. The Schedule 3 calculation is the first €10 million of gross premiums receivable for the previous financial year multiplied by 18 per cent plus any further premium income multiplied by 16 per cent (six per cent and five 1/3 per cent for health insurance based on actuarial principles). For the Schedule 4 calculation, gross claims incurred during the previous three financial years are converted into an annual figure. This is calculated as 26 per cent of the first €7 million plus 23 per cent of any further claims (8.67 per cent and 7.76 per cent for health insurance written on actuarial principles). The Schedule 3 and Schedule 4 calculations are each reduced for reinsurance by applying the ratio of net to gross claims up to a limit of 50 per cent.

4.6.3   *Asset and liability valuation*

The valuation methods to be applied to the assets and liabilities of a company are prescribed by the rulebook. These rules function as a loose proxy for investment restrictions, save that (except in the case of linked contracts) there is no prohibition on an insurance company investing in any asset which it sees fit; however, if the asset is not within the valuation rules, it will be left out of account in determining whether the company satisfies the solvency test.

4.6.4   *Lloyd's firms*

In addition to the Lloyd's market itself, the FSMA also brings within the FSA's regulatory scope underwriting agents and members' advisers. Lloyds already regulates the amount of capital which underwriters are required to maintain, and the FSA proposes to retain the Lloyd's requirements. Members' agents, however, have not previously been subject to a capital adequacy regime. The FSA points out that many members' agents are authorised by one or other of the SROs since the performance of their functions frequently requires investment business of one form or another. However it was felt that those who were not already regulated could not be left entirely outside the regulatory net, and as a result they have been subjected to the same minimum £10,000 regulatory capital requirement imposed upon corporate finance advisory firms.

Chapter 5

CONDUCT OF BUSINESS

Richard Stones
Partner and Head of the Financial Services Group
Lovells

5.1 Introduction

5.1.1 *Status of provisions*

In conducting its business a firm is subject to a hierarchy of principles, rules and guidance made by the Financial Services Authority (the "FSA") under the Financial Services and Markets Act 2000 (the "FSMA"). Broadly these comprise:

(a) the FSA's high level Principles for Businesses (*see* Chapter 2 of this Guide);

(b) mandatory rules of conduct (suffixed "R" in the Handbook);

(c) "evidential provisions" (suffixed "E": although these have the status of rules they do not as such require a firm to act or refrain from acting: instead they set out acts or omissions which may "tend to establish" that a firm is, or is not complying with a rule);

(d) guidance given under Section 157 of the FSMA (suffixed "G"). This is not binding, and need not be followed in order to achieve compliance with the relevant rule "So a firm cannot incur disciplinary liability merely because it has not followed guidance. Nor is there any presumption that departing from guidance is indicative of a breach of the relevant rule" (*see* Reader's Guide Instrument 2001). On the other hand, if a firm acts in accordance with guidance in the circumstances contemplated by the guidance the FSA will proceed on the footing that it has complied with the aspect of the rule to which the guidance refers. A fair amount of guidance relates to the Principles rather than to specific rules.

The upshot is that it will take a degree of self-confidence for a firm to act in a way which is discouraged by an evidential provision; on the other hand, it should in principle be possible to treat guidance as a "shield rather than a sword".

Both the Principles for Businesses and the Rules are, in formal terms, "general rules" made under Section 138 of the FSMA; the evidential provisions are made under Section 149. Breach of the Principles and of the "mandatory rules" will expose a firm to enforcement proceedings (*see* Chapter 10 of this Guide). Unlike the Principles, breach of a mandatory rule may also give rise to a right of action under Section 150 on the part of any person who suffers loss as a result. This right is, however, generally limited by Section 150 and the FSMA (Rights of Action) Regulations 2001 to "private persons", that is individuals who do not suffer the loss in the course of carrying on a regulated activity; and other persons who do not suffer the loss in the course of carrying on a business; and fiduciaries or representatives acting for the foregoing.

Compliance with FSA guidance will not necessarily provide a "safe harbour" against a claim under Section 150 that the firm is in breach of a related rule. In that context interpretation of the rules is a matter for the courts: at least in the FSA's own view rights conferred on third parties (such as firms' clients) by FSA rules cannot be affected by FSA guidance (*see* Readers Guide paragraph 30).

5.1.2 *The Conduct of Business Sourcebook; approach of this Chapter*

The rules, evidential provisions and guidance on conduct of business are set out in the Conduct of Business Sourcebook ("COB"). This Chapter aims to give a general guide to the content of COB. It is not intended to be comprehensive. For brevity:

(a) references to what is "expected" of a firm are to evidential provisions, and references "suggestions" are to guidance;

(b) unless otherwise stated, the provisions described apply only to "designated investment business" (*see* Section 5.2.2 below).

5.2 Scope of COB

5.2.1 *What firms do they apply to?*

In principle COB applies to *all* firms except investment companies with variable capital (i.e. UK open-ended investment companies): although they are technically authorised persons, they are in practice regulated through their authorised corporate directors, so that the direct application of COB to them is unnecessary (*see* 1.2.1R).

COB will generally apply to the "passported" business of an incoming Economic Area ("EEA") firm, except as regards client money and assets, which are the province of the home state (COB 1.2.1(1)R).

5.2.2 *What type of activity?*

The COB applies in principle to:

(a) *all* regulated activities (i.e. activities which fall within the scope of the Financial Services and Markets Act 2000 (Regulated Activities) Order 2001 ("RAO")), except where the particular rule has a narrower application; and

(b) to non-regulated activities only to the extent actually specified (1.3.1R).

It follows that there is no general exclusion for regulated activities which fall outside the historic scope of regulation under the Financial Services Act 1986 (the "FS Act"); however the preponderance of the COB provisions apply only to "designated investment business". This term simultaneously restricts and extends the scope of the provisions since:

(a) it applies only to activities relating to designated investments; (i.e. broadly securities, derivatives and investment related insurance) and thus excludes deposit taking, mortgage lending and general insurance; but

(b) it expressly includes those dealings as principal which would otherwise be excluded from the scope of the RAO by the exemptions in Article 15. Any dealing as principal in a designated investment will thus fall within the scope of the provisions concerned.

In practice the COB provisions apply only in very limited respects to non-designated investments. In particular:

(a) the financial promotions regime applies in part to all investments (*see* Section 5.5 below);

(b) COB Section 6 contains product disclosure requirements which apply to general insurance and pure protection insurance contracts (COB 6.8).

5.2.3   *Special cases*

The COB itself contains provisions which limit or modify its application in particular cases:

(a) only the rules on financial promotion (*see* Section 5.5 below) apply to:

   (i)   "service companies" (a category of firm designed to cover information and other service providers whose services may amount to "arranging" transactions, and whose Part IV permission will be limited accordingly);

   (ii) "UCITS qualifiers", that is, operators of EEA collective investment schemes established outside the UK which are recognised here under Section 264 of the FSMA (1.2.1R);

(b) only specified COB provisions will apply to:

   (i)   stock lending (COB 1.6.1R);

   (ii) corporate finance business (COB 1.6.3R): the restricted meaning of "client" in relation to corporate finance business also limits the scope of the rules in this connection (*see* Section 5.3.2 below);

   (iii) oil market activities undertaken by firms which are oil market participants (COB 1.6.5G);

(iv) a professional firm, as regards professional activities which (broadly) would have qualified for exemption under Part XX of the FSMA had they been carried on by themselves (COB 1.2.1R(4));

(c) the rules apply, but with significant modifications and additions:

(i) to the operator of a collective investment scheme as regards "scheme management activity", that is, management of the assets of the scheme, but excluding safe keeping of money or other assets (COB Chapter 10): an important point is that for certain purposes the scheme, rather than its participants, is treated as the firm's "customer" (*see* 10.2.3R(1));

(ii) to trustees and depositories (COB Chapter 11);

(iii) to activities relating to Lloyd's (COB Chapter 12).

More detailed explanations of these special regimes is beyond the scope of this Guide.

5.2.4 *Territorial scope*

In general COB (other than the rules on financial promotion (*see* Section 5.5 below)) applies in full to activities carried out:

(a) from an establishment of the firm in the UK; and

(b) from anywhere else if the activity is with or for a client in the UK.

However, the activities of a branch outside the UK will not (except as explained in Sections 5.2.6, 5.2.7 and 5.2.8 below) be subject to COB if, had the activity been carried out by a separate entity, that entity would not have needed to be authorised because of the "territorial" provisions of the FSMA or exclusions from the RAO (COB Section 1.4). This means that, broadly, the COB may not apply:

(a) if the activity would not in an ordinary sense be regarded as "carried on in the UK": however this phrase is given an extended sense by Section 418 FSMA and in the case of a UK company may apply where the "day-to-day management of the carrying on of the activity" is the responsibility of an establishment in the UK; or

(b) in the case of certain kinds of activity, if the business is not solicited by the firm, or is solicited in a manner permitted by the rules on financial promotion; or in certain circumstances where the activity involves another authorised person. (*See* COB 1.4 and Article 72 of the RAO.)

Some care is needed in determining where a particular activity is carried out "from". This will not necessarily be the place where an individual engaged in an activity happens to be. It is suggested that the reference must be to a place where he is based and it is unlikely that the courts will look kindly on artificial arrangements (e.g. if a substantively UK-based group arranges for its UK personnel to report to an office somewhere else). A representative in the field is likely to be treated as carrying on the activities concerned "from" the office to which he reports.

5.2.5   *Branches of UK firms in EEA Member States*

Such branches are regulated on the basis explained in Section 5.2.3 above (i.e. they will not normally be subject to COB unless they are providing services to UK clients, and then subject to the qualifications discussed). However such branches are subject to the client money and asset rules (reflecting that under the Investment Services Directive this is treated as a home state matter).

5.2.6   *Long-term insurance business*

The scheme of the EU Life Insurance Directives determines which country's rules will apply not by reference to the place where the business is done from, but by the habitual residence of the consumer. This means that certain provisions which reflect those Directives, that is, COB 6.5 (content of key features) COB 6.7 (cancellation rights) and COB 6.8 (insurance contracts):

(a) will not apply to business carried on in the UK if the consumer is habitually resident somewhere else; and

(b) conversely will apply in the case of a consumer habitually resident in the UK, even if the business is carried on from elsewhere (*see* COB 1.4).

5.2.7 *Disclosure*

Where a firm carries on business from an overseas place of business it must make a specified disclosure about the different regulatory system which will apply (*see* COB 5.5.7R and COB 5.5.8R):

(a) if it deals with a private customer in the UK; or

(b) if it deals with a customer anywhere else in circumstances where it states that it is an authorised person.

5.2.8 *Delegation of activities by the firm*

COB does not specifically make provision for outsourcing or delegation. However as a matter of general law a person who carries on an activity through the agency of another (whether that other be an employee or a sub-contractor) will normally be treated for legal purposes as carrying on the activity himself. It should thus follow that the COB will apply to the acts and omissions of the delegate. However the position will depend upon the obligations which the firm undertakes to its client: the above position will generally apply where the agreement with the client is silent on the subject of delegation. If, on the other hand:

(a) the contractual arrangements amount simply to an introduction of the firm to a third party; or

(b) (possibly) provide for sub-contracting to a third party on terms which specifically exclude any liability for the defaults of the sub-contractor;

it appears that the firm is not agreeing or purporting to carry on the regulated activity concerned, and there is no reason why it should be treated as carrying on the activity for the purposes of COB.

5.2.9 *Appointed representatives*

By virtue of Section 39(4) of the FSMA a firm is responsible for the acts and omissions of its appointed representatives when they are acting as such. In determining whether a firm has complied with any provision of COB, anything done or omitted by the firm's appointed representatives (when acting as such) will be treated as having been done or omitted by the firm (FSMA Section 39(4), COB 1.7.1G).

5.3 Clients and customers

5.3.1 *"Client"*

COB uses the term "client" in an extremely wide sense as "any person with or for whom a firm conducts or intends to conduct designated investment business or any other regulated activity".

The term expressly includes:

(a) potential clients; and

(b) clients of appointed representatives.

It will be noted that this definition will extend to a range of persons who will not be regarded as "clients" in any ordinary sense: for example the counterparties to market transactions.

COB has special provisions about who will be the client/customer:

(a) of the operator of a collective investment scheme (*see* Section 5.2.3 above);

(b) in relation to "OPS activities", that is, broadly, activities relating to the management of the assets of an occupational pension scheme or benevolent fund, if carried on by a firm which is the trustee of the scheme or fund, a related employer, or certain connected entities (*see* COB 1.5);

(c) of other trustees and depositories (*see* COB Chapter 11);

(d) in relation to Lloyd's (*see* COB 12.1.13R).

5.3.2 *Corporate finance and venture capital contacts*

An investment bank which advises a company on a corporate transaction might be regarded as providing investment advice "for" the company's shareholders, or as making arrangements "with" investors when (acting on behalf of the company) it places shares with them. To reduce the scope of the firm's regulatory responsibility the term "client" is cut back so as to exclude "corporate finance contacts". These are people with or for whom the firm carries on designated investment business as a result of carrying on "corporate finance business" for someone else or on its own account, provided that (broadly):

(a) the firm does not lead the person to believe he is being treated as a client; and

(b) it gives a clear indication to this effect.

"Corporate finance business" is defined in an elaborate way, but broadly includes the activities which would normally be regarded as corporate finance in the ordinary sense.

There is a similar exclusion for "venture capital contacts".

5.3.3   *Client classifications*

There are three sub-divisions of "client": *private customer, intermediate customer* and *market counterparty.* The "default" position is that a client is a private customer.

5.3.4   *Intermediate customers*

Certain categories of person automatically fall into the "intermediate" category unless they opt up or down (*see* Section 5.3.7 below):

(a) a local or public authority;

(b) a body corporate with shares listed or traded on an EEA exchange or on the primary board of any IOSCO member country official exchange;

(c) a body corporate (including a limited liability partnership) which has (or has a parent or subsidiary which has) a called up share capital or net assets of at least £5 million;

(d) a special purpose vehicle; that is, (broadly) a body established for the purposes of securitising assets which is assessed by a rating agency;

(e) a partnership with net assets of at least £5 million before deduction (in the case of a limited partnership) of partners' loans;

(f) a trustee of an Occupational Pension Scheme, a small self-administered scheme or a stakeholder pension scheme with at least 50 members and assets under management of at least £10 million;

(g) a trustee of any other trust with assets of at least £10 million in cash or designated investments;

(h) an unregulated collective investment scheme.

A *regulated* collective investment scheme will always be a private customer

5.3.5   Market counterparties

The following entities will fall into the category of market counterparty:

(a) a government, central bank or local authority;

(b) a supranational body with any of the above as members;

(c) a state investment body;

(d) a body charged with, or intervening in public debt management;

(e) in certain circumstances (*see* below) another firm or an "overseas financial services institution" (i.e. one which is regulated by the competent authorities of an EEA state or by a regulator which is a member of IOSCO); or

(f) an associate of a firm or an overseas financial services institution if the firm or institution consents.

A collective investment scheme which would otherwise fall into one of the above categories will not be a market counterparty.

5.3.6   *Agent and principal: who is the client?*

Complications arise when the person (referred to below as an "intermediary") who instructs a firm is acting as an agent for someone else: an example is where a professional fund manager, acting on behalf of clients, instructs a securities broker to buy and sell securities.

The starting point is that the intermediary will be the firm's "client" if:

(a) the firm is unaware that the principal exists;

(b) the intermediary is itself a firm or an overseas financial institution (*see* above); or

(c) in any other case provided that the main purpose of the arrangement is not to avoid the firm's duties to the principal. (In other words it is not open to a firm to channel business through (e.g.) an unregulated overseas associate.)

The principal will be the client if this is agreed between the firm and the intermediary or if the "avoidance of duties" test is not satisfied (*see* 4.1.5R).

5.3.7   *Opting up and opting down*

The COB permits clients who fall into one category to:

(a) "opt down" that is, to elect for a category giving greater protection; or

(b) "opt up" that is, to move to category giving less protection (in some cases the choice is that of the firm).

5.3.8   *Opting down – firms or overseas financial services institutions*

A firm or overseas financial services institution should normally be a market counterparty. This will largely deprive it of the protection of COB (*see* Section 5.3.12 below) and this may cause difficulties if it is in turn acting for a customer. On the one hand it will have obligations under the rules to the customer; on the other hand the firm which in turn provides it with services (the "service provider") is permitted:

(a) to treat it (and not the ultimate customer) as its client; and

(b) on this basis to treat it as a market counterparty, thus depriving it (and the ultimate customer) of the protections in COB.

The intermediary firm may therefore wish to be treated as an intermediate customer. In this respect the position differs depending on whether the activities concerned fall within the definition of "inter-professional business" (*see* Chapter 6 of this Guide).

(a) If they do, the intermediary firm has no *right* to demand intermediate customer treatment, but the service provider may agree to do so as long as the intermediary firm is acting for a customer and decides that it needs the benefit of intermediate customer protection in order to protect that customer.

(b) If they do not, the intermediary firm will normally be treated as an intermediate customer rather than the market counterparty, unless it has specifically indicated that it is acting on its own account.

Intermediate customer status will also be accorded to a life office when acting on behalf of its life fund (*see* COB 4.1.7R).

Finally (by way of exception), a firm will be private customer if it is a regulated collective investment scheme or an intermediate customer if it is an unregulated scheme.

5.3.9   *Opting down – market counterparty or intermediate customer to private customer*

The firm may elect to treat clients who are market counterparties or intermediate customers as private customers for the purposes of the COB if it wishes to do so and gives notice to the client. The client has no right to require such treatment (*see* COB 4.1.14R).

5.3.10 Opting up – "expert" private customer to intermediate customer

A private customer may "opt up" to intermediate customer status (COB 4.1.9R) if:

(a) the firm has taken reasonable care to determine that the client has sufficient knowledge and experience to waive private customer protections (*see* COB 4.1.10G);

(b) it has issued a written warning to the client explaining the protections he is losing (for expected contents *see* COB 4.1.11E); and

(c) the client has been given sufficient time to consider the implications and has given consent (which need not be in writing, so long as the firm can demonstrate that it has been given on an "informed" basis).

5.3.11 Opting up – "large intermediate customer" to market counterparty

Certain substantial corporate and institutional entities may opt up to market counterparty status. To qualify for this election the entity must fall into one of the following categories:

(a) a body corporate (including a limited liability partnership) which has (or has subsidiaries and/or parent companies which have) called up share capital of at least £10 million (note that this is a share capital and not a net assets test);

(b) a body corporate (possibly including a limited liability partnership) which meets (or has parents and/or subsidiaries which meet) any three of the following tests:

   (i) a balance sheet total of €12.5 million;

   (ii) net turnover of €25 million; or

   (iii) average of 250 employees during an (unspecified) year;

(c) a partnership (excluding a limited liability partnership) or an unincorporated association with net assets of at least £10 million (without deducting partners' loans);

(d) trustees of a trust who meet the test for qualifying as intermediate customers (*see* above).

To give effect to the "opt up" in these circumstances the firm must (*see* COB 4.1.12R):

(a) advise the client of its intention to treat it as a market counterparty;

(b) warn the client in writing that it will lose protections under the regulatory system (but with no obligation to explain what they are); and

(c) not be notified of objection (in the case of a body corporate) or obtain consent (in any other case).

5.3.12   *Effect of client categorisation*

The extent to which COB applies to a client will depend on its categorisation:

(a) COB is generally disapplied to inter-professional business between market counterparties: this is subject to the separate regime explained in Chapter 6 of this Guide. This position does not, however, amount to a complete disapplication since:

   (i)   the rules on Chinese walls (COB 2.4) and personal account dealings (COB 7.13) do apply;

   (ii) the definition of inter-professional business excludes the approval of financial promotions and the safeguarding and administration of investments, and the rules governing these activities will therefore apply to market counterparties in this context;

(b) where a firm is carrying on an activity with or for a market counterparty which is not inter-professional business, the application of the rules will depend on their specific scope: for example if (as in the case of custody) the rules apply to relations with "clients" they will apply to market counterparties, whereas those rules which relate only to "customers" will not;

(c) as between private and intermediate customers, the application of the COB provisions will again depend on their individual stated scope.

Opting up will not deprive a person who is "a private person" of his statutory right of action against a firm in breach of its obligation; however the effect of opting-up will be to reduce the number of rules to which the firm will be subject, and correspondingly its exposure to a statutory claim. Conversely an entity which "opts down" and is treated as a private customer will not thereby acquire any rights under the Financial Ombudsman Service or Compensation Scheme.

5.3.13 *Review and record-keeping*

COB 4.1.15R and 4.1.16R require periodic review of client classification and the keeping of records.

5.4 Communicating with customers

Any communication between a firm and a customer, however communicated, will be subject to regulation either:

(a) as a "financial promotion" (*see* COB Chapter 3); or

(b) where the rules on financial promotions do not apply, under the wider rules which govern fairness of communications (*see* COB 2.1).

It follows that in communicating with a customer a firm must always take reasonable steps to ensure that the communication is "clear, fair and not misleading" (referred to below as the "general duty of fairness").

In addition:

(a) in communicating with a private customer the firm must take reasonable steps to ensure that the customer is given adequate information about the firm's identity, the identity and status of employees or agents with whom the customer may have contact and the fact that the firm is regulated or authorised by the FSA (COB 5.5.3R). COB 5.5 lays down the expected standards for the information which should normally be provided (e.g. what should be on stationery and business cards);

(b) any communication which makes a specific recommendation to a particular customer may amount to advice which is subject to the rules on suitability and customers' understanding of risk (*see* Section 5.7 below);

(c) there are specific status disclosure requirements for those dealing with "packaged products" (*see* Section 5.13 below).

The FSA Handbook is intended to be "media neutral" and communications required to be "in writing" may generally be made by electronic media (*see* COB 1.8.1G). However the FSA suggests (COB 1.8.2G) that if it uses electronic media a firm should:

(a) adopt appropriate security arrangements;

(b) be able to show that the customer wishes to communicate electronically; and

(c) make it clear to the customer if a contractual relationship is to be created with legal consequences.

5.5   Financial promotion

5.5.1   *Scope*

"Financial promotion" is defined in Section 21 of the FSMA as (broadly) a communication of an invitation or inducement to engage in a "controlled activity" relating to a "controlled investment". These terms refer to activities and investments specified in Schedule 1 to the FSMA (Financial Promotion Order) 2001 and in general correspond to the investments and activities regulated under the RAO.

It should be noted that:

(a) it appears that the intent of a financial promotion must be promotional: that is, "an invitation or inducement";

(b) on the other hand the term will apply to any kind of communication in any medium and will in principle extend to one-to-one communications, whether or not solicited. A suggestion of a financial transaction in the course of a telephone conversation initiated by the customer may amount to financial promotion in the absence of an exemption;

(c) the restrictions apply only to communications made in the course of business;

(d) the definition in principle applies to communications relating to all kinds of investment, including deposits and general insurance, though the restrictions in this area are partially disapplied by exemptions in the Financial Promotion Order.

Under Section 21 of the FSMA the financial promotion may only be communicated by a person who is an authorised person or if the content of the communication is approved by such a person. This means that, with certain exceptions (*see* below) a firm will be free to issue or approve financial promotions, and the concern of COB is (broadly) to regulate the content of such communications.

5.5.2 *Exemptions*

The application of the requirements is limited by various exemptions:

The requirements do not apply to the communication of promotions of the following kinds: (except as regards unregulated collective investment schemes – *see* below) to:

(a) communications which could have been issued by a non-authorised person under the exceptions in the Financial Promotion Order (e.g. those directed at investment professionals, substantial companies and certain high net worth individuals; and "one off" real time communications);

(b) any kind of financial promotion "directed at" persons other than private customers (i.e. communicated only to persons established on reasonable grounds to be within this category, or otherwise in a way which may reasonably be regarded as so directed: the meaning of "directed at" is dealt with in COB 3.5.7R);

(c) "short form" or image communications, that is, communications which contain contact details, "brief factual descriptions" of the firm's activities, fees and/or products, and/or prices or yields of investments, and nothing else. (This would appear to exempt quite a wide range of possible communications, but the guidance suggests that the scope of the exemption is intended to be restricted;)

(d) personal quotation or illustration forms;

(e) a financial promotion which is subject to the Takeover Code or which has been exempted from complying with the Code by its terms or by a ruling of the Takeover Panel.

However, if a firm *approves* a promotion within (b), (c), (d) or (e) for the purposes of Section 21 of the FSMA, the general duty of fairness and various ancillary provisions about approvals will apply (COB 3.2.4R). (Where the firm communicates such promotions itself, the general duty of fairness will apply under COB 2.1 (*see* Section 5.4 above).)

In addition, the requirements in general will not apply if a firm ("A") communicates a financial promotion produced by another firm ("B"), so long as A takes reasonable care to establish that B properly approved it, that A communicates it only to recipients of the type intended by B, and that it has not ceased to satisfy the general duty of fairness (COB 3.6.5R).

In addition to the above general exemptions, there are partial exemptions for promotions relating to: deposits, general insurance contracts or pure protection contracts (3.2.3R). These are, in effect, subject only to the general duty of fairness and not to any other requirement (though certain specific information must be given in respect the cash deposit component of an ISA (COB 3.96R and COB 3.9.8R)).

5.5.3   *What is required?*

Although the term financial promotion covers all media, COB (following the Financial Promotions Order) distinguishes between "real time communications" (i.e. broadly, personal visits, telephone calls and other interactive dialogues) and "non-real time communications" (everything else). In the electronic medium it may not be as easy to make the distinction, but Article 7 of the Financial Promotion Order provides the following "indications" that a promotion is "non-real time":

(a) the promotion is communicated to more than one person in identical terms;

(b) the system of communication is such that in the normal course it creates a record which is available to the recipient to refer to it at a later time (e.g. material on a website or communicated by email); or

(c) the communication is made by way of a system which in the normal course does not require the recipient to respond immediately.

5.5.4   *Non-real time promotions*

In the case of a non-real time communication the firm must:

(a) before communicating or approving it, ensure that an individual or individuals with "appropriate expertise" confirm that it complies with the requirements of the COB (COB 3.6); and

(b) take reasonable steps to ensure that it is clear, fair and not misleading (COB 3.8.4R): the FSA's specific expectations in this regard are set out in COB 3.8.5E to 3.8.7G. (These include, in the case of deposits, general insurance and pure protection insurance, compliance with the applicable industry codes – COB 3.8.6G;)

(c) include its name and a point of contact (COB 3.8.2R);

(d) keep records containing specified information (COB 3.7).

In addition, unless exempted is mentioned above a non-real time financial promotion must comply with the detailed specific content requirements set out in COB 3.8.8R and following.

Additional detailed requirements apply to "direct offer promotions", that is promotions which:

(a) contain an offer by the firm to enter into an agreement with any respondent, or an invitation to the respondent to make an offer to the firm to do so; and

(b) specify the manner of response or include a form for doing so.

The key aspect of direct offer promotions (*see* COB 3.9) is that a response will immediately commit the respondent to take the product or service concerned, either by accepting the contractual offer or by himself making an offer which the firm can accept. Consequently, the promotion must contain sufficient information to enable the investor to assess the product or service without further advice. The rules make specific requirements for different kinds of advertising, and in relation to packaged products require the advertisement to contain the information specified for a key features document, or ISA "minimum information" (*see* COB 3.9.8, COB 3.9.10 and Section 5.13 below).

5.5.5   *Real time promotions*

The requirements for real time promotions depend on whether the promotion is solicited or unsolicited:

(a) the FSA suggests that many *solicited* real time promotions will fall within one of the general exemption (*see* Section 5.2.2 above) for example on the basis that they are "one off". Where they do not qualify, they will have to comply with the general fairness obligation as well as specific requirements about the time and method of communication (*see* COB 3.8.22R). The rules on record-keeping and approval procedures will not apply;

(b) real time *unsolicited* communications (i.e. broadly communications which are not initiated by, or made in response to an express request from the recipient (COB 3.10.1R)) are normally only permitted if:

(i) they fall within one of the general exemptions (*see* Section 5.5.2 above); or

(ii) the customer has an established existing customer relationship with the firm such that the customer envisages receiving such unsolicited promotions, and the call relates to a generally marketable packaged product other than a "higher volatility fund" or a life policy linked or potentially linked to a "higher volatility fund" (COB 3.10.3R).

In the first case the financial promotion rules as a whole will not apply: in the other cases the firm will have to comply with the rules on timing, and method of communication (referred to in (a) above).

Note that standard terms of business which permit calls to be made will not make them "solicited", though they may allow unsolicited calls to be made on the basis described above. Contrast a case where the customer signifies clearly, in addition to agreeing the terms, that such communications may take place: this will allow the communications to be treated as solicited (COB 3.10.1R(3)).

A real time promotion cannot be approved (COB 3.12.2R) and must therefore be communicated by an authorised person or within an exemption.

5.5.6   *Electronic media*

COB contains guidance on promotion by electronic media (COB 3.14). This suggests *inter alia*:

(a) that a website need not be designed so that key features and other required disclosures are actually read, so long as the firm makes it clear that they are available, and easily obtainable. A hypertext link can be used so long as it is not "hidden away";

(b) application forms or the preceding text should draw attention to the key features and/or contractual terms and stress the importance of reading them; and

(c) a hypertext link on a website will not of itself be regarded as causing the communication of any financial promotion to which it leads.

There is to be further guidance on financial promotion over the internet, including the treatment of banners and hypertext links in the Authorisation Manual.

5.5.7 *Prohibited and restricted advertising*

The regime described above turns largely on disclosure. However there are certain categories of promotion which an authorised person cannot issue at all, or can only issue subject to restrictions. These are:

(a) unsolicited real time communications (*see* Section 5.5.5 above);

(b) communications relating to unregulated collective investment schemes (*see* Section 5.8 below);

(c) direct offer promotions relating to derivatives or warrants, which may only be communicated if the firm has itself adequate evidence to suggest that the investment may be suitable for the customer to whom it is directed (COB 3.9.5R);

(d) direct offer promotions for broker funds (COB 3.9.5R);

(e) promotions relating to overseas entities (*see* Section 5.5.10 below);

(f) financial promotions relating to life policies offered by any person who is not an authorised person, an exempt person in relation to the relevant class of insurance business, certain EEA insurance companies or insurance companies authorised to carry on insurance business of the relevant kind in Guernsey, Jersey, the Isle of Man, Iowa and Pennsylvania (COB 3.13).

All such promotions are, however, permitted if they fall within the general exemptions referred to in Section 5.5.2 above)

5.5.8 *Unregulated collective investment schemes*

Financial promotion of unregulated collective investment schemes is only permitted if it:

(a) falls within an exemption under the FSMA 2000 (Promotion of Collective Investment Schemes) (Exemptions) Order 2001 (which contains exemptions similar to, but more restrictive than, those in the Financial Promotion Order); or

(b) is permitted by COB 3.11.2R (which sets out a further list of permitted types of scheme and investor).

The FSA suggests that promotion of an unregulated scheme on a website is permissible if the site is designed to reduce, so far as possible, the risk of participation in the scheme by non-permitted persons. This may be satisfied by stating clearly what are the permitted categories and putting in place a system for rejecting non-complying applications (COB 3.14.5G, paragraph 4).

Where permitted, any financial promotion of an unregulated scheme can only constitute a direct offer if the firm has adequate evidence that the scheme may be suitable for the customers concerned (COB 3.9.5R).

5.5.9 *Promotion of overseas products and services; introduction to overseas entities*

A firm may not communicate or approve a financial promotion which identifies a specific investment which may lead to an overseas entity carrying on investment business with a private customer in the UK, unless:

(a) the promotion includes specified warnings; and

(b) the firm has no reason to doubt that the overseas entity will deal with UK customers honestly and reliably.

(*See* COB 3.12.6) There are similar disclosure requirements where a firm makes an introduction to an overseas entity: *see* COB 5.5.3R and 5.5.7R.

5.5.10 *Territorial scope*

The application of the financial promotion rules turns on whether a promotion is "directed at" persons in the UK, as interpreted by Article 12 of the Financial Promotions Order (repeated in COB 3.3.6R). This lays down the following tests (broadly stated):

(a) an indication that the communication is directed only at persons outside the UK;

(b) an indication that it must not be acted upon by persons in the UK;

(c) the communication is not referred to in, or directly accessible from, any other communication by the same person which is directed at persons in the UK;

(d) the existence of proper systems and procedures preventing persons in the UK from engaging in any investment activity to which the communication relates;

(e) inclusion of the communication in a publication which is principally accessed in or intended for a market outside the UK, or a sound or television broadcast or teletext service transmitted principally for reception outside the UK.

The presence of (c) and (d) will be conclusive where the communication is directed from outside the UK; (a), (b), (c) and (d) will be conclusive if the communication is directed from inside the UK; any of the tests individually are simply indicative.

On this basis, rules on issue of communications apply:

(a) where the promotion is made to someone *in* the UK or directed at persons here; or;

(b) in addition, in the case of an unsolicited real time promotion where the promotion is made to a person *outside* the UK, or directed at persons there, unless it is made:

    (i) *from* outside the UK; *and*

    (ii) for the purposes of a business carried on exclusively outside the UK.

(*see* COB 3.31R; 3.3.5R.)

Where the firm is approving a communication:

(a) the rules will apply in full if it is sent to or directed at persons in the UK(CO 3.3.2);

(b) if it is directed elsewhere (and regardless of its origin) the general duty of fairness and the rules on approval of overseas advertising (COB 3.12) will apply.

The restrictions on promotion of unregulated collective investment schemes apply without territorial limitations (COB 3.3.3R(i)).

5.6   Taking on business

Before carrying on business with or for a client, a firm must:

(a) take reasonable steps to establish the classification of the client (*see* Section 5.3 above) (COB 4.1.4R);

(b) consider whether it needs to provide terms of business or a client agreement.

5.6.1   *Terms of business*

Principle 7 requires a firm to "pay due regard to the information needs of its customers". To support this COB may require the issue of terms of business (COB 4.2). Precisely what is required will depend on the circumstances:

(a) there is no requirement where the client has been categorised as a market counterparty;

(b) there are various specific exceptions to the requirement (4.2.1R and 4.2.9R): these include:

   (i) cases where the business is confined to arranging "execution only transactions" (but this does not apply to transactions in contingent liability investments with or for a private customer);

   (ii) transactions resulting from direct offer financial promotions (*see* Section 5.5 above);

   (iii) the supply of published recommendations;

   (iv) issue by a life insurance company of a life insurance policy;

   (v) the arrangement of a transaction in the shares of an investment trust by the operator of an investment trust savings scheme;

   (vi) (broadly) the performance of the functions of manager or trustee of a collective investment scheme (including acting as authorised corporate director or depository of an open-ended investment company.

Any activities outside these exceptions will require (one way) "terms of business". In addition, in the case of a private customer, the following activities require a "client agreement," that is, an agreement to which the customer has consented, normally in writing (*see* COB 4.2.7R):

(a) managing investments on a discretionary basis;

(b) a transaction in a contingent liability investment;

(c) stock lending;

(d) underwriting (except in respect of a life insurance policy).

5.6.2   *Timing*

In the case of a private customer the terms of business must be provided before conducting the business (with certain exceptions relating to ISAs and stakeholder pension schemes). Where a client agreement is required, the firm must not enter into it unless it has taken reasonable care to ensure that the customer has had a proper opportunity to consider its terms (COB 4.2.5R and 4.2.7R). (It does not follow from the rules as drafted that signature of the agreement must occur before the service is provided, but this is perhaps implicit.) In the case of a customer habitually resident outside the UK signature of a client agreement is not required if the firm has taken reasonable steps to establish that he does not wish to enter into such an agreement (COB 4.2.7(2)R). In the case of an intermediate customer the terms of business must be provided "within a reasonable period" of the firm beginning to act (COB 4.2.5(3)R).

5.6.3   *Content*

Terms of business (or a client agreement) must set out "in adequate detail" the basis on which the relevant business is to be carried on (COB 4.2.10R). The matters which the FSA expects to be included, as relevant, are set out in the tables at COB 4.2.15E and 4.2.16E. The terms should also include any further or alternative provisions that the customer has asked for, where relevant and practicable (COB 4.2.11E).

5.6.4   *Restriction of liability*

A firm may not in any communication (whether written or oral) seek to exclude or restrict, or to rely on any exclusion or restriction of:

(a) any duty or liability which it may have to a customer or the regulatory system; or

(b) in the case of a private customer, any other duty, unless it is reasonable for it to do so (COB 2.5).

5.6.5   *Risk warnings*

It is also usual to include in customer documentation the various risk warnings which may be required under the COB provisions on suitability and understanding of risk (*see* Section 5.7.6 below).

5.6.6   *Charges*

When dealing with a private customer:

(a) a firm's charges must not be excessive (COB 5.6.3R), taking account of market comparisons, the trust the customer has placed in the firm and the nature and extent of disclosure which has been made (COB 5.6.4G);

(b) the firm must disclose the basis or amount of its charges in writing, and the nature and amount of any other income receivable by it (or, to its knowledge, an associate) and attributable to the business concerned (COB 5.7.3R).

There are separate rules as regards:

(a) remuneration/commission in relation to packaged products (*see* Section 5.13 below);

(b) soft commission (*see* Section 5.10.4 below).

5.7   Advice and suitability

5.7.1   Scope of requirements

A firm will generally be required to take responsibility for the suitability of transactions arranged for a private customer if the customer has relied on the firm in relation to its choice, that is:

(a) there has been a "personal recommendation" (one made to the client specifically); or

(b) the firm is acting as an investment manager (which includes not only discretionary management but also the process of keeping a portfolio under review).

In the case of certain types of investments, some of the requirements apply even if there is no recommendation; for example in relation to pensions, derivatives and warrants: this is noted below.

The reference to "personal" recommendations means that the provisions in this area will not normally apply to direct offer promotions (*see* COB 5.3.3G): to reflect this, COB 3.9.7R requires that any direct offer promotion makes it clear that if the customer is in any doubt about the suitability of the agreement concerned he should contact the firm (or an independent intermediary if the firm does not offer advice). As an exception, a direct offer promotion of a personal pension scheme to a group of employees will be subject to suitability requirements (*see* Section 5.7.5 below).

COB rather confusingly refers in addition to "execution only transactions", that is, "transactions executed on the specific instructions of the client where the firm does not give advice on the merits of the transaction". It is not entirely clear whether this is exactly equivalent to a "transaction made without a personal recommendation". So when the FSA suggests in COB 5.2.3G that a firm which provides "limited advice" should not treat any resulting transaction as "execution only", the implications are not clear. It seems unlikely, however, that the suitability obligations will apply simply because the firm has provided the customer with factual information about available investments, so long as there has not in substance been any recommendation.

5.7.2 *Know your customer*

Where the suitability obligations apply a firm must take reasonable steps to ensure that it is in possession of sufficient personal and financial information about a private customer relevant to its services (COB 5.2.5R). Any information must be kept under regular review where the services are provided on a continuing basis; where services are provided occasionally any information should be reviewed on each occasion (COB 5.2.6G). If a customer fails to provide the relevant information, the firm must advise the customer that the lack of certain information may adversely effect the quality of the services which it can provide; however there is no absolute bar on continuing to act (COB 5.2.7G). The information collected must be recorded for periods which vary by reference to the type of transaction (COB 5.2.9R). The FSA suggest (in COB 5.2.11G) that the information obtained in the fact finding process should, at a minimum, provide an analysis of customer's personal and financial circumstances leading to a clear identification of his needs and priorities so that, combined with attitude to risk, a suitable investment can be recommended.

5.7.3 *Suitability*

The firm must take reasonable steps to ensure that it does not make a personal recommendation to buy or sell an investment, or effect a discretionary transaction for a private customer unless the recommendation for transaction is suitable for the customer, having regard to the facts disclosed by him (e.g. in the fact-finding process mentioned above) and other relevant facts of which the firm is, or should be, aware (5.3.5(1)R).

In the case of an investment manager (discretionary or otherwise) there is a corresponding obligation to ensure that the portfolio or account remains suitable (COB 5.3.5(2)R). In other words failure to effect or recommend transactions may breach the rule just as much as recommendation of unsuitable ones.

5.7.4 *Pooled vehicles*

In the case of pooled vehicles, slightly different rules may apply:

(a) where the funds of customers have been pooled with a view to the taking of common investment management decisions (e.g. in the case of a managed fund service) the suitability test has to be applied to the fund, having regard to its stated investment objectives (COB 5.3.5(3)R); and

(b) where the firm is the manager of an OPS or stakeholder scheme the suitability of transactions and of the investment portfolio under management must be tested by reference to the investment objectives specified in the portfolio mandate (COB 5.3.12R);

(c) special rules apply to collective investment schemes (COB 10.4).

5.7.5   *Specific cases*

There are additional suitability rules relating to the sale of packaged products including personal and stakeholder pensions (*see* Section 5.13 below). There are also specific rules applicable to the suitability of broker funds (COB 5.3.20R); pension transfers and pension opt outs (COB 5.3.21 to COB 5.3.27R); as well as guidance relevant for assessing the suitability of particular pension products (COB 5.3.29G).

In the case of pension transfers and opt outs the regime is particularly stringent:

(a) recommendations not made by a pensions transfer specialist must be reviewed by one (COB 5.3.21R);

(b) specific projections are required (COB 5.3.22R);

(c) a "suitability letter" may be required (COB 5.3.16 and *see* Section 5.13 below).

Where a firm arranges a pension opt-out or pension transfer on an execution only basis, it must obtain a clear record to evidence that no investment advice was provided (COB 5.2.10R).

A firm recommending a personal pension scheme to a group of employees must be satisfied that for the majority it will be as suitable as a stakeholder scheme (COB 5.3.28R).

5.7.6 *Understanding of risk*

Finally, the firm must take reasonable steps to ensure that a private customer understands the nature of the risks involved in the transaction concerned (COB 5.4.3R). This applies not only in the case of personal recommendations and discretionary management, but also in relation to:

(a) the arrangement of any transaction (recommended or not) in a warrant or derivative; or

(b) a proposal to engage in stock lending.

The FSA expects the general obligation to "take reasonable steps" to be satisfied in part by specified warnings which should be given in relation to:

(a) warrants and derivatives;

(b) investments which are not readily realisable, penny shares and securities subject to stabilisation; and

(c) stock lending.

(COB 5.4.5E to 5.4.10E.)

These warnings can normally be included in customer documentation. However COB 5.4.6E specifically indicates that the customer should be required to acknowledge receipt of the warrants and derivatives risk warning notice and to confirm acceptance of its contents (there is a similar exception for overseas customers to that mentioned in relation to client agreements above).

5.7.7 *Amendment of terms of business: business transfers*

If terms of business (including a client agreement) contain a right for the firm to make amendments unilaterally, it must give the customer at least ten business days' notice before doing business on the amended terms (COB 4.2.13R). (Note that this does not allow unilateral amendment if this is not permitted by the terms of business themselves, and the implications of the Unfair Terms in Consumer Contracts Regulation 1999 need to be considered.)

If one firm ("Firm A") transfers its business to another ("Firm B"), the customers of the Firm A will be new to Firm B, and the normal rules on customer classification and terms of business will, in principle, apply; there are no specific exclusions.

5.8 Dealing and managing

The following provisions apply to the process of dealing in securities with or on behalf of a customer, either in the context of a simple dealing service or of portfolio management.

5.8.1 Fair dealing

A number of provisions amplify Principle 6 (which requires a firm to pay due regard to the interests of its customers and treat them fairly). There is a danger that a firm dealing for a customer may:

(a) effect transactions which are designed to generate commission or transaction fees rather than to further the customer's interests ("churning");

(b) deal for its own account in the market when it knows it is about to publish a recommendation (thus enabling itself to benefit from any consequent market movement, potentially to the detriment of its customers – "dealing ahead");

(c) giving itself or favoured customers priority in effecting dealings which may be advantageous to them in a moving market or where there is limited available stock ("customer order priority");

(d) fail to obtain the best available price for the customer (failure to achieve "best execution");

(e) allow undue delay in executing an order (failure of "timely execution"); or

(f) aggregate orders from different customers and/or with own account orders. In certain circumstances this may disadvantage customers as regards to price. It is also necessary to ensure that subsequent allocation of the transaction between own account and customers is fair (assuming that less shares are brought or sold than the combined orders of the parties concerned) and that this allocation is done on a timely basis: it is an obvious temptation to see how the market moves and then to allocate beneficial positions to the firm itself or favoured clients.

Generally the approach of COB is not to lay down prescriptive requirements, but to impose an obligation to act reasonably and/or fairly.

5.8.2 *"Churning"*

The risk of churning (and the related risk of recommending switches within funds of a packaged product, or between packaged products) is addressed by a requirement that the firm may only recommend deals (and arrange them pursuant to a recommendation) if the firm has reasonable grounds for believing that a particular deal is in the customer's best interest, both individually and when viewed in the context of earlier transactions (COB 7.2.3R).

5.8.3 *"Dealing ahead"*

As regards "dealing ahead" a firm undertaking any own account transaction in the investment to which the research or analysis concerned applies may not deal for itself (and must take all reasonable steps to ensure that its associates do likewise) until the customers for whom the publication was principally intended have had (or are likely to have had) a reasonable opportunity to act on it (COB 7.3.3R). There are a number of exceptions (COB 7.3.4R) to allow acceptable dealings, for example:

(a) where a dealing could not reasonably be expected to have a significant effect on the price of the investment;

(b) where the firm acts in the normal course of market making, or to fulfil an unsolicited customer order;

(c) where the firm buys in order to place itself in a position to fulfil likely orders from customers following the publication, so long as it takes reasonable steps to ensure that doing so will not cause the price to move against the customers interests by a material amount.

More generally there is a safe harbour if the publication discloses that the firm may deal.

5.8.4   Customer order priority

In executing customer and own account orders the firm must act "fairly and in due turn" (COB 7.4.3R). The latter phrase does not have any precise meaning, but suggests that the dominant factor should be the order of receipt of instructions, but that the firm should not apply this rigidly. The guidance (COB 7.4.4G) specifically states that an own account order may be executed ahead of a current customer order (i.e. an order which is capable of being fulfilled immediately) if the instructions for the latter are received subsequently; or where the individual concerned neither knew or ought to have learnt about the unexecuted earlier order. The guidance also specifically allows for rearrangement of the order of transactions where this would give rise to a better price for both parties concerned.

"Own account orders" include orders for associates (a widely defined term). The guidance (COB 7.4.4G) provides relief where a strict application of the term might have inappropriate results: for example where an insurance company is dealing for its life fund (which as a matter of law belongs to it beneficially, but which is economically managed for the benefit of policyholders); similarly where the firm is dealing for an employee, or a connected investment trust or collective investment scheme, or its own OPS.

5.8.5   Best execution

When executing a customer order the firm must generally:

(a) take reasonable care to ascertain the price which is the best available for the particular order in the relevant market at the time for transactions of the size concerned; and

(b) execute the order at a price which is no less advantageous.

(COB 7.5.5R.)

The rule is disapplied in relation to the purchase of life policies or dealings in units in a regulated collective investment scheme with the operator of the scheme (COB 7.5.4(1)R). However it may apply to any other kind of investment, even where (e.g. in relation to a structured financial product or shares in a private company) there is no "market" as such and there may be nothing to compare the transaction with. It seems rational that the rule should not apply in these circumstances, but this is hard to reconcile with the wording, and it is therefore preferable in such circumstances to contract out of the obligation. This is permitted (COB 7.5.4(2)R) where agreed to by an intermediate customer (other than the trustee of an occupational pension scheme or of a trust where the firm acts as "permitted third party" to the trust).

Transactions effected through the London Stock Exchange's Electronic Trading Service ("SETS") are treated as providing best execution and the same will in principle apply where the firm betters or equals the price available on SETS at the material time. The test needs to be adapted where because of the size of the order, lack of prices displayed on SETS, or special transaction conditions an exact comparison is not possible (COB 7.5.6E). Firms are not currently required to have a feed for more than one price source, but if they do, they are required to compare them for determining the best price available (7.5.6(1)(b)E).

The best execution rule is becoming increasingly difficult to apply as markets become more fragmented and the use of alternative trading systems and/or direct dealings between major financial institutions become more common. While the benchmark remains the London Stock Exchange, its prices may be bettered by other means, leading to claims (frowned on by the FSA) of "better than best execution". The whole area is subject to discussion (*see* FSA Discussion Paper on *Best Execution*, April 2001).

5.8.6   Timely execution

A firm which has agreed or decided in its discretion to execute or arrange for the execution of a current customer order must do so as soon as reasonably practical, unless the firm takes reasonable steps to ensure that a postponement is in the best interests of the customer

(COB 7.6.4R and 7.6.5R) (e.g. where an improvement in liquidity is foreseeable, or where execution over a period may achieve a better price).

5.8.7   *Aggregation and allocation of orders*

In relation to aggregation and allocation of orders, the firm must act in accordance with a written policy on allocation which is consistently applied and fulfils the requirements explained below (COB 7.7.3R):

(a) it must be likely that the aggregation will not work to the disadvantage of each of the customers involved (COB 7.7.4(1)R);

(b) the firm must disclose (in its terms of business or otherwise) that the effect of aggregation may work on some occasions to the customer's disadvantage (7.7.4(2)R);

(c) allocation of an order which is effected on an aggregated basis must be "prompt" (COB 7.7.5R). (This means normally within one business day of the transaction; five business days where the transaction involves only intermediate customers who have agreed to the extension; and three business days in certain circumstances relating to ISAs and PEPs – in each case, an "allocation period".) For this purpose a series of transactions entered into for the purposes of a single investment decision or objective on a single business day may be treated as taking place at the time of the last transaction: but where executed over more than one day, the time limits will apply separately to each day (COB 7.7.6E);

(d) the allocation must not give unfair preference to the firm or to any of those for whom it is dealt: the firm generally must give priority to satisfying customer orders, unless it can demonstrate that the transactions could not have been executed on such favourable terms, or at all, if it had not participated itself (COB 7.7.9R). In this context the firm may treat certain associates as ordinary customers in the same way as explained in Section 5.8.4 above.

There are provisions for reallocation in certain circumstances where there has been an error or where an aggregated order has only been partially executed (*see* COB 7.7.11R).

Allocation (and, where relevant, reallocation) must be effected at the price at which the transaction was done, or at a volume weighted average of the prices, where there is a series of transactions involved (COB 7.7.12R).

5.8.8   Records

There are rules about the recording of allocations (COB 7.7.14R), and of the receipt and execution of customer orders generally (COB 7.12).

5.9   Other dealing matters

5.9.1   *Making markets in non-exchange traded securities*

Where a firm holds itself out as a market maker in security which is not traded on a recognised or designated investment exchange or any exchange in the EEA, and sells the security to a private customer it must (by written notice given no later then the sale):

(a) commit itself that a "reasonable price" for repurchase of security will be available for a specific period (not less than three months) after the sale; and

(b) warn the customer that sale thereafter may be difficult.

The provision contains guidance as to what amounts to a "reasonable" price: in particular fluctuations in the price offered must not be solely or mainly justified by reference to an absence of liquidity unless this reflects factors that are directly relevant to the particular security (COB 7.11).

5.9.2   *Programme trading*

There is guidance (based on Principle 6) in relation to programme trading, that is a single transaction or series of transaction executed for the purpose of acquiring or disposing all or part of a portfolio or a large basket of securities. The guidance (COB 7.14) suggests that the firm should:

(a) disclose whether it will act as principal or agent;

(b) ensure that neither it nor an associate executes any own account transactions in any investment included in the programme trade, unless it has notified the customer or can demonstrate that it has provided fair treatment; and

(c) provide best execution for each individual transaction forming part of the programme of trade (subject to the exceptions in the rule on best execution).

5.9.3   Non-market price transactions

COB 7.15 prohibits a firm from entering into a "non-market price transaction", that is one where:

(a) the dealing rate or price differs materially from the prevailing market rate or price; or

(b) the firm or the other party gives materially more or less value than it received;

unless the firm has taken reasonable steps to ensure that the transaction is not being entered into by the customer for an improper purpose. The prohibition does not apply to transactions which are subject to the rules of a Recognised Investment Exchange ("RIE").

5.9.4   Lending to customers; realisation of their assets

A firm may only extend credit to a private customer (or arrange for anyone else to do so) if:

(a) it has made and recorded an assessment of the private customer's financial standing;

(b) the firm has taken reasonable steps to ensure that the arrangements for the credit, and the amount concerned, are suitable for the type of investment agreement proposed or which the customer is likely to enter into; and

(c) the customer has given prior written consent to the maximum amount of the credit and the amount or basis of any interest or fees.

(COB 7.9.3R.)

"Credit" is very widely defined and will extend to any kind of financial accommodation. However the restrictions will not apply:

(a) where the firm settles a securities transaction because the customer has failed to pay or has paid late;

(b) the firm finances a margin call made on the customer for a period of no longer than five business days (or for a longer period in certain cases where the firm is permitted to leave the margin call outstanding (*see* Section 5.9.5 below)).

(COB 7.9.5R.)

If the firm wishes to realise a private customer's assets in order to discharge an obligation to the firm, it must set out in its terms of business the action it may take, the circumstances in which it may do so, and each type or class of assets over which it may exercise the right. It must also give the customer notice (oral or written) of its intention to exercise its rights at least three business days before it does so (COB 7.8).

5.9.5   *Derivatives*

Certain specific rules apply as regards to dealings in derivatives (i.e. futures, options and contracts for differences as defined in the RAO). The requirements apply in particular where the transaction is in a "contingent liability investment", that is, a derivative under the terms of which the client will or may be liable to make further payments (other than charges) when the transaction falls to be completed or is closed out.

The specific rules applying to derivatives generally are:

(a) the restriction of direct offer advertisements (*see* Section 5.5.7 above);

(b) the requirement of derivative risk warnings (*see* Section 5.6 above);

(c) the requirements of a (two way) client agreement in the case of transaction with or for a private customer in a contingent liability investment (*see* Section 5.6.1 above).

In addition:

(a) the firm is under an obligation to obtain payment by the customer of any margin which is payable to the firm (under the terms of its contract with its customer) or by the firm (under the terms in any relevant exchange or clearing house). In the case of an on-exchange transaction the minimum amount which must be collected is an amount or value equal to the margin requirements of the relevant exchange or clearing house (COB 7.10.3R);

(b) the FSA suggests that the firm should notify the customer of the circumstances in which it may be required to provide margin; the form in which it may be provided; the steps that the firm may be required or entitled to take if the customer fails to provide the margin; the fact that failure to provide margin may lead to the firm closing out the customer's positions within a specified time period; and finally any other circumstances that may lead to the firm closing out the customer's positions without prior reference to him (COB 7.10.4G);

(c) the firm must close out a private customer's open positions if a customer fails to meet a margin call for five business days unless either;

   (i) the firm has received confirmation from a relevant third party (such as a clearing firm) that the customer has given instructions to pay in full; and the firm has taken reasonable care to establish that the delay is owing to circumstances beyond the customer's control; or

   (ii) the firm decides to provide credit to the customer, but in this case the rules explained in Section 5.9.4 above will apply.

(COB 7.10.5R.)

The obligation to ensure that private customers meet their margin calls is one of the complex requirements designed to provide protection for clients' assets and monies which are put up to support contingent liability transactions (*see* Section 5.12.9 below).

5.9.6   *Reporting to customers*

COB lays down rules for:

(a) specific notices giving "essential details" of transactions ("confirmations" or "contract notes" COB 8.1); and

(b) periodic statements to customers (COB 8.2).

5.9.7   *Confirmations*

Confirmations must normally be provided in relation to all transactions in designated investments (other than life policies or personal pension contracts). There are exceptions (COB 8.1.6R):

(a) in the case of regular saving schemes for regulated collective investment schemes or investment trusts;

(b) where the customer has made a written request (either general or specific) not to receive confirmation (there appears to be no reason why such a request should not form part of a standard form client agreement);

(c) where the firm is acting as an investment manager or an ISA plan manager; this will only apply so long as the transaction is not in a contingent liability investment, and the firm has taken reasonable steps to determine the customer does not wish to receive confirmation (either generally or in specific circumstances);

(d) where the confirmation will duplicate information to be promptly provided by another party (other than information about the firm). This may apply, for example, where a firm acting as a fund manager instructs a broker which then provides confirmation direct to the customer. Where the firm itself receives the confirmation from the third party, it may pass it on, but will need to supplement it with any required information which the third party confirmation does not contain.

The exceptions in (b) and (c) above will only apply if the firm provides essentially the same information in a periodic statement (*see* below).

The obligation is to provide the confirmation "promptly"; the FSA expects (COB 8.1.5E) that this should be no later than the business day following the transaction or the business day following receipt of the confirmation received from a third party, if applicable. In the case of a regulated collective investment scheme, the information should be sent out at the latest on the business date following the day on which the price was determined.

A firm may provide confirmations by posting them on a website, so long as this is accessible only by the customer; in the case of a private customer, the firm is required to review the website to ensure that its customers view the confirmations, and must send the confirmation by a hard copy or by email if the customer does not access the relevant website page within five days of the information being placed there (COB 8.1.4G).

There are specific provisions (COB 8.1.15E – 19E) setting out the FSA's expectations as to the information on a confirmation.

5.9.8 *Periodic statements*

Periodic statements are required where the firm:

(a) acts as an investment manager; or

(b) administers any other account or portfolio which includes designated investments.

Periodic statements are also required where the customer's account includes uncovered open positions in contingent liability investments (COB 8.2.1R).

A periodic statement is not required:

(a) if the customer is habitually resident outside the UK;

(b) where the customer is an intermediate customer (unless the firm is an OPS firm (*see* below));

if, in either case, the customer has requested not to receive statements or the firm has taken reasonable steps to establish that he does not wish to receive them; or

(c) if it would duplicate a statement to be provided by someone else.

(COB 8.2.6R.)

The obligation under the rule is to provide "promptly and at suitable intervals" a written statement containing "adequate information" on the value and composition of the customer's account or portfolio. Evidential provisions (COB 8.2.7–15E) indicate:

(a) the expected content in particular circumstances;

(b) the expected standard of "promptness", this is normally 25 business days after the end of the period concerned (10 business days if the portfolio includes any uncovered open positions in contingent liability investments; 50 business days for venture capital business);

(c) the expected standard for "suitable intervals." In the case of a private customer, this should normally be six monthly (if there are open business positions), or if the customer indicates that he does not wish such frequent reports, it should be at least 12 monthly.

The firm may follow the wishes of an intermediate customer as to promptness and suitable intervals, where these wishes are expressed on the customers own initiative.

5.10   Conflicts of Interest

5.10.1   *General*

A firm (particularly an "integrated house" with multiple functions) will inevitably encounter conflicts of interest between the firm and its customers and between different customers. For example:

(a) the firm may hold knowledge in confidence for one client which would benefit another (e.g. a corporate finance division may have information of value to customers dealing in a company's shares);

(b) acting for one client may damage another;

(c) a firm may be remunerated in a way which encourages it to act against its customers' interests (e.g. commission paid by product providers to intermediaries; soft commission); and

(d) a firm's employees may take advantage of customers' information.

In this environment, *avoiding* all conflicts of interest is unrealistic, and significantly Principle 8 requires a firm to "manage" conflicts of interest fairly. This is amplified by COB 7.1.3R, which applies that if a firm has:

(a) a "material interest" in a transaction to be entered into with or for a customer;

(b) a relationship that gives or may give rise to a conflict of interest in relation to such a transaction;

(c) an interest in any transaction which is or may be in conflict with the interest of any of the firm's customers;

(d) customers, or customers and clients (i.e. including market counterparties), with conflicting interests in relation to transactions.

If so, it must not knowingly advise or deal in the exercise of discretion in relation to the transaction concerned unless it takes "reasonable steps to ensure fair treatment for the customer".

The rule does not specify what may amount to "reasonable steps". However the FSA expects (COB 7.1.4E) that they will comprise one or more of the following:

(a) disclosure of an interest; this may be either specific or general, but it must be made before the transaction in question, and the firm must be able to demonstrate that it has taken reasonable steps to ensure that the customer does not object to the interest which has been disclosed (*see* COB 7.1.6E);

(b) reliance on a "policy of independence", that is, a written policy requiring the relevant employees to disregard any material interest or conflict of interest when advising customers or dealing in the exercise of discretion. Such policy of independence must be accompanied by a general disclosure to customers that material interests or conflicts of interest may arise (COB 7.1.7G);

(c) the establishment of a Chinese wall (*see* below); or

(d) declining to act for the customer.

5.10.2   *Chinese walls and attribution of knowledge*

A Chinese wall arises (COB 2.4.4R) where the firm "establishes and maintains" arrangements (i.e. takes reasonable steps to ensure that they remain effective and are adequately monitored) that require information held by it in the course of carrying on one part of its business to be withheld from, or not to be used for, persons with or for whom it acts in the course of carrying on another part of the business.   For the purposes of managing a conflict of interest, individuals on "the other side of the wall" will not be regarded as being in possession of knowledge denied to them as a result of the Chinese wall (COB 2.4.7G): this means that, for regulatory purposes, no conflict which will arise where information held on a confidential basis for a client on one side of the wall is not used for one on the other.

Apart from conflicts of interest, there are numerous wider provisions of COB which turn on the firm acting with knowledge.   In this respect establishment of a Chinese wall will prevent the firm from being disciplined because knowledge on one side was not used on the other (COB 2.4.6R).   It will also (by virtue of Section 147 of the FSMA) provide a defence in relevant circumstances against proceedings under Sections 397(2) and (3) of the FSMA (statements and practices which are knowingly misleading) (*see* COB 2.4.5G). However:

(a) a Chinese wall must, in effect, be permanent and cannot be established within a department or function;

(b) the implication of 2.4.6R is that in the absence of a Chinese wall, knowledge in one part of a firm will be attributed to the firm generally for the purposes of the Rules.

5.10.3   Inducements

A firm must take reasonable steps to ensure that it, and any agent, does not:

(a) offer or give; or

(b) solicit or accept;

any inducement if it is likely to conflict to a material extent with any duty owed by the firm (or the recipient) to their respective customers (COB 2.2.3R). On an "anti-avoidance" basis the prohibition extends to directing or referring of any business to a third party (since an unregulated associate might give or receive an inducement in this connection).

There are more specific and stringent requirements in relation to packaged products (*see* Section 5.13 below).

5.10.4   "Soft Commission"

"Soft Commission" is a benefit provided by a broker or other intermediary to a fund manager or adviser (e.g. in the form of research and analysis, or linkages to electronic dealing systems) in exchange for an understanding that the manager/adviser will place a particular level of business with the intermediary. Such a practice is potentially abusive, since it may tempt the manager/adviser away from seeking best execution, while the cost of the benefits may fall indirectly on the manager's client (insofar as it is funded from the intermediary's commission which the client will usually bear). COB permits the practice (which is thus not a prohibited inducement) on the basis that:

(a) the goods and services are provided under a written agreement and do not take the form of cash or any other direct financial benefit;

(b) the intermediary has agreed to provide best execution;

(c) the firm has taken reasonable steps to ensure that the arrangements do not involve any comparative price disadvantage to the customer;

(d) where the intermediary acts as principal, the firm has taken reasonable steps to ensure that the commission paid to the intermediary will cover the value of the goods or services plus the cost of executing the deal (i.e. to ensure that the cost of the benefit is at least reflected in the (disclosable) commission, and not hidden in the price of the securities); and

(e) the goods or services are directly relevant to, and are used to assist, the provision by the receiving firm of:

    (i)   investment management services;

    (ii) advice on dealing and valuation;

    (iii) custody services for customers; or

    (iv) valuation or performance measurement.

(*See* COB 2.2.8R, 2.2.12R: there is guidance in COB 2.2.13G and 2.2.14G as to goods and services which are likely, or are unlikely, to qualify).

The firm must make disclosure (which may be general) of the existence of soft commission arrangements, and explain the firm's policy in this connection, before entering a client agreement which authorises it to deal under such arrangements (2.2.16R). It must also normally provide periodic details of the benefits it receives and the commission it pays under soft commission arrangements (2.2.18R) and there are record-keeping requirements (2.2.20R).

5.10.5   *Personal account dealing*

A firm must take reasonable steps to ensure that:

(a) any personal account transaction by an employee or an associate does not conflict with the firm's duties to its clients (note that these may include market counterparties);

(b) it receives prompt notification of, or can otherwise identify, any permitted personal account transactions (COB 7.13.4R).

These requirements do not apply to (broadly):

(a) employees who are not involved to a material extent in, and have no access to information about, the firm's designated investment business;

(b) transactions in government or public securities, life policies or regulated collective investment schemes; or

(c) discretionary transactions where there is no prior communication with the employee and the discretion is not exercised by the firm.

(7.3.15R; definition of "personal account transactions").

The FSA expects (COB 7.13.7E) that the "reasonable steps" will include:

(a) a written notice setting out the basis on which personal account transactions are permitted, which will form part of the employee's terms of employment;

(b) procedures requiring the firm's written consent to such transactions (either specific or by reference to particular types of investment) and designed to ensure compliance with the objectives in COB 7.13.4R (*see* above).

5.11   Clients' assets

5.11.1   Custody

The rules on custody relate to the regulated activity of "safeguarding and administration of investments", which in turn includes arranging such safeguarding and administration. The rules apply:

(a) principally   to designated investments ("safe custody investments") but in certain respects apply to other assets held in the same portfolio ("custody assets"); and

(b) where such assets are held for a "client" (so including market counterparties).

A firm may be affected by these rules in a variety of ways depending on the circumstances:

(a) its customer may make its own arrangements for custody, and may enable the firm to deal by giving the custodian authority to act on the firm's instructions;

(b) the same may be the case but the firm may have recommended the custodian;

(c) the firm may arrange custody, that is, the custodian will contract with the client, but the relationship will have been established by the firm;

(d) the firm may itself undertake responsibility for custody, which it may delegate to a third party; or

(e) finally the firm's main activity may be providing custody services.

5.11.2   *Mandates*

The firm must accept responsibility for any nominee company which it controls (*see* COB 9.1.11R).   Where custody is arranged independently by the customer, the custody rules as a whole do not apply to the firm which is managing the assets.   However, if it holds written authority under which it may control the client's assets it must comply with specified requirements as regards to recording the mandate, transactions entered into using the authority, and the procedures and authorities for the giving and receiving of instructions (*see* COB 9.2).

5.11.3   *Assessment of custodians*

Where the firm:

(a) holds safe custody investments with a custodian;

(b) arranges registration with a custodian; or

(c) recommends a custodian to a private customer;

it must undertake "appropriate risk assessment" of the custodian (COB 9.1.43-44R).   There is guidance (COB 9.1.46G, 47G) as to the tests to be applied in the assessment. Where a firm's arrangements entail the holding of a *customer's* securities outside the UK, appropriate risk disclosures must also be made (9.1.54R).

5.11.4   *Obligations where safe custody investments are held*

Where the firm itself holds safe custody investment it must comply with a number of requirements which are designed primarily "to restrict the commingling of client and firm's assets and minimise the risk of the client's safe custody investments being used by the firm without the client's agreement or contrary to the client's wishes, or being treated as the firm's assets in the event of its insolvency" (9.1.12G). Broadly the requirements are as follows:

(a) safe custody investments must be segregated from the firm's own investments (COB 9.1.28R). This means that clients' own account investments must be distinguished:

  (i)   in the firm's own records if it holds the assets in an account with itself (COB 9.1.30R);

  (ii) in the title of any accounts maintained by a third party custodian for the firm (COB 9.1.32R). Broadly this means that (where a custodian is used) the firm must maintain at least two accounts, one for proprietary holdings and one for its clients. For this purpose assets of an affiliated company, that is, a company in the same group, must normally not be held together with assets for clients, unless the affiliated company is holding the assets for a third party client or is being dealt with as the client on an arm's length basis (COB 9.1.9R(1)); 9.1.33R;

(b) *title* to safe custody investments must be registered in a manner which provides the client with "appropriate protection" COB(9.1.34G). To the extent practicable, this must be in one of the following ways:

  (i)   in the name of the client (or of the client's client if the client is an authorised person);

  (ii) in the name of a nominee company (i.e. a company whose business consists solely of acting as a nominee holder of investments or other property) which is controlled by the firm or an affiliated company; by a RIE or designated investment exchange; or by a "custodian" (a term which includes any entity which is authorised to carry on the activity of safeguarding and administering investments);

(iii) in the name of a custodian itself (rather than a nominee) if it is subject to the law or market practice of a jurisdiction outside the UK and the firm has taken reasonable steps to determine that for this reason it is in the clients best interests to register or record the holding in that way (or it is not feasible to do otherwise): in this case the firm has to notify the client in writing;

(iv) in the name of the firm, in similar circumstances to those mentioned in the last paragraph, but subject to the giving of risk warnings and (in the case of a private customer) his prior written consent;

(v) in the name of anyone else, if this is in accordance with the clients specific written instructions; in these circumstances the firm must warn the client that this is at his own risk (9.1.58R) and, in the case of a private customer, the person concerned must not be an associate of the firm.

COB 9.1.38R permits title to the firm's investments to be recorded in the same name as title to clients' safe custody investments without any separate designation in the books of the custodian, nominee or issuer, so long as there is a separate identification in the firm's own records. (This seems to be at odds with COB 9.1.32R, *see* 5.11.4 (a)(ii) above.)

Physical documents of title must be held (COB 9.1.40R):

(a) by the firm itself;

(b) in the case of a private customer, with a custodian in an account designated for clients' safe custody investments;

(c) in the case of a market counterparty or intermediate customer, with such a custodian; or

    (i) a person whom the firm has taken reasonable steps to determine as having a business including the provision of appropriate safe custody services; or

    (ii) in any other way which complies with the market counterparty's or intermediate customer's specific written instructions (subject to a warning that this is at his risk (*see* COB 9.1.58R).

5.11.5 Documentation

Where a firm provides safe custody services to a client:

(a) it must notify the client setting out the terms and conditions applying to the service. The rules set out matters which should be covered; in the case of a private customer, the firm must normally obtain the customer's written agreement to terms on instructions and any lien which the firm may seek over the customer's assets (COB 9.1.49R; 9.1.51R);

(b) it must give specific risk disclosures in relation to assets to be held overseas or in the firm's name (COB 9.1.58R).

Where the firm holds safe custody investments for or on behalf of a client with a custodian, it must have appropriate written terms and conditions with the custodian, including where applicable provisions specified in COB 9.1.69R.

5.11.6 Reporting and reconcilation

Where a firm is "accountable for" custody assets (i.e., presumably holds them itself or through its own nominee, or has appointed a custodian on behalf of the client) it must provide, at least annually, a statement in relation to those assets; this must be delivered within 25 business days of the date as of which it is made (COB 9.1.59R, 9.1.60R).

In addition it must carry out a reconcilation between its own records of the investments for which it is accountable (but does not physically hold) and statements obtained from custodians or, in the case of the dematerialised investments, from the person who maintains the record of legal entitlement. This must be done at least every 25 business days (with certain exceptions for holdings in mutual funds where the reconciliation must be done as often as statements are received from the funds and in any event no less than every six months) (COB 9.1.85R; 9.1.87R).

In addition the firm must, at least twice annually carry out:

(a) a count of all investments which it physically holds for clients and a reconciliation of this with its record of such investments; and

(b) a reconciliation between its record of client holdings and its record of the location of its safe custody investments (COB 9.1.89R).

This may be done in a variety of ways, including the counting and reconciliation of all safe custody investments on the same date or a "rolling" method which deals with one type of investment at a time. In any event discrepancies must be made good by the firm where there are reasonable grounds for concluding it was responsible (COB 9.1.93R, 9.1.94R).

There are also record-keeping requirements and an obligation to notify the FSA if the firm fails to comply with the reconciliation requirements (COB 9.1.97 – 99).

5.11.7   *Disapplication of rules*

The rules on custody are disapplied, or apply only to a limited extent, in certain circumstances:

(a) a "personal investment firm" (very broadly, a firm which advises on packaged products and/or manages its investments for private customers) is not subject to the rules if it temporarily holds investments belonging to clients which it forwards to the client as soon as practicable after receiving them, having retained them for no longer than necessary to check for errors. For more specific requirements *see* COB 9.1.9R(3);

(b) the rules are also disapplied in relation to investments held in respect of a delivery versus payment transaction through a commercial settlement system where the security concerned will either be due to the client within one business day following the client's fulfilment of a payment obligation, or due to the firm within a similar period following fulfilment of such an obligation; however the rules will apply if delivery or payment by the firm does not occur at the close of business on the third business day following the date of payment or delivery of the designated investment by the client (COB 9.1.13R).

In any event where the client has paid the purchase money and this is segregated under the client money rules (*see* Section 5.12 below) it is not necessary to segregate the investment as well (COB 9.1.14R).

Finally:

(a) different issues arise where assets are provided as collateral to secure the client's obligations (*see* Section 5.12.9 below).

(b) the rules apply in a qualified form to trustees and depositories (taking account of their general law obligations in the safe keeping of assets) and to the issuers of depository receipts (COB 9.1.16R – 20G; 9.1.23G – 26R).

5.11.8   *Stock lending*

A firm may only lend a private or intermediate customer's securities with the customer's agreement and on written terms, which are expected to include provisions specified in 4.2.15E(19) (*see* COB 9.1.74R, 9.1.75E). Stock held together for a number of customers cannot be lent at all unless all of them agree, or the firm has adequate procedures to ensure that only the investments of consenting customers are lent (COB 9.1.79R). These obligations will also apply where customer securities are held in any custody or settlement system which provides for "automatic" lending; the firm will need to be able to segregate holdings of customers who wish to lend from those of customers who do not (COB 9.1.81G).

Where stock is lent for a private customer, the firm is responsible for ensuring that collateral meeting the requirements set out in the definition of "relevant collateral" is provided by the borrower; this must be monitored daily and any shortfall made up by the firm, unless agreed otherwise by the customer in writing (9.1.78R).

Any dividends (or payments in lieu) stock lending fees and other benefits received for the customer's benefit will belong to the customer (COB 9.1.84G).

5.12   Client money

5.12.1   What is "client money"?

The COB provisions on client money apply where a firm receives or holds "money" from or on behalf of a client (i.e. including in principle a market counterparty) in the course of or in connection with designated investment business (COB 9.3.1R).

As a starting point, the rules apply where the firm "receives or holds" the money. This means that the rules will not apply where the money is held by a third party which is accountable directly to the client (e.g. a bank holding money in an account in the client's name), though in these circumstances the rules on mandates may apply (*see* Section 5.11.2 above) if the firm is able to give instructions in relation to the money. A firm will not avoid the client money rules by transferring money to a third party which holds the money for the *firm's* account.

5.12.2   Exceptions

There are a number of exceptions and qualifications to the rules:

(a) "money" includes cheques and other payable orders, but will not (it is suggested) include cheques payable to a third party (e.g. where a client sends the firm a cheque made out to, and to be sent on to, a product provider);

(b) the rules do not apply to the permitted activities of a life office or a friendly society. (This reflects the fact that the insurance companies deal as principal with their customers and consequently do not hold money at their behalf on a long-term basis; customers are in any event protected by the policyholders' protection regime) (COB 9.3.2R(1));

(c) money held by an approved bank (*see* below) in an account with itself is not normally client money (subject to, broadly, an obligation to notify the customer that the money is not held on trust; there is also guidance as to how the money is recorded so that the bank can account to all its clients for such monies at all times) (COB 9.3.2(R)(3); COB 9.3.5G).

In addition:

(a) (unless the firm is a sole trader) a market counterparty or intermediate customer may opt out of the client money rules, subject to acknowledging in writing that the money will not be segregated and that it will rank only as a general creditor of the firm (COB 9.3.9R);

(b) in the case of a service which is not governed by the Investment Services Directive or Banking Consolidation Directive there can be "one way" opt out which arises simply by giving notice to a market counterparty or intermediate customer; but this does not apply if the client is itself a firm (COB 9.3.11R).

Where a firm holding client money transfers it to another person (including another firm) it must not agree to an opt out or otherwise represent that the money is not client money (COB 9.3.13R).

There are a number of further relaxations which apply (broadly) where money is held briefly by the firm before being paid over to the client or to someone else entitled to it:

(a) money will not be client money in relation to delivery versus payment transactions through a commercial settlement system where it is due from the client to the firm or the firm to the client within one business day upon fulfilment of a delivery obligation (unless the delivery or payment by the firm fails to occur by the close of business on the third business day following the date of payment or delivery of the investments by the client) (COB 9.3.15R);

(b) where the firm is the manager or authorised corporate director of a regulated collective investment scheme, it will not be required to treat as client money, money which:

(i) it receives from the client in respect to its obligation to issue units unless the unit price is not determined by close of business on the next business day after receipt of the money from the client (or from a field representative (*see* Section 5.12.5 below);

(ii) arises on redemption of units, so long as the redemption proceeds are paid within the period specified by the Collective Investment Schemes Sourcebook (COB 9.3.16R). (As an exception to the general rule (*see* Section 5.12.6 below), money representing uncashed cheques representing such amounts will not become client money;)

(c) to avoid contamination from across a corporate group, money of an affiliated company of a firm will not normally be client money unless, broadly, the affiliated company is itself under client money or similar obligations, or is being treated as a client on an arm's length basis (COB 9.3.18R);

(d) there are special rules for solicitors (COB 9.3.25-26R) and trustees (COB 9.3.27-29R) reflecting the fact that they are subject to particular responsibilities for client money under statute or the general law;

(e) money due and payable to the firm is not client money (COB 9.3.19R). The FSA expects firms to treat fees and commissions as "due and payable" only if the amount has been definitively determined, whether by reference to a disclosed formula or basis of charging; by giving notice to the client which has not been objected to; or by agreement or legal or arbitral proceedings (9.3.20E).

5.12.3   Handling client money

Client money is held on trust (COB 9.3.31R, made pursuant to Section 139 of the FSMA) in accordance with the rules. Broadly the effect of the rules is that:

(a) it must be held in a segregated client bank account, that is, an account appropriately designated as containing client money (or in a money market deposit identified as client money) (COB 9.3.68R);

(b) the account must normally be with an "approved bank", that is, in practice, broadly a bank or building society authorised under the FSMA; an EEA bank; or bank established elsewhere which meets specified criteria of substance (*see* definition of "approved bank"). If a non-UK account is used, the client must be notified and a risk warning given (this can be a general notification – COB 9.3.90R);

(c) client money may be held by a non-approved bank only in limited circumstances where required for the settlement of transactions, or receipt of income, outside the UK: risk warnings must be given and the consent of private customers obtained (COB 9.3.74R);

(d) the bank must acknowledge the basis on which the client money is held (COB 9.3.82R): if it fails to do so the account must be closed (in the case of a UK account – COB 9.3.83R) or the client must be notified (in any other case – COB 9.3.84R);

(e) in the case of a private customer, a firm must account to the customer for all interest earned on his money, unless it has notified him in writing of an alternative position (e.g. that no interest will be payable, or that interest will be paid on a specified basis) (COB 9.3.60R).

5.12.4   *Selection of bank; bank failures*

The rules are aimed primarily at protecting clients on the default of the firm, not its bank. However:

(a) a firm must take reasonable steps to establish that any bank it uses is "appropriate", and must review its conclusions at least annually (COB 9.3.76R: the FSA suggests that firms should in some circumstances consider diversifying risk – COB 9.3.77G);

(b) the same will apply to a bank in the firm's corporate group – and this case the firm must disclose the relationship and the identity of the bank to clients (COB 9.3.80R);

(c) normally any loss caused by the failure of a bank in which client money is held will be shared by all clients for whom client money is held (COB 9.5.22R). However, more "tailored" arrangements are possible through the use of:

    (i) a "designated client bank account" (where a failure if the bank concerned affects only those clients who have agreed to their money being held in such account) (COB 9.3.69R; 9.5.24R); or

(ii)   a number of "designated client fund accounts" which form a group of accounts: any failure of one of the banks concerned will be borne only by the clients who have agreed to their money being held in that group of accounts (there must be separate groups of accounts for each permutation of client choices) (COB 9.3.70R, 9.5.25R).

Note that amounts in "designated" accounts will be pooled with all other client money accounts on a default of the *firm*.

5.12.5   Payments into client accounts

Money which is client money must normally be paid into a client bank within one business day of receipt, unless it is paid away within the same time-frame (COB 9.3.58R). The same applies when money becomes client money (e.g. because a payment becomes due to the client). There are special provisions about money received by appointed representatives or the firm's own "field representatives" or other agents: they may forward money to a specified address of the firm, but the arrangements must be such as to ensure that it will be received there by the close of the third business day after receipt (COB 9.3.49R).

An "alternative" approach is open to firms operating in a complex environment, provided they have specified systems and controls (COB 9.3.42R). Such a firm may receive all client money into its own bank account, and make payments due to clients out of the same account; but it must make transfers to and from its client bank accounts on a daily basis as necessary to maintain the amount required by the client money calculation explained below (COB 9.3.46R).

A firm may have limited control over money received for clients as dividends, etc., on securities they own where these are held by a separate custodian. It must, however, take reasonable steps to be notified promptly of such receipts (COB 9.3.53R) (e.g. by getting regular statements from overseas depositories – 9.3.54G). In the case of overseas income, the firm has a "grace period" of five business days from notification to pay the money away or into a client bank account (COB 9.3.55R); in the latter case it must be allocated to individual clients within a reasonable time (the expectation being 10 business days) after notification (COB 9.3.56R; 9.3.57E).

5.12.6   *Money ceasing to be client money*

Money will cease to be client money if paid:

(a) to the client or his representative;

(b) to a third party on the client's instructions (but *see* Section 5.12.10 below);

(c) into a bank account in the client's name; or

(d) to the firm, when due and payable to it.

   (COB 9.3.133R.)

Balances represented by uncashed cheques will remain client money (COB 9.3.135). There are provisions for dealing with unclaimed client money balances (COB 9.3.138R).

5.12.7   *Client money calculation; reconciliations*

A firm must do a calculation every business day to establish that the amount of money it holds as client money is sufficient to discharge its obligations to all its clients, taking into account transactions in the course of settlement (9.3.100R – 9.3.107R). In the event of a shortfall, the firm must make this good.

The firm must also conduct reconciliations between its own records and the underlying bank statements (or confirmation given by third parties holding client money – *see* Section 5.12.10 below) at least every 25 business days (COB 9.3.123R; 9.3.126R), and discrepancies identified and corrected (COB 9.3.128 – 131R).

5.12.8   *Default*

COB Section 9.5 deals with the pooling and the distribution of client money amongst those entitled to it:

(a) on a failure of the firm (a "primary pooling event"); or

(b) on the failure of a bank (a "secondary pooling event").

5.12.9 *Transfer of client assets to third parties; margin and collateral*

The client money regime is complicated by the fact that a firm may need to pay away money:

(a) to another broker or to a counterparty;

(b) to an exchange or clearing house;

to satisfy payment or delivery obligations incurred on the client's behalf (or on transactions effected for the client's benefit); or to provide security for their performance ("margin" or "collateral"). In many markets the firm will be treated as dealing as principal (or at least as being liable as such) and may therefore need to be able to pass on collateral provided by the client to meet its own obligations.

5.12.10 *Cash payments*

To provide some degree of protection to the client:

(a) a transfer of client money to a third party (other than on the client's instructions) is only permitted:

  (i) for the purpose of a transaction for the client; or

  (ii) to meet the client's obligations to provide collateral;

  and a private customer must be notified that this may happen (COB 9.3.64R).

(b) in the case of transfers in relation to contingent liability investments (*see* Section 5.9.5) the firm must:

  (i) notify an exchange, clearing house, broker or over-the-counter counterparty to which the money is paid that the firm is required to keep the money segregated;

  (ii) instruct the person concerned to credit the money to a "client transaction account"; and

  (iii) require acknowledgement that the account may not be combined with or set off against any other account;

If the person concerned fails to do so, the firm must cease to use the client transaction account (in the case of an account with a broker or counterparty) or warn the client (in the case of an account with an exchange or clearing house) (COB 9.3.86-89R).

(c) the firm must calculate (as part of the client money calculation mentioned above in Section 5.12.7) the sum of its clients' "equity balances", that is, broadly, the amount that the firm would be obliged to pay the client (or vice versa) if all the client's positions in contingent liability investments were liquidated; if these reflect a liability of the firm which exceeds what it would receive if all contingent liability transactions which it has arranged for clients were liquidated, it must make good the shortfall (COB 9.3.113R-115R; 9.3.105R).

5.12.11   *Use of collateral*

There are broadly two ways in which a client's assets can be used by a firm to secure the client's liabilities.

(a) the firm can have a simple charge over the assets, enforceable on the client's default (a "bare security interest"). In this case the normal custody rules will apply to the assets until the charge is enforced;

(b) the firm can be given the right to treat the asset as its own, and to recharge it ("rehypothecate" it) to, for example, an exchange or clearing house to secure its obligations under a transaction for the client. In this case:

  (i) the firm should apply the custody or client money rules until it exercises its right;

  (ii) thereafter, it must ensure that it maintains adequate records to enable it to meet future obligations, including the return of equivalent assets (9.4.8R).

5.13   Packaged products

5.13.1   Introduction

Packaged products are, as their name suggests, investments which provide exposure to the securities markets in an indirect or "packaged" form. Since they form the preponderance of investments sold to retail customers, they are subject to a stricter regime which is intended to provide a greater degree of consumer protection.

The definition of "packaged product" includes:

(a) a life insurance contract other than a "pure protection contract" (the latter being, broadly, a policy with an investment element and including a personal pension structured as an insurance contract);

(b) a unit in a regulated collective investment scheme (an authorised unit trust, UK open ended investment company, or overseas scheme "recognised" under the FSMA);

(c) an interest in an investment trust savings scheme; or

(d) a stakeholder pension scheme.

Neither a PEP nor an ISA is a packaged product in itself, but will in effect be subject to the same regime to the extent that its investments include packaged products within the above definition. (In addition, certain special disclosure rules apply to the cash component of ISAs, (*see* Section 5.13.9 below), and the rights of withdrawal explained in Section 5.13.10 may apply to all ISAs.

5.13.2   Polarisation

The first, and most contentious, aspect of the packaged product regime is "polarisation". This requires a firm which advises on packaged products to choose between:

(a) acting as an "independent intermediary", in which case it will be required to act in the best interests of its private customers when it gives advice (COB 5.1.16R) and to advise on the packaged products which are "generally available" in the market as a whole (COB 5.3.9R); or

(b) acting as a "provider firm", that is, as a "product provider" (i.e. unit trust manager, insurance company, etc) selling its own products or as a "marketing associate" of a product provider, tied to selling only its products or those of its "marketing group" (COB 5.1.7R). A "marketing group" is a group of product providers who need not be connected in ownership terms but who are allied together formally or informally for the purposes of marketing their packaged products.

An appointed representative will be "polarised" in the same way as its appointor, that is, an appointed representative of a provider firm can only advise on the products of the provider firm's marketing group (COB 5.1R).

The aim behind the polarisation regime is to ensure that investors are aware whether they are dealing with:

(a) an intermediary which owes them a duty of impartial advice; or

(b) a product provider or a marketing entity whose commercial objective is to maximise the sales of the group's products.

In particular the original aim was to avoid the confusion created by the "multi-tie", where an intermediary appears to provide independent advice by selling a range of products, but these are in fact from a restricted range of providers chosen by reference to their commission terms. However, it is a moot point whether the public has been any the wiser, and the regime gives rise to a number of difficulties:

(a) it applies (with the limited exception of stakeholder pensions (*see* below)) on an "all or nothing" basis: a marketing group can only sell its own products even if its product range is incomplete. It cannot "buy in" products to fill a gap. This causes particular problems for new market entrants;

(b) the development of investment "supermarkets" on the internet have led to pressure for the freedom to sell a range of competing products without undertaking any obligation to establish that they are the best available;

(c) the desire to "white label" products is difficult to reconcile with the regime, since for polarisation purposes a packaged product will normally be treated as that of the underlying product provider, and not that of the brand under which it is sold.

As a result the future of the regime as a whole is under review, and COB reflects certain interim relaxations. In particular (so as to safe-guard the development of Government sponsored stakeholder pensions), a marketing group is allowed to "adopt" these products from a third party supplier and treat them as if they were the products of its marketing group (COB 5.1.4R).

5.13.3   *Sales without recommendation; Investment Managers*

The polarisation regime applies only to transactions involving advice: it is therefore possible for a tied firm to sell non-group products:

(a) where no advice is given: the onus will, however, be on the firm to show that this is the case;

(b) by way of financial promotion, so long as the promotion makes it clear that no personal recommendation is being made, and suggests that if the customer is in doubt, he takes advice. (*See* COB 5.1.2G; 5.3.2G and 3.9.7R.)

Firms are not subject to the full polarisation rules if:

(a) (in the case of provider firms) they manage investments on a discretionary basis (COB 5.3.8G); and

(b) (in the case of independent intermediaries) they manage investments on a discretionary or non-discretionary basis (COB 5.3.10R).

5.13.4   *Groups of companies*

It is permissible to have an independent intermediary in the same corporate group as a product provider, and indeed to have two separate marketing groups in the same corporate group. However:

(a) a provider firm must not act in a way which may give the impression that it can advise on packaged products outside its marketing group (COB 5.1.11R). This requirement has been broadly interpreted by the regulators and means that, for example, it is difficult to maintain two marketing groups in a single corporate group unless they operate in sufficiently independent fashion to avoid creating such confusion;

(b) while a provider firm may refer customers to an associated independent intermediary (COB 5.1.13R – so long as the referrals do not amount to a prohibited inducement, *see* Section 5.13.11 below), an independent intermediary will have difficulty in recommending the products of product providers with whom it associates (*see* 5.13.6 below).

5.13.5   Status disclosure

A firm advising on packaged products must disclose "on first contact" whether it is tied (with or without "adopted products"), or independent, or acting as a discretionary manager (*see* COB 5.1.17-5.1.19R). There are specific expectations relating to disclosures on stationery and business cards of provider firms (COB 5.5.4E) as part of the general obligation to provide adequate information about the firm (COB 5.5R and *see* Section 5.4 above).

5.13.6   Advice and suitability

Apart from the general obligation to ensure that recommendations are "suitable" for private customers (*see* Section 5.7 above) a firm which makes a personal recommendation of a packaged product has a more specific obligation to ensure:

(a) (where it is a provider firm) that the product is the most suitable of those available from its marketing group (COB 5.3.6R): for this purpose it is permissible to ignore the fact that the same product may be available at a better price through an alternative distribution channel, or on special terms on a restricted basis: (COB 5.3.7R). If no group product is suitable, no recommendation may be made (COB 5.3.6(2)R); or

(b) (where it is an independent intermediary) that it is at least as appropriate as any other generally available product (COB 5.3.9R).

In addition, an independent intermediary may only recommend the products of a connected entity if it is *more* appropriate than any other generally available product: a test which will usually be extremely difficult, if not impossible to satisfy.

The obligation on a tied sales force to consider all the available products of the marketing group may cause difficulties in complex groups and/or where two marketing groups are merged following, for example, a corporate acquisition. The requirement is reinforced by an obligation to ensure that all sales personnel are in a position to sell all products, unless they are not competent to do so, in which case they must, if appropriate, refer the customer to a colleague who is (COB 5.1.12R).

5.13.7   Suitability letter

If, following such a recommendation, a private customer buys or sells a packaged product (or enters into certain specified transactions relating to packaged products) the firm must provide the customer with a "suitability letter" setting out why the firm has concluded that the transaction is suitable for the customer; containing a summary of the main consequences and any possible disadvantages of the transaction; and providing further explanations of the recommendation in specified cases (which include the need to justify the recommendation of a personal pension scheme or free standing additional voluntary contribution over a stakeholder pension scheme) (COB 5.3.14-16R). This requirement does not apply:

(a) to an investment manager which makes recommendations relating to regulated collective investment schemes (5.3.19); and

(b) in certain other cases, including small transactions and changes of premium.

(COB 5.3.19R.)

5.13.8   *With profits guide*

A life office which sells with products life policies must prepare a with profits guide containing specified information about its policies on bonuses and other matters. This must be supplied free of charge on request (COB 6.9).

5.13.9   *Disclosure: key features*

The basic scheme of COB is that a private customer who acquires a packaged product should receive "key features" relating to the product, containing specified information. The rules (at COB 6.5) set out in considerable detail the requirements for key features in relation to different types of product: Both content and format are prescribed and broadly require:

(a) a description of the nature of the product (COB 6.5.13(1)R);

(b) a description of risk factors (COB 6.5.13 (2)R;

(c) (in the case of a life policy) a projection illustrating how the principal terms of the transaction will apply to the customer: this will also apply to a collective investment scheme in certain circumstances (broadly where the customer's objective is to raise a specific sum (COB 6.5.15R)). The projection must be calculated as specified in COB 6.6, which will also apply to any projections which are made voluntarily for marketing reasons. The projection must be "customer specific" in relation to a life policy (other than a single premium policy; policies with values below specified maxima; or where the key features are part of a direct offer financial promotion (*see* COB 6.5.19R)). Where customer specific projections are not required, any projection must be provided by reference to figures which typically represent the type of business which the firm conducts in relation to the relevant product;

(d) a description of the product in the form of questions and answers (COB 6.5.20R);

(e) an explanation in tabular form of the effect of deductions (i.e. primarily, charges) on the return of the product. These must (broadly) be calculated by taking projected returns (on the basis of the standardised projections mentioned above) and deducting expected actual expenses. There are complex provisions determining how these calculations have to be made in particular circumstances (*see* COB 6.5.22G and the rules to which it refers);

(f) a commission statement (*see* below);

(g) further specified information (COB 6.5.40R).

The basic obligation to prepare key features rests with the product provider. They must be available in printed format on request unless the party concerned proposes to conduct its activities solely via electronic media in which case no hard copy is required (COB 6.1.4R). The key features must be produced and presented to at least the same quality and standard as associated sales or marketing material. In the case of a life policy, they must be free-standing (i.e. separate from other marketing materials). This is not obligatory in the case of collective investment schemes or stakeholder pensions, but in these circumstances they key features section of the document concerned must "appear with due prominence" (COB 6.5.1R).

The obligation to issue key features arises where a firm sells, personally recommends or arranges the sale of a packaged product (COB 6.2.7R; .2.22R): they must be issued before the customer completes an application form. There are certain qualifications to this Rule:

(a) where the customer has responded to a direct offer financial promotion, the promotion itself should have included the required information and there is no requirement to provide a further set (COB 6.2.8G; 6.2.23G);

(b) the product provider is not required to provide key features where the product is sold on a personal recommendation of, or arranged to be sold by, an independent or intermediary or marketing group associate (6.2.9 (1)R; 6.2.25R). In this case the obligation will rest on the intermediary concerned. It may (in principle) provide its own key features or pass on those of the product provider;

(c) where the product is purchased without a written application, the firm must ensure that it gives an adequate explanation of the main features of the product and must send the key features to the customer within five business days of the date on which the sale, recommendation is made (COB 6.2.9(2)R; 6.2.22(2)R).

In the case of collective investment schemes there are some additional exceptions, in particular:

(a) where the product is purchased on an execution-only basis; or

(b) where it is purchased by an investment manager exercising discretion; or by an investment manager who does not exercise discretion, if the customer has agreed that key features do not have to be provided; or

(c) in the case of repeat purchases, where there has been no intervening change of terms.

(COB 6.2.24R.)

Special disclosure requirements apply to various types of product and transactions (COB 6.4) including:

(a) sales of packaged products to the trustees of occupational pension schemes and self-invested personal pension schemes, where broadly the aim is to ensure that the members/beneficiaries are given the regulatory benefits of customer status, including receipt of appropriate disclosure (COB 6.4.5R; 6.4.6R);

(b) cash deposit ISAs (COB 6.4.13R) where specified information must be supplied instead of key features (COB 6.5.42R);

(c) stakeholder pensions: where the product is sold without a personal recommendation, the key features must include a prescribed "decision tree" (*see* COB 6.5.2(5)R; 6.5.8R), and the customer must be given formal notice that no advice has been given (COB 6.4.23R).

5.13.10 *Post-sale procedures; cancellation and withdrawal*

In the case of a life policy the product provider must normally provide a post-sale confirmation containing a repetition of the illustration, explanation of deductions and commission statement (COB 6.3). This applies everywhere, no key features have been provided because of an exception referred to in 5.13.9 above.

Section 6.7 of COB provides purchasers of certain types of investment (principally packaged products) the right either to withdraw from the transaction pre-contract ("withdrawal") or to cancel the contract after sale ("cancellation"). The Rules in this area are particularly complex but the position is broadly as follows:

(a) the pre-contract withdrawal right applies principally to PEPs or ISAs which will not be invested in packaged products; however

    (i) the manager of a PEP or ISA which may invest in packaged products has the choice of whether to offer withdrawal or cancellation;

    (ii) in the case of pension annuities or pension transfers, the basic principle is to provide for cancellation, but in certain circumstances firms can choose to operate a pre-sale right to withdraw (a "cancellation substitute") given the difficulty of restoring the status quo after the contract has been entered into;

(b) with these exceptions the right is to cancel: this will apply generally in the case of any insurance contract (life policy or pure protection); cash deposit ISAs and any stakeholder pension scheme;

(c) in relation to PEPS/ISAs, or regulated collective investment schemes the right will normally only arise if the customer has received advice (but this may have been given by the product provider or an intermediary);

(d) where there is a cancellation right the customer must normally be informed both before the agreement is concluded and afterwards (COB 6.7.30R), and the notices must contain specified information. The period of cancellation is 30 days for life policies (though the firm may reduce this by specifying a period of not less than 14 days in its notices); 14 days in the case of other investments (*see* COB 6.7.10R and 6.7.20R);

(e) in the case of certain investments a firm is entitled to deduct any "shortfall" on refunding the investor's subscription/premium monies, that is, in the amount reflecting any market fall between price paid by the customer and the ruling price of the date when the firm first becomes aware of the notice of cancellation (*see* COB 6.7.54R-6.7.58R).

5.13.11   *Commission*

An independent intermediary is responsible to its customer and one might expect that it would be precluded from receiving commission from the product provider altogether. As a matter of long standing tradition, such an arrangement is permitted, but it is tightly regulated. In contrast what is paid to a tied sales force (whether employed by a marketing group associate or an appointed representative) is generally less regulated, though:

(a) the sales force's remuneration structure must not distort advice (e.g. by paying a higher rate of commission for particular types of product)(COB 5.1.13R); and

(b) the commission or other remuneration paid to sales force will need to be disclosed and also taken into account in the calculation of expenses for key features disclosure purposes: (*see* below).

Commission paid by a product provider to an independent intermediary will be subject to the general COB provisions on "inducements" (i.e. the product provider must not provide any benefit which is likely to conflict with any duty which the recipient may owe to its customers (*see* below). In relation to packaged products there are more specific requirements. The FSA expects (COB 2.2.5E) that commission paid will not include:

(a) "volume overrides" (i.e. commission which is not calculated as a simple multiple of the commission payable on a per transaction basis);

(b) increases in commission beyond that disclosed to the customer, unless attributable to additional payments by the customer;

(c) commission on indemnity terms (i.e. which might enable the recipient to retain the commission even if the transaction was cancelled); or

(d) any payment (subject to certain exceptions) to anyone other than the firm responsible for the sale.

In addition there is extensive guidance as to permissible types of indirect benefits which may be made available to independent intermediaries (COB 2.2.6G); an independent intermediary must not enter into commercial arrangements which might be likely to affect adversely its ability to provide advice on an independent basis (COB 5.1.16R).

There is an obligation on both the product provider and on an independent intermediary to disclose commission in relation to packaged products "in cash terms" before effecting a transaction with or for a private customer. This obligation applies:

(a) in the case where an independent intermediary involved, to the remuneration which it receives;

(b) in the case of a tied sales force, to the commission or remuneration which the product provider or its associates pays to its employees or agents.

(COB 5.7.5R.)

There are extensive provisions about the benefits and services which the FSA expects to be included in determining employees' and agents' remuneration (COB 5.7.6R and 5.7.8E).

The requirement is excluded or modified:

(a) if the firm is acting as an investment manager;

(b) in certain circumstances where the customer is overseas; and

(c) if the firm has provided the customer with "example" key features (*see* above). However in this case the full disclosure must be made within five business days of the transaction.

(COB 5.7.9R.)

Chapter 6

THE INTER-PROFESSIONAL CONDUCT

Tamasin Little
Partner, Financial Services Group
SJ Berwin

6.1   Introduction

The Market Conduct Sourcebook ("MAR") will contain a chapter on Inter-Professional Conduct which replaces the draft Inter-Professionals Code which was first produced for consultation by the Financial Services Authority (the "FSA") in its CP47.   The Inter-Professional Conduct chapter (the "IPC") will in the new regime:

(a) replace the FSA's (formerly Bank of England's) Grey Paper and London Code of Conduct which currently applies to money market business falling under Section 43 of the Financial Services Act 1986 (the "FS Act"); and

(b) apply to the area of business which is currently excluded from almost all Conduct of Business Rules by virtue of The Securities and Futures Authority's ("SFA") and Investment Management Regulatory Organisation's ("IMRO") exclusion of "market counterparties" from their definition of "customer" (except in relation to client money and custody).

Its stated aim is to "provide some articulation of the standards expected in inter-professional business and, in so doing, to increase certainty about what regulatory requirements apply in this area". The FSA believes that this will promote market confidence without hampering the efficient functioning of London's markets or applying inappropriate and disproportionate regulation to inter-professional business (paragraph 1.94 CP47). It recognises that such business will in many ways remain self-disciplining.   Given the size and international importance of London's wholesale markets, let alone its other inter-professional dealings, it is essential for the prosperity of London as a financial centre that the FSA gets the balance right in this area of regulation.

For the most part the IPC amounts to guidance on the FSA's Principles, but it also contains a few rules together with "the FSA's understanding of certain market practices and conventions". Out of caution the IPC expressly specifies under Section 141(2) of the Financial Services and Markets Act 2000 (the "FSMA") that none of the rules in it can give rise to action for damages by a private person under Section 141(1) FSMA.

6.2 Who the IPC applies to and its jurisdictional limits

The IPC will apply to all firms which are authorised under the FSMA apart from:

(a) service companies. Service companies are those trade support service organisations which fall outside the Investment Services Directive, require regulation in the UK because they make arrangements with a view to others participating in investment transactions, but do not carry on any other form of investment business or take any responsibility for performance. Provided their business is kept within strict limits such companies have in the past been authorised directly by the FSA and subject to a very light regime. It is currently proposed that the existing light regime will continue with the few additions outlined in CP55. This is why the new IPC will not apply. However service companies are subject to the FSA's overall consideration of the market infrastructure and how it should be regulated, which may produce future changes. There is an element of illogicality about treating some service companies differently from, say, electronic trading, order matching and routing systems which are provided by authorised firms and subject to the IPC. However, that illogicality (as well as those associated with the differences between recognised investment exchanges ("RIEs") and such electronic systems) is currently an inevitable consequence of the different routes chosen by different businesses to obtain authorisation or exemption;

(b) those insurance companies and friendly societies which in do not come within the relevant Directive;

(c) operators trustees and depositaries of European Economic Area ("EEA") UCITS (that is, undertakings for collective investment in transferable securities falling within Directive 85/611/EEC) who are carrying on regulated activities in the UK by virtue of authorisation under Paragraph 1(1) Schedule 5 FSMA.

The range of firms to be covered by the IPC is an expansion when compared to those previously covered by the London Code of Conduct. This is principally because authorised investment businesses which do not carry on Section 43 business, and could therefore previously simply disapply their regulator's Conduct of Business Rules relating to customers without moving into the Section 43 wholesale regime, will become subject to the IPC. In addition, the number of authorised firms will be increased by the addition of most insurance companies and friendly societies, managers of collective investment schemes (who were regarded as "end users" under the London Code of Conduct) and some firms which are at present either "permitted persons" or subject to regulation by their professional body. All these firms could previously ignore the London Code of Conduct (except when they wished as end-users to rely on it) but will now have to concern themselves with the IPC.

The IPC applies only to relevant business (*see* Section 6.3 below) done by an authorised firm from a UK office of the firm. This includes business that the office does with counterparties worldwide. However, business done by an overseas office (whether of the authorised firm or an unauthorised entity) will not be covered. Generally this is a straightforward line to draw but difficulties can arise, particularly in relation to transactions which are wholly or partially carried out or arranged offshore but booked to a UK office or vice versa. FSA guidance (Mar 3 Ann 1G 9) does not give much assistance in solving these difficulties apart from saying that if a transaction arranged by one entity is booked to a UK legal entity the latter will be covered by the IPC. This approach was opposed in consultation but maintained by the FSA which stated that it did not believe any resulting conflict between regulatory jurisdictions will be significant or unmanageable.

In practice it will be wise to err on the side of caution in relation to the territorial application of the IPC. Certainly when a UK office effects or arranges the relevant transaction it should apply the IPC even if it then books the transaction to an offshore office or entity. This should not produce many practical problems, in fact more problems would probably arise if an attempt was made to identify and treat differently in terms of conduct transactions which are subsequently booked to different offices. More difficult in practice may be the application of the IPC (which will inevitably be less familiar to those carrying out the business) to transactions done offshore and then booked to London but given the FSA guidance it would still be wise to apply the IPC. It is to be hoped that the relatively flexible nature of the IPC (*see* Section 6.4 below) and its willingness to recognise the practices of other markets will make this feasible in practice.

Although the IPC will not apply to market counterparties who are not themselves authorised firms the FSA hopes that it will provide a guide to good practice which may help resolve bilateral disputes and lend itself to being adopted or endorsed by other market counterparties. Some global firms/groups may wish to adopt the IPC, or aspects of it, as part of their global practice/procedures – although it does not contain as many "commercial good sense" provisions as the London Code of Conduct.

6.3   What business the IPC covers

6.3.1   Elements of test

There is a three-fold test for establishing whether the IPC applies:

(a) the nature of the parties;

(b) the type of business activity; and

(c) the type of investment.

6.3.2   *Business done with market counterparties*

As has already been indicated the key point is that the IPC applies only to business done with "market counterparties". This is the rationale for cutting back on the application of Conduct of Business Rules and, in regulatory terms, a relatively "light touch".

The categories of person to be classified as "market counterparties" will include:

(a) properly constituted governments (including quasi-governmental bodies and government agencies) of any country or territory. It is an open question how the average market trader is meant to determine whether a government is improperly constituted;

(b) central banks and other national monetary authorities of any country or territory;

(c) supranationals whose members are either countries or central banks or national monetary authorities;

(d) state investment bodies or bodies charged with, or intervening in, the management of the public debt;

(e) authorised firms and overseas financial services institutions unless the relevant firm or institution:

(i) is a collective investment scheme; or

(ii) in relation to designated investment business (i.e. mainstream investment business rather than other regulated activities such as insurance and deposit taking) when that firm or institution has opted down to intermediate status under Conduct of Business Rule 4.1.7 (*see* Section 6.3.2 below);

It should be noted that "overseas financial services institution" is a new term which is not quite the same as the old "overseas person". The new definition means an institution authorised by a competent authority in another EEA state or by a regulatory body which is a member of the International Organisation of Securities Commissions ("IOSCO") in any other country. It does not include other firms which have activities which would be regulated investment business if done in this country but which do not require regulation in their home country.

(f) associates of authorised firms (apart from firms whose business relates to occupational pension schemes) and overseas financial services institutions if the relevant firm or institution (note, not the associate itself) consents; and

(g) large intermediate customers who opt-up to market counterparty status under COB 4.1.12R (*see* Section 6.3.2 below).

Excluded from the definition of market counterparties are those who, although they would otherwise be market counterparties, opt-down and require to be classified as private customers under COB 4.1.14R. (*See* Chapter 5, para 5.3.7 above for further detail on this.)

At present authorised firms only automatically count as market counterparties for SFA and IMRO purposes if they are regulated by the same regulator and carry on investment business of the same description in the same capacity, a test which is not always easy to apply and can reach anomalous results. The SFA, which is the main regulator at present for wholesale markets, simplifies the test to some extent by allowing authorised firms and some other entities which would not otherwise qualify as market counterparties to be reclassified as that category, provided they do not object. Under the new COB 4.1.7R all authorised firms and overseas financial services institutions will start with a market counterparty classification. In relation to business which would otherwise be inter-professional business such a firm (the "client firm") can only opt-down to intermediate customer status (the term which is to be used to refer, very broadly, to the category which is currently called "non-private customers") if the client firm is acting for an underlying customer **and** considers that in order to protect its underlying customer's interests under the Conduct of Business Rules the client firm should benefit from the protections available to intermediate customers. Even then the agreement of **both** firms is needed for the opt-down to be effective, although the FSA appears to envisage implied agreement as being sufficient (*see* Section 6.8 below).

The main areas where authorised firms with underlying customers may seek intermediate customer status are where they owe their customers duties such as those of best and timely execution and need to rely on the counterparty to provide that service. Agreement may be given in relation to all underlying customers or on a customer by customer basis. If the other firm refuses to agree to the opt-down then the firm wanting protection for its underlying customers will have to look elsewhere for the service concerned. In addition it should be noted that the "opted-down" reclassification only applies in relation to inter-professional business done for underlying clients.

Perhaps the more interesting group of potential market counterparties, and certainly one of the groups for which proper classification procedures will be most important, is intermediate customers who are reclassified as market counterparties ("opting-up" to that status). Under COB 4.1.12R this will be possible for "large business customers" but not for individuals, however wealthy or sophisticated.

Intermediate customers capable of reclassification will include:

Corporates

(a) companies and other bodies corporate (including limited liability partnerships) which have (or any of whose holding companies or subsidiaries have) called up share capital of at least £10 million (or equivalent in another currency);

(b) companies or other bodies corporate which meet (or any of whose holding companies or subsidiaries meet) at least two of the following tests:

   (i) a balance sheet total of €12.5 million (or equivalent);

   (ii) a net turnover of €25 million (or equivalent); and

   (iii) an average number of 250 employees in the year;

provided that in each of (a) and (b) above a one way notice has been given of the proposed classification, warning of the relevant losses of regulatory protections and delivered to an appropriately authorised (and presumably senior) person at the client and the relevant client has not notified the firm of any objection to the classification.

Non-corporates

(a) a local or public authority;

(b) partnerships (other than limited liability partnerships) or unincorporated associations with net assets of at least £10 million (calculated in the case of a limited partnership without deducting loans owing to partners);

(c) trustees of trusts (other than pension schemes) with assets of at least £10 million calculated by aggregating cash and designated investments but before deducting liabilities (i.e. broadly the same as the current non-private customer level. It was originally proposed that the test should be of net cash and designated investments but the FSA presumably realised that this would be hard to calculate if only certain types of asset are relevant; would one, for instance, need to deduct liabilities under mortgages secured on land from the trust's net assets without being able to include the land itself as an investment);

(d) trustees of pension schemes where the trust has or had at any time in the previous two years:

(i) at least 50 members; and

(ii) assets under management of not less than £10 million (or equivalent);

provided in the case of each of (a) to (d) the authorised firm not only gives a classification and warning notice to an appropriate person but also receives back a written consent, or can otherwise demonstrate that consent has been given.

Thus many of those who qualify for intermediate customer status, such as listed companies, companies and partnerships with assets of between £5 and £10 million and expert private customers will not be allowed to opt-up to market counterparty status however willing they may be to be treated in this way. Logically, collective investment schemes, if they are large enough, should be dealt with under the relevant corporate, partnership, unincorporated association or trust heading even though they do not qualify as market counterparties automatically as authorised firms. However, the definition of intermediate customer separately classifies unregulated collective investment schemes as intermediate customers and excludes regulated collective investment schemes which are therefore always treated as private customers and this treatment is confirmed in COB 4.1.7R. The managers and trustees of the schemes will, however, apparently on the current wording be treated in the same way as other authorised firms or companies/trustees (apart from trustees of authorised unit trusts which according to the rule definitions, though not the policy statement, will be treated as private customers). However, the Association of Unit Trusts and Investment Funds ("AUTIF"), the trade body whose lobbying was largely responsible for the classification of regulated collective investment schemes as private customers, is lobbying for that classification to be extended to cover their managers and trustees in all circumstances.

A number of the proposed tests differ significantly from those which were familiar from past practice and if implemented in full at N2 would require a major reclassification exercise. The transitional arrangements which will apply to prevent the need for wholesale reclassifications are set out in Section 6.8 below. Some of the changes, particularly the two out of three test for large corporates in (b) above, derive from the Forum of European Securities Commissions ("FESCO") Paper of March 2000 on the categorisation of investors for the purpose of Conduct of Business Rules. Significant departures from the FESCO outline classification are that the FESCO Paper does not have the single £10 million test as an alternative for corporates and would treat all partnerships (rather than just those which qualify as bodies corporate) in the same way as companies. The FESCO Paper would also treat all collective investment schemes, pension funds and their managers as professionals and allow any listed company to be treated as a professional.

It is strange, and may prove highly inconvenient, that the tests for moving into the market counterparty category (subject to warnings and, where necessary, consent) do not (except in the case of pension funds) allow for the tests to be satisfied at any time in the last two years, unlike the tests for intermediate customer status. Some comfort may be obtained from the fact that, under the Conduct of Business Rules, classifications only have to be reviewed annually (or less often if there is a gap of more than 12 months between occasions on which investment business is done). Even so finding up-to-date evidence of clients meeting size tests, rather than, for instance, relying on the latest audited accounts, can be nearly impossible. In practice this will presumably be addressed by seeking warranties and comfort letters to cover the period after any accounts which have been obtained but it is not clear what the FSA expects here, or why exactly the change has been made.

Records will need to be kept of the classification process, including the basis of assessment and evidence of consent, in the usual way.

6.3.3   *Types of business*

The IPC will apply to dealing, arranging deals or agreeing to do so and giving transaction specific advice, or agreeing to do so, and ancillary activities. Thus:

(a) it will not apply to other regulated activities such as investment management, running collective investment schemes, custody, insurance business and deposit taking;

(b) it will, however, apply to dealing and arranging deals which is done by insurance companies, investment managers and managers of collective investment schemes;

(c) in the field of advice only what is called "transaction specific" advice is covered. This means advice given in the course of IPC dealing or arranging deals (or with a view to carrying on any such activities) with or for the market counterparty to whom the advice is given. More wide-ranging advice falls outside the IPC and accordingly will normally be subject to full Conduct of Business Rules. Adding advice of this kind to the IPC regime is a helpful clarification. In the past the Section 43 regime did not in fact apply to giving advice but many market participants (and to some extent the London Code of Conduct itself) proceeded on the basis that it did;

(d) ancillary activities, that is, unregulated activities which are carried on in connection with regulated activities or are held out as being for similar purposes, are also covered.

It does not matter how the dealing or arranging takes place. Thus electronic trading and matching services (unless provided by a service company) will be covered just as direct telephone or other communications are.

Some activities are expressly excluded from the IPC. They are:

(a) the approval of financial promotions (but not their issue);

(b) activities between operators, or between operators and trustees, of the same collective investment scheme when acting in that capacity. Presumably this is meant to relate to transactions of a kind which are covered by the constitution of the scheme, such as the issue and redemption of units, whether in return for cash or for in specie transfers of investments. Although this is not entirely clear it seems to be implied by the reference to the capacity in which the action is taken. It is not necessarily appropriate to exclude from the IPC transactions which are straightforward market purchases of securities by the manager on behalf of the collective investment scheme simply because they happen to be made from the trustee of the scheme. However, if AUTIF is successful in establishing that the operators and trustees of regulated collective investment schemes are always to be treated as private customers they will fall outside the IPC;

(c) safekeeping and administration of securities, or agreeing to do so. Custody on behalf of market counterparties will continue to be treated as subject to the same rules as those applying to other customers. This is partly because of the importance of safeguarding others' property and the fiduciary obligations which normally arise as a matter of law and partly because custody falls under Article 10 of the Investment Services Directive which, *inter alia*, requires adequate arrangements to be made to safeguard the ownership rights of all investors, rather than under Article 11 which relates to Conduct of Business Rules and, unlike Article 10, allows for the possibility of differentiation by reference to the professional nature of the client.

6.3.4   *Types of investment*

The third test which has to be satisfied before the relevant business falls under the IPC relates to the type of investment involved. The dealing, arranging or transaction specific advice must not only be with or for a market counterparty but must also relate to what is called an "inter-professional investment". This is fairly straightforward because the term includes all:

(a) shares;

(b) debt securities;

(c) warrants;

(d) depositary receipts;

(e) futures;

(f) options;

(g) contracts for differences; and

(h) interests in any of the foregoing;

in each case whether on or off-exchange but excludes all insurance contracts, deposits and (perhaps more surprisingly) units in collective investment schemes.

Thus it is very significantly wider than the types of investment covered by the Section 43 and the London Code of Conduct regime. It does exclude some non-investment products, notably wholesale deposits, spot and forward foreign exchange and bullion which were covered in the London Code of Conduct even though they did not fall under the FS Act. More logically in regulatory terms (if not perhaps for market participants) these will now be covered by a Non-Investment Products Code which is being produced by the Bank of England.

6.4   What the IPC requires

6.4.1   General

The IPC is quite short, under 20 pages, and would be shorter still if the FSA's standard, rather formal, handbook style and layout was not used. Apart from the application provisions it contains just two substantive rules which are:

(a) a prohibition on off-exchange non-market price transactions ("NMPT"), unless the firm has taken reasonable steps to ensure that the transaction is not illegal or otherwise for an improper purpose (MAR 3.5.3R) and a requirement that when it does so it retains records on the steps taken (*see* Section 6.4.5 below);

(b) a requirement that if a name passing broker compensates a market counterparty for a difference that difference must be settled in money (which may include discounted or rebated commission) (*see* Section 6.4.7 below).

There were two other rules in the consultation version of the IPC in CP47, one saying that if voice recordings were used to comply with statutory record-keeping requirements they had to be retained in accordance with the relevant statutory requirements (something of a statement of the obvious) and one saying that Investors Compensation Scheme information must be provided if an investor requests it.

A focus on rules promulgated in the IPC is not, however, particularly relevant since the bulk of the IPC involves guidance of one kind or another, and this covers a much wider range of matters than the provisions which are described as "rules". The basic concept, as expressed in MAR 3.4.2G, is that the FSA will interpret both the Principles and the IPC itself on the basis that each market counterparty is responsible for its own decisions.

6.4.2 *Communications and advice*

The central IPC and Principle 7 requirement in relation to communications is simply that communications by a firm to a market counterparty should not be misleading. Not only is there no obligation to consider suitability, or to make sure the counterparty understands the risks or to give advice, but also:

(a) there is no obligation even to provide information and silence by the firm is not to be treated as a breach of Principle 7 unless it amounts to misleading the counterparty. A grey area therefore remains over how far, if at all, a firm needs to disabuse its counterparty of misconceptions it has;

(b) giving information is not to be taken to amount to assuming responsibility for giving advice;

(c) if information is volunteered then, in the absence of a formal advisory arrangement and provided of course that the information is not misleading, the firm is not required to advise the market counterparty about the reliability, relevance or importance of the information. As a matter of general law it may be wise for the firm to warn the counterparty against reliance in any event. Although courts sometimes override such warnings to the extent that they are willing to respect disclaimers of this kind the courts may also respect the guidance of the Code as an important factual indication of the level of protection to be expected by those dealing in these circumstances;

(d) if information is given and the transaction is not executed immediately the firm is not obliged to update the information given unless it has agreed to do so. It must follow that there is no need at all to provide or update information after a transaction (such as a derivatives transaction where changing facts are relevant for exercise) in the absence of a contractual commitment to do so. This guidance would not, of course, override general obligations, for instance to keep a prospectus up-to-date to the time of issue of the securities.

Generally the relationship between firms and their market counterparties is taken to be an arm's length execution-only one unless and until there is an agreement to the contrary. This is the foundation for the absence of obligations to advise and the limited responsibility for information provided. It should however be noted that the obligation to avoid misleading communications has some weight. It is not phrased just as an obligation to take reasonable care to avoid misleading communications. In practice it is to be hoped that such a "reasonable care" qualification will be implied. An absolute obligation to get all communications correct could be much more onerous than the IPC seems to envisage. This is why the express statement that there is no obligation to update information given is particularly helpful. There are many circumstances where a statement made at one date would be misleading if repeated later. The IPC makes it clear that it is not concerned with statements "becoming" misleading in this way, unless there is an agreement to keep the counterparty updated.

In some circumstances a firm may act for a market counterparty in situations where duties are owed to the latter, and there is an obligation to act in its interests under the general law or the law of contract. Examples given are where the firm acts as agent for the counterparty, agrees to advise it or otherwise owes it fiduciary duties. In such circumstances the IPC only requires that the firm should either manage the conflict by the operation of internal Chinese walls or, before transacting, disclose the nature and extent of any material conflict between its own interests (or those of an affiliated company). The specific example given is that where a firm is arranging a transaction for a market counterparty and is also affiliated to the other principal to the trade this should be disclosed to the market counterparty for whom the firm acts. The IPC does not indicate whether a general disclosure of possible conflicts is sufficient (which is the normal practice) or whether specific disclosure is required in relation to an individual transaction. The way the example is phrased suggests the latter. It does, however, make it fairly clear that it considers that disclosure is all that is required to overcome the conflict for regulatory purposes. This is an area where it is by no means clear that the general English law on conflicts of interest, which continues to develop, would be as lenient as the IPC.

6.4.3   *Identification of status*

Whether or not a conflict of interest requires disclosure, guidance in the IPC requires firms to ensure that it is clear to their counterparties **before** the relevant transaction whether the firm is acting on its own account, as agent or as arranger. If it is acting as a "wholesale market broker" it should indicate whether it is a "name passing broker" (i.e. arranging the deal between two counterparties on mutually acceptable terms and then passing their names to one another for settlement purposes) or a "matched principal broker" (i.e. one which takes the transaction onto its own books, albeit only on a fully matched basis so that it should have no real exposure). These are the only two types of broker which fall into the definition of a "wholesale market broker". The distinctions between different types of "broker" are partly ones of legal form (principal, agent or not party to the transaction at all), partly regulatory classification (e.g. "arranging" falls under paragraph 25 of the Regulated Activities Order while dealing as agent falls under paragraph 21) and partly market terminology (e.g. name passing). The disclosure requirement may change market terminology to some extent; in the past the term "arranger" has hardly been used and the term "broker" is commonly used to cover a much wider range of activities.

Once a firm has agreed with a market counterparty to act in one capacity for a transaction it needs the latter's consent before changing its capacity for the transaction. For instance a firm which bids to transact on an agency basis should not without consent execute any part of the trade against its own book. The example given would in fact fit the conflicts guidance as well as the guidance on clarity of role, or status. The latter guidance, unlike the guidance on conflicts, presumably applies equally when a firm has stated that it is acting as principal – it should not then fill the deal as agent. In practice, however, this is unlikely to be relevant as the firm could instead simply enter into a back-to-back (or matched) principal trade.

The guidance also notes that it is inconsistent with acting solely as an arranger or name passing broker to take positions, even fleetingly, or act on a matched principal basis. It does not say the same about brokers generally and although the term "broker" is defined in the IPC as a firm acting as agent some, for instance interdealer brokers, commonly act on a matched principal basis as is made clear in the IPC. Even the majority who do not may, by reason of exchange or clearing rules or otherwise, sometimes be left with a position on failed trades. The restriction on arrangers is more one of regulatory permissions and capital than an IPC requirement. Nevertheless it may be worth a counterparty noting that although in some circumstances a broker may be liable on a transaction an arranger never should be. Arrangers also need to take particular care on this point since, as mentioned above, it is not simply a matter of disclosure of status under IPC guidance and the prohibition on misleading statements, it may affect their permission to do the business at all and regulatory capital requirements.

6.4.4   Incentives and inducements

There are only two pieces of guidance given on the acceptability or otherwise of marketing incentives, inducements and payments in kind and both require significant exercise of judgement:

(a) the first is that a firm should take reasonable steps to ensure that neither it, nor anyone acting on its behalf, offers, gives, solicits or accepts any inducement which is intended or likely to conflict to a material extent with any duty of the recipient firm to another person. It is pointed out that inducements can include entertainment and soft commissions. CP47 had included under this heading a requirement that any payment for broking or arranging services should be in cash unless otherwise agreed in writing. That provision has now been moved to more general guidance in relation to the broking/arranging function (MAR 3.7.9G) and in this Section it is instead pointed out that firms who deal for a customer through an intermediary, even if the intermediary is a market counterparty, may be subject to COB 2.2R, relating to inducements and soft commission. COB 2.2R, *inter alia*, requires firms to be sure that neither they nor anyone acting on their behalf offer inducements or direct business if it is likely materially to conflict with a duty to customers and also sets out permitted and prohibited types of indirect benefits and soft commissions;

(b) firms are expected to have, and to implement, appropriate systems and controls and policies to avoid inducements which conflict with duties (whether on the paying side or as recipients). This underlines the nature of the IPC obligation. It is not in itself an absolute obligation to prevent the relevant inducement being given (or offered or solicited) - although the offeror and /or the recipient may well be under an absolute ban as a matter of general law – but more one of having systems and controls in place to minimise the risks of occurrence.

It is worth noting the IPC reference to a conflict "to a material extent" with a "duty". According to the IPC entertainment and gifts are not inappropriate as such but care has to be taken to see that they are not excessive or in breach of the "material conflict" requirement, bearing in mind the level and type of regular business undertaken between the firm and the market counterparty.

This is a difficult area where most firms lay down formal, and often quite low, permitted bands but have scope for much higher levels to be cleared. In practice whether an inducement is intended or likely to give rise to a material conflict, in the sense of any real likelihood of breach of duty varies greatly from individual to individual and it can be very hard to distinguish between normal networking, courtesy, and improper inducements. The difficulty is particularly acute given the different nationalities working in London and their different home traditions of hospitality, gift giving, and expected returns.

It should also be noted that various provisions of the general law also apply in this area such as statutory bans on inducements offered to certain public officials, the liability of agents to account and more general restitutionary remedies.

6.4.5 Transactions at non-market prices

Transactions at non-market prices are one of the few areas where the IPC contains a rule, rather than mere guidance. The FSA is concerned with market integrity and sensitive to the risk that a transaction at a rate or price which is not in line with the current market may be designed to conceal profit or loss, or may distort the market. Although it is not mentioned in the IPC such transactions may also involve money laundering or be part of wider criminal activity. Equally, there may be perfectly good reasons for the transaction.

The rule laid down in the IPC is that a firm must not enter into (whether as agent or principal) an off-exchange deal (the rule does not apply to business which is subject to the rules of a RIE) under which it deals in an IPC investment if either:

(a) the dealing rate or price paid by the firm or its market counterparty differs from the prevailing market rate or price to a material extent; or

(b) in so doing it or its market counterparty otherwise gives materially more or less in value than it receives;

unless it has taken reasonable steps to ensure the transaction is not being entered into by its market counterparty for an improper purpose.

The second limb of the test for a NMPT bears an interesting relationship to the absence of an obligation under the IPC to check suitability. Market counterparties are presumed to be able to look after themselves, but if the transaction is materially disadvantageous it seems that they cannot be left to lose their money without any check at all. The nature of the check is, however, only that they are not in some way fiddling the books or otherwise acting improperly.

In CP47 the question was whether the transaction itself was "illegal or otherwise for an improper purpose". The revised version focuses solely on the propriety or otherwise of the counterparty's purpose. In addition following consultation brokers and others who are arranging IPC transactions are not expected to inquire into the motivation of the principals to the transaction.

Guidance states that the question of whether a transaction is a NMPT is to be judged at the time it is effected, and not with hindsight, but also that a variation or rollover of an existing transaction must be regarded as a new transaction. Thus if there is a variation or rollover whether the price or rate is "non-market" must be judged at the time of the variation or rollover, not the original pricing.

It can often be very difficult to make inquiries into a suspicious transaction, particularly since the reasons for the transaction may be commercially confidential and, even when they are not, the other party may resent the enquiry and/or threaten loss of business. This is presumably why the obligation is imposed in a rule, not in mere guidance. Moreover although the rule does not impose an absolute obligation it does not stop at merely making an enquiry. It requires the firm to "take reasonable steps to ensure" that the transaction is not for an improper purpose and then keep records of the steps taken for at least three years. This is intended to give regulators or other investigators a good chance to track down problems.

An explanation to the rules sets out the minimum required to amount to such "reasonable steps". Firms should:

(a) have procedures in place to identify NMPTs, have a policy and procedure of having NMPTs reviewed, **in advance of commitment,** by a senior individual in the firm. The degree of seniority required may depend on the nature of the transaction. It does not say that the senior individual should be separate from the executive in the firm proposing the transaction, but that would seem to be a sensible precaution whenever possible;

(b) ensure the review considers the reasons for the transaction; and

(c) (in one of the negatives which are so popular in the new legislation and rules) check whether the firm has not been put on notice that the transaction is for an improper purpose.

However, following consultation, the IPC does not insist on senior level sign-off on a transaction by transaction basis if:

(a) the firm establishes a policy and procedure which is itself approved by a senior individual and sets out the categories of transaction which can be reviewed by a more junior person (albeit one whom the person approving the policy is satisfied has the appropriate level of skills);

(b) the transaction falls into one of those categories;

(c) the firm can demonstrate that it routinely enters into transactions of those categories and that the categories are defined so that there is a high probability that transactions coming within them will be for proper purposes (and the firm keeps under review whether this continues in fact to be the case);

(d) the factors defining the categories do not themselves involve judgement over the propriety or otherwise of the purpose;

(e) the policy provides for matters to be referred to more senior levels in "appropriate circumstances"; and

(f) the policy has due regard to segregation of responsibilities, which presumably means that at this level the one proposing the transaction should not be the same as the one approving it.

The use of more or less automatic clearance procedures for some transactions is a shift from the FSA's position in CP47, which would only have allowed general policies of this kind for transactions with other group members.

Another change from the position at the time of CP47 is that some types of transactions which CP47 regarded as justifiable as being for legitimate purposes are in the IPC regarded as not being NMPTs at all. Two main examples are given. One is transactions which have more than one component and the individual components are entered into at non-market rates or prices but the sum of the whole transaction produces an overall market price or rate (e.g. asset swaps or other swaps where one or both legs do not show implied forward rates or prices but instead involve up-front or final payments). Another is the purchase and sale of out of the money options where other factors, such as the level of premium, are as important as the strike price. Other factors which may result in a transaction being at a different price without it necessarily being an NMPT are where the transaction is not for a marketable amount, or is done outside normal market hours, over a period of time or has a non-standard settlement.

The advantage of this reassessment of what amounts to an NMPT is presumably that in these cases it is not necessary to go through the assessment and record-keeping process at all, even at a more junior level. However this is not entirely clear, and certainly cannot be relied on for absolute protection, because elsewhere guidance states that where a NMPT has more than one component the assessment of whether or not the transaction is improper should be made by reference to the transaction as a whole but that a firm may conclude, in making such a judgement, that the rationale for one component would cause it (i.e. the transaction) to be in breach.

Some of the lack of clarity is because the language of the IPC slips between saying that a judgement must be made as to whether a transaction "constitutes a non-market price transaction" and saying that a judgement must be made as to whether it is for an improper purpose.

Very little guidance is given on what constitutes impropriety, apart from saying that examples of impropriety include the perpetration of a fraud, improper concealment of a profit or loss, market abuse, transactions which are vulnerable under the insolvency legislation and year-end "window dressing" to conceal the true financial position. Even less guidance is given on what constitutes propriety. The only comment is that transfers between a firm and its nominee or intra-group transfers for risk management purposes will normally be for proper purposes provided that the firm has established and acted in accordance with an established policy, on the subject and can show it has considered the consequences of participating in such transactions. Although the IPC does not say so, such consequences could include the weakening of the financial viability of the firm in potential group insolvency situations.

If a firm does decide to enter into an NMPT then the senior personnel considering the transaction have to consider the justification and rationale of the other parties and whether the decision to enter into it was taken by the parties concerned at a senior level and not by an individual trader or treasurer. It is not said whether high level approval is meant to guarantee or improve the likelihood of propriety but the implication is that a transaction approved at a high level is more likely to have been approved properly. That may be the case in the event of traders seeking to cover up their fraud, or losses, but the really major problems may have high level support (e.g. a policy of cleaning up the balance sheet for the year-end).

In any event, once the transaction is to go ahead the senior personnel should be sure that all material terms (e.g. payments and receipts, netting, offset against other transactions etc.) of the NMPT have been agreed in advance and are promptly recorded (along with the steps taken to ascertain whether the counterparty had an improper purpose).

The FSA does recognise that a firm may be unable to ascertain its counterparty's rationale for entering into the transaction even after taking all reasonable steps to do so. It is then left to the firm to decide whether it is appropriate to deal. Charmingly the IPC says that a relevant consideration in deciding whether to do so is whether or not the market counterparty is itself an authorised firm. If it is then, in the absence of information to the contrary, the first firm is "entitled to assume that the other firm is acting properly".

Interestingly the guidance only says that firms operating electronic matching systems should "consider" implementing appropriate systems to identify NMPTs and that in these circumstances it may be appropriate for such identification and appropriate resulting action to occur after the transaction has taken place. This is a relatively realistic approach but it is worth noting that if the guidance is taken at full value it overrides the rule and seems to mean that those operating electronic matching systems are not obliged to follow the rule.

In theory the new provisions are less onerous than the London Code of Conduct which said that deals at non-market rates should only be undertaken, if at all, on rare occasions and then after most careful consideration by both parties and approval on a deal by deal basis by their senior management, including seeking written confirmation from the counterparty at senior management level of the reasons for the transactions. In practice just because they are phrased as a rule, and sufficiently flexible to be capable of being followed, they may well prove to have a greater effect, particularly since they apply to all authorised firms doing IPC business.

6.4.6 Taping

The guidance given by the IPC on taped and other records starts from the premise that firms are expected to ensure that the material terms of, and other material information about, all transactions to which it is a party are promptly recorded in its books and records. Information which is not material to the relevant firm does not need to be recorded (e.g. an arranger generally does not need to know about payment and settlement). The records can include voice recordings, written trading logs or blotters or automated electronic records but they should be capable of being accessed promptly, be in legible and comprehensible form (or be capable of being reproduced legibly and comprehensibly) and be subject to procedures intended to avoid unauthorised alteration.

Written or electronic confirmations can be regarded as adequate records of transactions (and be substituted for the original records). The records of an electronic trading, matchmaking and order routing system can also be sufficient.

As far as tape recording itself is concerned firms are only expected to keep under review whether and to what extent to make and keep voice recordings of its front and back office phone lines and also to make and implement policies on the length of time it keeps tapes. Relevant matters for consideration when reviewing taping policy are that such recordings:

(a) provide an immediate record which may help resolve disputes;

(b) may help to identify whether staff or counterparties are involved in "inappropriate behaviour";

(c) may give comfort to the market counterparties which whom dealing takes place, since they know there is an instant, reliable record; and

(d) can provide a rationale for a particular trading strategy or other matters and thus a defence to the firm.

What the FSA does not say in the IPC is that the pleasure of listening to hours of taped calls is a key part of its enforcement activity and not infrequently provides evidence of behaviour for which the firm or individual is disciplined.

Firms are expected to make and implement policies on the length of time they keep tapes but are not expected to keep them as long as ordinary records are kept, except, of course, where they are being used to fulfil statutory record-keeping requirements.

Curiously, and probably accidentally, although there is no longer the rule proposed in CP47 relating to taped records there is still a rule rather than mere guidance excluding from the relevant guidance in the IPC those establishing, operating or winding up a collective investment scheme, insurers and firms which are subject to Conduct of Business Rules on record-keeping for the relevant transaction.

6.4.7   Name passing and settlement of differences

As mentioned above, the IPC does try to clarify the use of various terms for brokers. The need to recognise some market terminology and the fact that different terms are used in different markets can make it rather confusing all the same. According to the IPC it regards "name passing brokers" "in simple terms" as what arrangers are called in some markets so that the two terms are virtually interchangeable and the IPC generally tries to use both. On the other hand name passing brokers and matched principal brokers are both subsets of wholesale market brokers. The IPC says that the use of the latter term is intended to reduce confusion but it is hard to see how this optimistic statement is justified.

Setting aside any confusion (which in any event is likely to loom larger in the minds of lawyers than of market participants) a fair amount of guidance is given by the IPC in this area, though perhaps less than the London Code of Conduct used to give.

Name passing brokers are told that they should not disclose names of prospective counterparties until, at least, both sides display a serious intention to deal but should disclose them as soon as the material terms of the transaction have been agreed. It is not only permissible but good practice to keep secret the name of the objecting party if one market counterparty's name is unacceptable to the other. It would not in fact always be possible if disclosure was really as mutual and immediate as the guidance suggests. In the "good practice" guidance annexed to the IPC, however, it is recommended that firms which regularly use a particular name passing broker should tell or give the broker a list of the counterparties with which the firm is not prepared to deal. Such indications should be given in a way which would not damage or lower the reputation of the rejected counterparty, in the estimation of other reasonable market counterparties who got to know it, and should in any event be kept confidential by the name passing broker.

Both name passing brokers and firms who use them are required (as a rule, not mere guidance) to ensure that if the broker compensates a market counterparty for a difference (i.e. a difference between the rate or price quoted by the name passing broker and that at which the transaction is ultimately concluded) the difference is settled in cash.

Guidance on this rule explains that when non-electronic arrangers are trying to achieve a mutual and immediate exchange of names based on a firm price there are inevitably sometimes occasions when the transaction is not completed at the original price (for instance because the firm quote has been hit by someone else). It points out that name passing brokers cannot take positions and therefore a name passing broker should not normally accept liability for differences and should provide its services on the basis that it does not do so. However where a difference arises the IPC does allow name passing brokers to compensate the market counterparty for some or all of the difference if it does so to preserve the relationship or for other legitimate commercial reasons and only in the form of money or discounted or rebated commission.

Where a price has been missed and a difference arises the firm acting as principal:

(a) should not in the ordinary course ask for compensation for the difference; and

(b) is normally expected to proceed at the next available price through the original name passing broker, rather than prejudice the smooth operation of the market.

However, the guidance accepts that the firm may not proceed with the transaction provided. If so it must first consider whether its withdrawal would affect the market and should not refuse to enter into the transaction at the new price if it would breach a reasonable expectation by the name passing broker that it would proceed. It should also notify the broker immediately if it is not going to proceed.

Generally brokers and arrangers should not "unfairly" favour one market counterparty client over another, unless that other has expressly agreed to the treatment.

Firms should not use brokers and arrangers as a form of private enquiry agent, placing orders in order to find out the identity of the broker's clients or information about transactions in which there is interest. The example given is that a firm which wants to buy 1,000 bonds should not use an arranger to buy 100 bonds in order to find out who the seller is and buy another 900 direct.

6.4.8   Adoption of Codes

In CP47 it was proposed that the IPC should adopt the Stock Lending and Repo Committee's Gilt Repo Code and Equity Repo Code and noted that other codes may also be relevant if those dealing in the relevant business generally expect others to observe the standards set out in the relevant code. This has now been watered down even further to say that the FSA does not endorse any other codes of practice but will take into account "the differing standards and practices operating in markets" in interpreting the application of the Principles to inter-professional business. In addition non-compliance with relevant codes may raise issues on the integrity and competence of authorised firms.

6.4.9   Good market practice

After the blend of rules and guidance in the body of the IPC (mostly guidance) Annex 3 sets out general guidance on good market practice which apparently has an even lower status in regulatory terms than normal guidance. It is closer to the blend of commercial sense, statements of the obvious and regulatory caution which used to characterise the London Code of Conduct.

For example it points out that confidentiality conditions are normally enforceable and can be broken by practices such as having loudspeakers in broking and dealing rooms which are close to other lines of communication (and can therefore be overheard).

At the negotiation stage of transactions it says that firms should agree expressly all the economic terms of a transaction before committing itself and should then negotiate the remaining terms in good faith as soon as possible. On the other hand it also says that firms should regard themselves as bound to transact once the rate or price and any other key commercial terms (it is not clear whether the FSA sees this as the same as "all the economic terms") have been agreed, whether orally or in writing, unless the parties explicitly and unambiguously agree to the contrary. The IPC's recommendation for "agreement" not to agree at this stage seems excessive. If one party makes it very clear that it is not contracting and will not do so until other terms are concluded or clearances obtained that is sufficient to prevent a contract arising. However, the general assumption that agreement on key market terms is sufficient to create a contract seems in line with English contract law, as well as market practice.

Some provisions relating to "firm" quotes which appeared as full-scale guidance in CP47 have been relegated to the lower level of "general information on good market practice" in the IPC. Firms are advised to follow market conventions regarding quotations unless they have specifically agreed otherwise with the counterparty. Essentially it should be clear to the market counterparty with whom the firm deals:

(a) whether or not the quote is firm;

(b) whether it is subject to conditions, and if so what they are;

(c) for how long the quote remains firm, though this is qualified by reference to the limited practicability of doing so in fast moving markets; and

(d) whether it is firm only for the normal marketable amount (if appropriate, otherwise the size of quote should be given).

Express clarification of these matters is not regarded as necessary to the extent that the quote is in accordance with the relevant market convention or exchange rule. This does, of course, beg the question of what market convention is in any particular case. It is possible that the guidance will affect conventions which are established in future.

Generally once a firm rate or price has been quoted to a market counterparty (directly or through a broker or arranger) the firm giving the quote must stick to it and neither withdraw it or refuse to deal on it during the firm period. Whatever the IPC says on this point, clearly it must not do so if it would be in breach of contract to do so. Some leeway is, however, given by the IPC if the firm gave the quote without knowing the identity of the counterparty and, once known, the name turns out to be unacceptable, for instance because of credit risk. Firms which wish to take advantage of this flexibility would be wise to make it clear that the acceptability of the market counterparty is a condition of the quote. Otherwise, unless they can prove a well known and generally accepted convention to that effect which has to be implied into the quote, they may find themselves bound as a matter of contract notwithstanding the apparent flexibility in the IPC.

Those who accept limit orders are warned that they should have policies on the circumstances in which, and terms on which, they will accept such orders and also systems and controls for carrying them out.

The approach now taken to out of office and out of hours dealing moves away from the London Code of Conduct. This, particularly out of office dealing, was viewed with deep suspicion by the London Code of Conduct as one of the most fruitful areas for malpractice. Changing business practices and technology have made it much more normal but the opportunities for abuse remain. The IPC, in line with its general approach of making firms responsible for looking after themselves, just says that it is good practice to issue guidelines to staff on transactions entered into outside normal hours or off-site, whether by mobile phone or otherwise. The guidelines are expected to cover:

(a) permitted types of transaction;

(b) permitted locations and counterparties;

(c) permitted limits;

(d) how and when such transactions should be booked into and recorded on front and back office systems; and

(e) how and when they are to be confirmed.

On the most practical level it is recommended that if answering machines are being used for instant reporting and recording of transactions which are effected off-site they should be installed and located so that they cannot be altered or erased without senior management approval. It is also said that it is positively bad practice for mobile phones to be used for business purposes from within the dealing room except in an emergency.

Moving on to the type of good practice it can be tempting to overlook but is important for proper functioning of the market, the guidance says that those who become aware of settlement errors in their favour should inform the counterparty promptly and reverse the error and brokers who become aware that they are holding assets for a counterparty because of a settlement error which adversely affects the latter should also promptly inform the relevant firm and try to rectify the situation.

For off-exchange business it is strongly recommended that confirmations should be exchanged in writing as soon as possible after the transaction is agreed or executed in order to reduce dealing errors and as an important element of control of the relevant business and exposures. It is recommended that the firm arranging a transaction should try to make sure that the parties agree who is to issue the relevant confirmation(s). Although one way confirmations are acceptable, if a firm makes significant use of one-way confirmations it should identify, and address in its risk control policies, the legal and other risks involved. Standard forms (under any relevant master agreement or market practice) should be used for confirmations unless there is a good reason not to do so.

It is emphasised that the point of confirmations is largely as a control. Thus electronic matching systems are an acceptable substitute for confirmations provided that they make and retain records of transactions which can be used by back offices to verify the details of transactions entered. Equally the relevant dealer should normally not issue or receive the confirmations, or even be responsible for checking them, and if the individual dealer is responsible for this he should be subject to independent monitoring.

It is said that it is good practice for firms to make and implement policies on the use of standard settlement instructions ("SSIs") in a secure and verifiable format, particularly when the firm has a relationship with a market counterparty under which there may be regular payment of significant amounts since the use of SSIs can reduce the incidence and size of differences from mistaken settlement of funds. However, unlike confirmations, firms arranging the relevant transaction are not expected to enquire into whether SSIs are in place.

The use of master agreements is encouraged and the FSA points out that **executed** documentation can and should be used as an effective risk management tool, particularly when it includes, as is normally the aim, valid close out netting provisions. Reference is made to the capital adequacy benefits of having such arrangements in place. The guidance goes on to say that if the firm has a policy of using master agreements it should also make and implement policies on what transactions should be subject to which master agreements and have systems and controls to enforce that policy. In addition if the policy is that transactions are only to be entered into once a master agreement is in place then exceptions to this policy should be subject to appropriately senior clearance. This is a recognition, and discouragement, of the fact that very frequently firms are very dilatory about negotiating and executing master agreements.

After passionate representations by brokers the FSA has included in the IPC, albeit in this lowest level of good practice information, a statement that it is good practice for firms acting as principals to pay brokerage bills promptly. The FSA had originally been minded to leave this as a commercial matter which it could not influence but it accepts that overdue payments can result in a regulatory capital hit for the unfortunate broker so the least the FSA can do is advocate prompt payment.

Finally the IPC statements of good practice recommend settling disputes between the parties, and where this cannot be done that established arbitration or mediation services should be used. Although the FSA is dropping out of providing the arbitration service it used to provide itself under the London Code of Conduct it does not list the main alternative providers such as the City Review Panel.

6.5   What the IPC does not require

The advantage of falling within the IPC is the exclusion of a great swathe of the Conduct of Business Rules which will apply to those doing non-IPC business with customers. The detail of those rules is set out in Chapter 5 of this Guide but it is worth noting here that among the provisions which will not apply are all the detailed rules on:

(a) communications disclosure of soft commission, disclosure of information about the firm, disclosure of charges, remuneration and commission;

(b) restrictions on exclusion of liability;

(c) financial promotion when the firm itself is making the communication, (rather than approving a communication by someone else);

(d) terms of business and customer agreements;

(e) know your customer, suitability, risk warnings;

(f) conflicts of interest, though the IPC itself addresses this area and it is also subject to the general law on the subject;

(g) churning and switching, dealing ahead, customer order priority, best and timely execution, aggregation and allocation;

(h) remedies against private customers, margin requirements, off-exchange dealing for and lending to them;

(i) programme trading; and

(j) almost as important as any of the above, all the multifarious record-keeping and reporting requirements relating to them.

The one area where the IPC was arguably more rigorous than the Conduct of Business Rules, that is, NMPTs, has now had rules and guidance equivalent to the IPC provisions inserted into the Conduct of Business Rules.

6.6 What still applies even though it is not covered by the IPC

Inevitably, it is not the case that those falling within the IPC really can ignore all 500 odd pages of the Conduct of Business Rules and other codes applying to regulated firms and refer only to the 30 odd pages of the IPC (in fact 19 pages plus definitions). Some provisions have to be considered before even falling within the IPC, notably customer classification. Others apply because of limitations on the definition of IPC business. The most important of these are the rules on safeguarding and administering client assets and money, which are excluded from the IPC and apply in full to any client assets and money held in the course of IPC business, subject to any waivers permitted and agreed because of the status of the client (e.g. a market counterparty can opt-out of client money protections). This is consistent with the current position under the SFA and IMRO Rules, where market counterparties are included in the definition of customer for the purposes of safekeeping and client money rules even though they are excluded for most other purposes.

Other areas which are excluded from the definition of IPC business and therefore subject to the mainstream Conduct of Business Rules are approving financial promotions for others and corporate finance business (although in the latter case the IPC may apply to some dealings done in the course of corporate finance business).

There are also parts of the regulatory system which apply separately and affect those doing IPC business. In particular:

(a) market professionals are naturally subject to Sections 118 to 131 of FSMA relating to the new "civil offence" of market abuse and to the Code of Market Conduct which is the statutory code which the FSA issues under Section 119 setting out its views on what might, and might not, amount to market abuse (*see* Chapter 7 of this Guide). It is worth noting that NMPTs may also be market abuse;

(b) "approved persons", that is, the individuals in authorised firms holding key positions of a type which require prior approval by the FSA (*see* Chapter 3 of this Guide), are subject to their own Principles and Code of Practice which apply directly and independently from the Principles applicable to their firm and are therefore not affected by the IPC's interpretation of the latter. Nevertheless despite the express statement in the IPC that the Approved Persons Code and Principles are not qualified or modified by the IPC it is inconceivable that the level of duties of approved persons would not in practice sometimes be affected by the fact that the business being done was IPC business.

Finally some of the Conduct of Business Rules simply continue to apply in any event, notably those on Chinese walls and personal account dealing.

6.7 Changes from the previous position – comparison tables

There are set out in an Appendix to this Chapter tables of some of the key differences between the IPC and the regime formerly applicable under the London Code of Conduct and the regime formerly applicable to SFA regulated business, together with key differences between the treatment of market counterparties. These tables are based on those supplied by the FSA in CP47, revised to take account of the "near final" text of the IPC on which this Chapter is based.

6.8 Transitional provisions

Generally there will be no transitional provisions for the application of the IPC and it will come into force in full at N2. This is subject to the very major qualification that there are complex transitional provisions relating to customer classification. In addition, as far as those firms who were previously subject to Section 43 of the FS Act (rather than regulation by the SFA or another self regulatory organisation) for the relevant business are concerned there is a one year period of grace (from the date of N2) before they are obliged to apply the new client money rules. If they take advantage of this transitional provision such firms must continue to comply with the Grey Paper provisions on segregation of money and other assets belonging to counterparties.

The transitional provisions for ex-Section 43 firms and for other previously authorised firms (referred to as "pre-N2 firms") on client classification differ.

Ex-Section 43 firms are again given a one year period of grace from the date of N2 for client classification purposes. Until that date they are allowed to treat all their former Section 43 clients (who may include some people who would under the new regime be intermediate or even private customers) as market counterparties. They must, however, conduct the new client classification exercise by the end of that one year period. While the ex-Section 43 firm is taking advantage of these transitional provisions on client classification it has to continue to comply with paragraphs 31-37 (on "know your customer" and "duties to clients") of the London Code of Conduct and the FSA will also continue to make its arbitration service available for disputes which arise in relation to business done in the pre-classification period.

Thus the IPC, although it will apply from N2, will not do so on a completely "clean" basis. It will have some elements of the London Code of Conduct overlaid on top of it for ex-Section 43 firms.

Pre-N2 firms are generally allowed to continue with previous classifications so that if they properly classified a client pre-N2 as a market counterparty or non-private customer that classification will continue in effect (in the case of market counterparties) or be automatically converted to an intermediate customer classification (in the case of non-private customers). A reclassification exercise would be needed, however, if a client was previously classified as a market counterparty only for a particular transaction or type of business or if the firm wished to take advantage of the new "opting up" provisions to reclassify an intermediate customer as a market counterparty.

The other point pre-N2 firms need to note is that there are no transitional provisions relating to the reclassification of other authorised firms and overseas financial services institutions. They automatically become market counterparties at N2 **unless** they are entitled to, and do, opt-down to intermediate customer status under COB 4.1.7R. In this context it is worth noting that the FSA in guidance on these transitional provisions says that the agreement of both firms (which is required for an effective "opting down") can be achieved by the client firm serving notice that it wishes to be treated as an intermediate customer and stating in the notice that agreement will be implied if the other firm continues to do business with it after N2. Firms will need to be on the watch for notices of this kind in order to object if they are not willing to accept the "opting-down", or to note and apply the classification if they are willing to accept it.

APPENDIX

Changes for Section 43 firms

Table A1

Existing arrangements for Section 43 firms	Proposed arrangements post-N2 covered elsewhere in the Handbook
1 Wholesale counterparties are divided into two groups: (a) core principals; and (b) end users.	It is proposed that investors will be categorised within one of three groups: (a) market counterparties; (b) intermediate customers; and (c) private customers.
2 Under Section 43 there is no requirement for individuals to be registered. The London Code of Conduct ("LCC") covers firms and employees, and holds firms liable for their employee's actions.	Specified groups of individuals will be subject to approval and covered by the Approved Persons Code.
3 No provisions for Chinese walls.	The IPC cross-refers to Chinese wall provisions in the Conduct of Business Sourcebook ("COB").
4 Requirements on record-keeping are currently drawn from the Grey Paper.	Record-keeping requirements appear in the Handbook. The IPC adds some guidance.
5 Client money segregation rules are currently drawn from the Grey Paper.	Client money rules in COB will apply.

Existing arrangements for Section 43 firms	Proposed arrangements post-N2 covered elsewhere in the Handbook
6 The LCC refers to the potential conflict of interest arising from employees dealing for their own account in any of the products covered by the LCC. (*See* paragraph 56 of LCC.)	Personal account dealing rules in COB will apply.
7 The LCC refers to money laundering guidelines and makes special provisions for name passing brokers. (*See* paragraph 20 of LCC.)	The FSA's rules on money laundering will appear in the Money Laundering Sourcebook.
8 Mismarking is a breach of the LCC, although guidance is not explicit.	The Interim Prudential Sourcebook for investment firms will take account of mismarking.
9 The LCC currently has a requirement for firms to train staff adequately. (*See* paragraph 16 of LCC.)	The requirements for training will appear as part of the Training and Competence Sourcebook, with a 24 month transitional period for current Section 43 business.
10 A single code is applicable for all relevant markets and also covers certain non-investment products.	The IPC covers all inter-professional investments in the same way. Non-investment products will be covered by a separate industry code.

Existing arrangements for Section 43 firms	Proposed arrangements post-N2 covered elsewhere in the Handbook
11 Undisclosed principal requirements: LCC requires listed firms to ensure that they properly consider the risks before undertaking such activity.	The Interim Prudential Sourcebook for investment firms will take account of undisclosed principal requirements.
12 The Grey Paper contains guidance on transaction reporting.	Transaction reporting will be covered in the Supervision Manual.

Table A2

Existing arrangements for Section 43 firms	IPC
1 LCC requires clarity on whether a quote is firm or indicative. (*See* paragraph 73.)	The IPC contains good market practice information on this subject. *See* Annex 3 – paragraphs 7-9.
2 Specific guidance is given on: (a) dealers/brokers visiting each other's dealing rooms and the location of business execution; and (b) the sharing of confidential or market sensitive information whereby the onus of confidentiality is placed on management.	The IPC contains good market practice information on confidentiality and out of hours/office dealings but these are less detailed (in comparison with the guidance in the LCC). *See* Annex 3, paragraphs 2, 3 and 12-14.
3 The LCC contains provisions on restricting entertainment, gifts and gambling.	The IPC provides guidance on undertaking marketing incentives, inducements and payments in kind in accordance with Principles 1 (integrity) and 5 (proper standards of market conduct). *See* MAR 3.4.13G – 3.4.16G.
4 The LCC recognises dealing mandates as useful in certain cases and gives guidance on their content where this is so.	The IPC does not contain guidance on dealing mandates for market counterparties as these are considered only appropriate for customer transactions.
5 Guidance is given on prompt payment of brokerage in the LCC.	The IPC contains a good market practice information on this subject.

Existing arrangements for Section 43 firms	IPC
6 Under the LCC, Section 43 firms are required to tape deals and keep them for two months or obliged to "persuade FSA" of why the firm is not taping. In the case of FSA arbitration of a dispute, particular relevance would be attached to the lack of taping.	The IPC contains guidance on records including taping which is less prescriptive than the LCC provisions. *See* MAR 3.6.1G – 3.6.11G.
7 The FSA offers mediation to Section 43 firms for disputes concerning activities under the guidance of the LCC.	The FSA will cease offering a mediation service in this area (except in relation to transactions which took place before the introduction of the IPC even though the dispute arose later) but supports the use of alternative dispute resolution procedures.
8 Some OTC transactions are regulated under the LCC and some by the SROs.	Level playing field (in regulatory terms) for all relevant OTC investment transactions (and normally for on-exchange transactions). *See* MAR 3.1.2R.
9 Confirmations: LCC provides guidance on the effect that confirms are exchanged and checked promptly.	IPC contains good market practice information on this subject which is less detailed (compared with the guidance in the LCC). *See* Annex 3, paragraph 17-23.

Existing arrangements for Section 43 firms	IPC
10 There are currently no provisions for exchange rules in the LCC.	In the case of exchange business, any statement on what the Principles do and do not require of a firm in a particular situation should be read subject to any exchange rule that applies.
11 Non-market price transactions ("NMPTs"): LCC has requirements on firms when conducting "historic rate rollovers" and "off-market rate" deals. The objective is to prevent fraud/concealment of losses.	The IPC has rules and guidance on this subject. Ultimately, the practical outcome will be the same, or slightly less onerous since the rules no longer require a sign-off from the counterparties. *See* MAR 3.5.1G – 3.5.21G.

Changes for SFA regulated firms

Table A3

Existing arrangements for SFA regulated firms	Proposed arrangements post-N2 covered elsewhere in the Handbook
1 Investors are classified into two broad categories: (a) non-customers, which comprise market counterparties; and (b) customers, which can be sub-divided into non-private and private.	It is proposed that investors will be categorised within one of three groups: (a) market counterparties; (b) intermediate customers; and (c) private customers.
2 Rule 5-3 of the SFA Rulebook deals with conduct regarding use of Chinese walls.	The IPC cross refers to Chinese walls provisions in COB.
3 Rule 5-54 of the SFA Rulebook deals with record-keeping.	Record-keeping requirements appear in the Handbook. The IPC adds some guidance.
4 Chapter 4 of the SFA Rulebook deals with segregation of customer assets and client money.	Client money rules in COB will apply.
5 Rule 5-51 in the SFA Rulebook relates to personal account dealing.	Personal account dealing rules in COB will apply.
6 Rules on money laundering safeguards can be found in SFA Board Notice 159.	The FSA's rules on money laundering will appear in the Money Laundering Sourcebook.

Existing arrangements for SFA regulated firms	Proposed arrangements post-N2 covered elsewhere in the Handbook
7 Market practice is covered in Principle 3 of the Principles of Business by which market counterparties must operate. Guidance is given in a few specific areas.	Standards of market conduct are specified within the Code of Market Conduct, as well as in the IPC.
8 Mismarking is considered a prudential issue and is, therefore, disciplinable under the FSA Principles.	The Prudential Sourcebook will take account of mismarking.
9 Misleading financial adverts and financial promotions: Rule 5-9 of the SFA Rulebook deals with advertising and marketing and applies generally to a firm.	Financial promotion: is covered in COB which will exempt market counterparties from rules and guidance on the subject when issuing, but not when approving, financial promotions.
10 Rule 5-40 within the SFA Rulebook refers to reportable transactions.	Transaction reporting rules will be in the Supervision Manual.
11 Currently, Rule 5-8 in the SFA Rulebook on soft commissions is switched off for inter-market counterparty deals.	IPC includes guidance on inducements.

Table A4

Existing SRO arrangements	IPC
1 No SRO rule on taping.	The IPC contains guidance on records including taping. *See* 3.6.1 to 3.6.11.
2 Currently the SRO Rulebooks have no guidance with regards to firmness of quotation.	IPC provides good market practice information on the firmness of quotation. *See* Annex 3 paragraphs 7-9.
3 Some OTC transactions regulated by the LCC and some by the SROs.	Unified regulatory regime for all OTC investment transactions (and generally for on-exchange transactions).
4 There is no requirement for firms to issue confirmations when dealing with market counterparties.	IPC provides good market practice information on this subject. *See* Annex 3, paragraph 17-23.
5 After hours/out of office dealing: no guidance currently.	The IPC provides good market practice information on this issue. *See* Annex 3, paragraph 12-14.
6 Passing of names: no guidance currently.	The IPC provides guidance on this issue. *See* MAR 3.7.3G.
7 Definition of a broker's role: no guidance at present. Are confined to activities of their relevant ISD category.	Some guidance is given on the role of the broker in the IPC *see* MAR 3.7. The permissions given to each broker will limit that broker's role.
8 Confidentiality: no requirements currently.	The IPC annex contains good market practice information on confidentiality. (*See* Annex 3, paragraphs 2 and 3).

Existing SRO arrangements	IPC
9 Stop loss orders: no specific requirements currently.	The IPC provides good market practice information on this issue. *See* Annex 3, paragraphs 10 and 11.
10 Exchanging of Standard Settlement Instructions ("SSIs"): no requirements currently.	The IPC provides good market practice information for exchange of SSIs in a simplified LCC format. *See* Annex 3, paragraphs 24 and 25.
11 Exchange rules: firms expected to follow exchange rules.	In the case of exchange business, any statement on what the Principles do and do not require of a firm in a particular situation should be read subject to any exchange rule that applies.
12 Negotiation of deals: no requirements currently.	IPC provides good market practice information on negotiation of deals. *See* Annex 3, paragraph 4-6.
13 Settlement of differences: no requirements currently.	Rules and guidance on how to settle differences in name passing business. *See* MAR 3.7.4R-3.7.8G.
14 Marketing incentives: no requirement currently.	The IPC provides guidance on marketing incentives, inducements and payments in kind. *See* MAR 3.4.13G-3.4.16G.
15 Third party codes: no inclusion currently.	The IPC also does not include third party codes.

Existing SRO arrangements	IPC
16 Master agreements: currently no requirements.	The IPC offers good market practice guidance on master agreements. *See* Annex 3 paragraphs 26-27.
17 Deals using a connected broker: no specific requirement currently beyond general requirements on "conflicts of interest".	Guidance now focuses on disclosure. *See* MAR 3.4.7G–3.4.9G.
18 Non-market price transactions: no specific provisions currently.	Rules and guidance in IPC. *See* MAR 3.5.1G-3.5.21G.

Table A5

Summary of differences in protections for dealing, arranging and related advice to be given to market counterparties and intermediate customers

	Market counterparty	*Intermediate customer*
Know your customer	No	Yes
Suitability	No	Yes, limited
Customers understanding of risk	No	No
Information about the firm	No	Yes
Disclosure of charges	No	No
Conflict of interest and material interest	Some disclosure	Yes
Churning/switching	No	Yes, but limited
Dealing ahead	No	Yes
Customer order priority	No	Yes
Best execution	No	Yes, but opt-out allowed
Timely execution	No	Yes
Allocation	No	Yes
Confirmations	Guidance	Yes, but flexibility
Fair and clear comments	Communication not to be misleading	Principle 7 applies in full

	Market counterparty	*Intermediate customer*
Marketing incentives, inducements	Guidance	Yes
Customer assets	Yes	Yes
Client money	Yes, but opt-out allowed	Yes, but opt-out allowed

Chapter 7

MARKET CONDUCT AND THE MARKET ABUSE REGIME

Tamasin Little
Partner, Financial Services Group
Charles Abrams
Partner
SJ Berwin

7.1　　Introduction

The Code of Market Conduct (the "Code") which forms the first chapter of the Market Conduct Section of the FSA Handbook is a Code which the Financial Services Authority (the "FSA") is required to produce under Section 119 of FSMA in order to give "appropriate guidance to those determining whether or not behaviour amounts to market abuse". It fulfils a unique function under the FSMA, perhaps even a unique function in all UK legislation. It is a new tool of statutory interpretation under which a body (other than the courts or Parliament itself) provides guidance which is given some statutory force by Section 122 FSMA. Section 122 provides that generally the Code (as in force at the time particular behaviour takes place) has a strong evidential character which can be relied on so far as it indicates whether or not that behaviour should be taken to amount to market abuse. Moreover if the Code positively states that the relevant behaviour does not in the FSA's opinion amount to market abuse, Section 122 goes further and provides that such behaviour **will not be** market abuse for the purposes of FSMA. The FSA is therefore able in the Code to provide definitive safe-harbours from the legislation. In providing them the FSA has gone further than might have been expected and has made the offence much fairer (and narrower) than appears in FSMA.

Given that the Code is an interpretation tool, not a stand-alone set of rules it is necessary to read the Code together with Sections 119 to 131 of the FSMA relating to the offence of market abuse. The FSA has issued for consultation several drafts of the Code and this Chapter describes the latest version which was issued with a detailed policy statement in April 2001. The FSA has stated that this version will be the final one but if there are any changes this Chapter must be read in light of them.

7.2 Overview

The new offence of market abuse, which is set out in Part VIII of the FSMA, is the only truly novel part of the new regime. It is an offence which can be committed by anyone, not just FSMA-authorised firms, even without any intention to abuse the market or otherwise do anything which involves committing the offence, even merely by unknowingly issuing a misleading takeover offer document or other company circular, and, in the case of markets in or accessed electronically from the UK, even by conduct outside the UK. Accordingly, it can be committed even by honest directors or employees of quoted companies or their subsidiaries and even by non-UK securities firms or banks without a UK branch.

The new offence will apply not only to firms authorised in the UK under the FSMA and non-UK securities firms and banks but also to any other person and is not restricted to "market participants", as the Government had originally indicated. References in this Chapter to "firms", include not only stockbrokers, broker-dealers, investment or commercial banks and investment or fund managers, and individuals working for them but also all these other persons. The offence is based on the existing criminal offences of insider dealing (contained in Part V of the Criminal Justice Act 1993) and market manipulation (currently in Section 47 of the Financial Services Act 1986 (the "FS Act") and replicated in Section 397 FSMA) both of which will continue but it goes much wider and is more uncertain in scope.

The FSA will police and enforce the new offence and will be empowered to impose an unlimited fine on "market abusers" or issue public censures and obtain injunctions and remedial orders against them; it can also require the "abuser" to compensate everyone who suffered loss as a result of the market abuse (even if they are not his clients or counterparties) and to surrender any profits made by him (Section 384 FSMA). In addition, the FSA can impose an unlimited fine on anyone who has required or encouraged another person to engage in market abuse, and, again, can require him to pay compensation and to surrender his profits from the abuse (referred to below together as "restitution").

One of the policies behind the introduction of the new offence is to enable action to be taken against an offender who is not a FSMA-authorised firm or someone employed by a FSMA-authorised firm (a "FSMA-regulated person") for behaviour falling short of the criminal offences of insider dealing and market manipulation but which nonetheless is considered to prejudice the integrity of the market. The FSA will often be able to impose unlimited fines on FSMA-regulated persons, and throw them out of the industry, for failing to comply with its regulatory requirements to conduct their business with integrity and observe proper standards of market conduct. In these cases, it therefore does not need to allege the new offence against them at all. Accordingly, it is likely that the persons who will be prosecuted by the FSA will often be outside the regulatory regime and amongst the most likely candidates for accusations of market abuse would therefore be market practitioners who are not FSMA-regulated persons. It should, however, be noted that the FSA has indicated that it will prosecute FSMA-regulated persons for market abuse (or, indeed, insider dealing or market manipulation) if the alleged facts are sufficient.

There are, in fact, four separate offences relating to market abuse. There are three primary ones: misusing inside information and other non-public information, creating false or misleading impressions (which can be referred to in short as "misleading the market" provided that it is remembered that the offence does not need to have anything to do with the market at all and covers misleading even just one person) and distorting the market, which appear in Section 118 of the FSMA. There is also a secondary one: requiring or encouraging someone else to commit market abuse (which appears only in the penalty provisions in Section 123). It is only the first three offences which are technically the offences of market abuse. Importantly, in their case, the offending behaviour is only market abuse if it is likely to be regarded by a reasonable "regular user" of the relevant market as "a failure on the part of the person concerned to observe the standard of behaviour reasonably expected of a person in his position in relation to the market". This is a very helpful requirement as it means that in many cases non-practitioners will not commit the offence. However, it is in itself probably of little help to investment firms, even if they are from outside the UK (but *see* below), or to directors of quoted companies which issue misleading company circulars.

The FSMA defines "behaviour" to cover both action and inaction (Section 118(10)), and therefore any failure to correct a mistake or indeed to file required information (e.g. that a particular holding of shares has been bought or sold) could in itself constitute market abuse. Behaviour will constitute market abuse only if it occurs in relation to qualifying investments traded on a prescribed market. However, there is no need for the market abuse to relate to on-market dealings. Indeed, market abuse can be engaged in without any securities transaction at all, whether on or off market. This was made abundantly clear by the Economic Secretary to the Treasury (Melanie Johnson MP) in a debate in the Commons Committee on 2 November 1999, when she gave as an example of market abuse the issue of a misleading press release by a UK quoted company. Indeed, the issue of any circular or even individual letter which contains a misleading statement can in itself be market abuse, if for example the misleading statement would lead someone to buy or sell securities.

Importantly for firms outside the UK, the offence does not have any territorial limitations as such. The offence can therefore be committed by conduct outside the UK and this extra-territorial application goes far further than in the case of the existing criminal offences of insider dealing and market manipulation (which will as noted above, also continue). This means that non-UK firms will have to be fully aware of the scope of the market abuse offence.

7.3   Extra-territorial effect

The Treasury can prescribe for the purposes of market abuse any markets they like, even if the market is outside the UK. However at present the Treasury in FSMA (Prescribed Markets and Qualifying

Exchanges) Order 2001 has only prescribed those markets which are from time-to-time established under the rules of a UK recognised investment exchange. These are at present the London Stock Exchange, LIFFE, the LME, the IPE, OM London, virt-x plc (formerly Tradepoint), COREDEAL and Jiway. The formulation used in the Order will pick up new UK recognised investment exchanges as and when they are recognised.

However, even behaviour which is clearly outside the UK can be treated as constituting market abuse if it relates to qualifying investments traded on a prescribed market which is situated in the UK which can be accessed electronically from the UK. This is because behaviour can be treated as occurring "in relation to" qualifying investments even if it does not relate to the particular investments themselves. Section 118(6) of the FSMA spells out that behaviour will be regarded as occurring in relation to qualifying investments even if it relates only to their subject matter (e.g. silver since silver futures are prescribed), or to anything whose price or value is expressed by reference to the price or value of those investments (e.g. spread betting on securities quoted in London) or, indeed, if it occurs in relation to investments based on or referenced to qualifying investments traded on a UK exchange (e.g. options or contracts for differences on shares quoted on the London Stock Exchange). Accordingly, the grant by a broker-dealer in New York to a buyer in Zurich of an option over shares quoted in London will be market abuse if he had inside information about the shares at the time he granted it. Similarly, behaviour in Canada relating to a particular silver mine is covered merely because silver futures are traded on the London Metal Exchange. Accordingly, if a silver producer in Canada sells a quantity of silver at below market price, because he needs to find funds to pay a tax bill, and it was reasonable for market players to think that this low price was only because he had a large supply of silver (which he did not) so that the price of silver (and silver futures) consequently fell, he could in principle be treated as committing the market abuse of misleading the market.

The fact that there is no need for the market abuse to relate to on-market dealings, or indeed any dealings at all, only widens the scope of the offence even more. If a New York newspaper publishes a report about a company quoted in London which is false or misleading, the journalist could be guilty of market abuse, and subject to an unlimited fine, even if he wrote his report when in New York. It is easy to see why non-UK internet service providers publishing articles by companies on websites they are hosting have grounds for concern.

7.4   Markets and investments covered

As mentioned above, under the Prescribed Markets and Qualifying Investments Order 2001 all markets established under the rules of a UK recognised investment exchange are prescribed for the purposes of the market abuse regime. Investments qualify if they fall under the very broad definition of investments specified under Section 22 of the FSMA by the Regulated Activities Order 2001 ("RAO") **and** are traded on one of the relevant markets. Because there was some doubt as to whether "traded" meant that there actually had to be a market transaction, rather than being merely a description of the investments, the Government spelled out in Committee in the House of Commons that the latter was the correct interpretation (as indeed seems quite clear from the terms of the offence).

The FSA in the Code expands on this by confirming that "traded on" a prescribed market means "traded subject to the rules of" that market and by setting out the categories of investments which would be regarded as being "traded on" a prescribed market (MAR 1.11.3G). They include not only those which are currently traded on that market but also those which have not yet traded (which will be regarded as traded on that market from the moment that they start trading, including the first trade) and those which have been so traded in the past and can still be traded under the market's rules, even if trading is not active. However, it also points out (as a matter of guidance only) that generally unless there is an ongoing market it is unlikely that behaviour will amount to market abuse. This is because it is unlikely that the other conditions for the offence will be satisfied because market participants are unlikely to rely on the relevant market for price discovery or formation and trading which is not associated with that market is unlikely to damage confidence in the market. Although helpful, this does not seem entirely persuasive; for example, the price of the market transaction may be misleading, and damaging confidence in the market is no longer a required part of the offence as it was in its first draft. Accordingly, this FSA statement must not be regarded as meaning that the possibility of market abuse can definitely be ignored if there is no ongoing market.

7.5   Important points when reading the Code

There are a few important points to bear in mind when reading the Code:

(a) it is not an exclusive or exhaustive description of market abuse. Despite its importance as an interpretative tool it is still possible for the FSA, Tribunal or courts to find someone guilty of market abuse based directly on the statute. Equally, the FSMA makes it clear that the FSA's opinion that particular behaviour constitutes market abuse is not determinative, albeit that it is persuasive. Accordingly, the allegation of market abuse can be rebutted not only by showing that the facts alleged by the FSA are not correct but also by showing that, even if they are correct, they do not amount to market abuse. A finding by the FSA of market abuse can be appealed to the independent Financial Services and Markets Tribunal and then, on a point of law, to the courts; a decision that proven behaviour constitutes market abuse would be just such a point of law which can be appealed against to the courts;

(b) complying with the Code does not exempt anyone from compliance with all the other laws, rules and regulations applicable to them, including, for instance, those relating to insider dealing or market manipulation, and, in the case of FSMA-regulated persons the very general Statements of Principle which require them to comply with high standards of market conduct, a much more general high level obligation which may not be satisfied by merely avoiding committing market abuse;

(c) the Code itself uses a complex notation system giving different weight to different provisions in it. Paragraphs marked "C" are full-scale safe harbours under Section 122(1) of the FSMA and so narrow the scope of the offence. Paragraphs marked "E" are statements of the FSA's opinion which are given evidential force under Section 122(2) but do not necessarily narrow the scope of the offence although, probably, they do bind the FSA. Sections marked "G" are technically not part of the Code and not to be relied on under Section 122 but are only guidance given under the FSA's general powers to give guidance under Section 157; accordingly they may not even bind the FSA as the Government refused to accept an amendment proposed by the Opposition Treasury Team that guidance should be binding;

(d) the FSA is obliged under Section 124 to issue a statement of its policy on penalties in relation to market abuse. That statement of policy forms part of the Enforcement Manual and is not dealt with in this Chapter;

(e) although the FSA is a quasi-legislator in issuing the Code under Section 119 FSMA, it is also a prosecutor which imposes and enforces penalties under Section 123 FSMA. The accused can refer the case to the independent Financial Services and Markets Tribunal for it to determine the allegation of market abuse itself; this is not technically an appeal because the Tribunal is empowered to hear the case again from scratch (technically, *de novo*). It is only the possibility of a reference to the Tribunal that prevents the FSA being also a judge; however, even if the accused does not refer the case to the Tribunal, the Government is of the view that the FSA should not be regarded as acting as a judge even though it decides that its allegations are proven and it imposes a penalty. Appellants to the Tribunal who are individuals can obtain some legal assistance before the Tribunal if the FSA imposes a penalty (Section 134 FSMA). Appeal to the court from the Tribunal can only be made on points of law, although this includes a decision of the Tribunal on whether proven behaviour constitutes market abuse at all;

(f) there has been extensive debate as to how far the market abuse regime is a "criminal" rather than (as it purports to be) a "civil" one and, to the extent that it is, the impact this has on both the standard of proof and the rights which the accused have under the Human Rights Act 1998 and the European Convention on Human Rights. This debate is not covered in detail in this Chapter. However, where the FSA is seeking to impose a fine (or, as the FSMA calls it, a "penalty", which sounds less criminal) the regime is more properly classified for ECHR purposes as criminal, rather than civil. Indeed, the Treasury stated in writing on 14 May 1999, in evidence to the Joint Committee (of both Houses of Parliament) on Financial Services and Markets (the Burns Committee), which in a novel form of pre-legislative scrutiny reviewed the draft Bill before it was formally put into Parliament, that it accepted that there was a "real possibility" that proceedings for market abuse penalties would be treated as criminal for ECHR purposes, even though they were civil for UK domestic law purposes. It should be noted, however, that the FSA states in the Code that it considers that only the civil "balance of probabilities" standard of proof applies to charges of market abuse. However, this approach does not appear to be clearly justified on the case law even in UK domestic law and it is outlawed by the ECHR where the offence is criminal for ECHR purposes (*see* above). In addition, the fundamental ECHR "due process" requirement of a fair hearing by an impartial and independent tribunal (Article 6(1)) applies even if market abuse is civil for ECHR purposes. It is for this very reason that the concept of a Tribunal hearing an appeal from scratch was introduced into the FSMA. For the same reason, in the Government's, the FSA does not have to comply with the "due process" requirement even if there is no reference to the Tribunal; it is acting only as a prosecutor not as a judge;

(g) the Code correctly spells out the statutory tests which must be satisfied in order to establish (primary) market abuse (MAR 1.1.3G). These are:

(i) the behaviour must occur in relation to qualifying investments traded on a prescribed market;

(ii) the behaviour must fall in at least one of the three categories of "abusive behaviour" (*see* Section 7.6 below); and

(iii) the regular market user must be likely to regard the behaviour as falling below the appropriate standards.

In each of its sections dealing with the three categories of abusive behaviour, the Code calls the behaviour "market abuse". However, as the Code states in the first paragraph of each section detailing the categories of abusive behaviour, it is assuming that test (i) is satisfied. It should, of course, also have assumed that test (iii) is satisfied. Unless it is, the behaviour is not market abuse even if it satisfies tests (i) and (ii). This is a rather unfortunate omission, especially as test (iii) is often a helpful statutory defence and the FSA knows that it cannot be satisfied merely because the FSA think that it is.

7.6　The three basic types of market abuse

The three primary categories of market abuse are:

(a) behaviour which is based on information that is not generally available to those using the market but which, if available to him, would or would be likely to be regarded by a regular user of the market as relevant when deciding the terms on which he would buy or sell (or effect another transaction in) the relevant investment (Section 118(2)(a));

(b) behaviour which is likely to give a regular user of the market a false or misleading impression of the supply of, demand for or value or price of an investment of the kind in question (Section 118(2)(b));

(c) behaviour which a regular user of the market would, or would be likely to, regard as likely to distort the market in investments of the kind in question (Section 118(2)(c)).

7.7　No need for intention

None of the three main heads of market abuse have any requirement that the alleged "abuser" should have intended (either positively or by reckless or negligent disregard of the possible effect of the behaviour in question) to commit the offence. An element of intention may perhaps be implied in the first head (misuse of information) in the sense that the behaviour must be "based on" the information which is not generally available. It is difficult to see how this can be the case unless the accused intended to use the information. However, even that was not entirely clear until the FSA provided a safe harbour where the abusive behaviour is not "influenced" by the information (MAR 1.4.21 C).

What is clear is that the Government, though pressed very hard and repeatedly by the Opposition with the argument that no-one should be found guilty of market abuse unless he had some intention to mislead the market, or at least some anticipation that the market might be misled, refused to introduce any such requirement. The Treasury also refused the calls for an intent requirement which were made by three of the main associations of market practitioners: the London Investment Banking Association ("LIBA"), the Association of Private Client Investment Managers and Stockbrokers ("APCIMS") and the British Bankers' Association ("BBA") and, because they were well aware of the risks which the new offence might pose to their members, also the Confederation of British Industry ("CBI"). The Government emphasised repeatedly that market abuse was to be an "effect-based" offence rather than a "intent-based" one and that its purpose was to protect the market rather than to penalise transgressors. There are, however, very extensive potential penalties and, indeed, the offence is not really even "effect-based". On the wording of the FSMA it is quite possible to be guilty of market abuse if the effect could be said to be "likely" even if it did not in fact occur, no-one was misled and the market was not distorted in any way. It is evident that the offence is supposed to be a deterrent rather than merely something which protects the market. What is not evident is how someone can be deterred from doing something he did not know he was doing.

7.8   The regular market user test

Instead of an "intention" or "*mens rea*" requirement of the FSMA qualifies the three main heads of market abuse by saying that in each case the behaviour in question needs to be likely to be regarded by a regular user of that market who is aware of the behaviour as a failure on the part of the person or persons concerned to observe the standard of behaviour reasonably expected of a person in his or their position in relation to the market (Section 118(1)(c)).

The "regular user" in relation to any particular market is defined as "a reasonable person who regularly deals on that market in investments of the kind in question". He may therefore differ depending both on the market in question and on the relevant type of investments. He is meant to be a sophisticated market equivalent of the "man on the Clapham Omnibus".

The "regular user" test was introduced by the Government to bring in an "objective" standard, but it seems actually to introduce a subjective standard by using the presumed likely opinion of those firms which are likely to be regarded as "regular users". It seems fairer to create a more truly objective test, by seeing whether the behaviour falls short of the standards reasonbly expected of a person in the position and with the attributes of the accused (which would be similar to the UK test for negligence by a director). That approach was, however, rejected by the Government. The "regular user" test seems to make the position rather worse for market practitioners and, indeed, the FSA, but the Government would not move from it. Essentially, therefore, a compliance officer advising his firm (or an FSA prosecutor considering whether to bring a prosecution) has to put himself in the position of a regular market user and then decide what view that regular market user would take of the behaviour. Accordingly, the market abuse offence of "misleading the market" is going to be committed by anyone doing anything which might be misunderstood by a regular user of the market, provided only that in the view of the regular user he should have known better. The scope for differences of opinion as to what a "regular user" of a market may think is obvious. Users of the markets, and their views on what is acceptable, vary widely.

The FSA has tackled this question in the Code by setting out its own views on what is required under the "regular user" test. Many of the FSA's views on what it considers the expectations of a regular market user are helpful both in clarifying the offence and in introducing an element of intent (*see* below). Essentially at a number of points, it assumes that a market user has some moral sense which condemns intentional bad behaviour much more than accidents. The Code says (MAR 1.2.5E-6E) that although intention is not essential for behaviour to fall below the objective standards required in some circumstances the determination whether behaviour falls short of those standards will depend on the purpose of the alleged abuser. A mistake is considered by the FSA to be unlikely to fall below the standards required provided that the person concerned has taken reasonable care to prevent and detect the occurrence of such mistake.

Nevertheless one of the points put forcefully in consultation was that it is not appropriate for the FSA as regulator rather than market user to say what a regular market user might or might not expect. The FSA in its response to consultation accepted that it could not set itself up as the regular user nor could it require the regular user to act in any particular way, take any particular factor into account or give any specific weight to a particular factor. Nevertheless it considered that it could give guidance on the behaviour which, in its opinion, the regular user would be likely to consider as amounting to market abuse and the standards he is likely to accept. This must be correct. The Code is required to give guidance to those seeking to determine whether or not behaviour amounts to market abuse. The regular user test is a key element of the definition of market abuse and it would therefore be a failing if the Code did not address that element.

It remains, however, dangerous territory. This is partly because of the normative effect of the FSA's statements in the Code which could by shifting the expectations of market users, or some market users, diminish market efficiency if inappropriate. At the other extreme, it is also partly because the FSA's views on what the views of the regular market user would be may clearly be overruled and, even before that, might be widely rejected by the markets. In either case their removal would potentially damage or unbalance the remainder of the Code.

A number of the FSA's general statements about the regular user test in MAR 1.2 are uncontroversial. It says (in MAR 1.2.3E) that a hypothetical reasonable person familiar with the market in question would consider all the circumstances of the behaviour including:

(a) the characteristics of the market, the investments traded on it and its users. The example given is that the disclosure standards currently expected in equity markets differ from those in commodities markets;

(b) the rules and regulations of the market in question and any applicable laws;

(c) prevailing market mechanisms, practices; and

(d) the position of the person in question and the standards reasonably to be expected of that person at that time in the light of that person's experience, level of skill and standard of knowledge.

Thus it says that the standards which it would be reasonable to expect from a retail investor are likely to be different from those to be expected of an industry professional (MAR 1.2.3(4)E) and when considering the standards to be expected of public sector bodies it is likely to be relevant to take into account their statutory and other official functions (MAR 1.2.7G).

Going a little further the Code offers a limited degree of protection against the extra-territorial effect of the market abuse provisions by saying that if a person is based overseas it may be relevant to consider the extent to which the behaviour is in compliance with the standards prevailing in that overseas jurisdiction. As a matter of guidance only, the FSA says that where relevant behaviour takes place on an overseas market (but has an effect on a prescribed UK market) the regular user is likely to consider it relevant to have regard to local rules, practices and conventions in the overseas market and whether or not the person concerned is in the UK (MAR 1.2.9G). It stresses, however that compliance with such rules will not of itself be determinative. It is however not clear that the regular market user would expect a local firm acting only in its overseas market to have regard to anything other than its local rules, practices and conventions. The COMARC also addresses the situation where an overseas firm or investor deals directly into the prescribed market; it confirms that compliance with local standards "may" be relevant to the view formed by the regular market user (MAR 1.2.3(2)E). However, the Economic Secretary (Melanie Johnson MP) stated in the 2 November 1999 debate in the Commons Committee that the regular market user would expect such a person to deal in accordance (only) with his local standards and the regular market user would probably indeed take that view, unless perhaps the alleged abuser was aware that the behaviour was not allowed in the UK.

In some other respects the pronouncements of the Code on the regular user test are a little more controversial. It adds as a basic consideration which a regular user would, in its view, always bear in mind "the need for market users to conduct their affairs in a manner that does not compromise the fair and efficient operation of the market as a whole or unfairly damage the interests of investors". While this may be desirable there are plenty of market theorists who would not say that fairness is a necessary part of efficiency nor that all market users should necessarily conduct their affairs to avoid damage to investors, or at least "unfair" damage, whatever that might be.

This attribution of morality to the markets is taken a step further when the Code goes on to say that regular users would only find it relevant, not determinative, that the behaviour conforms with standards that are generally accepted by market users. According to the FSA the fact that the users of a particular market do accept a particular standard of behaviour does not necessarily make it acceptable. Indeed the fact that behaviour complies with the rules of the relevant recognised investment exchange, the Takeover Code or even the FSA's Code own rules, all of which firms are not merely expected but actually required to obey, is also regarded by the FSA as a matter which a regular market user would regard as relevant, not determinative (apart from certain specific rules for which safe harbours are given, *see* below). In its answers to consultation the FSA gave the example of a large on-exchange position, properly built up in accordance with exchange (and presumably the Takeover Code) rules might form part of a strategy of behaviour amounting to market abuse (paragraph 5.9 of the 21 April policy statement).

The Code takes the line that the regular user test is looking at whether the behaviour in question is acceptable, not whether it is actually accepted. Where standards are generally accepted (or a range of practices are generally accepted) such standards will, in the FSA's view, only be acceptable where they promote the fair and efficient operation of the market as a whole and do not unfairly damage the interests of investors.

In fact the FSMA does not refer to either "accepted" nor "acceptable" behaviour. The question is whether the alleged abuser met the standards reasonably "expected". It seems reasonable to take the view that regular users expect what is actually accepted and happens (provided that the "accepted" behaviour is known to regular market users and universally, or at least generally, accepted), not what would happen if the world and the markets were "fair". The alternative approach adopted by the Code is more like a teacher or regulator saying mournfully "I expected better of you". Indeed, it is arguable that a regular market user would not regard any behaviour as falling short of expected standards if there is no intent to engage in the activities constituting market abuse, or recklessness or negligence in doing so, or if the behaviour results from a mere mistake (and even if there were no protective procedures in place as required by the FSA). This is therefore an area where the FSA may be vulnerable to the criticism that in assessing the likely views of a regular market user it is putting itself in the place of the market user.

The FSA does say that it does not expect there to be many cases where accepted standards are lower than those expected by the regular user and indicates that if such a case arises the FSA will consider giving further guidance rather than proceeding direct to enforcement actions. In its response to consultation the FSA said that enforcement action rather than guidance or supervision might be appropriate when the behaviour is "egregious or heinous and quite clearly abusive".

7.9   Misuse of information

There are four elements to this first head of market abuse, apart from the regular user/standards of behaviour test:

7.9.1   *Based on information*

(a) the behaviour must be based on information;

(b) the information must not be generally available;

(c) the information must be such that, if available to a regular user of the market, would or would be likely to be regarded by him as relevant when deciding the terms on which transactions in the investment in question should be effected;

(d) the information must relate to matters which the regular user would reasonably expect to be disclosed to users of the particular market involved.

Arguably unnecessarily, since this requirement is written into the statute itself, the Code gives a specific safe harbour for dealing or arranging deals where possession of the relevant information did not influence the person in question's decision to deal or arrange a deal (MAR 1.4.21C). In addition, but only as explanation rather than a formal safe harbour, the Code says that it will be presumed that the information did not affect the decision if a firm decision had been taken to deal before having the information and the terms of the proposed transaction did not alter after the information was received (MAR 1.4.22E). In addition where the person concerned is an organisation within which only some individuals have the relevant information it will be presumed (MAR 1.4.23E) that such possession had no influence on the decision to deal or arrange the deal if none of those individuals:

(a) had any involvement in the decision to deal/arrange the deal;

(b) behaved in such a way as to influence, directly or indirectly, the decision to engage in the dealing or arranging; or

(c) had any contact with those who were involved in the decision making whereby the information could be passed on.

This explanation of circumstances where it can be presumed that the information did not influence the decision making (and therefore the dealing was not based on the information so there was no market abuse) leads on to a specific safe harbour for effective Chinese walls or arrangement or equivalent to them in relation to the particular information (MAR 1.4.24C). (A Chinese wall is defined as an arrangement which requires information held by a person in the course of carrying on one part of its business to be withheld from or not to be used for persons with or for whom it acts in the course of carrying on another part of its business.) It is worth noting the stress on an "effective" Chinese wall. A Chinese wall may in practice sometimes be broken by the chief executive overlooking the wall or even information being passed through the compliance department. In addition, the Chinese wall will not be "effective" if an individual behind it requires or encourages a person in front of it to deal or arrange deals which the individual behind the Chinese wall on the basis of material information which he knows to be not generally available, even if the person in front of it does not know the information.

Finally in this context an express safe harbour is given where the dealing or arranging was required in order to comply with a legal (including contractual) or regulatory obligation in circumstances where the obligation existed before the relevant information was in the person's possession (MAR 1.4.20C). In these circumstances it is not clear whether it matters that the terms of the deal might change after receipt of the information. Logically it should matter and arguably if the terms change it is no longer a "pre-existing" obligation.

7.9.2   Not generally available

There was a good deal of debate during the consultation process over what amounted to information being "generally available". The FSA in the Code have taken a liberal approach to the subject (MAR 1.4.5-8). Section 118(7) of the FSMA says that information can be treated as being generally available if it can be obtained by research or analysis conducted by or on behalf of market users. The FSA adds to this that information which has been obtained through any "other legitimate means" including observation of a public event and any information which is discussed in a public area or can be observed by the public without infringing rights of privacy, property or confidentiality" can be regarded as generally available. Specific examples given of information which is regarded as "generally available" are formal material such as:

(a) information disclosed to a prescribed market through an accepted channel for dissemination of information or otherwise under the rules of the market; or

(b) information contained in records which are open to inspection by the public;

but also material of a less formal nature such as:

(c) information otherwise made public, including through the Internet or some other publication, or which is derived from information which has been made public; or

(d) information which can be obtained by observation, giving the famous hypothetical case of a passenger on a train seeing a burning factory and promptly calling his broker to sell shares in the factory's owner.

These examples show that "generally available" is interpreted very widely in the Code. The fact that most market users do not have the information does not prevent it being "generally available". Thus FSA guidance gives as an example of information which might be obtained by research information which is available only overseas and has not been published or otherwise made available in the UK or information which is only available on payment or a fee. The Code says that "the fact that in practice other users of the market cannot obtain the information because of limitations in their resources, expertise or competence does not mean that the information cannot legitimately be obtained".

This liberal approach to the meaning of "generally available" is helpful in encouraging wide ranging research and analysis. It is perhaps a little less helpful in identifying wrong doing because it does not address the position where someone has information which is subject to rights of privacy, property or confidentiality in his hands (including classic "inside" information) but which is also "generally available" because, for instance, it has been put on the Internet in an obscure site in another language. Having the restricted information early enables one to overleap those who only obtained the information legitimately. In the field of intellectual property and confidential information this is known as the "springboard effect."

When considering the offence of insider dealing this was not an issue. Until the price sensitive information was made public through the official channels it could not be used. Once it had been made public it could be used. The line for "generally available" information is much less clear. The statements in the Code that people are free to use information they have obtained by legitimate means implies that they are not free to use information they have obtained by illegitimate means and possibly not even information that they know or believe to have been obtained by others illegitimately. But that is not said expressly in the Code and is not what Section 118(2) says. Section 118(2) is just concerned with whether the information is "generally available" or not. Merely putting the information on the Internet would seem to make it public and therefore "generally available" even if the information in question was an insider tip of deeply confidential price sensitive information (though *see* below on whether the act of putting it on the Internet would amount to requiring or encouraging others to commit market abuse).

7.9.3   *Relevant information*

The Code sets out factors which it thinks a regular user would consider in deciding whether a particular piece of information was or was not relevant. They include how far it is:

(a) specific and precise (a term picked up from insider dealing legislation where anything less was not considered to be inside information);

(b) material;

(c) current;

(d) reliable, including how near the person providing the information is, or appears to be, to the original source of the information and the reliability of that source. Thus, although it is not necessary for the information in question to be "inside" information for the offence to be committed if it is inside information it is more likely to be "relevant" and thus involve commission of the offence if it is acted on;

and whether:

(a) there is other material information which is generally available to inform the market;

(b) the information differs from information which is generally available and can therefore be said to be new or fresh information;

(c) if it relates to possible future developments, whether the information provides with reasonable certainty grounds to conclude that those developments will actually happen; and

(d) if it relates to possible future developments, the significance those developments would assume for the market user if they did occur.

The specific examples of relevant information given in the Code (MAR 1.4.11) are all fairly straightforward:

(a) in the case of a share issued by a company or a derivative on it, information on the business affairs or prospects of the company as a related company would be relevant;

(b) in the case of a commodity derivative information or events affecting the deliverable supplies of the commodity, such as information on the business operations of major suppliers would be relevant; and

(c) more generally information on official statistics and fiscal and monetary announcements before they are made could be relevant.

The Code does give two more express safe harbours for dealing or arranging deals based on trading information or (in limited circumstances) in relation to takeover bids. Absent such safe harbours it seems clear that the regular market user would have regarded the information in question as relevant (as well as not being generally available).

The first is a safe harbour for dealing or arranging deals based on information about the actual trading or trading intentions of any person (i.e. not just one's own dealing and intentions). Thus those with access to extensive deal flow information from their own transactions and those of their clients can profit from it without risk of committing market abuse. There are two qualifications to this safe harbour. Information on a possible takeover bid is excluded (it has its own more detailed safe harbour – *see* below) Information about new offers, issues, placements or other primary market activity is also excluded as it is regarded as different in kind from secondary market deal flow.

It should be noted that, at least as far as FSMA regulated firms are concerned, even if it will not amount to market abuse there are a number of other rules which have to be considered before dealing whether it is permissible to act on trading information including the rules prohibiting front running, governing personal account dealing and requiring deals to be placed fairly and in due turn, with timely and best execution.

The takeover bids safe harbour is similar in outline but different in detail from that given in connection with "market information" dealing under the Criminal Justice Act 1993. The Code (MAR 1.4.28) provides a safe harbour for dealing or arranging deals in connection with the acquisition or disposal of an equity or non-equity stake in a company for the sole purpose of making that acquisition or disposal and for the sole benefit of the person making the acquisition or disposal. The safe harbour is available not only to the person concerned but also for his associates and those acting for him but it is only available if the information in question is only one or more of the following facts:

(a) that investments of a particular kind have been or are to be acquired or disposed of, or their acquisition or disposal is under consideration;

(b) the number of investments involved in the actual or possible acquisition or disposal;

(c) the price (or range of prices) involved;

(d) the identity of the people involved, or likely to be involved, in any capacity in an acquisition or disposal.

Specific examples given of permitted behaviour includes seeking irrevocable undertakings to accept or reject an offer, making arrangements for an issue of those securities which are to act as consideration for or fund a takeover offer (including making arrangements for underwriting or placing those securities) and making arrangements to offer a cash alternative. The Code does not, however, allow the safe harbour to cover all types of transaction which might be considered before or in the course of, a takeover battle. Specifically it says that the safe harbour given for taking certain steps for the purposes of stake-building or otherwise directly in connection with the takeover does **not** mean that the bidder (and its associates and agents) may undertake other types of transaction in the target company's shares or other investments (e.g. contracts for differences or securities in other companies in the sector in relation to which the information is also relevant information).

The Code says that a bidder would be engaging in market abuse if it entered into transactions in investments which provide merely an economic exposure to movements in the price of target company shares. This is a clear reference to the Northern Electrics case which involved the use of equity derivatives to recover the bidder's costs (*see SIB Guidance Release 4/96, Equity-related derivatives: use of inside information*). It also says that those acting for the bidder would be guilty of market abuse if they used the information to deal for their own benefit in securities or related products for which it was relevant.

7.9.4   *Regular user would expect disclosure*

The FSA in the Code imposes the above consideration in the "misuse of information" head of market abuse in addition to the three conditions in the legislation itself. It is quite a significant further limitation and it is worth considering why, and how, it has been added in the Code. No explanation is given in the Code itself or in the Policy Statement published with the Code in April 2001. The explanation is to be found in Consultation Paper 59, published July 2000, which says that the FSA "in applying the regular user test to the type of behaviour, has identified an additional element which has the effect of narrowing the range of information which is potentially covered by the market abuse regime". The FSA says that there will always be times when some market users have information which is not generally available and that they may be able to take advantage of that information by trading on it without necessarily damaging the wider interest of the market. It takes the view that the reality of markets is that it is impossible for every piece of information to be made available on an equal and simultaneous basis and the regular market user has no expectation that it should be so.

Without stating it in the Code, the FSA has therefore reached the conclusion that a regular market user would not consider conduct to have fallen below expected standards unless the information on which the conduct is based relates to matters which the regular user would reasonably expect to be disclosed to the particular prescribed market. Having inserted this new element (MAR 1.4.9E(4)) the Code then goes on to analyse it in a fairly legalistic way. It distinguishes between:

(a) information which has to be disclosed in accordance with any legal or regulatory requirement ("discloseable information"). This would include, for example, information required to be disclosed under the Takeover Code, SARs, Listing Rules or rules of a Recognised Investment Exchange ("RIE");

(b) information which is routinely the subject of a public announcement although not subject to any formal disclosure requirement ("announceable information"). This would include, for instance, information which is to be the subject of official announcements by Governments, central monetary or fiscal authorities or regulatory authorities, changes to published credit, ratings and changes to the constituents of a securities index. It would <u>exclude</u>, according to the FSA, surveys or research based on information generally available, in which category the FSA would put CBI surveys and MORI opinion polls.

Provision is made that where the information concerned is about possible future developments it should normally only be regarded as "disclosable" or "announceable" if it contains with reasonably certainty grounds to conclude that the possible further developments will take place and accordingly that a disclosure or announcement will in due course be made.

There is also an attempt to distinguish between information which is discloseable or announceable in different markets so that, for instance, it is suggested that sometimes information about a commodity producer would be discloseable or announceable information in relation to the equities market, so as to prevent dealings based on it in that market, while potentially not being disclosable or announceable in respect of the relevant commodity futures market, so that dealings could, without market abuse take place in commodities futures using the same information which could not be used in the equities market. This is a difficult area where each case would need to be analysed quite carefully on its facts. In consultation commodity producers argued strongly that they should be able to hedge (in the commodities derivatives market) their contractual delivery obligations before disclosing the relevant information and also that information required to be disclosed in relation to the equity market would not be required in the commodities market so its use in dealing on the latter would not be regarded by the regular user as a failure to meet accepted standard. It appears that these arguments have been accepted for the purposes of the Code and market abuse. However the FSA pointed out that obligations under the Listing Rules may require disclosure of significant new developments without delay.

If, of course, disclosure was made, even to the equity markets, then the information would in any case became "generally available" so that dealing on the basis of the information could not in any event be market abuse. It seems however that some commodity producers see a window between the time at which something is sufficiently clear to require them to hedge their commodities position and the time at which it is so clear that an announcement is needed to the equity markets.

It is certainly true that there can be such gaps. The Code identifies the example where a listed company would need to make an announcement on entering into a significant contract with a major supplier which might lead to substantial movement in the price of the listed securities. Information about the negotiations, or proposed contract, would in the FSA's view come into the market abuse regime at an earlier stage, that is to say once there are grounds to conclude, with reasonable certainty, that the contract will be entered into and that disclosure of the contract will have to be made.

It is apparent that these will, like all instances of market abuse, be highly fact dependent and also that the FSA has taken a particular view of what a market user might think. Others might take the view that dealings on the basis of inside information about the negotiations could still be market abuse even if it could not at that point be said with reasonable certainty that the contract would be concluded successfully.

7.9.5 *Comparison with insider dealing*

Although for convenience it may be useful to refer to this category of market abuse as misusing inside information there are important differences between this category of market abuse and insider dealing:

(a) the market abuser does not have to be an insider or tippee, although it is likely that in most cases he would be;

(b) the information which is not generally available does not need to be price sensitive for market abuse although it does for insider dealing; for market abuse it is sufficient that it is relevant to deciding the terms on which a transaction will be entered into, which in principle does not need to be restricted to terms as to price;

(c) a transaction can be market abuse even if it is entered into off-exchange and no professional intermediary is involved; in those circumstances, there cannot be insider dealing;

(d) there is no defence in terms where both parties to the transaction know the information; there is such a defence in the case of insider dealing. Hopefully, the regular market user would take the view that in these circumstances there is no failure in expected standards (so that there is no market abuse);

(e) the alleged market abuser can be guilty even though he was acting as a market maker on an RIE; there is a defence in these circumstances in the case of insider dealing;

(f) an alleged market abuser can be guilty even if he did not know that the information was not generally available; conversely, there can be no insider dealing unless a person "has information as an insider" which means that he must actually know that the information has not been made public;

(g) for the moment at least, securities traded only on a non-UK market are not subject to the market abuse regime; conversely, insider dealing can be committed if the securities are quoted on any of the many European markets covered by that regime or, indeed, on NASDAQ or NASDAQ Europe;

(h) as indicated below, information is generally available (and so outside this category of market abuse) even if it has not been made public in the UK; in these circumstances, information is still to be treated as non-public for the purpose of insider dealing unless the court decides that it should be treated as made public; and

(i) in contrast to insider dealing, market abuse is a corporate offence. Accordingly, a company can commit the misusing information category of market abuse (and be subject to an unlimited fine) even though it cannot be guilty of insider dealing. However, an effective Chinese wall, or similar confidentiality arrangements, constitutes a safe harbour, although one may not in fact be needed (*see* below).

7.10   False or misleading impressions

Just as the "misuse of information" head of market abuse has some similarities with the offence of insider dealing, so also the "false or misleading impression" head overlaps to some extent with the offence of market manipulation. In some senses this heading is central to the concept of market abuse. As the Code says (MAR 1.5.3E) the prescribed markets provide a mechanism by which the price or value of investments may be determined according to market forces and those trading expect the price or value of investments and volumes of trading to reflect the proper outcome of market forces, rather than outcome of improper conduct by other market user. Improper conduct which gives market users a false or misleading impression results in their no longer being able to rely on the prices formed in markets or the volumes of trading as a basis for investment decisions, this undermining confidence in market integrity.

The elements of the "false or misleading impressions" head of market abuse are that the behaviour must be likely to give the regular user a false or misleading impression as to the supply or demand for, or as to the price or value of investments of the kind in question.

The Code in stating the elements of the test elaborate it in four important ways:

(a) that the behaviour may actually give rise to a price or value or volume of trading which is false or misleading or may merely give an impression of such price, value or volume;

(b) that it should be <u>materially</u> false or misleading; and

(c) that, in the FSA's view, the word "likely" does not mean a 50 per cent or higher chance of producing the wrong effect. It would be sufficient in the FSA's view for the "likelihood" to be "real and not fanciful". This approach appears to downgrade the word "likely" to "possible" but the FSA has reviewed the case law and considers that its approach is justifiable. Any challenge to the low level of "likelihood" required by the FSA to generate a charge of market abuse would therefore have to be made in court or in front of the FSA's own Tribunal;

(d) less controversially, the FSA says that the behaviour in question may be likely to give rise to more than one effect, including the undesirable one of misleading the market. The latter does not have to be the only effect.

The Code then divides its analysis of "false or misleading impressions" between:

(a) general factors which are considered relevant;

(b) certain types of behaviour which the FSA considers would amount to market abuse; and

(c) a few safe harbours for behaviour the FSA does not consider would amount to market abuse under this head.

It notes that there is an element of overlap between this head and distorting the market. This is hardly surprising given the generality of the statutory provisions. There is also some overlap with the first head of misuse of information.

7.10.1   General factors

The general factors identified by the FSA as relevant to whether the market user is likely to be given a false or misleading impression appear completely non-controversial, though a little vague to be helpful. They are:

(a) the knowledge and experience of market users;

(b) the structure of the relevant market including its reporting, notification and transparency requirements;

(c) the legal and regulatory requirements of the market concerned and accepted market practices;

(d) the identity and position of the person responsible for the behaviour which has been observed (if known); and

(e) the extent and nature of the visibility or disclosure of the person's activity.

7.10.2 Behaviour which the Code indicates will amount to market abuse

The Code identifies four types of possible market abuse under the "false or misleading impressions".

7.10.2.1 Artificial transactions

The first type of behaviour identified by the Code as potential market abuse under the "false or misleading impressions" head is artificial transactions where:

(a) someone enters into a transaction or series of transactions in a qualifying investment or relevant product; and

(b) the principal effect of the transaction or transactions on the market will be or will be likely to be to inflate, maintain or depress the apparent supply or demand, price or value so that a false or misleading impression is likely to be given to the regular user; and

(c) the person <u>knows</u> or could <u>reasonably be expected </u>to know that the above will be or will be likely to be that stated above <u>unless</u> the regular user would regard:

    (i) the <u>principal rationale</u> for the transaction as a legitimate commercial rationale; and

    (ii) the way in which the transaction is to be executed is proper.

Thus in its formulation of an artificial transaction the FSA has brought in a form of intention at two levels. The first is that the alleged abuser must have known, or ought to have known, of the likely adverse principal effect of the transaction(s). The second is that his principal rationale for the transaction should not have been a legitimate commercial one.

The Code then goes into considerably more detail on the elements of its definition of artificial transactions.

To begin with simply aiming to make a profit or avoid a loss (directly or indirectly) does not necessarily amount to a "legitimate commercial rationale" for these purposes. That would be far too easy an escape route. More specifically a transaction will rarely be regarded as having a legitimate commercial rationale where the purpose was to induce others to trading or to position or move the price of a qualifying investment or relevant product. This makes sense. Otherwise it would drive a hole through the section. It should, however, be noted that the FSA only requires that purpose to be "an actuating purpose", not the sole purpose for the transactions. Thus even if there was another legitimate commercial rationale for the transaction it could be treated as market abuse if price positioning or a volume increase was also a purpose.

The term "actuating purpose" which is defined as "a purpose which motivates or incites a person to act" is used at a number of places in the Code where the word "intention" (actual or presumed) might have been used had it not been for the extended quarrel over the latter term during the legislative process.

Factors the Code identifies as <u>relevant</u> (but not necessary, nor determinative) when considering there has been one or more artificial transactions include:

(a) whether the transaction causes or contributes in an increase or decrease in supply/demand/price/value and the person concerned has an interest in the level of that supply/demand/price/value (e.g. because he directly benefits by having a holding or short position, or has indirect benefits from a change in the market price or may be rewarded by, or is otherwise in collusion with, those who do benefit);

(b) whether the transaction involves the placing of buy orders higher than the market price, or sell orders lower, or the placing of buy and sell orders which increase the volume of trading;

(c) whether the transaction coincides with a time at or around which the volume or pricing is relevant, either for the market as a whole or for the person in question, in calculating reference prices, settlement prices or valuations;

(d) whether those involved are connected parties;

(e) whether the transaction causes a change in the market price which immediately thereafter returns to its previous level;

(f) whether a bid/offer is placed outside the previous price only to be removed before it is executed.

An important factor is whether the transaction opens a new position, creating an exposure to market risk or closes a position, removing pre-existing market risk. Where this is the case it is a strong indication that the transaction will be regarded as having a legitimate commercial rationale and not amounting to market abuse provided it is executed "properly".

As noted above proper execution is regarded by the FSA as being just as important in avoiding an artificial "abusive" transaction as is the requirement that the principal purpose of the transaction should be a legitimate commercial one. Its comments on the subject are, however, not very clear and have circular tendencies. According to the Code a transaction will only be executed in a "proper" way if it is executed in a way which takes into account the need for the market as a whole to operate fairly and efficiently. This would not be the case if a transaction was executed in a particular way with the purpose of creating a false or misleading impression. It notes that the rules of most prescribed markets have a requirement that transactions be executed in a proper way, for example by rules on reporting and executing cross trades but does not remind the reader at this point that there is no safe harbour for complying with exchange rules on crosstrades. Compliance with those rules would therefore seem to be necessary but not sufficient to avoid market abuse. However the Code does at least say that transactions would not "necessarily" be considered to be executed in an improper way simply because the way in which they were executed did not disclose the firm's positions or intentions to the market.

Moving on to circumstances which the Code identifies as possibly giving rise to a false or misleading impression without having a legitimate commercial rationale, examples given in the Code (MAR 1.5.14) are:

(a) arrangements (other than normal repo or stock borrowing or lending) for sale or purchase where there is no change of beneficial ownership or market risk or the transfer of beneficial interest or market risk is only between people acting in concert or collusion;

(b) transactions (other than normal nominee holdings) designed to conceal ownership of a qualifying investment or relevant product.

The final example the Code gives, without further explanation, of an "artificial transaction" is a "fictitious transaction".

A couple of safe harbours are given in the Code for transactions which would not be regarded as artificial transactions offending under this head of market abuse. They are:

(a) arbitrage transactions which take or unwind a position so as to take legitimate advantage of differences in the taxation of income or capital gains (no reference is made to other taxes such as stamp duty and value added or sales tax) generated by investments or commodities (whether the differences arise by reason of the identity of the recipient of the income or gains or otherwise) or differences in the prices of investments or commodities as traded in different locations; and

(b) lending or borrowing qualifying investments or commodities to meet an underlying commercial demand for them.

It should be noted, however, that these are very limited, indeed positively rock strewn, safe harbours because they are only available if it can be shown that:

(a) the principal rationale for the transaction was a legitimate commercial one; and

(b) they are executed in a proper way.

Since the way in which the safe harbour transactions are defined sets out their purpose in some detail it is confusing to add a "legitimate commercial rationale" test. The addition might suggest that in some cases those purposes (i.e. tax or other arbitrage or satisfying underlying commercial demand) might <u>not</u> be a legitimate commercial rationale. It is to be hoped that such doubt was not intended and the extra test is only designed for those who actually have an abusive purpose so that arbitrage, or the commercial demand, although it exists, is something of a facade.

7.10.2.2   *Disseminates information (generally)*

The second type of behaviour identified as potentially market abuse under the "false or misleading impressions" head is where:

(a) a person disseminates information which is, or if true would be, relevant information (the test for "relevance" is the same as under the misuse of information head i.e. information a regular user would consider relevant when determining the terms of transactions);

(b) the person knows, or could reasonably be expected to know, that the information is false or misleading; and

(c) he disseminates it in order to create a false or misleading impression. This need not be the sole purpose of disseminating the information but once again must be an "actuating purpose".

Thus here again the Code writes in two "intent" elements, a knowledge test and a purpose test.

In this context it is relevant in considering the person's purpose to see whether he has an interest in a qualifying investment or relevant product to which the information relates. If he does it will tend to suggest the existence of the improper purpose. However the Code says the absence of any such interest does not conclusively demonstrate the absence of market abuse.

The example given in the Code is of posting false or misleading information on an Internet bulletin board or chat room site. No comment is made on the position of the Internet Service Provider or host of the bulletin board or chat room but the "purpose" elements which the Code has introduced in this context would seem to give them a significant degree of protection provided at least that they had no reason to suppose the information was false or misleading. What is unclear is how far they would need to be ready and in a position to remove information if it became apparent (or likely) that it had been posted in order to create a false or misleading impression. The question of how far policing or censorship of Internet sites by the host is necessary or desirable, or how far repeated intervention will lead to the host being seen as having taken on a "vetting" role and accordingly positive responsibility for content, is a perpetual tension. It does not seem to have been addressed to any significant extent in the Code (though *see* Section 7.12 below).

7.10.2.3   *Disseminating information through official channels*

The third type of market abuse the Code identifies under this heading is a variant of the first. It relates to the submission of information to an "accepted" channel for the dissemination of information. Such a channel is defined, in relation to any prescribed market, as an approved channel of communication whereby information concerning investments traded on the market is formally disseminated to other market users on a structured and equitable basis. Such channels include but are not necessarily limited to those required to be used under the rules of a particular market (e.g. Regulatory News Service, LIFFE Connect).

Where relevant information which is likely to give a false or misleading impression is disseminated in this way the Code imposes a much lower knowledge/purpose test. The person concerned does not have to know that the information is false or misleading. There is not even a statement that he ought to have known of its falsity. Nor is any level of purpose (actuating or otherwise) required. All that is required is that the person concerned has not taken reasonable care to ensure that it is not misleading. The FSA points out that users of information which is disseminated in this relatively formal way should be able to rely on the accuracy and integrity of information carried through those channels. Those disseminating information through them, whether the company itself, its financial advisers or its public relations advisers, should therefore take reasonable care to ensure that the information is not inaccurate or misleading.

This approach is a useful warning for companies, their advisers (including public relations advisers, some of whom can be less careful than others) about the importance of formal releases. It is, however, as interesting for what is left unsaid as for what is said. It seems that press releases not made through "accepted channels" are subject to the tougher knowledge (actual or deemed) and purpose tests even when they come from "official" sources such as the company and its advisers. In addition no mention is made in the Code of the potentially false and misleading effect of <u>failing</u> to disseminate information (rather than positively disseminating information which is false or misleading).

It is clear under the legislation that "behaviour" includes inaction as well as action and in the course of the legislative process the example was given of a company or other person which failed to make a required disclosure or failed to correct an onerous impression which was known to be current in the market. It is strange therefore that this situation is not addressed expressly in the Code. It is possible that the FSA considers that silence is also a form of "disseminating information" although this would be a very unusual use of language. The possibility is suggested because a safe harbour given by the Code under this heading is that making a report or disclosure would not of itself give rise to a false or misleading impression if it was made in the way specified by any applicable legal or regulatory requirement and it was expressly required or expressly permitted by the FSA rules, the rules of a prescribed market, those of the Takeover Code or SARs or other applicable statute, regulation or rules. When giving examples of such disclosure the Code identifies certain provisions which allow announcements to be delayed or otherwise affect their timing rather than those positively requiring disclosure.

The other safe harbour given in relation to misleading markets by disseminating information generally is for Chinese walls (*see* Section 7.9.1 above). Where someone within an organisation disseminates information which he would know, or could reasonably be expected to know, is false or misleading if he were aware of the information held by others in the organisation then the organisation will not be held to know (or to be reasonably expected to know) that the information was false or misleading if:

(a) the other information is held behind an effective Chinese wall or is restricted using other similarly effective arrangements; and

(b) there was nothing which was known (or should have been) by the individual who disseminated the information which should have led him to conclude it was false or misleading.

Cross references are made to MAR 1.4.24C and 1.4.25G on the facts which will help to establish that there was an effective Chinese wall or equivalent arrangements. Since those parts of the Code relate to dealing and decisions to deal they are not entirely illuminating when an attempt is made to apply them to circumstances of disseminating information.

As a rule of thumb, however, it seems it can be assumed that Chinese walls which are strong enough to hold in the dealing situation will also hold in the dissemination of information situation.

It should be noted that the Chinese walls safe harbour is not given in the Code where information is disseminated through accepted channels. In those circumstances there is no suggestion that the obligation to take reasonable care to ensure that information is not false or misleading can be blocked by the existence of a Chinese wall.

7.10.2.4   *Course of conduct*

The fourth type of market abuse identified by the Code under the heading "false or misleading impressions" could be said to be a variant of, or rather a wider description of, the first. It is where a person engages in a course of conduct:

(a) the <u>principal effect</u> of which will be, or is likely to be, to give a false or misleading impression to the regular user as to the supply/demand/price/value of a qualifying investment or relevant product; and

(b) the person concerned knows, or could reasonably be expected to know, of this actual or likely principal effect;

unless the regular market user would regard:

(c) the principal rationale for the conduct as a legitimate commercial one; and

(d) the way in which the conduct is engaged in as proper.

Once again the Code includes two levels of information in this type of market abuse: knowledge (actual or implied) coupled with the illegitimate "principal rationale".

Both examples given of possible market abuse under this heading relate to the commodities markets. They are the movement of physical commodities, or of an empty cargo ship, in a way which might create a misleading impression as to the supply of or demand for or price or value of a commodity or the deliverable into a commodity futures contract.

7.11   Distortion

7.11.1   *Main elements*

The elements of the third main category of market abuse, as elaborated in the Code, are:

(a) that the behaviour must be such that a regular user would, or would be likely to regard it as behaviour which would or would be likely to distort the market in the investment in question;

(b) behaviour will amount to market abuse if it interferes with the proper operation of market forces and is made with the purpose of positioning prices at a distorted level. This need not be the sole purpose of entering the transaction or transactions but it must be an actuating purpose;

(c) in order to be likely there must be a real and not fanciful likelihood that the behaviour will have such an effect. However, this effect need not be more likely than not and can be only one of several different effects.

Paragraph (a) above is the statutory definition. Paragraphs (b) and (c) are added by the Code. It should be noted that there is a double "likely" in the statutory definition. Although the Code addresses only the FSA's view of meaning of "likely" when applied to the effect of the behaviour presumably the FSA would have the same "less than 50 per cent likelihood is sufficient" approach when considering the likelihood of a regular user coming to a view on that effect.

The Code also inserts an intention, or "actuating purpose" test, though not a knowledge test.

The Code takes the view that the purpose of this heading is to prevent behaviour that interferes with the proper operation of market forces and supply and demand and therefore says that it is unlikely that the behaviour of market users trading at times and in sizes most beneficial to them and seeking the maximum profit from their dealings will amount to distortion. It even adds, in a curious formulation, that it is "unlikely" that prices trading outside this normal range will "necessarily" be "indicative" that someone has engaged in abusive behaviour with the purpose of positioning prices at a distorted level. Although the wording used is double-edged, the general statements about freedom to trade and to make profits without being too concerned about the price range and the recognition that high or low prices relative to a trading range can be the result of the proper interplay of market demand give some comfort on concerns that monitoring the "distortion" head of market abuse could itself involve distorting the market because it would inhibit proper trading.

The Code goes on to give two examples of behaviour amounting to market abuse: price positioning and abusive squeezes. The former could often also be caught under the "false or misleading impression" heading of market abuse. The latter arguably could not.

7.11.2 *Price positioning*

Price positioning is described as entering into a transaction or series of transactions with the purpose (i.e. an actuating purpose) of positioning the price of a qualifying investment or relevant product at a distorted level. The Code notes that trading in significant volumes for a proper purpose (e.g. index trading) and in a proper way is unlikely to distort the market even if it causes the market to move.

It then goes on to identify the following factors which the FSA considers should be taken into account when determining whether someone has positioned the price at a distorted level:

(a) the extent to which the timing of the transaction(s) coincided with a time at which the price was relevant (whether for the market as a whole or for the person in question) for the calculation of reference prices, settlement prices or valuations;

(b) the extent to which the person concerned had a direct or indirect interest in the price or value of the investment or product in question;

(c) the volume or size of the transaction(s) in relation to reasonable expectations of the depth and liquidity of the market at the time in question;

(d) the extent to which price, rate or option volatility movements and the volatility of these factors for the investment in question occur which are outside their "normal intraday, daily, weekly or monthly ranges";

(e) the extent to which the transaction(s) caused the market price of investment in question to increase or decrease, following which the market price returned immediately to its previous level;

(f) whether a person has successively and consistently increased or decreased his bid, offer or the price he has paid for a qualifying investment or relevant product.

It is worth noting that points (a), (b) and (e) above also feature as relevant factors when considering whether there have been artificial transactions creating a false or misleading impression but the other factors diverge significantly. This is because under the "distortion" heading the transaction concerned may well be "real" in the sense that full commercial risk is taken for the transaction and, indeed, the resulting price may even be said to be "true" within the conventions of the relevant market.

Nevertheless, they have been structured to have a disproportionate effect on the market so that the price is "distorted" even if it is arguable that it is not misleading.

Four examples are given in the Code of abusive price positioning all of which are fairly clearly improper. Only the first of them would clearly fall within the Code's description of artificial transactions giving a false or misleading impression, although arguably all could fall within the statutory wording for misleading the market as well as for market distortion.

They are:

(a) a trader simultaneously buying and selling the same investment which is relevant to the calculation of the settlement price of an option at a price outside the normal trading range. He has a position in the relevant option and the purpose of the dealing is to position the price to give him a profit or avoid a loss on the option;

(b) a trader buying just before the close of trading a large volume of commodity futures the price of which is relevant for the settlement value of a derivatives position held, again in order to distort the price and profit from the derivatives position;

(c) a trader holding a short position which would show a profit if a particular investment falls out of the index and placing a large sell order on that investment just before the close of trading in order to reduce its price sufficiently for it to drop out of the index;

(d) a fund manager wishing to improve his quarterly performance and doing so by placing a large order to buy relatively illiquid shares of a kind contained in the portfolio just before the end of the quarter.

7.11.3   *Abusive squeezes*

The second type of market abuse identified by the Code under the Distortion heading is "abusive squeezes", which are not defined as a form of sexual harassment but as situations where:

(a) someone has a significant influence over the supply of, demand for or delivery mechanisms for a qualifying investment or relevant product; <u>and</u>

(b) a position (directly or indirectly) in an investment under which quantities of the relevant investment or product are deliverable; <u>and</u>

(c) engages in behaviour with the purpose (which as usual need not be sole but must be "actuating") of positioning at a distorted level the price at which others have to deliver, take delivery or defer delivery to satisfy their obligations.

Factors which the Code says will be taken into account when determining whether or not someone has engaged in an abusive squeeze are:

(a) the extent to which, and price at which, he is willing to relax his control or influence in order to help maintain an orderly market;

(b) the extent to which his activity causes or risks causing settlement default by other market users on a multi-lateral basis and not just a bilateral one;

(c) the extent to which prices under the market delivery mechanisms differ from those for delivery of the investment or its equivalent off market;

(d) the extent to which the spot or immediate market, compared to the forward market, is unusually expensive or inexpensive, or the extent to which borrowing rates are unusually expensive or inexpensive.

The Code states that these factors are not intended to impose new obligations on market users so that, for instance, it does not create an obligation for someone with a long position, even a very significant one, to lend investments. The FSA considers in guidance that other market users should normally also be expected to protect their own interests and put themselves in a position to be able to fulfil their obligations in a manner consistent with the standards of behaviour on that market. It thinks that the regular user is likely to expect others not to put themselves in a position where they have to rely on the holders of long positions lending when they may not be inclined to do so and may be under no obligation to do so.

Even so the Code also says that willingness to lend means behaviour is less likely to amount to an abusive squeeze. Although it is not said in the Code, given the prevalence of lending in some markets, it may already be, or become, open to question whether regular users could sensibly assume that loans would always be available for settlement. What, for instance, would the position be if a person who normally participated in a clearer's automatic lending programme pulled out unexpectedly? If an inappropriate "actuating purpose" could be found this might be market abuse.

The example given of an abusive squeeze in the Code is, however, much narrower and clearer. It is where a trader with a long position in bond futures, buys or borrows large amount of the cheapest-to-deliver bonds and either refuses to re-lend them or lends only to those he believes will not re-lend to the market and his purpose in doing this to position the price at which those with short positions have to deliver to satisfy their obligations at a materially higher level, making him a profit.

The only safe harbour given by the Code under the "distortion" heading of market abuse is for certain LME rules generated by its 1998 report into market aberrations dealing with the behaviour expected of holders of long positions on that market. There is a slight oddity here in that the provisions of those rules are equally applicable to the "false or misleading impressions" head of market abuse. The commentary in the Policy Statement issued with the Code suggested that the safe harbour was being applied to that section but this does not seem to have happened in the Code itself.

7.12   Requiring or encouraging

7.12.1   Main elements

The final form of market abuse is a secondary one, but no less important than the three main categories. The FSA can impose penalties, and other provisions of the FSMA also apply, not only where it is satisfied that one of the three types of market abuse described in Section 118 of the FSMA have taken place but also where the FSA is satisfied that the relevant person has, "by taking or refraining from taking any action required or encouraged another person or persons to engage in behaviour which, if engaged in by [the first person] would amount to market abuse".

The somewhat convoluted wording is designed to prevent an obvious avoidance technique under which otherwise a sophisticated market user, or one with improper information or purposes, uses relatively innocent or unsophisticated players to carry out the relevant behaviour. The fact that the latter may have a defence, under the statute itself or under the "regular user" test or under the Code, so that they have not committed "market abuse" should not prevent the former from being held liable.

All the various provisions of the Code will be applied in the normal way when putting the hypothetical "encourager" into the shoes of the person encouraged to see if market abuse would have been committed. In addition the Code has a few additional pieces of guidance on the subject, mostly relating to situations which the FSA would, or would not, normally regard as requiring or encouraging market abuse. There are no additional safe harbours given by the Code, however, under this heading. It should be noted that there is no extra "regular user" test applied to whether particular action or inaction amounted to "requiring or encouraging". That question is left to the FSA. It should also be noted that the whole of the section in the Code in "requiring or encouraging" is technically just guidance by the FSA under Section 157 of the FSMA and does not have any special status under Section 122 of the FSMA.

As general comments the FSA says that whether someone might be regarded as "requiring or encouraging" will depend on circumstances such as acceptable market practices, the experience, level of skill and standard of knowledge of the person concerned and the control or influence the person has in relation to the person who engages in the behaviour in question. Thus it seems that the FSA will apply to this heading at least some of the elements which in other circumstances it lists as part of the "regular user" test.

7.12.2   Examples

Examples given in the Code of behaviour which may be regarded as "requiring or encouraging" are:

(a) a director of a company while in possession of relevant discloseable information, other than trading information (*see* above) which is not generally available instructs an employee of the company to deal in relevant investments or products;

(b) someone simply recommends or advises someone else to do something which, if he had done it himself, would have amounted to market abuse (this would normally include someone with relevant discloseable information advising or encouraging someone else to deal);

(c) except in limited circumstances (*see* below) making an early or selective disclosure of information which a regular user would expect market users to have.

Examples given in the Code of behaviour which would not be regarded as "requiring or encouraging" are:

(a) in the context of a takeover offer, an adviser to the person considering the relevant acquisition or disposal advising that an acquisition or disposal should be made of a kind which is permitted without breach of the Code under MAR 1.4.28C (*see* above);

(b) an intermediary acting on a transaction where the originator appears to have engaged in market abuse, unless the intermediary knew or ought reasonably have known that the originator was engaging in market abuse. This, although helpful as far as it goes, does not give much assistance to brokers and other intermediaries in establishing how far they have a duty to monitor their clients activities and may themselves be held guilty of requiring or encouraging market abuse if they fail to do so.

7.12.3   *Early or selective disclosure of information*

Most of the commentary in the Code on the "requiring or encouraging" head relates to early or selective disclosure of information which the regular user would expect market users to have.   The FSA assumes that such disclosure will involve "encouragement" to deal, although the CBI in consultation argued that this was not necessarily the case.   The FSA says that such disclosure will generally be regarded as abusive unless:

(a) there is a legitimate purpose for the disclosure. Examples of legitimate purposes are given as disclosures required or permitted under exchange rules, those of the FSA or the Takeover Code; and

(b) it is accompanied by a statement at or before the time the information is passed that the information is given in confidence and that the recipient should not base any behaviour in relation to the qualifying investment or relevant product on the information until the information is made generally available.

It is not clear in this context whether the FSA means "generally available" to have the extended meaning given to it earlier in the Code or whether it should be restricted to the time at which the information is actually released to the market. If it is the former then, as noted above, the restrictions could be circumvented by placing the relevant information on the Internet in an obscure language and place, possibly even on a subscription basis. In principle "disclosing" information in this way (particularly if restricted to a subscription website) should be regarded as a form of selective distribution which could itself potentially amount to requiring or encouraging market abuse. It is not, however, clear that this would be the result under the Code as drafted.

The Code does address more traditional situations. It gives as examples of situations where disclosure might be regarded as being for a "legitimate purpose" (though still needing to be coupled with the confidentiality provision):

(a) giving information to group employees and fellow employees on a "need to know" in order to do their jobs basis;

(b) giving information to professional advisers for the purpose of obtaining advice;

(c) giving information to those with whom a commercial, financial or investment transaction is being negotiated (including prospective underwriters or places of securities) in order to facilitate the transaction;

(d) giving information to those from whom irrevocable undertakings or expressions of support are being sought in a takeover, in order to get those commitments;

(e) giving information to representatives of employees or trade unions in fulfilment of a legal obligation (e.g. redundancy consultations);

(f) unsurprisingly, giving information to any Government department, the Bank of England, the Competition Commission, the Takeover Panel or any other statutory or regulatory authority to fulfil a legal or regulatory obligation or otherwise in connection with the performance of that body's functions.

It is worth noting the emphasis placed on stating at or before the time the information is handed over that it is given in confidence and not to be the basis for behaviour by the recipient before it is generally available. This statement can be incorporated in the express or implied terms of any contract governing the relationship of the people concerned.

In some circumstances it is already normal to have confidentiality agreements in place so all that is needed is to extend the standard wording of these agreements so that they pick up the requirements of the Code. In others, such as employment relationships, it may be that relevant provisions can be implied into the employment contract but specific warnings would be preferable. In others again either no formal warning has normally been given (e.g. disclosures to statutory authorities) or they have not been reduced to writing and recorded. In future, bearing in mind the level of penalties which may be imposed for market abuse, it will be advisable always to give and record a formal written warning, preferably obtaining written agreement to the restriction

7.13   Complying with other rules

As mentioned above, complying with other rules, even those the firm is bound to obey, is under the Code normally not a full defence against a charge of market abuse but only a factor to be taken into account when applying the regular user test.

Although the Government initially indicated that behaviour conforming with FSA rules would not be regarded as market abuse, they retreated somewhat from that in the House of Lords, and the revised position has been maintained in the Code. The FSMA now provides in Section 118(8) that this "safe harbour" only applies if the rule itself includes a provision that behaviour conforming with the rule does not amount to market abuse. The reason for this reduced safe harbour is that the Government thought that a safe harbour which is constituted by FSA rules generally will be too wide. However, it is difficult to see that behaviour "conforms" with an FSA rule if it consists of dealing on information which is not generally available, or misleading or distorting the market. What the reduced safe harbour means is that, in particular cases, the firm might have to choose between being at risk of an unlimited fine by complying with the rule and consequently committing market abuse and being at risk of an unlimited fine by avoiding market abuse by not complying with the rule. This could put a firm in an intolerable position but the Government refused to move from it.

Similarly, compliance with the FSA's Code of Market Conduct would not in itself necessarily mean that the firm will not be subject to an accusation of market abuse by so doing. The FSMA makes it clear that the safe harbour given by compliance will only apply if the Code states expressly that the given behaviour, in the FSA's opinion, does not amount to market abuse; if it does not, the Code is only evidential in that it may be relied on only insofar as it indicates whether or not particular behaviour should be taken to amount to market abuse. Full safe harbours are given only by the very limited number of provisions in the Code which are marked "C".

The restriction of safe harbours under the Code is rather more understandable than the position in relation to FSA rules. First, there is no provision that a rule can be taken as evidence as to whether or not behaviour does or does not amount to market abuse. Secondly, and more importantly, the firm does not have to comply with what is provided for in the Code, although of course it is at risk if it does not, but it has no choice as to whether or not to comply with actual FSA rules.

Despite urging by the Conservative Party's Treasury Team, the FSMA also does not provide any safe harbour for compliance with the rules of a RIE as such or even require the FSA to have regard to whether the accused was complying with existing market practice. It is again unfair that firms dealing on the RIE should run the risk that complying with RIE rules (e.g. the rules of the London Stock Exchange) may constitute market abuse, as the FSA has authority over the RIEs and can make sure that the rules do not actually require something which the FSA regards as market abuse.

In practice the FSA has gone through its rules and given express safe harbours to those acting in compliance with a number of them, in particular:

(a) those relating to price stabilisation (MAR 2);

(b) those relating to Chinese walls (as noted above safe harbours for effective Chinese walls or equivalents have also been written into the Code in a number of places);

(c) various Listing Rules on the timing, dissemination or availability, content and standard of care applicable to disclosures, announcements, communications or releases of information;

(d) Listing Rule 15.1(b) in relation to share buy-backs.

The FSA understandably does not comment on whether it otherwise regards its own rules as requiring market abuse (one must assume that it generally does not). It does say, as a matter of guidance only, not officially forming part of the Code, that it is satisfied that the RIE Rulebooks do not permit or require behaviour which amounts to market abuse (MAR 1.2.13G).

7.14   The Takeover Panel

The last political battle on the FSMA which was fought in Parliament related to the involvement of the FSA in takeover bids and the position of the non-statutory Takeover Panel (the "Panel"). The Panel became very concerned that somebody could commit market abuse during a bid and this would allow the FSA to get involved in the bid and interfere in the takeover bid process. The Opposition Treasury Team therefore put forward an amendment on behalf of the Panel that the Panel could agree with the FSA that certain provisions of the City Code on Takeovers and Mergers, which is issued and administered by the Panel (the "Takeover Code") would constitute safe harbours for market abuse. The Government did not want to allow this (because the FSA is supposed to be the only securities regulator and, perhaps, because the Takeover Panel represents the last example in the City of London of self-regulation) and therefore insisted that, although the Panel and the FSA could indeed agree safe harbours, the FSA could only agree them with the consent of the Treasury. In addition, and importantly, the Government wanted the FSA to have the last word on what constituted market abuse and therefore on what sort of behaviour was permitted or required by the Takeover Code and so fell within whatever safe harbour was agreed. Although the Government lost an important vote on this amendment in the last lengthy debate in the House of Lords and the amendment giving primacy to the Panel was passed, the Government succeeded in reversing this when the Bill went back to the House of Commons and their own amendment was then passed when the debate went back to the House of Lords.

The end result was Section 120 of the FSMA which gave the FSA (without requiring consent from the Panel) a limited power to include in its Code provisions that, in its opinion, behaviour conforming with the Takeover Code does not amount to market abuse (either generally or in specified circumstances or when done by specified persons). The limitations were that the Treasury's consent is required for any such provision and that if such provisions are included the FSA must keep itself informed of the way in which the Panel interprets and administers the relevant provisions of the Takeover Code. Ironically, since otherwise the FSA has a general power to grant safe harbours, this means that in law (if not in practice) it is more difficult to grant a safe harbour for behaviour conforming with the Takeover Code than with, for example, the rules of a foreign regulator such as the National Association of Securities Dealers ("NASD") in the US or with guidance issued by a trade association such as the British Bankers Association (BBA) in the UK. Indeed the FSA has given safe harbours (*see* below) in the Code in relation to the SARs (Substantial Acquisition Rules, which are also produced and interpreted by the Takeover Panel) without requiring Treasury consent.

Accordingly, if a party to a bid makes misleading statements in its offer or defence document, or engages in a share support operation, the FSA can interfere in the bid and, in extreme cases, apply to the court for an injunction stopping it; the mere application could stop the bid in its tracks even if it failed. It was in order to prevent this happening, and also because the Takeover Panel is so well regarded, that the House of Lords originally insisted that primary responsibility for takeover bids should remain with the Takeover Panel. The Government did actually agree to this but made it clear that, ultimately, if there was disagreement between the Panel and the FSA as to the meaning of a particular rule in the Takeover Code, the final decision as to what it meant lay with the FSA, and not the Panel. Indeed, if the FSA disagrees with the Panel, the FSA will seemingly be able to require the Panel to change its rules, or at least their interpretation of them, with the threat always in the background that the FSA would remove its safe harbours.

This whole debate (which was really the last stand of the City against an over-mighty regulator) was somewhat misdirected. First, the FSA was not under any obligation to agree any safe harbour at all. Secondly, the safe harbour is only for behaviour "conforming with" the Takeover Code. Although the Takeover Code provides that, for example, the offeror normally must issue its offer document within 28 days after announcing the offer, and the issue of the document within that period would therefore conform with the Code, it cannot sensibly be argued that the making of misleading statements in that document also conforms with the Code. Accordingly, whatever agreement is reached, the FSA can always interfere in a bid, if they believe the relevant documents mislead, and the UK will therefore have to become used to the idea of references to the FSA, even if only to double-guess the Panel and delay the bid, becoming a regular part of takeover bids in the UK.

The FSA has in the Code in this area as in many others sought to reduce the risks posed by the breadth of the legislation. As far as the Takeover Code and SARs are concerned it has given specific safe harbours from the "misleading impressions" and "distortion" heads of market abuse for:

(a) various rules relating to the timing, dissemination or availability, content and standard of care applicable to disclosures, announcements, communications or releases; and

(b) behaviour conforming with Rule 4.2 of the Takeover Code (relating to restrictions on dealings by the offeror and concert parties).

provided, in each case, that the General Principles set out in the City Code, as well as the express rules, are followed. No safe harbours are given in relation to the "misuse of information" head but that is not surprising.

More generally, and without giving a full safe harbour, the FSA says that it is satisfied that the remainder of the Takeover Code and SARs do not permit or require behaviour which amounts to market abuse since, for example, many of them relate to ensuring that an offer or stakebuilding is conducted in an orderly manner or that shareholders in a company are treated similarly. It also says that sometimes the existence of these rules would be taken in to account by a regular user in considering whether behaviour falls below the standards reasonably to be expected. As usual, however, the FSA does not consider that compliance with such rules will necessarily avoid market abuse. It gives as an example a situation where the SARs are followed in building up a stake but the decision to build up that stake was based on a misuse of relevant information which was not generally available.

7.15   The statutory defence

There is one other defence written into the FSMA. Section 123(2) of the FSMA says that the FSA cannot impose penalties if it is satisfied that the person concerned:

(a) believed on reasonable grounds that his behaviour did not amount to market abuse (of any of the four kinds); or

(b) took all reasonable precautions and exercised all due diligence to avoid behaving in a way which amounted to market abuse.

It is not a full defence because it only prevents a fine or restitution (and perhaps a censure) and the behaviour concerned still ranks as market abuse. It may therefore still be regarded as a breach of FSA Principles for FSMA-authorised persons and the FSA can still enforce other remedies, such as exemptions.

It also has the weakness that in order to rely on the defence it is necessary to think about the possibility of committing market abuse. Those who are too innocent or ignorant to do so cannot avail themselves of the defence. Those who do think about possible market abuse will often find that the question only arises in situations where they are arguably at fault so that the defence is again not available. The defence does, however, provide a further reinforcement of the Code. Establishing systems and procedures which are based on the Code and testing proposed actions against the Code will be of assistance when seeking to use this defence.

7.16   Further action and guidance

Although it is the Code alone which has a special statutory function in relation to market abuse the FSA does plan to give some further assistance to those who are trying to avoid committing market abuse. It will give guidance on individual difficult situations provided full and clear disclosure is made. It will also publish simplified descriptions of market abuse and "decision trees" on the subject, although it is hard to see how useful these will be except in the simplest situations. It will also continue to consult its specialist Practitioners Group on the subject over the implementation period and is planning to issue a "Frequently Asked Questions" ("FAQ") bulletin. Such a bulletin may be of considerable assistance in bridging the gap between very specific individual cases and the general material in the Code.

In addition certain trade associations, notably a joint working group of BBA and LIBA, are planning to work on guidance on hypothetical situations and examples which they do or do not regard as market abuse.

All of these additional initiatives may be of assistance in applying the difficult and uncertain areas of the law which is market abuse. However, as further guidance and FAQs are dealt with, it would be desirable to have them incorporated as far as possible in a regularly revised version of the Code, thus clarifying the level of reliance which can be placed on them.

Chapter 8
MONEY LAUNDERING

Ruth Fox
Partner
Slaughter and May

8.1   Introduction

Money laundering has been described by the Financial Services Authority (the "FSA") as "the process by which the proceeds of crime are converted into assets which appear to have a legitimate origin, so that they can be retained permanently or recycled to fund further crimes".[1]

Money laundering has been the subject of a good deal of legislative attention in the UK over the last 15 years. While it is beyond the scope of this Chapter to analyse in detail all of the related statutes and regulations (quite apart from common law issues such as the tort of conversion), it is necessary, in order to understand the new role of the FSA in this field, to look briefly at the existing regime and at the roles of the various other bodies which are engaged in attempts to combat money laundering in this country.

The Criminal Justice Act 1988 (as amended by the Criminal Justice Act 1993), the Prevention of Terrorism (Temporary Provisions) Act 1989 (as amended by the Criminal Justice Act 1993), the Drug Trafficking Act 1994, the Criminal Law (Consolidation) Scotland Act 1995, the Criminal Justice (Scotland) Act 1987, the Criminal Justice (Confiscation) (Northern Ireland) Order 1990, the Northern Ireland (Emergency Provision) Act 1991, the Proceeds of Crime (Northern Ireland) Order 1996 and the Criminal Justice (International Co-operation) Act 1990 each create specific offences relating to the handling of the proceeds of crime. These offences include assistance in arrangements to facilitate the retention or control of the proceeds

---

[1]   CP46, paragraph 2.1.

of criminal conduct, concealment of the proceeds of criminal conduct, knowing acquisition of the proceeds of criminal conduct, the tipping-off of persons engaged in money laundering as to any investigation, and failure to disclose the provision of financial assistance for criminal conduct. The criminal conduct in question covers not only drug trafficking (the original focus of most money laundering legislation) and terrorism, but all criminal activities.

In addition, financial institutions (including banks, building societies and other credit institutions, all individuals and firms authorised to conduct investment business under the Financial Services Act 1986 (the "FS Act") and all insurance companies covered by the EC Life Directive) are subject to the Money Laundering Regulations 1993,[2] which were introduced pursuant to the Criminal Justice Act 1993 in order to implement into English law the European Community's Money Laundering Directive.[3] These Regulations impose requirements as to record-keeping, verification of identity, internal reporting and systems and training of employees. They are designed to ensure that financial institutions maintain procedures and systems, aimed at deterring money launderers from using such institutions as conduits for their illegal activities by requiring these institutions to:

(a) identify the ultimate source of funds ("know your customer");

(b) identify and report suspicious transactions; and

(c) keep an audit trail for use in any subsequent investigations.

Failure by a relevant institution to comply with the Regulations is a criminal offence punishable by a fine or imprisonment or both.

---

2   SI1993/1933.

3   (1991/308/EC). A second EU Money Laundering Directive is currently under consideration.

The Joint Money Laundering Steering Group (which is made up of 14 trade associations within the financial services sector)[4] has produced detailed Guidance Notes,[5] which are intended to provide financial institutions with practical assistance in complying with the Money Laundering Regulations. By virtue of Regulation 5(3)(b), these may be taken into account by a court in determining whether particular conduct by a financial institution was compliant. They were substantially revised in February 2001 in order to take into account the FSA's proposals for its Money Laundering Sourcebook.

The Government has announced proposals to amend the criminal law in respect of money laundering[6] by, *inter alia*, consolidating the existing offences under the primary legislation referred to above and extending the existing offence under the Money Laundering Regulations of failing to disclose known or suspected money laundering to cover circumstances where the person concerned had "reasonable grounds for such knowledge or suspicion" (i.e. introducing an objective "ought to have" known or suspected test in place of the existing test of actual knowledge or suspicion). In addition, the draft proposes the establishment of a criminal assets recovery agency, and to give financial investigators powers to require financial institutions to provide details of the accounts of persons who are under suspicion.

Money laundering was not historically addressed directly by the rules of the self-regulating organisations ("SROs") established under the FS Act. Instead, the SROs took the approach of drawing the

---

4   Association of British Insurers, Association of Friendly Societies, Association of Private Client Investment Managers and Stockbrokers, Association of Unit Trusts and Investment Funds, British Bankers' Association, Building Societies Association, Council of Mortgage Lenders, Foreign Banking and Securities Houses Association, Futures and Options Association, IFA Association, Institutional Fund Managers' Association, Large Networks Association, London Investment Banking Association, Wholesale Market Brokers' Association.

5   Revised and consolidated June 1997, updated August 1998, April 1999; substantially revised February 2001.

6   Draft Proceeds of Crime Bill published 5 March 2001.

requirements of the relevant statutes and of the Money Laundering Regulations to the attention of their members and noting that members were expected to comply with these laws. The Securities and Futures Authority (the "SFA") stated that a member firm which failed to have the systems and to provide the necessary staff training required by the Money Laundering Regulations might be in breach of Principle 9 (the obligation of an authorised firm to organise and control its internal affairs in a responsible manner) and the continuing fit and proper requirements, and that as part of its normal monitoring of member firms it would seek confirmation that adequate systems and controls were in place.[7] The Investment Managers' Regulatory Organisation (the "IMRO") stated that members might be asked to confirm that they had money laundering procedures in place which conformed with the Money Laundering Regulations, and that a negative response or subsequent infringement of the law relating to money laundering would be treated as having a bearing on the fitness or properness of that member.[8] The Personal Investment Authority (the "PIA") stated that it would regard any shortcoming of a firm in respect of the legislation relating to money laundering as a serious matter which might call into question the fitness and properness of the firm and/or relevant members of the firm's staff.[9]

The National Criminal Intelligence Service (the "NCIS") is the police body responsible for investigating and prosecuting money laundering offences, and it is to the NCIS that financial institutions are required to report suspicions of money laundering pursuant to the Money Laundering Regulations.

Money laundering is also the subject of high level inter-governmental and other international action. The Financial Action Task Force (the "FATF") on Money Laundering was established by the then Group of Seven at their summit in Paris in 1989 to examine

---

[7]   *See* SFA Board Notice 159 issued on 13 December 1993.

[8]   IMRO Notice to Members ("The Money Laundering Regulations") issued on 14 March 1994.

[9]   PIA Regulatory Update 29 issued in March 1997.

measures to combat money laundering. In April 1990 FATF issued a report containing a programme of 40 recommendations in this area which are designed to provide a comprehensive blueprint for action against money laundering, covering the criminal justice system and law enforcement, the financial system and its regulations, and international co-operation. These are regarded as internationally accepted minimum standards in the effort to combat money laundering.

In addition, the Council of Europe Strasbourg Convention 1999 seeks to facilitate international co-operation on investigative assistance in relation to search, seizure and confiscation of the proceeds of serious crime.

Most recently, a group of major international banks[10] announced on 30 October 2000 that they had agreed to a set of global anti-money laundering guidelines for international private banks, to be known as the Wolfsberg Anti-Money Laundering Principles.

8.2 The New Role of the Financial Services Authority under the Financial Services and Markets Act 2000 (the "FSMA")

One of the FSA's statutory objectives is the reduction of financial crime – that is, reducing the extent to which it is possible for a business carried on by a regulated person (or a person who ought to be regulated) to be used for a purpose connected with financial crime.[11] Financial crime for these purposes is stated to include any offence involving:

(a) fraud or dishonesty;

(b) misconduct in, or misuse of information relating to, a financial market; or

---

10   ABN AMRO Bank N.V., Banco Santander Central Hispano, S.A., Barclays Bank, The Chase Manhattan Private Bank, Citibank, N.A., Credit Suisse Group, Deutsche Bank AG, HSBC, J.P. Morgan, Société Générale and UBS AG.

11   The FSMA Section 2(2)(d) and Section 6.

(c) handling the proceeds of crime.

The FSA is required, in pursuance of this objective, to have regard in particular to the desirability of:

"(a) regulated persons being aware of the risk of their businesses being used in connection with the commission of financial crime;

(b) regulated persons taking appropriate measures (in relation to their administration and employment practices, the conduct of transactions by them and otherwise) to prevent financial crime, facilitate its detection and monitor its incidence;

(c) regulated persons devoting adequate resources to the matters mentioned in paragraph (b)."

For the purpose of these provisions, "regulated person" means any authorised person and any recognised investment exchange or recognised clearing house.

The FSA is given power by the FSMA to make rules specifically in relation to the prevention and detection of money laundering in connection with the carrying on of regulated activities by authorised persons.[12] In addition, the FSA is given power by the FSMA to institute proceedings for offences under regulations relating to money laundering prescribed for this purpose by the Treasury,[13] and the Money Laundering Regulations have been prescribed for this purpose. The FSA has stated that it does not currently propose to exercise this power to institute proceedings outside the sphere of its regulatory regime (i.e. it does not intend to take proceedings against anyone other than authorised persons or those who ought to be authorised) "except where circumstances make it particularly appropriate for it to do so in pursuing the regulatory objectives".[14] It is at present unclear in what circumstances this exception might be relied upon.

---

[12]   The FSMA Section 146.

[13]   The FSMA Section 402.

[14]   CP46, paragraph 4.12.

Against the background of the existing anti-money laundering regimes described above, which the FSA has itself acknowledged to be complex,[15] it may be relevant to question whether the position is likely to be improved by the imposition of a further layer of regulation at the level of rules promulgated by the FSA. In the FSA's view, however, the absence in the past of a specific role for the UK regulators in relation to money laundering has contributed to a perception that confidence (i.e. confidence that high standards apply in this area in regulated business) and co-operation (i.e. co-operation between the various relevant law enforcement and regulatory authorities) is not as good as it might be.

The FSA has acknowledged that the systems and controls which a financial services business should have in order to be vigilant and effective against money laundering are very largely those which are already regarded as best practice in the industry, both because of the existing legal requirements and also because it is in the interests of the financial institution itself and its customers to have such systems and controls in place. It has stated that the FSA should use its new role, not to set new standards, but "primarily to increase confidence that the industry is consistently and effectively meeting existing standards". It has also referred to a "joined up" philosophy, indicating that it intends actively to pursue co-operation between the law enforcement authorities, the industry and the regulators.

The FSA has also acknowledged that the standards it regards as appropriate in relation to money laundering are reflected at a high level in its Principles and Rules. For example, an FSA regulated firm must conduct its business with integrity and "take reasonable care to organise and control its affairs responsibly and effectively, with adequate risk management systems".[16]

Nevertheless, the FSA has concluded that the right course is for it to produce a "full set" of money laundering rules, encompassing matters arising out of the more general Principles and Rules as well

---

15   CP46, paragraph 2.8.

16   *Policy Statement – the FSA Principles for businesses (Response on CP13)* October 1999, Principle 3.

as other matters, and to do so in a way which it has acknowledged to be significantly more detailed than much of the rest of the Handbook. The FSA has said that this approach is appropriate in order to "complement" the existing Regulations and Guidance Notes. It is apparently no longer regarded as appropriate for money laundering to be a matter solely for the criminal regime, since this might "deny or restrict the benefits which regulatory powers and processes can bring". These, although they are not specified in the consultation document, are presumably thought to be the greater flexibility, in relation to enforcement and penalties for rule breaches, than is enjoyed in relation to prosecution for criminal offences (although it is to be noted that regulatory action in respect of failures to operate appropriate anti-money laundering systems and controls could be brought under the FS Act regime if a breach of, for example, Principle 9 could be established).

Additional complexity is added by the decision of the FSA not to disapply Section 150 of the FSMA for the purposes of the Money Laundering Sourcebook. Section 150 provides that a contravention by an authorised person of a rule is actionable by a private individual who suffers loss as a result of that contravention, but the Section may be disapplied by the FSA in respect of contraventions of particular rules. The FSA has announced that it will disapply the Section in respect of breaches of the Principles for business and the general rules about senior managers and systems and controls but, despite the close connection between these rules and the Money Laundering Sourcebook, it has made the decision not to extend the disapplication to the Sourcebook. Where a failure by a financial institution to comply with its Sourcebook obligations can be shown to have caused a loss to a private individual (e.g. where the victim of a fraud can show that his funds would have been recoverable but for the failure of a firm to detect and report a suspicious transaction on the part of the fraudster, where that failure arose out of systems and procedures which did not comply with Sourcebook requirements) that individual will have the right under Section 150 to sue the financial institution for his loss. Fears were expressed during the consultation process that this decision by the FSA would expose financial institutions to unjustified claims because of their perceived "deep pockets", but the FSA did not accept that the possibility of such claims was in itself grounds to disapply Section 150.

8.3 The Money Laundering Sourcebook

The Money Laundering Sourcebook contains eight separate chapters and a schedule of transitional provisions. Each of the chapters is discussed briefly below.

8.3.1 *ML 1 – application and purpose*

The Sourcebook is stated to apply to "relevant firms", which are all authorised firms other than those whose only regulated activity consists of certain types of insurance business (essentially general insurance, long-term insurance business falling outside the First Life Directive, permanent health insurance, insurance relating to funeral expenses and certain Lloyd's business)[17] and Undertaking for Collective Investment in Transferable Securities ("UCITS") qualifiers (operators, trustees or depositaries of recognised collective investment schemes authorised under Schedule 5 to the FSMA).

The UK branches of passporting EU firms are also caught within the definition to the extent that their activities are conducted in the UK, reflecting the fact that the Money Laundering Directive is designed to apply on a "host State" basis. EU firms which are operating on a services only basis in the UK are not within the definition.

The exclusion for certain types of insurance business has, it appears, been made because of a mismatch between the scope of the FSMA and the scope of the Money Laundering Regulations. The latter apply to most financial institutions, but not to companies conducting insurance business of the type identified in ML 1.1.4 R(2). The FSA has for the moment taken the view that its Rules should not apply more widely than the Money Laundering Regulations, presumably because it views its role as reinforcing the existing standards embodied in those Regulations rather than as imposing new standards, and has therefore excluded firms carrying on such insurance business from the application of the Rules. It has, however, issued a warning that it will reconsider the position if that seems necessary, and might at the same time ask the Treasury to

---

[17]   ML 1.1.4 R(2).

consider extending the scope of the Money Laundering Regulations to cover general insurance so as to maintain the connection between the two sets of requirements.[18]

It is to be noted, however, that mismatches remain, which are outside the power of the FSA to remedy. For example, bureaux de change activities are not regulated under the FSMA, with the result that the FSA's Rules cannot apply to them. They are, however, regulated under the Money Laundering Regulations. In this connection the FSA has noted that when unregulated activity of this type is carried on by an authorised person or by a subsidiary of an authorised person, it will regard such activity as relevant to the performance of the FSA's authorisation and supervision functions in relation to the authorised person because of the reputational, managerial, financial or other exposure which could arise from such activities.

ML 1.1.5R states that the Sourcebook applies only in relation to activities carried on from an establishment in the UK. The FSA has, however, noted that where a UK authorised firm is able to exercise control over business carried on outside the UK, it will look into the way in which such control is exercised in the prevention and detection of money laundering in the non-UK business. Once again, it cites reputational, managerial, financial or other exposure of the relevant firm as the justification for this broad approach. It is not clear whether the FSA will regard compliance with host state rules as sufficient in these circumstances.

ML 1 also contains guidance (but no substantive rule) as to the purpose of the Sourcebook, which it identifies as being to require authorised firms to have effective anti-money laundering systems and controls so as to reduce the opportunities for money laundering in relation to relevant firms, and also to require firms to ensure that approved persons exercise appropriate responsibilities in relation to anti-money laundering systems and controls.[19]

---

[18] CP46, paragraph 4.10.

[19] ML 1.2.1G.

The guidance draws attention to the ways in which the Sourcebook is relevant to the FSA's regulatory objectives[20] and states that the Sourcebook provides support, in relation to money laundering, for a number of other parts of the Handbook, such as Principle 3,[21] the statements of principle for approved persons, the requirements as to senior management arrangements, systems and controls and the Training and Competence Sourcebook. It is stated in the guidance that, because the Sourcebook relates to regulatory requirements rather than requirements imposed by the criminal law, it does not constitute "relevant supervisory or regulatory guidance" for the purposes of Regulation 5(3) of the Money Laundering Regulations 1993.[22] The FSA has said that it has taken this position in order to maintain as a safe harbour in respect of the Money Laundering Regulations the Guidance Notes issued by the Joint Money Laundering Steering Group[23] (because guidance issued by representative bodies has "safe harbour" status under Regulation 5(3) only in the absence of relevant supervisory or regulatory guidance).

The definition of money laundering for the purposes of the Sourcebook is essentially the same as for the purposes of the Money Laundering Regulations: any act which constitutes an offence under specified sections of the various pieces of primary legislation dealing with money laundering, or any act committed outside the UK which would have constituted such an offence if committed in the relevant part of the UK.

---

[20]   FSMA, Section 2 – *promoting marketing confidence and public awareness, protecting consumers and reducing financial crime.*

[21]   *See* footnote 16 above.

[22]   "In determining whether a person has complied with any of [the requirements under the Money Laundering Regulations] a court may take account of - (a) any relevant supervisory or regulatory guidance which applies to that person ...."

[23]   *See* footnote 5 above.

8.3.2   ML 2 – *general money laundering duties*

A firm to which the Sourcebook applies is required to set up and operate arrangements which are designed to ensure that it and any person appointed to act on its behalf are able to comply, and do comply, with the requirements set out in the remainder of the Sourcebook. These arrangements must include the appointment of an individual, who must be an approved person, as its Money Laundering Reporting Officer ("MLRO") in accordance with the obligations set out in ML 7 (*see* below).

Guidance explains that the MLRO is the key person in the relevant firm's implementation of anti-money laundering strategies and policies.

Guidance also draws attention to the fact that the firm's responsibilities to comply with the Sourcebook extend to appointed representatives carrying on regulated activities on its behalf.

8.3.3   ML 3 – *identification of the client*

ML 3 contains the main obligations imposed by the Sourcebook in relation to the identification of clients. It requires a relevant firm "to take reasonable steps to find out who its client is", and to do so by obtaining "sufficient evidence" of the identity of any client who comes into contact with the relevant firm as to be able to show "that the client is who he claims to be".[24]

Guidance draws attention to the use of the term "client" in the Sourcebook, specifically designed to differentiate the application of the Sourcebook's provisions from other parts of the Handbook where the term "customer" is used. "Client" is defined to mean any person engaged in, or who has had contact with the relevant firm with a view to engaging in, any transaction with that firm either on his own behalf or as agent for someone else. This appears to have the result that the firm will be subject to the identification obligation contained in ML 3.1.3R in respect of every person who approaches it with a view to a possible transaction (which includes the giving of advice,

---

[24]   ML 3.1.3 R(1).

so also extends well beyond its natural meaning), notwithstanding that the approach is not followed up (although it may be thought that the more absurd applications of this will be avoided by reliance on the fact that the obligation is to take "reasonable steps" to identify a client).

As with the Money Laundering Regulations, the Sourcebook obligation to obtain evidence of identity extends to any third party for whom the client is or appears to be acting.

In its initial proposals for Chapter 3 of the Sourcebook, the FSA included a number of provisions specifying the types of identification evidence upon which a relevant firm might rely in satisfying its identification obligation. These provisions were heavily criticised during the consultation process as being likely to generate confusion as to the respective roles of the Sourcebook and the Money Laundering Regulation Guidance Notes, from which they differed in a number of respects. The FSA has accepted these arguments up to a point, and has replaced the proposed rules with guidance to the effect that, in assessing a relevant firm's compliance with its identification obligation, the FSA will have regard to the relevant firm's compliance with the Guidance Notes (although this appears to fall short of being a "safe harbour" in respect of such compliance).

A separate provision is, however, still included (despite opposition during the consultation process) in order to reflect the Government's concerns about financial exclusion.[25] Its purpose is to enable a person whose circumstances are such that he cannot reasonably be expected to produce the standard forms of identification evidence (e.g. a passport or driving licence) to access financial services. In these circumstances, it is stated in guidance that a firm may accept a letter or statement from a person in a position of responsibility who knows the client that tends to show that the client is who he says he is and

---

[25] See *Access to Financial Services: The Report of Policy Action Team 14*, published by H.M. Treasury in November 1999.

confirms his permanent address if he has one. For these purposes, it is stated that examples of persons in a position of responsibility would include solicitors, doctors, ministers of religion, teachers, hostel managers and social workers.

It is emphasised in the guidance to this provision that the relaxation does not override the general requirement that the firm must take reasonable steps to check who its client is. It seems that these provisions will be of relevance mostly to banks or building societies in connection with the opening of basic accounts.

ML 3.1.8R states that the obligation under ML 3.1.3R to obtain identification evidence must be performed "as soon as reasonably practicable" after the firm has contact with the client with a view to agreeing to carry out a particular transaction or to establish a relationship. If the relevant evidence is not obtained within that timescale, the firm is required to discontinue any regulated activity that it is conducting for the customer and to terminate any "understanding" it has reached with him unless in either case the relevant firm has notified the NCIS (which may require the firm to continue the transaction or relationship for the purposes of its own investigations). The provision clearly contemplates the possibility that, in certain circumstances, the firm may begin to deal with the client before the identification evidence is obtained. The provision mirrors Regulation 7 of the Money Laundering Regulations, but it should be noted that the Guidance Notes suggest that certain checks must be completed "at the outset", and it would clearly be unwise for a financial institution to operate on the basis that it is not, in almost every case, essential to obtain identification of a potential customer before embarking on a transaction or a relationship.

ML 3.1.9R states, rather oddly, that nothing in the preceding rule requires a relevant firm to continue with a transaction which conflicts with its obligations in relation to rights of a third party. Since ML 3.1.8R (2) does not require a firm to continue with a transaction in any circumstances, this is presumably an oblique reference to the possibility that the NCIS may do so.

ML 3.2 lists a number of exceptions to the obligation to obtain identification evidence, but notes expressly that none of the exceptions apply in circumstances where the firm knows or suspects that the client (or any person on whose behalf the client is acting) is engaged in money laundering. It appears that the "knowledge or suspicion" in question is actual knowledge or suspicion on the part of a member of the staff of the firm who is handling the transaction, or on the part of any member of staff who is managerially responsible for the transaction.

The specific exceptions are as follows:

(a) the client is a credit institution (for the purposes of the Banking Consolidation Directive)[26] or a financial institution which is covered by the Money Laundering Directive (note that the test here is purely factual, rather than based on the reasonable belief of a firm as is the case in the similar provisions of the Money Laundering Regulations; if the firm is wrong about the status of the client, the rule is breached although the Regulation may not be);

(b) the transaction is a "one-off transaction" with a value of less than €15,000 (or is one of a number of transactions which are related and which together have a value of less than €15,000);

(c) where, with a view to carrying out a one-off transaction, the client is introduced by a third party who provides written assurance that in all such cases he obtains and records identification evidence, and that the third party is itself in one of the categories described in (a) above or is subject to regulatory oversight by a relevant overseas regulatory authority (i.e. one

---

[26]   (2000/12/EC).

which falls within Section 82 of the Companies Act 1989)[27] and to legislation at least equivalent to that required by the Money Laundering Directive. Note that it is not adequate for these purposes (or for the purposes of the equivalent exception in the Money Laundering Regulations) that the third party has provided an assurance that adequate checks have been carried out in relation to the particular client: the assurance must refer to the procedures undertaken by the introducer in all such cases;

(d) where the proceeds of a one-off transaction will be payable to the client but are to be invested on his behalf, will be the subject of a record, and can thereafter only be either reinvested on behalf of the client or paid directly to him; and

(e) where the transaction concerns a long-term insurance contract:

> (i) taken out in connection with a pension scheme relating to the client's employment or occupation, if the policy contains no surrender clause and cannot be used as security for a loan; or

---

[27]   Companies Act 1989 Section 82(2):

(2) An "overseas regulatory authority" means an authority which in a country or territory outside the UK exercises:

(a) any function corresponding to: (i) a function under the FS Act of a designated agency, transferee body or competent authority (within the meaning of that Act); (ii) a function of the Secretary of State under the Insurance Companies Act 1982, the Companies Act 1985 or the FS Act; or (iii) a function of the [FSA] under the Banking Act 1987; or (b) any function in connection with the investigation of, or the enforcement of rules (whether or not having the force of law) relating to, conduct of the kind prohibited by [Part V of the Criminal Justice Act 1993 (insider dealing)]; or (c) any function prescribed for the purposes of this Subsection by order of the Secretary of State, being a function which in the opinion of the Secretary of State relates to companies or financial services.

An order under paragraph (c) shall be made by statutory instrument which shall be subject to annulment in pursuance of a resolution of either House of Parliament.

(ii) where the premium is a single payment not exceeding €2,500; or

(iii) where the premium payments do not exceed €1,000 in any calendar year.

This exception matches precisely the equivalent provisions of the Money Laundering Regulations.

ML 3.2.4R also mirrors (although in rather different language) a provision of the Money Laundering Regulations in that it permits a firm to regard the evidential requirements as satisfied if payment for the relevant transaction is made from an account with an authorised bank or passported or authorised credit institution, provided that the payment is sent or confirmed by post or electronically and it was reasonable for the payment to be sent or confirmed in that way, and the payment is not made in order to open an account which may be used for the making of payments to someone other than the client.

ML 3.2.5R provides that a firm may regard "evidence" as sufficient for the purposes of the identification obligation if it establishes that the client is itself bound by the Sourcebook or is otherwise covered by the Money Laundering Directive (although it appears from ML 3.2.2R that in these circumstances there would be no obligation to obtain evidence in any event), or is acting on behalf of another person and has given a written assurance that it has obtained and recorded evidence of the identity of the person in question, and the client is itself subject to regulatory oversight by an overseas regulatory authority which falls within Section 82 of the Companies Act 1989 and to legislation at least equivalent to that required by the Money Laundering Directive. Guidance adds that the firm is expected to take "reasonable steps" to determine whether the client falls within the second exemption. Note that in this context the written assurance to be obtained does not relate to the general procedures of the intermediary (as required by ML 3.2.2R(3) referred to at (c) above), but only to the evidence actually obtained in respect of the specific person for whom the client is acting.

The FSA has pointed out that the requirements of ML 3 are closely related to requirements in other parts of its Handbook, in particular the "know your customer" obligations. It has, however, formed the view that the purposes of the various provisions are distinct and that the requirements should therefore be kept separate with the result that it will be necessary for a relevant firm, in devising and up-dating its account-opening or equivalent procedures, to keep in mind two separate sets of Rules within the Handbook (as well, of course, as the Money Laundering Regulations and Guidelines).

Transitional provisions contained in the Schedule provide that where a firm has an "established client relationship" with any person immediately before the date of commencement of the Sourcebook, it will not be required to re-establish the identity of that client. The term "established client relationship" is not defined in the Sourcebook, and it is not clear whether it is intended to imply any requirement for the relationship to have been established in accordance with existing customer identification requirements. The Money Laundering Regulations use a similar term – "established business relationship" – which is defined as a business relationship in connection with the formation of which the relevant firm has obtained satisfactory evidence of the identity of the applicant for business in accordance with its procedures established under the Regulations.

8.3.4   *ML 4 – reporting*

ML 4.1.2R(1) requires a relevant firm to take "reasonable steps" to ensure that any member of staff who handles, or is managerially responsible for the handling of, transactions which may involve money laundering makes a report promptly to the MLRO if he knows or suspects that a client, or the person on whose behalf the client is acting, is engaged in money laundering.

The rule does not specify what those "reasonable steps" will consist of, beyond providing that they must include arrangements for disciplining any member of staff who fails, without reasonable excuse, to make a relevant report. Presumably, the steps will essentially consist of the maintenance and application of written procedures for staff to follow in these circumstances. It would appear that procedures already in place for the purpose of compliance with the Money Laundering Regulations would be likely to satisfy the requirements of ML 4.1.2R(1). Guidance refers to the possibility that firms may wish to set up systems which allow staff to consult with a line manager before sending a report to the MLRO, but warns that such systems should not be allowed to prevent reports reaching the MLRO when staff have stated that they know or suspect that a transaction may involve money laundering. A system involving the automatic notification to the MLRO of all reports may therefore be appropriate.

ML 4.2.1R requires a firm to take reasonable steps to give its MLRO, or any person to whom the MLRO's duties have been delegated, access to any "know your business" information which it has. "Know your business" information is defined as information about the financial circumstances of the client or any person on whose behalf the client is acting, and the features of the transactions which the firm has entered into with or for the client or that other person. Guidance states that, in order to do his job properly, the MLRO is likely to need access to information of this type before taking a decision as to whether to report any matter to the NCIS. It is emphasised that the requirement is not intended to increase the amount of information which a firm is required to gather and keep about its clients, but rather is intended simply to ensure that a firm uses existing client information effectively by making it readily available to the MLRO.

In the earlier draft of the Sourcebook, a much wider obligation was proposed, whereby a firm would be required to deploy its "know your business" information throughout the firm so as to be readily available to all staff in order to facilitate the identification of potential money laundering. Significant objections to this were raised during the consultation process, relating both to potentially high compliance costs as well as to issues of client confidentiality and, in some cases, Chinese walls. The FSA has acknowledged these difficulties and has replaced the original wide obligation with the provisions now appearing in ML 4.2.1R, but comments in the policy statement of January 2001 suggests that this is an issue which the FSA may wish to review in the future.[28]

---

[28] Policy Statement of January 2001 (*Money Laundering: The FSA's new role*) paragraph 3.18.

ML 4.3.2R requires a relevant firm to take "reasonable steps" to ensure that any report made to the MLRO under ML 4.1 is considered by the MLRO or his duly appointed delegate and that if, having considered the report and any relevant "know your business" information to which he has sought access, the MLRO suspects money laundering, he reports that promptly to the NCIS.

This rule closely mirrors the requirements of the Money Laundering Regulations in relation to the role of the "appropriate person" including the requirements (appearing here as ML 4.3.3E(1)) that the person concerned should be required to consider any report received by him "in the light of all relevant information accessible to or reasonably obtainable by" him and should be permitted access to information in the firm's possession which could be relevant. The rule also adds that the firm should ensure that a report by the MLRO is not subject to the consent or approval of any other person.

ML 4.3.4R requires that a sole trader who has no other employees and who knows or suspects that a client or a person on whose behalf a client is acting is, or has been, engaged in money laundering must himself make a report promptly to the NCIS.

8.3.5   ML 5 – using national and international findings on material deficiencies

ML 5 obliges a relevant firm to take reasonable steps to ensure that it obtains and makes proper use of any government (i.e. UK Government or government department) or FATF findings of material deficiency in the anti-money laundering arrangements in any other state or jurisdiction. "Findings" for these purposes are published notices issued by the UK Government or any UK Government department or the FATF, and the FSA has said that in order to assist firms it will publish such findings on its website.

"Proper use" of any relevant finding is stated to include applying the information in connection with customer introductions, applying the information to "know your business" information and disseminating information in the course of dealing with awareness and training of staff.

Commenting on this chapter,[29] the FSA has drawn attention to the fact that several of the exemptions relating to customer identification rely on the notion that other jurisdictions have legislation in respect of money laundering equivalent to that in force in the UK, and has suggested that the mechanism provided by ML 5 will assist in identifying those jurisdictions that are considered not to meet equivalent or minimum standards. Thus, in applying its customer identification standards, a relevant firm must check not only whether an overseas customer is subject to an equivalent legislative regime, but also whether any relevant body has issued any notice of findings which may be relevant for ML 5 purposes.

8.3.6 ML 6 – awareness of and training for staff

The Money Laundering Regulations oblige relevant businesses to take appropriate measures to make those employees whose duties include the handling of relevant financial business aware of the firm's procedures and the law relating to money laundering, and to provide those employees with training in the recognition and handling of transactions which may involve money laundering. ML 6 imposes essentially the same obligation, although the categories of staff to whom it applies are extended to include both those who handle, and those who are managerially responsible for handling, relevant transactions, and the matters of which such staff are required to be made aware are stated to include the potential effect of any breach of the law on the firm, its employees and its clients.

The evidential provisions require that the firm should provide information "whether recorded in writing or otherwise" covering all of the matters of which the employees are required to be aware, which must be brought to the attention of any new member of staff who starts work in any capacity which is relevant to money laundering and remain available to him as long as he works in that capacity. The "otherwise" in this context is presumably intended to refer to electronic methods of communication.

---

29   CP46, paragraph 4.21.

ML 6.3.1R requires a firm to take reasonable care to provide anti-money laundering training for all staff who handle, or are managerially responsible for handling, transactions which may involve money laundering. It is stated that training must take place with sufficient frequency to ensure that within any period of 24 months it is given to substantially all of the relevant staff, although guidance states that the requirements do not preclude a rolling programme of training under which training on different subjects takes place on different dates.

8.3.7 ML 7 – the Money Laundering Reporting Officer, compliance monitoring and record-keeping arrangements

ML 7.1.5R requires a firm to appoint an individual as its MLRO and to operate arrangements that are designed to ensure that it and the MLRO comply with the relevant obligations contained in chapter 7. The position of MLRO has been designated as a controlled function; the individual carrying out the role must therefore be an approved person. The individual must be someone who is employed within the relevant firm or within another relevant firm in the same group (so cannot be, for example, an outside contractor or consultant). The firm must ensure that its MLRO is able to monitor the day-to-day operation of its anti-money laundering policy and to respond promptly to any reasonable request for information made by the FSA. The firm must make its MLRO responsible for receiving internal reports under ML 4.1, taking reasonable steps to access any relevant "know your business" information, making external reports to the NCIS under ML 4.2, obtaining and using findings under ML 5, taking reasonable steps to establish and maintain adequate arrangements for awareness and training and making annual reports to the firm's managers under ML 7.2. If the position of MLRO falls vacant, the relevant firm must appoint another individual in his place.

It is expressly required by ML 7.1.7R that a relevant firm must ensure that its MLRO has a sufficient level of seniority within the firm and sufficient resources, including his own time and if necessary support staff, in order to carry out his functions effectively.

Guidance points out that the function of acting as MLRO is a controlled function for the purposes of Section 58 of the FSMA, with the result that the individual is subject to prior approval by the FSA. Transitional provisions contained in the Schedule permit an individual who has been approved for these purposes prior to the commencement of the Sourcebook, or whose application for approval is pending on that date, to continue to act in that capacity.

Certain of the functions to be discharged by the MLRO for the purposes of the Sourcebook are similar to those required of the "appropriate person" whom firms are required to identify for the purposes of the Money Laundering Regulations, and ML 7.1.4G acknowledges that, where convenient, a firm may decide that the same person can carry out both roles. There is, however, no indication in the Money Laundering Regulations as to the level of seniority required for such an appointment, and the role is essentially confined to receiving internal reports of suspicions of money laundering, considering those reports in the light of other relevant information and dealing with the making of external reports.

Guidance acknowledges that a firm which is a member of a group may decide to appoint as its MLRO an individual who performs that function for another relevant firm within the group, and that relevant firms with a number of branches or offices in different locations may wish to permit the MLRO to delegate his duties within the relevant firm. It is made clear, however, that the FSA will expect the MLRO himself to take ultimate managerial responsibility for ensuring that the duties imposed on him by the Sourcebook are complied with. There is an evidential provision stating that a relevant firm should ensure that its MLRO is based in the UK.

The compliance monitoring provisions of ML 7 consist only of evidential and guidance provisions. They cross refer to SYSC 3.2.6R (senior management arrangements, systems and controls) and spell out what the FSA expects of firms, with reference to money laundering, under the more general rule about compliance monitoring.

ML 7.2.2E states that a firm should have in place arrangements under SYSC 3.2.6R which include requirements that, at least once in every calendar year, the firm commissions from its MLRO a report which assesses its compliance with the Sourcebook, indicates the way in which any new findings under ML 5 have been used during the year, and provides details of the number of reports made in accordance with ML 4.1 by staff of the firm, dealing separately if appropriate with different parts of the firm's business. The firm's senior management are required to consider the report and to take any necessary action to remedy deficiencies identified by it.

The provision has the effect, no doubt intended, that senior management of a firm will have to look in considerable detail at the firm's performance in relation to obligations under the Sourcebook.

ML 7 cross refers to SYSC 3.2.20R (senior management arrangements, systems and controls) which deals with the making and retaining of adequate records. In relation to money laundering arrangements, ML 7.3 amplifies this requirement and, indeed, extends it in terms of the time during which records are required to be kept for the purposes of consistency with the requirements of Regulation 12 of the Money Laundering Regulations (although, as elsewhere, the two sets of requirements are differently worded and the Sourcebook adds some obligations not included in the Regulations).

ML 7.3.2R(1) requires the firm to make and retain for the relevant periods:

(a) in relation to identification evidence, either a copy of the evidence obtained or a record of where it can be obtained or a record of how the details given in it can be obtained and, in appropriate cases, a record of the firm's reasons for accepting evidence in accordance with ML 3.1.5G to ML 3.1.7G (financial exclusion);

(b) a record containing details of every transaction (for these purposes, not including advice when the advice is followed by a transaction with a monetary value) carried out by the firm with or for the client in the course of regulated activity;

(c) where the firm's client has become insolvent and it has taken steps to recover all or part of the debts owed to it by the client, a record of those steps;

(d) records of actions taken under the internal and external reporting requirements of the Sourcebook (not required by the Money Laundering Regulations); and

(e) where the MLRO has considered information relating to the possibility of money laundering but has not made a report to NCIS, a record of that information (not required by the Money Laundering Regulations).

The records in question are required to be retained for five years from:

(a) in the case of identification evidence, the end of the firm's relationship with the customer;

(b) in the case of transaction records, the date when the transaction was completed;

(c) in the case of an insolvency, the date thereof; and

(d) in all other cases, the date of obtaining the information or creation of the record.

It is also noted in ML 7.3.4G that records kept by the firm under SYSC 3.2.20R should include details of all anti-money laundering training, including dates, the nature of the training and details of the names of staff who have received it, and money laundering reports made by the MLRO together with details of the consideration given to these reports and of any action taken as a consequence.

8.3.8   *ML 8 – sole traders and professional firms*

ML 8.1.1R specifies those requirements of the Sourcebook which apply to a sole trader with no employees apart from himself. A sole trader is not required to appoint a MLRO or to set up arrangements for internal reporting of suspicions and money laundering but is otherwise generally required to comply with the Sourcebook. A sole trader for these purposes is an individual who is an authorised person. A company with only one employee is apparently bound to comply with all of the provisions.

Pursuant to ML 8.2.1R an authorised firm which is a member of a profession which is supervised and regulated by a designated professional body is bound by the Sourcebook except in respect of those activities which would have been exempt if the firm had not been an authorised person.

8.4 Conclusion

It is apparent from the above summary that the provisions of the Sourcebook have very largely been dictated by the existing provisions of the Money Laundering Regulations and the Guidance Notes. They cover the same ground, but in a number of respects use different terminology and in a few respects, most notably in relation to the role of the MLRO, impose different or additional obligations.

At a time when authorised firms are already facing a very significant task in assimilating the new Handbook and adapting their systems and procedures to comply with it, and are also likely to have to make further adjustments in the relatively near future to take account of proposed changes in the criminal law relating to money laundering, it must be questionable whether the FSA's new approach to money laundering is the most efficient one which could have been adopted. While it may well be desirable to provide regulatory as well as criminal sanctions in this difficult area, where the absence of significant numbers of criminal convictions may give rise to political issues, it is not clear why this could not have been achieved by an approach more like that previously used by the SROs. The FSA could have adopted the Money Laundering Regulations as, in effect, a part of its Handbook and, to the extent that it is thought that the Regulations are inadequate, could have worked with the Government to improve them. Instead, subject to a small number of concessions made during the consultation process, the FSA has stuck to its "parallel but separate" approach, and has chosen to write its own "full set" of money laundering rules, thereby adding another layer of detailed regulation in an area which is already complicated, and has significantly increased the compliance burden on authorised firms.

It remains to be seen whether this increased burden will be justified by a proportionate increase in the amount of money laundering which is detected and prevented.

Chapter 9

AUTHORISATION AND SUPERVISION PROCESSES

John Tattersall
Partner
PricewaterhouseCoopers

9.1   Introduction

The creation of a single regulator under a single piece of legislation has given the Financial Services Authority (the "FSA") the opportunity to introduce common processes for authorisation and supervision of firms. These processes are spelt out in the Authorisation and Supervision Manuals which, together with the Enforcement Manual and the Decision making Manual, form the regulatory processes block of the FSA Handbook.

The FSA intends that the single authorisation regime should reduce overlap and duplication as well as improving the consistency in assessing applicants to determine whether they will satisfy and continue to satisfy the threshold conditions. The objectives of this regime are set out in the FSA's publication – *A New Regulator for the New Millennium* and states:

> "Vetting at entry aims to allow only firms and individuals that satisfy the necessary criteria (including honesty, competence and financial soundness) to engage in regulated activity. Experience in the UK and elsewhere shows that regulatory objectives are more likely to be achieved by setting and enforcing standards for entry, rather than having to deal with major problems later."

This objective means that the authorisation process will be a challenging hurdle for applicant firms, though it is not intended to be insuperable, and the checks and balances introduced by the Government and monitored by the Office for Fair Trading should ensure this. Equally, however, some potential problems are bound to escape detection: the intention is to reduce the risk of such problems arising after authorisation!

The Authorisation manual sets out the relationships between the FSA and those applying for permission to carry on a regulated activity or overseas firms seeking to exercise their rights to carry on regulated activities in the UK under relevant directives.

The Supervision Manual sets out an integrated approach to the supervision of firms once they have been authorised, reflecting the requirements and processes in the Financial Services and Markets Act 2000 (the "FSMA"). It contains both guidance on the procedures set out in the FSMA and rules designed to enable the FSA to pursue its regulatory objectives. Essentially it spells out the:

(a) FSA's approach to monitoring firms and the use of its regulatory toolkit (*see* Section 9.4.4 below);

(b) FSA's requirements and procedures for dealing with changes to a firm's circumstances; and

(c) information that the FSA requires from firms to fulfil what it regards as its monitoring obligations.

It also contains sections on the appointment of auditors and on FSA's use of "skilled persons" to complement its own supervisory staff's enquiries. While the rules and guidance contained in the Supervision Manual apply to all firms, the FSA will be able to focus its efforts on those firms which, in its view, constitute higher risks: in *A New Regulator for the New Millennium*, it states:

> "Supervision of individual firms allows the FSA to monitor, identify and deal with firm-specific risks, and provides an insight into industry developments. This may, for example, involve changing capital requirements in response to a changing risk profile, or the instigation of focused reviews of particular business or control areas, whether by supervisors themselves or by reporting accountants working to a brief agreed by the FSA."

Inevitably, the approach to supervision will develop with time, particularly in areas where the integrated approach to monitoring represents the greatest change. The burden of making the supervisory processes work will fall upon the regulator's staff and their success will depend on the FSA's ability to recruit and keep staff of the right calibre.

The Decision Making Manual is principally concerned with the FSA's processes for issuing statutory notices as part of its supervisory and enforcement processes.

This Chapter provides a guide to the Authorisation and Supervision Manuals as they stand at the date of publication, though they will continue to be updated.

9.2   Authorisation process

9.2.1   *The need for authorisation*

Under the FSMA, a firm (described in the FSMA as a "person") must be authorised if it carries on or purports to carry on activity which is defined in the Regulated Activities Order as a regulated activity (taking account of various exclusions) and carries on a business of engaging in that activity:

(a) from an establishment maintained by that firm in the UK;

(b) otherwise in a way which constitutes the carrying on by the firm of a business in the UK subject to certain exclusions for "overseas persons";

(c) in another European Economic Area ("EEA") State if its registered office or, if it has no registered office, its head office is in the UK, it is entitled to exercise rights under one of the Single Market Directives;

(d) it is carrying on in that other EEA State a regulated activity to which the relevant Single Market Directive applies;

(e) is the manager of an Undertaking for Collective Investment in Transferable Securities ("UCITS") whose registered office or, if it has no registered office, its head office is in the UK if a person in another EEA State is invited to become a participant in the

UCITS; or elsewhere than in an EEA State if its registered office or, if it has no registered office, its head office is in the UK and the day-to-day management of the regulated activity is in the responsibility of that office or of another establishment maintained by the firm in the UK; and

(f) is not exempt from needing authorisation to carry it on.

Firms that carry on regulated activities in the UK will require authorisation from the FSA unless they are subject to exemption or are automatically authorised by or under the FSMA (e.g. EEA passported rights). A firm obtains authorisation from the FSA by obtaining Part IV permission from the FSA under Section 42 of the FSMA to carry on one or more regulated activities. Existing authorised persons or firms (authorised under predecessor legislation to the FSMA) should obtain authorisation automatically at N2 under the FSMA by means of the Transitionals Order which provides for the "grandfathering" of activities that were carried out immediately prior to N2.

Under Section 23 of the FSMA it is a criminal offence to conduct activities in breach of Section 19 of the FSMA, punishable by a maximum of two years imprisonment and a fine. It is a defence under Section 23(3) of the FSMA for the accused to show that he took all reasonable precautions and exercised all due diligence to avoid committing the offence. In addition, agreements entered into by a person carrying on a regulated activity in breach of Section 19 of the FSMA are potentially unenforceable against the other party.

9.2.2 *Regulated activities*

The regulated activities are set out in Part II of the Regulated Activities Order. They may relate to all specified investments or to a particular specified investment, or only to designated investments. In general terms, regulated activities are:

(a) accepting deposits;

(b) effecting or carrying out contracts of insurance;

(c) establishing, operating or winding up a collective investment scheme, acting as trustee or depository of such a scheme or acting as sole director of an investment company with variable capital (or agreeing to do any of these things);

(d) buying, selling, subscribing for or underwriting designated investments either as principal or as an agent (or agreeing to do any of these things);

(e) making or agreeing to make arrangements:

    (i) for another person (whether as principal or agent) to buy, sell, subscribe to or underwrite a particular designated investment; or

    (ii) in which persons participate (whether as principal or agent) with a view to buying, selling, subscribing to or underwriting designated investments;

(f) safeguarding and administering, or arranging for the safeguarding and administration of assets belonging to someone else, where those assets:

    (i) consist of or include designated investments; or

    (ii) where the arrangements under which they are safeguarded and administered have at any time been held out as ones under which such designated investments would be safeguarded and administered, or agreeing to safeguard and administer assets in these circumstances or agreeing to arrange to do so;

(g) sending, on behalf of someone else, dematerialised instructions relating to securities by means of either a relevant system in respect of which an operator is approved under the Uncertificated Securities Regulations 1995 or a computer-based system established by the Bank of England and the London Stock Exchange, through the medium of which specified securities may be transferred or allotted without the need for a written instrument (or agreeing to do any of those things); or causing instructions to be sent in this way (or agreeing to do so);

(h) managing, on a discretionary basis, assets which belong to someone else and which consist of or include designated investments, or managing assets, on a discretionary basis, where the arrangements for their management are such that those assets may consist of or include designated investments and either the assets have at any time since 29 April 1988 done so or the arrangements have at any time been held out as arrangements under which the assets would do so (or agreeing to manage assets in any of these circumstances);

(i) giving or agreeing to give advice to:

    (i) investors or potential investors;

    (ii) agents for investors or potential investors;

on the merits of their:

    (i) buying, selling, subscribing to or underwriting a particular designated investment; or

    (ii) exercising any right conferred by such an investment to acquire, dispose of, underwrite or convert such an investment;

(j) advising an underwriting member of Lloyd's to become a member of a particular syndicate or to continue or cease to be a member of a particular syndicate;

(k) managing the underwriting capacity of a Lloyd's syndicate as a managing agent at Lloyd's;

(l) establishing, operating or winding up a stakeholder pension scheme;

(m) entering as provider, into a funeral plan contract; and

(n) entering into (as lender) or administering a regulated mortgage contract.

9.2.3   *Excluded activities*

A number of activities are specifically excluded from the definition of regulated activities. Among the most significant exclusions are those relating to:

(a) casual deposit-taking;

(b) certain cases in which a person deals as principal in designated investments;

(c) groups and joint enterprises;

(d) sale of goods and supply of services;

(e) employees share schemes;

(f) sale of a body corporate;

(g) trustees and personal representatives;

(h) the issue by companies of their own shares, loan notes or warrants;

(i) dealing and making arrangements and (where acting as an attorney only) managing using authorised third parties;

(j) overseas persons;

(k) advice, arrangements and safeguarding and administering of investments when they are a necessary part of services provided by a business or profession which does not otherwise consist of a regulated activity;

(l) introducing; and

(m) advice given in certain newspapers, journals, magazines and other periodical publications and television and radio broadcasts.

Guidance on how the FSA will approach the issue of certificates confirming that the exclusion relating to advice given in certain newspapers, journals and other periodical publications is applicable is to be contained in Chapter 7 of the Authorisation Handbook.

9.2.4 *Non-commercial activities*

Under Section 23 of the FSMA, an activity will be a regulated activity only if it is carried on by way of business. HM Treasury has power, under Section 419 of the FSMA, to make an order providing that persons who would not otherwise be regarded as carrying on a regulated activity by way of business are to be regarded as doing so and vice versa. HM Treasury is expected to use this power to require persons such as trustees who manage the assets of an occupational pension scheme where those assets include designated investments to be authorised unless:

(a) the generality of all decisions or all day-to-day decisions relating to designated investments are taken on behalf of that person by an:

  (i) authorised person;

  (ii) exempt person; or

  (iii) overseas person who does not need to be authorised under the FSMA; or

(b) the scheme is a small self-administered scheme that meets specified conditions.

9.2.5   Exemptions

There are various exemptions from the need for firms to be authorised to carry on regulated activities in the UK. There is, however, no general provision for firms to apply for exemption.

The following lists the categories of firms or persons where the exemptions are available:

(a) *appointed representative:* persons may be exempted if they are appointed representatives of an authorised person. This will require that they enter into a contract with the authorised person. It is also necessary for the authorised person to accept responsibility in writing for the activities carried on by its appointed representatives;

(b) *recognised investment exchanges and recognised clearing houses:* investment exchanges and clearing houses which are recognised under Part XVIII of the FSMA are exempt persons;

(c) *members of Lloyd's:* a member of the Society of Lloyd's does not, therefore, need to obtain Part IV permission in respect of the insurance business carried on by them in connection with or for the purposes of insurance business at Lloyd's. However, the making of arrangements that enable members to carry on insurance business and the giving of advice in relation to the participation in a Lloyd's syndicate are regulated activities and, therefore, managing agents and members' agents will need to be authorised;

(d) *members of the professions:* subject to specific conditions, a firm or person providing professional services which are supervised and regulated by a professional body which has been designated by HM Treasury under Section 326 of the FSMA, may carry on regulated activities without the need to be authorised. The conditions are that the:

   (i) person must be a member of a profession or controlled or managed by one or more such members;

   (ii) person must not receive from a person other than his client any pecuniary reward or other advantage, for which he does not account to his client, arising out of his carrying on of any of the activities;

   (iii) manner of the provision by the person of any service in the course of carrying on the activities must be incidental to the provision by him of professional services;

   (iv) person must not carry on or hold himself out as carrying on, a regulated activity other than one which rules made by the designated professional body to which he is subject allow him to carry on or one in relation to which he is an exempt person;

   (v) activities must not be of a description, or relate to an investment of a description, as may be specified by HM Treasury; and

   (vi) activities must be the only regulated activities carried on by the person (other than regulated activities in relation to which he is an exempt person).

(e) *miscellaneous exemptions:* various firms or persons are exempt persons, either in their entirety or only in relation to particular regulated activities, under the exemptions order. For the most part, these exemptions apply to supranational bodies of which the UK or another EEA State is a member or persons whose activities are, to a certain extent, subject to control or oversight by the Government (e.g. the Bank of England, the International Monetary Fund, the National Grid Company and the Scottish Development Agency).

Automatic authorisation is available for the following persons:

(a) an EEA firm, meeting certain qualifying conditions, which is seeking to establish a branch in or provide cross-border services into the UK in the exercise of an EEA right arising under any of the Single Market Directives;

(b) a Treaty firm, meeting certain qualifying conditions, which is seeking to carry on in the UK a regulated activity which the firm has a Treaty right to carry on;

(c) the operator, trustee or depository of a recognised collective investment scheme constituted in another EEA State;

(d) the Society of Lloyd's is an authorised person under Section 315 of the FSMA.

Further details of regulated activities, investments and the relevant exclusions and exemptions are found in Chapter 2 of the Authorisation Manual. There are Appendices to the Authorisation Manual which give guidance on how the provisions and exemptions relating to Financial Promotion work, and also set out the FSA's views on the definition of open-ended investment companies.

9.2.6   *Limitations*

The FSA may incorporate appropriate limitations in a description of the regulated activities included in a Part IV permission (e.g. limitations on the circumstances in which an activity may be carried on).

Limitations that may be imposed upon a firm by the FSA or for which an applicant may apply as part of its application might, for example, take one or more of the following forms:

(a) a limit on the client categories that a firm may deal with. This would be used either where an applicant's business plan makes it clear that it only intends to provide services to a specific client category or categories, or where the FSA wishes to limit the client categories a firm can deal with;

(b) a limit on the number of clients a firm may deal with for an initial period of operation. This might be used where, for example, a firm's systems are not yet adequate to be able to process high-volume transactions;

(c) a limit on the types of specified investments that a firm can deal in. This would be used either where an applicant's business plan makes it clear that it only intends to provide services in respect of certain specified investments or where the FSA wishes to limit the categories of specified investments a firm can deal with; or

(d) a limit on the type of insurance business which a firm may carry on in connection with certain categories of specified investments in relation to which Part IV permission may be granted (e.g. a limit specifying that only reinsurance business may be carried on).

The FSA has designed a framework based around three client categories, in order to apply appropriately differentiated market conduct and conduct of business provisions based on the expertise of the different clients. The categories are:

(a) private customer;

(b) intermediate customer; and

(c) market counterparty.

In practice, a firm will be permitted to carry on regulated activities in relation to specified investments with one, or more, of these client categories. Following the grant of Part IV permission, a firm can apply to vary that Part IV permission, including any limitation, at any time.

9.2.7 *Requirements*

The FSA has the power to include such requirements in a Part IV permission as it considers appropriate. A requirement may be imposed on a firm to:

(a) take a particular action; or

(b) refrain from taking a particular action.

The requirement may extend to activities which are not regulated activities and the FSA may specify a time at which the requirement expires.

There may be cases in which an applicant wishes to apply for a requirement in order to be subject to the prudential rules applicable to a particular category or sub-category of firm.

Examples of requirements which may be imposed on a firm or for which an applicant applies might, for example, include a requirement:

(a) not to hold or control client money; or

(b) not to carry on regulated activities in certain business areas (e.g. ISA management, operating an Investment Trust Savings Scheme, Broker Fund management), unless an applicant is able to demonstrate to the FSA that it can satisfy the threshold conditions in respect of these business areas; or

(c) that the activities of a firm may only be carried on within the defined scope in which an applicant has demonstrated to the FSA that it is able to satisfy, and continue to satisfy, the threshold conditions. This might be used when an applicant applies for Part IV permission to carry on activities which fall within specific differentiated regulatory regimes, for example, those for oil market participants, locals, venture capital firms, corporate finance advisory firms or service companies. For example, an applicant wishing to act as a corporate finance adviser may be granted Part IV permission to carry on the activities of giving advice and arranging deals subject to a requirement that the firm only carries on these activities within the definition of a corporate finance adviser;

(d) not to exceed a specified amount of insurance premium income, deposits, or client assets under management. This might be used to minimise the risks to consumers that can arise in the initial period of operation of any new business; or

(e) to submit financial returns more frequently than normal, for example during the firm's first months or years of business; or

(f) to submit periodic independent compliance reviews, performed by an appropriate person, during the first months or years of business.

As part of the application process, an applicant will need to determine which prudential category it falls into and, in some cases, which sub-category. In some cases, a requirement may form part of the description of such a category or sub-category, in which case an applicant may wish to apply for Part IV permission subject to appropriate requirements.

Following the grant of Part IV permission, a firm can apply to vary that Part IV permission, including any requirement at any time.

9.2.8   *Threshold conditions*

The FSA must, in granting Part IV permission or imposing any requirement, ensure that the applicant will satisfy and continue to satisfy, the threshold conditions in relation to all of the regulated activities for which it has or will have Part IV permission. The threshold conditions are set out in Schedule 6 to the FSMA.

There are five threshold conditions:

(a) the first two threshold conditions prescribe criteria that must be met. These are the threshold conditions that prescribe the legal status that the applicant must have if it wishes to carry on certain regulated activities and the requirement that:

   (i)   a body corporate constituted under the law of any part of the UK must have its head office, and if it has one, its registered office, in the UK; and

   (ii) a non body corporate incorporated with its head office in the UK must carry on business in the UK;

(b) the last three threshold conditions require the FSA to assess whether the applicant will satisfy and continue to satisfy them; these are the threshold conditions that relate to the effect of close links on supervisability, the adequacy of an applicant's resources and the suitability of the applicant. These three threshold conditions enable the FSA to assess the applicant in the light of the activities that it wishes to carry on and, in particular, make it clear that suitability to carry on one regulated activity does not mean that the applicant is suitable to carry on all regulated activities.

The FSA would seek to determine whether an applicant satisfies and continues to satisfy the threshold conditions by considering whether the applicant can demonstrate that it is willing, ready and organised in order to comply with the specific regulatory obligations. These regulatory obligations are as applied for by the applicant in order to carry on the regulated activities detailed in its application for Part IV permission. In addition, the FSA have regard in assessing an applicant's compliance with the threshold conditions to the adequacy of its auditor's skill, resources and experience to meet their obligations to report to the FSA in respect of that applicant.

The FSA Handbook explains the specific regulatory obligations, for example:

(a) senior management arrangements and high level systems and controls;

(b) the conduct of business rules;

(c) the prudential rules contained in the Interim Prudential Sourcebooks; and

(d) the obligations in respect of the firm's relationship with the FSA contained in the Supervision Manual.

Therefore, if an applicant wishes, for example, to hold client money it will be expected to be ready, willing and able to comply with the client money rules and senior management responsibilities and high level systems and controls.

9.2.9   Connected persons

In considering an application for Part IV permission, the FSA may also take into consideration any person in a relationship with an applicant which is relevant. This person is known as a connected person.

The FSA will assess whether a particular relationship is relevant in light of the particular circumstances of each application. Examples of persons who might be considered connected with an applicant include, but are not limited to:

(a) a controller of the applicant;

(b) an applicant's directors, partners or members of its governing body; or

(c) a company in the same group as an applicant.

As part of the application procedure, the FSA will require information on an applicant's controllers, directors, partners or members of its governing body. The FSA will assess whether the applicant's:

(a) controller is a fit and proper person to have control over the firm;

(b) directors, partners and members of the governing body who will be performing controlled functions are fit and proper persons to be granted approval under the approved persons regime.

The FSA may also request information from the applicant regarding persons who are currently connected persons and/or are likely to become connected persons under any proposed transactions or relationships.

9.2.10   *The application for permission*

An applicant for Part IV permission must apply in writing in the form contained in the application pack provided by the FSA.

An application should be accompanied by the application fee set by the FSA.

An application pack and accompanying Guidance Notes are available from the corporate authorisation department at the FSA. There is also a Reader's Guide available with the Authorisation Manual, which is of considerable assistance to applicants.

9.2.11   *What information will the FSA require?*

The application forms request, *inter alia*, the following information from applicants:

(a) a business plan which describes the regulated activities and any non-regulated activities which the applicant proposes to carry on, the management and organisational structure of the applicant and details of any proposed outsourcing arrangements. The level of detail required in the business plan will be appropriate to the risks to consumers arising from the proposed regulated and non-regulated activities. For an applicant seeking to carry on insurance business, the business plan should include a scheme of operations in accordance with Appendix II to the Supervision Manual (*Insurers and friendly societies: schemes of operation*);

(b) appropriately analysed financial budgets and projections which demonstrate that the applicant expects to comply with the relevant financial resources requirements appropriate to the applicant's prudential category (and in some cases sub-category);

(c) details of systems to be used (which do not have to be in place at the time of initial application), compliance procedures and documentation;

(d) details of the individuals to be involved in running the proposed firm and any connected persons.

The application forms also require a statement from one or more members of the applicant's governing body confirming, to the best of their knowledge, the completeness and accuracy of information supplied.

The FSA may require the applicant to provide, at its own expense and as part of the application, a report by an accountant, actuary or other qualified person approved by the FSA, on such aspects of the information provided or to be provided by the applicant as the FSA may specify. Such reports may include, but not be limited to:

(a) a report from an applicant's auditor or an accountant confirming, for example, that, in their opinion, there is reasonable evidence to support the answers given by the applicant in respect of its systems and controls;

(b) a certificate from an actuary confirming the appropriateness of the projections for the business and, in respect of an application for effecting or carrying out long-term insurance contracts, the adequacy of premium rates and technical provisions and margin of solvency and how quickly capital strains from effecting new business will be overcome.

Applicants which will need permission from the Council of the Society of Lloyd's to conduct business as underwriting agents should apply for such permission in addition to applying to the FSA for Part IV permission.

Applicants should be aware that there might be a delay in processing applications if the information submitted to the FSA is inaccurately compiled or incomplete, for example, if the business plan for an application does not provide adequate details of the regulated activities for which the applicant seeks Part IV permission. Applicants should consider seeking appropriate professional advice if necessary.

As part of the application, an applicant will be required to provide the following:

(a) a controller's Form A; and

(b) except if the controller is a UK authorised person, one or more controller's Form B.

The application pack requires the application to be accompanied by other information which the person making the notification reasonably considers the FSA should be aware of for the purposes of determining the application, along with any relevant supporting documentation.

An applicant will also be required to submit information about its directors, partners and members of the governing body who will be performing controlled functions.

In certain circumstances, the interests of the customers of an applicant would be significantly affected by the death or incapacity of an individual within the applicant. Where this is the case, an applicant will be required to provide information on its arrangements to protect the interests of customers in that event. For example, arrangements to enable urgent transactions to be carried out and unfinished transactions to be completed. The information should include the name and address, and such other details as the FSA may reasonably require, of an authorised person with whom arrangements have been made for the protection of customers.

At any time after receiving an application and before determining it, the FSA may give notice to the applicant to require it to provide additional information or documents. The circumstances of each application will dictate what additional information or procedures are appropriate.

In addition, in considering the application, the FSA may:

(a) carry out any enquiries which it considers appropriate, for example, discussions with other regulators or exchanges;

(b) request the applicant, or any specified representative of the applicant, to attend meetings at the FSA to answer questions and explain any matter the FSA considers relevant to the application;

(c) require any information provided by the applicant to be verified in such manner as the FSA may specify;

(d) take into account any information which it considers appropriate in relation to the application, for example any non-regulated activities which the applicant carries on or proposes to carry on; and/or

(e) request to visit the premises that the applicant intends to use as its place of business.

The FSA expects the firm to commence its regulated activity as soon as possible following grant of Part IV permission and applicants should take this into consideration when determining when to make an application to the FSA. Applicants should discuss any issues with respect to the commencement of regulated activity with the corporate authorisation department.

The FSA may exercise its own initiative powers to vary or cancel firms' Part IV permissions if they do not start a regulated activity for which they have Part IV permission within 12 months of the date of grant.

9.2.12   *How long will an application take?*

Under Part IV, Section 52 of the FSMA, the FSA has six months from the date of receipt of a completed application to make its determination. However, within these time limits, the length of the process will relate directly to the complexity of the application.

The FSA publishes standard response times on its website setting out how long the application process is expected to take in practice. These response times are likely to be dependent upon the regulatory risk posed by the applicant. Therefore, should an applicant be classified as a low risk/complexity category their application is likely to take eight-12 weeks for consideration whereas an application that is classified as a high risk/complexity category firm is likely to take 16-26 weeks.

The response time is also subject to the FSA receiving a complete application. Where the FSA receives an application which is incomplete, that is, where information or documents required to be submitted as part of the application are not provided, the FSA is required by the FSMA to determine such incomplete applications within 12 months of the initial receipt of the application. It is worth noting that, unless the FSA considers it is appropriate to do so, the FSA will not grant an application for Part IV permission until the applicant has provided all the information and documents which the FSA has requested for in connection with the application.

9.2.13   *How will the FSA make the decision?*

Upon satisfactory receipt of all the information and documents relating to the application form, the FSA would present the application document to the Regulatory Decisions Committee (the "RDC") for approval.

The RDC is appointed by the FSA board and has responsibility for all decisions concerning applications for Part IV permission or approval of a person under Section 59 of the FSMA in respect of which, the FSA's staff have recommended the giving of a warning notice or decision notice.

The RDC has also delegated the responsibility of authorisation decisions to FSA staff (within corporate authorisations) in certain situations. In making these decisions, the FSA staff members are subject to the FSA internal staff procedures. These decision undertaken relate to:

(a) decisions to grant an application for Part IV permission on the terms applied for, including decisions to grant an application for Part IV permission subject to limitations or requirements applied for by the applicant; or

(b) decisions to grant an application for approval under Section 59 of the FSMA.

As part of an application for Part IV permission, an applicant may apply for permission which includes a limitation (e.g. a limitation in respect of customer categories), or a requirement, (e.g. a requirement not to hold or control client money).

9.2.14   Can an applicant for Part IV permission withdraw an application before the FSA makes a decision?

An applicant for Part IV permission may withdraw an application in relation to a candidate for approval at any time by writing to the FSA. This will only be accepted by the FSA if the withdrawal has the consent also of the candidate and the person by whom the candidate is, or will be, employed, if this is not the applicant for Part IV permission.

9.2.15   Will the FSA give notification of approval?

Whenever it approves an application, the FSA will confirm this in writing to all interested parties. However, where the applicant for Part IV permission is not yet an authorised person, approved person status will only be effective from the date the applicant for Part IV permission receives permission.

Further to a written notification upon authorisation, the FSA will update the FSA register with a general description of the regulated activities the firm has permission to carry on. The FSA Register is statutory requirement imposed on the FSA for the purposes of maintaining a public record containing certain details about all firms, including information as to the services they hold themselves out as able to provide.

The FSA register can be accessed at www.fsa.gov.uk.

9.2.16   *What if the FSA needs further information?*

Before making a decision to either grant the approval or give a warning notice, the FSA may request further information from the applicant for Part IV permission about the candidate. If the FSA does this then:

(a) the three month approval period will stop on the day the FSA requests the information; and

(b) will start running again on the final day on which the FSA receives all the requested information.

9.3   Other powers relating to the scope of Part IV permission

In determining an application for Part IV permission, the FSA may:

(a) specify a narrower or wider description of regulated activity than that for which Part IV permission was originally sought; or

(b) grant Part IV permission for a regulated activity which was not originally applied for.

The FSA expects to use its power to grant Part IV permission for an applicant to carry on a regulated activity for which it did not originally apply when, as a result of correspondence and discussion with an applicant, it becomes clear that it needs Part IV permission to carry on different categories of activities or activities relating to different categories of specified investments than those it had originally applied for.

The FSA will not use the power to grant Part IV permission for a regulated activity which was not originally included in the application if an applicant is applying for Part IV permission to carry on insurance business.

9.3.1   Specific requirements

There are specific requirements that relate to firms that are not bodies corporate. The following paragraphs highlight the key information that should be taken into account in an application for Part IV permission.

9.3.2   Partnerships and unincorporated associations

For the purposes of the grant of Part IV permission, all partnerships and unincorporated associations are treated as if they were legal persons hence any application for Part IV permission should be undertaken in the name of the partnership or unincorporated association.

Once a partnership or an unincorporated association is authorised by the FSA, then under Section 32 of the FSMA:

(a) it is authorised to carry on the regulated activities concerned in the name of the partnership or unincorporated association; and

(b) its authorisation is not affected by any change in its membership provided that the substantive continuity test is met.

If a partnership or unincorporated association is dissolved, its authorisation continues to have effect in relation to any partnership or unincorporated association which succeeds to the business of the dissolved partnership or unincorporated association, provided:

(a) the members of the resulting partnership or unincorporated association are substantially the same as those of the dissolved partnership or unincorporated association; and

(b) the succession is to the whole or substantially the whole of the business of the dissolved partnership or unincorporated association.

9.3.3   *Applicants seeking to undertake insurance business*

Under threshold condition 1 (legal status), an applicant seeking Part IV permission to carry on the regulated activities of effecting or carrying out of contracts of insurance, other than pure re-insurance, must be a body corporate or a registered friendly society.

Applicants should note that a firm with Part IV permission to carry on regulated activities relating to insurance business must not carry on commercial business in the UK, or elsewhere other than insurance business and activities arising directly from that business.

Except as indicated in the Authorisation Manual ("AUTH") 3.12.3G, the FSA will, therefore, not grant an applicant seeking to carry on insurance business, Part IV permission, other than for insurance business.

An applicant for Part IV permission which includes effecting or carrying out long-term insurance contracts may, however, also apply for Part IV permission to carry on activities arising directly from the insurance business they are intending to carry on; for example, a long-term insurer might also have permission to provide advice on its own products.

An applicant with its head office outside the EEA, that seeks to carry on insurance business in the UK, should refer to AUTH 3.12.14G to AUTH 3.12.17G.

An applicant with its head office outside the EEA, which is seeking a Part IV permission to carry on insurance business should appoint a Principal UK Executive and an Authorised UK General Representative.

Applicants should also be aware that generally the FSA will not grant Part IV permission to carry on both long term and general insurance business, unless:

(a) the applicant's long-term business will be restricted to reinsurance; or

(b) the applicant's general insurance business will be restricted to accident or sickness contracts (or both).

If an applicant is uncertain whether the FSA will grant Part IV permission in respect of a particular combination of activities, it should seek professional advice and discuss the matter with the FSA before making a formal application for Part IV permission. These discussions with the FSA will not, however, constitute part of the application process.

In applying for Part IV permission to carry on insurance business, applicants will need to determine the specified investments for which Part IV permission will be necessary having regard to whether certain classes of contract may qualify to be effected or carried out on an ancillary or supplementary basis. Part IV permission to effect or carry out certain classes of contracts of insurance includes permission to effect or carry out certain classes of general insurance contracts on an ancillary or supplementary basis. A firm should not apply for Part IV permission to effect or carry out contracts which can be effected or carried out on an ancillary or supplementary basis.

Part IV permission to effect or carry out life and annuity business includes permission to effect or carry out accident or sickness contracts (or both) on a supplementary basis. However, a friendly society may not effect or carry out any general insurance contracts, whether or not on an ancillary basis, other than those permitted under the Friendly Societies Act 1992.

Part IV permission to effect or carry out any class of general insurance contract includes permission to effect or carry out any other class of general insurance contract on an ancillary basis other than credit, suretyship or subject to the AUTH 3.12.9G, legal expenses insurance.

Part IV permission to effect or carry out any classes of general insurance contract includes permission to effect or carry out legal expenses business:

(a) if the main risk relates solely to the provision of assistance provided for persons who fall into difficulties while travelling, while away from home or while away from their permanent residence; or

(b) where it concerns disputes or risks arising out of, or in connection with, the use of sea-going vessels.

A class of contract of insurance will qualify to be effected or carried out on an ancillary basis if:

(a) the business in question is to be the subject of the same contract as the principal business and covers the same object; and

(b) the risks covered by the principal business and those covered by the ancillary business are the same.

In determining the classes of specified investments for which Part IV permission is required, and those which may qualify to be written on an ancillary or supplementary basis, an applicant may need to take professional advice and may also wish to discuss this with a member of the FSA's Corporate Authorisation department.

The application for Part IV permission will need to provide information about the insurance business to be carried on by the applicant in the categories of specified investments for which Part IV permission is requested and also that qualifying to be carried on an ancillary or supplementary basis.

An applicant for Part IV permission which includes insurance business should be aware that specific reporting requirements apply during its first two years of operation.

9.3.4   *Applicants seeking to carry on deposit taking activities*

Under threshold condition 1 (legal status), an applicant who seeks to carry on the regulated activity of accepting deposits must be either a body corporate or a partnership.

9.3.5   *Applicants seeking to hold or control client money*

An applicant seeking to hold or control client money must complete the relevant sections of the application forms for Part IV permission. The applicant must be able to demonstrate to the FSA that it can satisfy and continue to satisfy the threshold conditions should the application for Part IV permission be granted, including demonstrating that it is ready, willing and organised to comply with the relevant requirements in the Conduct of Business sourcebook.

9.3.6 Applicants seeking to establish a collective investment scheme or to act as a manager of a regulated collective investment scheme

An applicant seeking to establish a collective investment scheme should consult the collective investment schemes sourcebook for detailed requirements and guidance.

An applicant that is seeking Part IV permission to act as an authorised unit trust manager should note the Collective Investment Schemes Sourcebook, chapter 16 Section 16.5, which restricts the activities that the manager may engage in.

9.3.7 Applicants seeking to establish a branch in, or to provide services into, another EEA State

An applicant for Part IV permission that is seeking to establish a branch in, or provide cross-border services into, another EEA State using its rights under one of the Single Market Directives or the Treaty should refer to AUTH 4 and SUP 13 for guidance on the additional requirements and procedures under Schedule 3 to the FSMA. In some circumstances, it may be possible to submit a notice of intention to passport along with an application for Part IV permission.

9.3.8 Applicants with a principal place of business outside the EEA seeking to establish a branch in the UK

The guidance in AUTH 3.12.14G to AUTH 3.12.17G applies to applicants from outside the EEA. The exercise of passport rights by EEA firms and Treaty firms is dealt with separately in AUTH 5.

Where an applicant has its principal place of business in a country or territory outside the EEA, the FSA will, in assessing the application for Part IV permission, have regard to the applicant as a whole and not just the proposed UK branch. As part of the process, the FSA may, if reasonable in the circumstances, take into consideration information supplied by the relevant overseas regulator in that country or territory.

For example, the FSA may have regard to whether the relevant overseas regulator referred to above, informs the FSA that it is satisfied with respect to the prudent management and overall financial soundness of the applicant, in assessing whether the applicant has satisfied threshold condition 4 (adequate resources).

In considering the weight to be given to the information supplied by such an overseas regulator, the FSA will have regard to the scope of the supervision exercised by that authority.

The Prudential Sourcebook applies to non-EEA branches, except where it is explicitly stated that it does not. Waivers and requirements, for example, will be used to ensure that appropriate prudential requirements apply to the branch, taking into account the nature of the non-EEA applicant's home country supervisory arrangements and the particular circumstances of the applicant.

An applicant with its head office outside the EEA seeking permission to carry on direct or direct and reinsurance business in the UK should note that specific prudential requirements apply, including the requirements to have assets in the EEA equal to the required margin of solvency and in to make a deposit when required to do so by the FSA.

9.3.9 *Passporting into another EEA State from the UK*

This Section applies to an applicant for Part IV permission, with its head office in the UK, that wishes to exercise an entitlement to establish a branch in, or provide cross-border services into another EEA State under a Single Market Directive. Such entitlement is referred to in the FSMA as an EEA right, and its exercise is referred to in the Handbook as passporting.

An applicant that wishes, if the FSA grants it Part IV permission, to passport on or shortly after the grant of Part IV permission is advised to contact the FSA's Corporate Authorisation department before completing an application. In some circumstances, it may be possible to submit a notice of intention along with an application for Part IV permission.

9.3.10   *Automatic authorisation under the FSMA*

An automatic authorisation of EEA firms is available under Schedule 3 to the FSMA. This applies to a:

(a) Treaty firm that wishes to exercise rights under the Treaty in respect of financial services not covered by the Single Market Directives and become automatically authorised under Schedule 4 to the FSMA; and

(b) UCITS qualifier, that is an operator, trustee or depositary of a recognised collective investment scheme, constituted in another EEA State, and which is automatically authorised under Schedule 5 to the FSMA.

This Chapter does not apply to any insurance activity which is provided by a person participating in a Community co-insurance operation otherwise than as leading insurer. Such a person is exempt from the general prohibition, on the basis that a Community co-insurance operation is treated as authorised on completion by the leading insurer of the requirements of Schedule 3 to the FSMA.

Under Treasury Regulations to be made under Section 409 of the FSMA, a Gibraltar firm will be treated as an EEA firm under Schedule 3 to the FSMA if it is:

(a) authorised in Gibraltar under the Insurance Directives; or

(b) authorised in Gibraltar under the First and Second Banking Co-ordination Directives.

At present, if it complies with the relevant notification procedures, a Gibraltar insurance company is allowed to passport its services into the UK. Similarly, a Gibraltar credit institution is allowed to passport into the UK to provide banking services. This does not yet extend to investment services. Gibraltar investment firms have not yet been granted the right to passport into the UK.

9.3.11   How do Treaty firms obtain automatic authorisation under the FSMA?

Under Section 31 of the FSMA, a Treaty firm is authorised for the purposes of the FSMA if it qualifies for authorisation under Schedule 4, that is the:

(a) Treaty firm seeks to carry on a regulated activity; and

(b) conditions set out in paragraph 3(1) of Schedule 4 to the FSMA are satisfied.

The conditions in paragraph 3(1) of Schedule 4 to the FSMA are that:

(a) the Treaty firm has received authorisation under the law of its home state to carry on the regulated activities it seeks to carry on (a Treaty firm is not to be regarded as so authorised unless its home state regulator has so informed the FSA in writing); and

(b) the relevant provisions of the law of the firm's home state:

  (i)   afford equivalent protection; or

  (ii) satisfy the conditions laid down by community instruments for the co-ordination or approximation of laws, regulations, or administrative provisions of EEA States relating to the carrying on of that activity; and

(c) the Treaty firm has no right to passport in relation to that activity under one of the Single Market Directives in respect of that activity.

Under paragraph 3(3) of Schedule 4 to the FSMA, home state provisions afford equivalent protection if, in relation to the Treaty firm's carrying on of the regulated activity, they afford consumers protection which is at least equivalent to that afforded by or under the FSMA in relation to that activity.

If a Treaty firm wishes to carry on regulated activities in or into the UK as such, it must give the FSA notice in writing, by completing and submitting an application pack, as provided by the FSA.

9.3.12   How do UCITS qualifiers obtain automatic authorisation under the FSMA?

Under Schedule 5 to the FSMA, a UCITS qualifier is an authorised person. A UCITS qualifier has permission, under paragraph 2 of Schedule 5 to the FSMA, to carry on, as far as it is appropriate to the capacity in which it acts in relation to the scheme:

(a) the establishing, operating or winding up of a collective investment scheme; and

(b) any activity in connection with, or for the purposes of, that regulated activity.

A UCITS qualifier should refer to the separate section of the FSA Handbook dealing with Collective Investment Schemes for details of obtaining recognition of a scheme under the FSMA and of applicable rules and guidance.

9.3.13   EEA firms establishing a branch in the UK

9.3.13.1   The conditions for establishing a branch

Before an EEA firm can establish a branch in the UK, the FSMA requires it to satisfy the establishment conditions, as set out in paragraph 13, Part II of Schedule 3 to the FSMA. These conditions are that:

(a) the FSA has received notice (a consent notice) from the EEA firm's home state regulator that it has given the EEA firm consent to establish a branch in the UK;

(b) the consent notice:

  (i)   is given in accordance with the Single Market Directive under which the applicant is passporting;

  (ii) identifies the activities to which the consent relates; and

  (iii) includes the requisite details of the branch; and

(c) the FSA has informed the EEA firm of the applicable provisions or two months have elapsed beginning with the date on which the FSA received the consent notice.

For the purposes of paragraph 13(4), Part II of Schedule 3, to the FSMA, the applicable provisions are the FSA's rules with which the EEA firm is required to comply when carrying on a passported activity through a branch in the UK.

9.3.13.2   *The notification procedure*

When it receives a consent notice from the EEA firm's home state regulator, the FSA will, under paragraphs 13(2), (b), (c) and 13(3), Part II of Schedule 3 to the FSMA, notify the applicable provisions (if any) to:

(a) the EEA firm; and

(b) in the case of an EEA firm passporting under Insurance Directives, the home state regulator;

before the end of the two-month period beginning with the day on which the FSA received the consent notice.

In some circumstances, an EEA firm may find it helpful to contact the FSA before giving its notice of intention to its home state regulator, in order to facilitate the efficient commencement of its operations.

9.3.13.3   *EEA firms providing cross-border services into the UK*

An EEA firm should note that the requirement under the Single Market Directives to give a notice of intention to provide cross-border services applies whether or not:

(a) it has established a branch in the UK; or

(b) those cross-border services are regulated activities.

9.3.13.4   *Conditions for providing cross-border services into the UK*

It is a requirement of the Single Market Directives that, before an EEA firm can provide cross-border services into the UK, it must satisfy the service conditions, as set out in paragraph 14, Part II of Schedule 3 to the FSMA. These conditions are that:

(a) the EEA firm has given its home state regulator notice of its intention to provide cross-border services into the UK (a notice of intention);

(b) if the EEA firm is passporting under either the Investment Services Directive or the Insurance Directives, the FSA has received notice (a "regulator's notice") from the EEA firm's home state regulator containing the requisite details; and

(c) if the EEA firm is passporting under the Insurance Directives, its home state regulator has informed the EEA firm that it has sent the regulator's notice to the FSA.

9.3.13.5   *The notification procedure*

On receiving a regulator's notice or other notification from an EEA firm's home state regulator, the FSA will, under paragraphs 14(2) (b) and 14(3), Part II of Schedule 3 to the FSMA, notify the EEA firm of the applicable provisions (if any) before the end of a period of two months, beginning on the day on which the FSA received the regulator's notice or was informed of the EEA firm's notice of intention to its home state regulator, in order to facilitate the efficient commencement of its operations.

9.3.13.6   *The rules for an incoming EEA firm*

An incoming EEA firm or incoming Treaty firm carrying on business in the UK must comply with applicable provisions including relevant UK legislation. For example, where the business includes:

(a) business covered by the Consumer Credit Act of 1974, then an incoming EEA firm or incoming Treaty firm must have regard to the provisions of that FSMA, as modified by paragraph 15(3) of Schedule 3 to the FSMA; or

(b) effecting or carrying out contracts covering motor vehicle third party liability risks as part of direct insurance business, then an incoming EEA firm or incoming Treaty firm is required to become a member of the Motor Insurers Bureau.

*9.3.13.7   Regulated activities outside the scope of the Single Market
           Directives*

If a person established in the EEA does not have an EEA right,
permission as a UCITS qualifier or does not have, or does not wish
to exercise rights under the Treaty then to carry on a particular
regulated activity in the UK, it must seek Part IV permission from the
FSA to do so. This might arise, for example, where the activity is
outside the scope of the Single Market Directives. If a person also
qualifies for authorisation under Schedules 3, 4 or 5 of the FSMA as
a result of its other activities, the Part IV permission is referred to in
the Handbook as a top-up permission.

Where the FSA grants a top-up permission to an incoming EEA firm
to carry on regulated activities for which it has neither an EEA right
nor a right under the Treaty, the FSA is responsible for the prudential
supervision of the incoming EEA firm to the extent that the
responsibility is not reserved to the incoming EEA firm's home state
regulator.

Top-up permission will normally be required in respect of, for
example:

(a) the carrying on of reinsurance business;

(b) the marketing of life insurance contracts by intermediaries; and

(c) dealing, arranging or advising in relation to commodity
     derivatives.

9.3.14   The FSA's approach to approved persons

As part of an applicant's application for Part IV permission, the FSA
would require applicants to obtain its approval before people may
perform any controlled function under certain arrangements entered
into by the applicant for Part IV permission or its contractors
(including appointed representatives).

The people who perform controlled functions are likely to be
individuals but in some cases these functions may be performed by
others, (e.g. bodies corporate). Except where otherwise indicated,
references to people in this Section should be read as including
reference to these other persons.

This regime covers individuals who perform controlled functions in the capacity of, or employed by, an appointed representative. The regime does not cover an appointed representative itself unless it is a natural person. (For further details relating to appointed representatives, *see* Section 9.3.19 below.)

However, an introducer, that is, a person, other than an appointed representative, who is appointed by a firm to effect introductions between customers and the firm but not to give investment advice, will not be an approved person although there are certain obligations on these persons.

9.3.15   *What is a controlled function?*

A controlled function is a function specified by the FSA which cannot be performed by:

(a) a person under an arrangement entered into by the applicant for Part IV permission; or

(b) one of its contractors;

until approval for this has been given by the FSA. An application for approval from the FSA is required for each controlled function to be performed by a person.

Section 59 of the FSMA allows the FSA to specify a description of a controlled function on the basis that one of the following conditions is met:

(a) the function is likely to enable the person responsible for its performance to exercise a significant influence on the conduct of the authorised person's affairs, so far as relating to the regulated activity (Section 59(5) of the FSMA); or

(b) the function will involve the person performing it in dealing with customers of the authorised person in a manner substantially connected with the carrying on of the regulated activity (Section 59(6) of the FSMA); or

(c) the function will involve the person performing it in dealing with the property of customers of the authorised person in a manner substantially connected with the carrying on of the regulated activity (Section 59(7) of the FSMA).

The FSA has specified in Chapter 10 of the Supervision Manual which functions within a firm are controlled functions for the purposes of Section 59 of FSMA. These comprise:

(a) the **Governing** functions, which all firms must have, including executive, managing and non- executive directors;

(b) the **Required** functions, which again all firms must have, and which include the Apportionment and Oversight function (designated investment business only), the Compliance Oversight function, the Money Laundering Reporting Officer, and (where relevant) the EEA Investment Business Oversight function and the Appointed Actuary;

(c) the **Systems and Controls** functions, including those responsible for finance, risk assessment and internal audit;

(d) the **Significant Management** functions; and

(e) the **Customer** functions, covering those dealing with customers and/ or their property.

Functions (a) to (d) constitute the **significant influence** functions. Chapter 10 of the Supervision Manual gives further details on how to determine whether or not particular jobs in a firm constitute controlled functions, and the requirements that this creates for the firm.

9.3.16   *What is an approved person?*

An approved person is a person whose performance of one or more controlled functions has been approved by the FSA.

9.3.17   *How does a person become an approved person?*

Where a person will be performing one or more controlled functions, the applicant for Part IV permission should apply to the FSA for the person to receive approved person status before he starts performing these functions. This is true whether the person is acting under arrangements entered into by the applicant for Part IV permission or one of its contractors, including an appointed representative.

The application should be made using the FSA Form A, copies of which are available on the FSA website at www.fsa.gov.uk or from the individual vetting and registration department.

9.3.18 *What will the FSA take into account when making a decision?*

The FSA may grant an application only if it is satisfied that the person is a fit and proper person to perform the controlled function(s) specified in the application form.

When assessing the fitness and propriety of a person, responsibility lies with the applicant for Part IV permission making the application to satisfy the FSA that the person is fit and proper to perform the controlled function(s) applied for.

When considering an application for approval, the FSA will consider all relevant matters, including:

(a) the honesty, integrity and reputation of a person;

(b) his experience, competence and capability; and

(c) his financial soundness.

For further guidance on criteria for assessing fitness and propriety is appended to the application form.

In determining whether a person has the competence and capability to perform the relevant controlled function(s), the FSA may, *inter alia*, have regard to whether the candidate has:

(a) a relevant qualification;

(b) undergone training or is currently a trainee; or

(c) appropriate experience or competence;

having regard to requirements set out in the Training and Competence Rules (*see* T&C).

9.3.19   *The FSA's approach to appointed representatives*

Applicants for Part IV permission, an EEA firm or a Treaty firm, seeking to carry on designated investment business, are entitled to appoint representatives to conduct regulated activities on their behalf and under their supervision. The Authorisation Manual (AUTH 1) provides guidance on the meaning of the term "appointed representative" and the status of an appointed representative as an exempt person under the FSMA. However, the main guidance in respect of appointed representatives is contained in SUP 12.

Before an applicant, an EEA firm or a Treaty firm can permit a person to carry on regulated activities as an appointed representative, the applicant, EEA firm or Treaty firm itself must have permission to perform those activities.

An applicant, an EEA firm or a Treaty firm that wishes to appoint an appointed representative once authorised should refer to Chapter 12 of the Supervision Manual which contains:

(a) the FSA's rules and guidance relating to the appointment of an appointed representative; and

(b) guidance on the implications, for the applicant, EEA firm or Treaty firm itself, of appointing an appointed representative.

A separate leaflet has been produced to give guidance to appointed representatives themselves. Copies of this leaflet can be requested from the corporate authorisation department.

9.3.20   *What is an appointed representative?*

In order to become an appointed representative, a person must meet the requirements under Section 39 of the FSMA. These are that:

(a) the person cannot be an authorised person (Section 39(1) of the FSMA);

(b) the person must have entered into a contract with an authorised person, referred to in the FSMA as the "principal", which:

(i) permits or requires it to carry on business of a description prescribed by HM Treasury (Section 39(1)(a)(i) of the FSMA); and

(ii) complies with any requirements that may be prescribed by HM Treasury (Section 39(1)(a)(ii) of the FSMA); and

(c) the principal must have accepted responsibility, in writing, for the activities of the person in carrying on the whole, or part, of that business (Section 39(1)(b) of the FSMA).

If these requirements are satisfied, the person appointed under the contract has the status of an exempt person under the FSMA in relation to any regulated activity comprised in the carrying on of that business for which the authorised person has accepted responsibility. Section 19 of the FSMA states that no person may carry on a regulated activity in the UK, or purport to do so, unless they are an authorised person or an exempt person. A person who is exempt as a result of meeting these requirements is referred to in the FSMA as an appointed representative.

9.4 Supervision process

9.4.1 The FSA's approach to supervision and risk assessment of individual firms

The cornerstone of FSA's supervision of its authorised firm members is embodied in the requirement of the FSA to "maintain arrangements designed to enable it to determine whether persons on whom requirements are imposed by or under this FSMA are complying with them" (paragraph 6(1) of Schedule 1 to the FSMA).

The FSA's approach to supervision is primarily driven by the regulatory objective to secure an appropriate degree of protection for consumers, hence the FSA aims to focus and reinforce the responsibility of management of each firm to ensure that it takes reasonable care to organise and control the affairs of the firm's responsibly and effectively and develops and maintains adequate risk management systems. It is the responsibility of management to ensure that the firm acts in compliance with its regulatory requirements.

In designing its approach to supervision the FSA has regard to the "principles of good regulation" set out in Section 2(3) of the FSMA. In particular, the FSA's regulatory approach aims to focus and reinforce the responsibility of the management of each firm (Section 2(3)(b) of the FSMA) to ensure that it takes reasonable care to organise and control the affairs of the firm's responsibly and effectively, develops and maintains adequate risk management systems. It is the responsibility of management to ensure that the firm acts in compliance with its regulatory requirements.

Where a firm or individual falls short of regulatory requirements, the FSA expects that senior management will take steps to remedy this and to deal fairly with any consumers who have been disadvantaged as a result.

Where a firm or individual falls short of regulatory requirements, the FSA will seek to ensure that action is taken to correct this and to address the risks involved. Where consumers have suffered loss, the FSA will seek to ensure that redress is provided. Wherever appropriate the FSA will use persuasion and dialogue. However, in some cases it will be appropriate for the FSA to use its powers on its own initiative to set individual requirements for a firm (*see* SUP 7). In certain cases, the FSA may use its enforcement powers as soon as a regulatory issue is identified. These enforcement powers are covered in Chapter 10.

In pursuing the objective of reducing the extent to which it is possible for a business to be used for a purpose connected with financial crime, the FSA will take account of compliance with the Money Laundering Regulations 1993; and in assessing such compliance will have regard to a firm's compliance with the Joint Money Laundering Steering Groups' Guidance Notes for the Financial Sector. For more detail on the FSA's general approach to money laundering *see* Chapter 8.

For a firm which undertakes business internationally (or is part of a group which does), the FSA will have regard to the context in which it operates, including the nature and scope of the regulation to which it is subject in jurisdictions other than the UK. For a firm with its head office outside the UK, the regulation in the jurisdiction where the head office is located will be particularly relevant. As part of its supervision of such a firm, the FSA will seek to co-operate with relevant overseas regulators, including exchanging information on the firm. Different arrangements apply to an incoming EEA firm, an incoming Treaty firm and a UCITS qualifier.

In order to enhance the efficiency and effectiveness of the process of supervisions, the FSA has taken a risk-based approach to supervision. The FSA uses a standard risk assessment process applied consistently across all of its activities. It involves assessing the risk to the FSA's regulatory objectives posed by the firm against a number of impact and probability factors.

The impact of a firm is therefore assessed by reference to a range of factors derived from the regulatory objectives, including:

(a) the extent to which prudential failure, misconduct, market malfunction, market manipulation or the need to contribute to the reconstitution of compensation schemes may be detrimental (directly or indirectly) to consumers;

(b) the extent to which the firm may pose risks to the achievement of the objective of promoting public understanding;

(c) the incidence and materiality of any financial crime which may be perpetrated through or by the firm; and

(d) the degree to which risks, were they to materialise, would damage market confidence.

The risk assessment process applies equally to all member firms. The key driver to this process is the ongoing communication between the firm and the FSA. The FSA aims to ensure consistency through a peer review process within the FSA.

9.4.2   *The FSA's approach to gathering information about firms and the firms reporting requirements*

The FSA is required to monitor a firm's compliance with requirements imposed by or under the FSMA. To meet this requirement and to undertake its supervision, member firms are required to deal with their regulators in an open and co-operative way and must tell the FSA promptly anything relating to the firm of which the FSA would reasonably expect prompt notice.

The FSA employs the following techniques to collate information about the firms:

(a) reports requested from skilled persons;

(b) appointment of investigators;

(c) application for a warrant to enter premises;

(d) supervision visits made by FSA staff members;

(e) undertaking "mystery shopping" without notification.

Supervision visits may be made by representatives or appointees of the FSA to firms, on a routine basis after notification, for special purposes such as theme visits (looking at a particular issue across a range of firms), or without advance notice. Firms' employees, agents and appointed representatives may be requested to attend at the FSA's offices. The FSA may also seek information by electronic communication, over the telephone or in writing.

The FSA's representatives or appointees may, without notifying the firm, assume the role of a retail customer or potential retail customer during contact with a firm, its agents or its appointed representatives. This activity may be carried out:

(a) in conjunction with a programme of visits (looking at a particular issue across a range of firms) in order to obtain information about a particular practice of firms or a class of firms in carrying on regulated activities or ancillary activities or in communicating or approving financial promotions;

(b) in conjunction with focused visits (concentrating on particular aspects of a firm's business) in order to obtain information about the practices of a firm in carrying on regulated activities or ancillary activities or in communicating or approving financial promotions where the FSA has particular concerns about those practices; and

(c) to assist in regulatory investigations.

Telephone calls and meetings held while assuming the role of a customer or potential customer may be recorded.

As part of FSA's supervisory role, the FSA needs timely and accurate information about the firms it supervises. As such, the FSA requires firms to submit the following reports on an on-going basis:

(a) *annual controllers report: list* of all controllers as at the firm's accounting reference date. These reports must be submitted within four months of the firm's accounting reference date;

(b) *annual close links reports:* list of all the persons with whom the firm has close links as at its annual accounting reference date. These reports must be submitted within four months of the firm's accounting reference date;

(c) *compliance reports;*

(d) *financial reports:* both the compliance and financial reports have detail reporting specific to the type of firm, this is detailed within the FSA's Supervision Manual. Submission of these reports may be on a quarterly or annual basis dependent on the type of firm.

Further details are provided in Chapter 16 of the Supervision Manual

Over time, the FSA expects to shift the balance towards thematic regulation and to carry out a number of focused theme projects each year. The FSA has indicated a number of pilot theme projects. Topics include:

(a) e-commerce;

(b) the implications of a low-inflation environment;

(c) money laundering: customer identification and related requirements;

(d) treating customers fairly after point of sale;

(e) the implications of an ageing (and therefore gradually disinvesting) population; and

(f) harnessing market forces to support regulatory efforts.

Further details of the above are available in the FSA's document: *A New Regulator for the New Millennium.*

9.4.3   *Notification requirements*

A firm must notify the FSA immediately if it becomes aware that any of the following has or may have occurred or may occur in the foreseeable future:

(a) the firm failing to satisfy one or more of the threshold conditions;

(b) any matter which could have a significant adverse impact on the firm's reputation;

(c) any matter which could affect the firm's ability to continue to provide adequate services to its customers and which could result in serious detriment to a customer of the firm;

(d) any matter in respect of the firm that could result in serious financial consequences to the financial system or to other firms.

In addition, there are detailed requirements to require firms to notify the FSA of:

(a) significant rule breaches, breaches of Statements of Principle, or breaches of requirements of FSMA;

(b) significant civil proceedings, disciplinary measures or sanctions against the firm;

(c) significant fraud by an employee against a customer or by any person against the firm;

(d) any act of insolvency by the firm or actions taken to wind up the firm;

(e) changes in any of the key individuals who control or have significant influence over the firm; and

(f) changes in core information in relation to the firm (such as name, address, legal status and other regulators).

A notification required from a firm under any of the FSA's notification rules must be given in writing, by letter or by electronic mail, unless:

(a) the notification rule states otherwise; or

(b) the notification is provided solely in compliance with Principle 11 relating to dealing with the regulators in an open and co-operative manner.

Further details of notification requirements are provided in Chapter 15 of the Supervision Manual.

9.4.4   Tools of supervision

The FSA uses a variety of tools to monitor whether a firm, once authorised, remains in compliance with regulatory requirements, and to address specific risks identified in firms. They include:

(a) desk based reviews;

(b) liaison with other agencies or regulators;

(c) making recommendations for preventative or remedial action;

(d) meetings with management and other representatives from a firm;

(e) on-site inspections;

(f) reviews and analysis of periodic returns and notifications;

(g) reviews of past business;

(h) setting individual requirements, and issuing individual guidance for a firm;

(i) transaction monitoring;

(j) use of skilled persons;

(k) varying a firm's permission.

The FSA also seeks to rely on opinions from a firm's auditors as part of the process of supervision. Details of requirements relating to the appointment of auditors is contained within Chapter 3 of the Supervision Manual.

Firms should have in place an auditor who will be able to provide an opinion on the firm's annual financial statements and annual financial return and on a review of the firm's internal control system and also, where relevant, on its procedures for segregating clients' assets from its own. In assessing whether firms meet the threshold conditions for permission under Part IV of the FSMA, FSA will have regard to whether the firm's auditors have the required skill, resources and experience to fulfil these requirements, commensurate with the complexity of the business of the firm that they are auditing. Firms are also required by the FSA to take reasonable steps to ensure that their auditors are independent under their professional body's independence requirements. Chapter 3 of the Supervision Manual also sets out the access that firms must allow to their auditors.

The FSA may seek to apply the same criteria and reliance on reports on which opinions are expressed by a firm's actuaries.

Both auditors and actuaries of regulated firms are subject to a statutory duty to report to the FSA where they believe that they have information which would be of material significance to the regulator in deciding whether to take action against their client. Further details of the obligations of auditors and actuaries are spelt out in Chapter 3.

As at the date of publication of this guide, details of the regime relating to the use of skilled persons by the FSA had not yet been included in the Supervision Manual, though a Consultative Paper (CP 91) has been issued. However, it is expected that the final Supervision Manual will include a section on the use of skilled persons.

As part of FSA's power to gather information and conduct investigations set out in Part XI of the FSMA, Section 166 provides a power for the regulator to require regulated firms to commission reports from a "person" nominated or approved by the FSA and appearing to them to have the skills necessary to make a report on the matter concerned. This power will normally be used to commission reports from firms of accountants, lawyers, actuaries or information technology consultants, and in most cases will be from a professional services firm nominated by the regulated firm. This power is not just to be used to gather information to allow the regulator to assess the risks that a regulated firm creates to the FSA's regulatory objectives: it is seen as a means of assisting the firm to take action to remedy issues that the regulator has identified. The FSA has also indicated that it will not use this power where an adequate result could be obtained by requesting that a report be obtained from a firm's internal resources, for example from its internal auditors. It is also not seen as a means of compensating for any lack of resources that the FSA may suffer, but as a means of accessing skills and experience additional to those conventionally employed by the regulator.

9.4.5 *Specific variations: additional requirements imposed on an individual firm, waivers and modification of rules and individual guidance*

The circumstances in which the FSA may seek to vary a firm's Part IV permission on its own initiative or to give a firm individual guidance include the following:

(a) If the FSA determines that a firm's management, business or internal controls give rise to risks that are not fully captured by its rules then the FSA may seek to vary the firm's Part IV permission and impose an additional requirement or restriction on the firm.

(b) Similarly, the FSA may consider it necessary or desirable to issue individual guidance to a firm. For example, some of the FSA's requirements are expressed in general terms as the FSA recognises that the detailed steps which a firm should take to comply with the rules depend on factors which may be specific to an individual firm (e.g. the requirement for a firm to take reasonable care to establish and maintain appropriate systems and controls). However, there may be instances where the FSA considers that, in order to comply with a requirement, a firm should act or refrain from acting in a particular way. In such cases, the FSA may give individual guidance to the firm setting out how it considers the requirement should be met.

(c) Where a firm becomes, or is to become, involved with new products or selling practices which present risks not captured by existing requirements, the FSA may seek to vary the firm's Part IV permission in respect of those risks.

(d) Where there has been a change in a firm's structure, controllers, activities or strategy which generate uncertainty or create unusual or exceptional risks, then the FSA may seek to vary the firm's Part IV permission or issue individual guidance.

In certain circumstances, firms may apply to the FSA for permission to modify or waive the FSA's rules. If a firm wishes to request a waiver, it must write to a member of its supervision team. This request must include:

(a) a clear explanation, based on a thorough researching of the facts (in relation to the Handbook), of why the firm wants a waiver. This must include details of any special requirements, for example the date by which the waiver is required or relating to the publishing of waivers, and all relevant information that the firm reasonably believes should be brought to the FSA's attention; and

(b) sufficient information to enable the FSA to decide whether the criteria set out in Section 148(4) of the FSMA have been satisfied.

Under the transitional arrangements for the implementation of the new regime, the FSA intends to "grandfather" existing written concessions to firms at 30 November 2001 for a limited period of 12 months. Written concessions relating to the Interim Prudential Sourcebook or the compliance and financial returns (required by Chapter 16, Sections 6 and 7, of the Supervision Manual) can be carried forward until the Integrated Prudential Sourcebook is implemented.

Individual guidance includes guidance given to one particular firm or other person in relation to its own particular circumstances or plans. It may be oral or written, but will not normally be published. In exceptional circumstances, at the FSA's discretion, individual guidance may be published. No grandfathering arrangements are proposed for individual guidance.

The FSA does not expect to enter into discussions on a "no-name" basis about the affairs of an individual firm.

A firm, or a professional adviser acting on behalf of the firm, should make its request for guidance to the firm's supervision team within the FSA, and should normally do so in writing. Oral queries will not always result in substantive written guidance, although it is open to firms to confirm oral guidance in writing for positive ratification by the FSA.

Before entering into discussion with a firm's professional adviser, the FSA will need to be satisfied that the professional adviser is acting with the firm's full permission.

9.4.6 The individuals in authorised firms: approved persons, controller and appointed representative

Any changes to a person's job involving persons registered as an approved person and appointed representative of the firm would require a notification to the FSA. This would also apply for any changes in ownership or change in controller information. The Supervision Manual provides further details regarding the application forms and frequently asked questions and answers regarding this.

9.4.7 Transaction reporting

When a firm (whether on its own account or on behalf of another) effects a reportable transaction, it must make a transaction report to the FSA. This requirement is applicable to all securities and futures firms, personal investment firms undertaking ISD type of business and credit institutions.

A firm need not make a transaction report to the FSA if:

(a) the firm complies with a requirement on it to report the reportable transaction to its home state regulator; or

(b) the reportable transaction is transacted on one of the exchanges listed in the Supervision Manual and the firm reports the reportable transaction to that exchange.

There are certain exemptions for investment management firm or a personal investment firm in relation to transaction reporting. This is detailed in the Supervision Manual.

The obligation for firms to report their transactions to the FSA is primarily aimed to protect investors and ensure the smooth operation and transparency of the markets in transferable securities. Transaction reports also form a useful part of the FSA's arrangements for monitoring and can assist the FSA in assessing the type of business carried out by a firm and the conduct of that business.

9.4.8 *The FSA's decision making process for supervision*

In the course of its supervision functions the FSA proposes to give a supervisory notice, a warning notice or a decision notice, in respect of which there are specified procedures and specific actions and protections.

The FSA's decisions in relation to the giving of warning, decision and supervisory notices in the course of its supervision are made either by internal procedures within the FSA, that is by the FSA staff at an appropriate level of seniority or depending on the nature of the decision, by procedures involving the RDC.

The allocation of responsibility for decision-making between executive procedures and the RDC is set out in the Decision Making Manual.

9.4.9 *Emergencies*

There are inevitably occasions where it would be unreasonable for the FSA to expect firms to comply with all the relevant rules. The High Level Standards section of the Handbook therefore provides relief for firms from the need to comply with specific rules provided that the firm notifies the FSA of the emergency immediately and of the steps which it is taking or proposes to take, and the emergency:

(a) could not have been realistically avoided by the firm, had it taken all reasonable steps to do so;

(b) is such that it is impracticable for the firm to comply with the specific rules; and

(c) remains outside the control of the firm.

·

Chapter 10

DISCIPLINE AND ENFORCEMENT

Alistair Graham
Partner
Margaret Chamberlain
Partner
Travers Smith Braithwaite

10.1 Introduction

This Chapter provides an overview of the new discipline and enforcement powers available to the Financial Services Authority (the "FSA") under the Financial Services and Markets FSMA 2000 (the "FSMA").

In May 2001, following a period of consultation, the FSA published the "final" text Enforcement and Decision Making Manuals which specify how the FSA proposes to exercise its new disciplinary and enforcement powers. References in this Chapter to the Enforcement Manual (the "Manual") will be to ENF 1 (i.e. chapter 1). Similarly, references in this Chapter to the DEC Manual (the "DEC Manual") will be to DEC 1 (i.e. chapter 1). In the case of both Manuals, although "final" texts were published in May 2001 and Rules "made" in June 2001, they remain subject to possible change to achieve consistency with other parts of the Handbook which have yet to be finalised but the underlying policy will only be changed in what are described as "exceptional circumstances".

The Manual runs to 18 chapters and over 300 pages and contains many flow charts and helpful diagrams. The DEC Manual, although shorter, also contains a large number of diagrams and flow charts. It is therefore not possible in this overview to deal with every matter raised in those Manuals. We have therefore focused on the measures which are likely to be most regularly used in practice, namely:

(a) *Information Gathering Powers (Sections 1 to 7)*: under this heading we cover Sections 165-169 and 284 of the FSMA and ENF 2 which deal with the powers to appoint investigators to require information and documents from firms and to obtain reports by "skilled persons".

(b) *Main Disciplinary Measures (Sections 8 to 12)*: under this heading we cover Sections 205 (Public Statements and Public Censure) and 206 (Financial Penalties) of the FSMA, Private warnings, and ENF 12 and ENF 13, which explain the criteria the FSA applies in determining whether to take disciplinary action.

(c) *Other Enforcement Measures (Section 13)*: under this heading we cover Sections 45, 46 and 47 and ENF 3 which deal with variations of Part IV permissions on the FSA's own initiative; Section 194 and ENF 4 which deals with intervention against incoming EEA firms; Section 44 and ENF 5 which deals with cancellation of Part IV permission; ENF 6 which deals with injunctions; Section 63 and ENF 7 which deals with withdrawal of approval; Section 56 and ENF 8 which deals with prohibition of individuals; Section 382-4 and ENF 9 which deals with restitution and redress; ENF 10 which deals with insolvency proceedings and other miscellaneous matters.

(d) *Statutory Notices and the Decision Making Process (Section 14)*: under this heading we cover Sections 387-395 of the FSMA and DEC 2 which deals with warning notices, decision notices, final notices and supervisory notices.

(e) *The Regulatory Decision Committee (RDC) (Section 15)*: under this heading we cover Section 395 of the FSMA and DEC 4 which deal with the RDC's constitution, and procedures and settlement and mediation.

(f) *Hearings and Appeals (Section 16)*: under this heading we cover Section 132 and Schedule 13 of the FSMA and DEC 5 which deal with the Financial Services and Markets Tribunal (the "Tribunal"), its composition, procedure, evidence, decisions, appeals and costs.

10.2   Background and information-gathering powers

10.2.1   *Guiding principles flowing from A New Regulator for the New Millennium*

In its paper, *A New Regulator for the New Millennium*, the FSA considered its future regulatory approach, and noted that it has a range of regulatory tools to enable it to meet its statutory objectives. The FSA regards its ability to take formal disciplinary action, and its related powers to conduct investigations, to vary a firm's permission and to obtain restitution, as an important aspect of its role as a regulator.   However, it acknowledges that there are other preventative aspects which are also key.   For example, the requirement for authorisation of firms and approval of individuals is of assistance in ensuring that only persons who meet the criteria for honesty, competence and financial soundness are able to carry on regulated activities.   On-going supervision by the FSA allows it to monitor firms and, hopefully, identify risks before they can cause material harm.

The FSA also seems keen to stress that formal disciplinary action will not always be appropriate when a firm or approved person has breached a regulatory requirement.   Where a breach is detected as a part of the FSA's supervision and monitoring programme, the FSA may conclude that, provided the breach is remedied to its satisfaction, no formal action is appropriate.

The FSMA expressly requires the FSA to prepare and publish statements of policy and procedure on the exercise of some of its enforcement powers.   The Manual therefore contains statements of policy and procedures on matters such as the imposition of financial penalties (required by Sections 69 and 210 of the FSMA).   In addition, the Manual contains guidance in accordance with Section 157(1) of the FSMA on the FSA's use of its enforcement powers including its powers to vary a Part IV permission on its own initiative (ENF 3); to apply to the court for injunctions (ENF 6); and to obtain restitution (ENF 9).   In considering matters of discipline and enforcement it is therefore important to have regard not just to the provisions of the FSMA but also to relevant provisions of the Manual. It will also be necessary from time to time to consult two of the other manuals which form the regulatory processes part of the Handbook, namely the Supervision Manual (SUP) and the DEC Manual. The Supervision Manual sets out the relationship between the FSA and authorised persons. The DEC Manual is principally concerned with setting out the FSA's decision-making procedures for decisions that involve the issue of statutory notices.

10.2.2   *Information gathering and investigation powers*

The FSA's powers to gather information and appoint investigators are contained in Sections 165 to 169 and 284 of the FSMA. They are dealt with in the Manual at ENF 2 starting at ENF 2.3.1G. In summary they are:

(a) requiring information and documents from firms;

(b) requiring reports on firms by "skilled persons";

(c) general investigations of firms and appointed representatives;

(d) investigations of specific contraventions, offences and other matters;

(e) investigations in support of overseas regulators; and

(f) investigations into collective investment schemes.

The first four of these provisions are likely to be those most frequently used.

10.2.3   *Section 165 – requiring information and documents from firms*

FSMA Section 165 applies to information or documents "reasonably required" by the FSA in connection with the exercise of functions given to it, by or under the FSMA, it specifies the ways in which the FSA may require information and documents from firms:

(a) under Section 165(1) the FSA may, by notice in writing, require a firm to provide specified information or information of a specified description or produce a specified document or documents of a specified description. The firm must do this within a reasonable period of time. The firm must provide the information in any form which the FSA may reasonably require;

(b) under Section 165(3) an officer authorised by the FSA may require a firm without delay to (a) provide him with specified information or information of a specified description or (b) produce to him specified documents or documents of a specified description;

(c) under Section 165(7) the FSA may also use the power to impose requirements to provide information or to produce documents on a person who is "connected" with an authorised person;

(d) under Section 165(11) a person is "connected" with an authorised person ("A") if he is, or at any relevant time has been:

    (i)   a member of A's Group;

    (ii) a controller of A;

    (iii) any other member of a partnership of which A is a member;

    (iv) a person mentioned in Schedule 15(i) of the FSMA such as an officer, or manager of the firm who is a corporate body.

The FSA recognises that the powers under this Section to require information and documents will be used both in support of its supervisory function as well as its enforcement function.

10.2.4   *Section 166 – reports on firms by skilled persons*

Section 166 specifies the FSA's power to require firms to provide a report by a skilled person. The FSA may require any of the following who are or were at the relevant time carrying on a business, to provide it with a report made by a "skilled person" on any matter about which the FSA has required or could require the provision of information or documents under Section 165:

(a) a firm (A);

(b) any other member of A's Group;

(c) a partnership of which A is a member;

(d) a person who has at any relevant time been one of the above.

The FSA may specify the form in which it requires the report be made. There is no definition of what constitutes a skilled person, but under Section 166(4) the person appointed to make the report must be nominated or approved by the FSA and appear to the FSA to have the skills necessary to report on the matter concerned, so who is appointed will depend on the nature of the problem to be investigated. Section 166(5) gives the skilled person powers to require assistance which may be reasonably required from the firm being investigated in order to complete the report. The FSA may apply for an injunction to enforce this obligation. The FSA may use its Section 166 power to require reports by skilled persons in support of both its supervision and enforcement functions. Consultation Paper 91 published in May 2001, proposes an approach which is common across all financial service sectors and covers both FSA's supervisory and enforcement roles. It proposes a risk-focused approach, with the decision whether to appoint a skilled person to report being made on a case-by-case basis. In deciding whether to use the "skilled person" power, the FSA proposes to have regard to such factors as:

(a) whether the need can be met without use of statutory powers;

(b) circumstances relating to the firm (e.g. firm's attitude, history of similar issues);

(c) alternative tools;

(d) legal procedural considerations (e.g. statutory powers available);

(e) the objectives of the FSA's enquiries (e.g. for gathering historic information or obtaining expert analysis);

(f) costs;

(g) the expected benefit to the firm;

(h) considerations relating to the FSA resources (availability of the FSA expertise).

10.2.5   Section 167 – general investigations of firms and appointed representatives

Section 167 of the FSMA relates to the appointment of investigators to conduct general investigations into firms and appointed representatives. Under Section 167(1), if it appears to the FSA that there is "good reason" to do so, then it may appoint one or more competent persons to conduct an investigation into:

(a) the nature, conduct or state of the business of a firm of an appointed representative;

(b) a particular aspect of that business;

(c) the ownership or control of a firm.

Under Section 167(2) if the person appointed to investigate thinks it necessary for his investigation, he may also investigate the business of a person who is or has at any relevant time been (a) a member of the group of which the person under investigation (A) is a part; or (b) a partnership of which (A) is a member.

10.2.6 *Section 168 – investigations of specific contraventions, offences and other matters*

Section 168 of the FSMA relates to the conduct of investigations and to certain specified contraventions, offences or other matters. The FSA's powers to appoint investigators are contained in Sections 168(3) and 168(5) and the circumstances in which it can do so are listed in Sections 168(1), (2) and (4) of the FSMA and include issues such as market abuse, financial promotion, money laundering and a number of other specific contraventions.

10.2.7 *Section 169 – investigations in support of overseas regulators*

Section 169 specifies the FSA's powers following a request from an overseas regulator to use its powers to acquire documents or information under Section 165 or to appoint a person to investigate any matter. The FSA's policy on how to use this power is set out at ENF 2.8.

10.2.8 *Investigations into collective investment schemes*

Section 284(1) specifies the FSA's powers to investigate the affairs of collective investment schemes. The FSA's policy on how it will use its powers under Section 284 is set out at ENF 2.9.

10.3 Powers of FSA investigators

The nature and extent of an investigator's powers depend on the provision of the FSMA under which he was appointed. Broadly speaking, there are three levels of powers:

(a) the basic powers for Section 167 general investigations into authorised firms and persons "connected" with those under investigation;

(b) the same basic powers plus the power to interview and get information from other persons not the subject of the investigation and not "connected" to any such person where "necessary and expedient" for Section 168(1) or (4) investigations; and

(c) the widest possible powers for Section 168(2) investigators which can require persons who are neither the subject of the investigation nor connected with any such person to attend before the investigator, answer questions and provide information if the investigator considers they may have relevant information.

10.3.1 *Powers of Section 167 investigators*

The powers of a Section 167 investigator are contained in Sections 171 and 175 of the FSMA (described in ENF 2.4.2G to 2.4.5G and ENF 2.4.10G to 2.4.12G). In summary, Section 171 states that an investigator conducting a general investigation under Section 167 of the FSMA may require the person who is the subject of the investigation or any person connected with the person under investigation:

(a) to attend before the investigator at a specified time or place to answer questions; or

(b) otherwise to provide such information as the investigator may require.

Under Section 171(2), the investigator may also require any person to produce at a specified time and place any specified documents or documents of a specified description. Section 171(3) contains a limitation, namely that the investigator may only impose a requirement so far as he reasonably considers the question, provision of information or production of documents to be relevant to the purposes of the investigation.

10.3.2   *Powers of Section 168(1) and (4) investigators*

Under the FSMA, the powers of Section 168 investigators depend upon precisely which matter they are appointed to investigate. Lesser powers apply where the investigation is for matters listed in Sections 168(1) and (4) than those listed in Section 168(2). In respect of Sections 168(1) and (4), the applicable powers are those contained in Sections 172 and 175 (described in ENF 2.4.6G to 2.4.7G and ENF 2.4.10G to 2.4.12G). In summary, these are the same as the powers given for Section 167 investigators. However, under Section 172(2), an investigator will also have the power to require a person who is *not* subject to the investigation *nor* a person connected with the person under investigation, to attend before him at a specified time and place and answer questions or otherwise to provide such information as he may require for the purposes of the investigation. However, this additional power may only be imposed if the investigator is satisfied that it is necessary or expedient for the purposes of the investigation.

10.3.3   *Powers of investigators appointed as a result of Section 168(2)*

Section 173 of FSMA sets out the powers of an investigator appointed as a result of Section 168(2). Under this Section, if an investigator considers that any person is or may be able to give information which is or may be relevant to the investigation, he may require that person to:

(a) attend before him at a specified time and place to answer questions;

(b) provide such information as the investigator may require for the purpose of the investigation;

(c) produce at a specified time and place any specified documents which appear to the investigator to relate to relevant matters;

(d) give the investigator all assistance in connection with the investigation which he is reasonably able to give.

10.3.4   *Powers of Section 169 investigators*

Section 169(2) states that an investigator appointed in support of an overseas regulator has the same powers as an investigator appointed as a result of Section 168(1) (*see* ENF 2.4.6g to 2.4.7G and ENF 2.4.10G to 2.4.12G).

Some powers are common to the investigators whether they be under Section 167 or Section 168. Section 175 provides that the FSA, or an investigator appointed by it under Section 167 or Section 168, has the power to require a person to produce a document and if it appears the document is in the possession of a third person the FSA or investigator may use that power in relation to the third person.

10.3.5   *Powers of a Section 284 investigator*

Section 284(3) states that if a Section 284 investigator considers a person may be able to give information which is relevant, he may require him to produce any documents in his possession or control relevant to the investigation to attend before him and otherwise give all assistance which he reasonably can give.

10.4   **The FSA's policy on exercising its investigation powers in relation to firms**

ENF 2.5 represents the FSA's policy in relation to its different statutory powers. In relation to reports by skilled persons under Section 166 and investigations under Sections 167 and 168, which are most likely to be the most commonly used powers, the FSA states that if information available to it raises a "regulatory concern" about a firm or an approved person's conduct or fitness of propriety, it may need to make further enquiries by using its powers to require a skilled person's report or to appoint investigators. The types of concern that may prompt the FSA to make further enquiries cannot be exhaustively listed, but broadly speaking will be circumstances which suggest that:

(a) the firm or approved person may have acted in such a way as to prejudice the interest of consumers;

(b) the firm or approved person may have acted in breach of the requirements of the legislation or the rules;

(c) the firm may no longer meet any special conditions imposed by the FSA or an approved person within a firm may not be fit and proper to perform controlled functions;

(d) the firm may have been used or may be being used for the purposes of financial crime or laundering the proceeds of crime;

(e) the FSA should be concerned about the ownership or control of the firm, including whether a person who has acquired influence over a firm meets the requirements for FSA approval;

(f) the conduct of certain types of regulated activity in which a firm is involved are a cause of serious public concern over the way in which those activities are being conducted.

The FSA's policy on investigations into suspected market misconduct, unauthorised business, assistance to overseas authorities and in relation to collective investment schemes is set out at ENF 2.7, 2.8 and 2.9 respectively.

In some circumstances, the provision of a report by a skilled person under Section 166 may not be appropriate or may be insufficient. For example, there may be a need to ask persons to answer questions or produce documents and in such cases the FSA will appoint an investigator under Section 167 or 168. In other cases the FSA may appoint an investigator under Section 167 or 168 as a result of information obtained in a Section 166 report. Investigators will usually be members of FSA staff.

Where the FSA has a general concern about a firm or appointed representative but the circumstances do not at that stage suggest any specific breach or contravention, it will usually rely on the more limited powers in Section 167 of the FSMA. Where it appears to the FSA that circumstances suggest specific contraventions or offences set out in Section 168, the FSA will appoint investigators under that section, whose powers will be wider than those available to investigators under Section 167 (as an investigator appointed under Section 168 may also require persons who are neither the subject of the investigation nor connected with the person under investigation to attend before him and answer questions and provide information).

10.5 Preliminary findings letter

The FSA will generally send a preliminary findings letter to a firm or approved person before considering whether to recommend that enforcement action be initiated, unless it is not practical to do, such as in cases of urgency. The letter will set out the facts which the FSA staff consider relevant to the matters under investigation and will invite the person concerned to confirm that those facts are complete and accurate. The FSA will normally allow a reasonable period (28 days) for a response to that letter. The FSA staff will take into account any response they receive within the period stated in the preliminary findings letter. Where the FSA has sent a preliminary findings letter and decided not to take any further action, the FSA will communicate this decision promptly to the person concerned. In CP65 (the draft Enforcement Manual) it was not clear whether the FSA would, as a normal rule, send out preliminary letters. As part of the consultation process, the FSA recognised the usefulness of such letters and the final text has therefore made clear that the general rule is that such preliminary letters will be sent out.

10.6 Protected items, banking confidentiality and admissibility of statements

Under Section 413 of the FSMA, certain items are referred to as "protected". Under Section 413(1) a person may not be required under the FSMA to produce, disclose or allow inspection of protected items, which principally are communications between a professional legal adviser and his client.

10.6.1 Banking confidentiality

Under Section 175(5) and Section 284(8) of the FSMA a person may not be required to give information or produce a document in respect of which he has an obligation of banking confidentiality, unless the person to whom the obligation is owed is the person under investigation or a related company, or the person to whom the duty is owed consents to this disclosure or the requirement to disclose has been specifically authorised by the FSA.

10.6.2   *Admissibility of statements*

Under Section 174(1) a statement made to an investigator by a person who has been required to provide it can in general be used as evidence in any proceedings (as long as the evidence complies with any requirements governing the admissibility of evidence). However, under Section 174(2) such a statement cannot be used as evidence in criminal proceedings in which the person who made the statement is charged with an offence or in proceedings relating to an action against a person under Section 123 of the FSMA (penalties for market abuse). (This is because of the higher levels of protection afforded by Article 7 of the European Convention on Human Rights which the FSMA recognises in relation to criminal matters and in respect of which specific provision has been made in relation to the market abuse regime.) The FSA's policy on the use of voluntary rather than compulsory interviews appears at ENF 2.14. It is clear that because compelled interviews cannot be used as widely in enforcement cases as voluntary ones, the FSA will try to persuade people to give voluntary interviews.

10.6.3   *Section 170(2) – notification of persons under investigation*

Section 170(2) of the FSMA requires that the person under investigation must be given written notice of the fact of the investigation and the reasons for it. The FSA must also notify any change in the scope and conduct of the investigation if in the FSA's opinion the person under investigation is likely to be significantly prejudiced by it.

10.7   The FSA's power to enforce requirements

10.7.1   *Search warrants*

The FSA and its investigators may apply for a warrant to search and seize documents or information. Section 176 lists the grounds when a Justice of the Peace or Sheriff can issue a warrant. A search warrant will authorise a constable to enter premises, search premises, take possession of documents or information (or take steps to protect or preserve them), take copies and require any person on the premises to explain any document or information or state where it may be found. The FSA's policy is to ensure that the FSA investigator is named on the warrant and entitled to accompany the constable on the search.

10.7.2   Section 177 – prosecutions

Section 177 of the FSMA creates three criminal offences in relation to non-co-operation with the FSA, information gatherers authorised by the FSA under Section 165(3) of the FSMA, and investigators. Under Sections 177(3), (4) and (6) a person commits an offence if he:

(a) knows or suspects that an investigation is being or is likely to be conducted; and:

    (i) falsifies, conceals, destroys or otherwise disposes of a document which he knows or suspects is, or would be, relevant to the investigation; or

    (ii) causes or permits the falsification, concealment, destruction or disposal of such a document;

    unless he shows that he had no intention of concealing facts disclosed by the documents from the investigator (*see* Section 177(3)); or

(b) in purported compliance with a requirement placed on him under Part XI of the FSMA, gives information which he knows to be false or misleading in a material particular, or recklessly gives information which is false or misleading in a material particular (*see* Section 177(4)); or

(c) intentionally obstructs the use of any rights conferred by a warrant (*see* Section 177(6)).

10.7.3   Certification procedure

Section 177(1) states that if a person other than the investigator fails to comply with a requirement imposed on him under Part XI of the FSMA, the person imposing the requirement may certify that fact in writing to the court. If the court is satisfied that that person has no reasonable excuse for failing to comply, it may deal with him as if he were in contempt. If the person is a body corporate, the court may deal with any director or officer as if he were in contempt (Section 177(2)).

10.8 Disciplinary measures

10.8.1 *Introduction and general*

In this section we consider the guidance provided by the Manual as to how authorised firms and approved persons may be *disciplined*. We consider the general approach of the FSA to what are its main disciplinary tools, namely public censure and public statements and financial penalties. We also deal (more briefly) with the other enforcement tools available to the FSA where it considers it necessary to take protective or remedial action (rather than disciplinary action) such as injunctions and restitution. Disciplinary measures are only one of the regulatory tools available to the FSA. They are not the only tool, and it may be appropriate to address many instances of non-compliance without recourse to disciplinary action. However, the FSA believes the effective and proportionate use of its powers to enforce the requirements of the FSMA, the rules and the Statements of Principle will play an important role in buttressing its pursuit of its regulatory objectives. The imposition of disciplinary measures shows that regulatory standards are being upheld and helps to maintain market confidence, promote public awareness of regulatory standards and deter financial crime. An increased public awareness of regulatory standards also contributes to the protection of consumers.

The main formal disciplinary measures available to the FSA are contained in Part XIV of the FSMA and are:

Section 205:   Public statements and public censure (described at ENF 12).

Section 206:   Financial penalties (described at ENF 13).

The procedures relating to disciplinary measures are also contained in Part XIV of the FSMA, but are dealt with not in the Manual but the DEC Manual. The DEC Manual gives guidance on the FSA's decision making and other procedures for giving statutory (i.e. warning, decision and supervisory) notices and also the FSA's procedures for using its powers under Part XXIV (insolvency order), Part XXV (injunctions and restitution) and Part XXVII (criminal offences).

For these principal disciplinary measures, the decision making and warning notice/decision notice procedure referred to below in Section 10.14.3 and at DEC 2.2 and 2.3 applies.

In addition to its formal disciplinary powers the FSA has, through the consultation process following Consultation Papers 17, 25 and 65, recognised the importance of more informal methods of approaching discipline. In particular, the FSA has in the Manual recognised the value of using private warnings to avoid in suitable cases the need for more formal discipline (ENF 11).

10.8.2   Private warnings

In certain cases, the FSA may consider that although a contravention has taken place it may not be appropriate, having regard to all the circumstances of the case, to bring formal disciplinary action against the firm or approved person. The examples given in the Manual when such private warnings will be appropriate are where a contravention is only minor in nature or degree or the firm or approved person has taken immediate and full remedial action (ENF 11.3.2G). A private warning will state that:

(a) the FSA has had concerns arising from a firm's or approved person's conduct but has not made a determination of any rule breach;

(b) the FSA does not presently intend to take formal disciplinary action, having regard to all the circumstances of the case;

(c) the private warning will form part of the firm's compliance history, and may be taken into account in deciding whether the FSA brings disciplinary action against the firm or approved person in the future; and

(d) the FSA requires the firm or approved person to acknowledge receipt of the warning letter and invites the firm or approved person to comment on the private warning if they wish to.

The firm may make a response to a private warning. Where the firm or approved person takes its obligations under the FSMA seriously and a close relationship exists with its supervisor, a private warning may constitute a useful tool by which the FSA can gently nudge the firm or approved person onto what it believes is the right path.

The use of private warnings has generally been welcomed by practitioners as a useful and appropriate method of control. However, one practical issue which arises from such informal discipline is whether, if a party receives a private warning and it feels that it should not have been warned, it can itself raise the matter with the Regulatory Decisions Committee. The reason that this issue may be important is because a private warning, together with any comments in response to it, will form part of a firm or approved person's compliance history. The Manual states that the warning "may be taken into account in deciding whether the FSA brings disciplinary action against the firm or approved person in the future" (ENF 11.3.4G). The Manual makes clear that an earlier private warning will not be relied upon in subsequently determining whether a breach has taken place or in determining the level of sanction, if any, to be imposed (ENF 11.3.6G). It seems logical that if, having had a private warning for a particular matter, the firm or approved person subsequently gives the FSA further cause for similar concern, recourse should be had in deciding appropriate disciplinary action to the earlier private warning. However, if the subsequent matter is in no way related to the previous private warning, a party may feel aggrieved if the earlier matter is one of the factors weighed against it in taking disciplinary action. Being an informal method of discipline it is likely private warnings will be the subject of negotiation between the FSA and a firm, and no doubt firms will stress that there is a difference between complaints in respect of which remedial action has been taken and repeated examples of the same type of conduct.

10.8.3   *What criteria does the FSA rely on in determining whether to take disciplinary action?*

Given the wide scope of disciplinary powers and the potential circumstances in which they might be deployed, it is perhaps not surprising that the criteria given in the Manual at ENF 11.4.1G state that the FSA will consider "the full circumstances of each case". It then gives a non-exhaustive list of the factors it will bear in mind:

(a) the nature and seriousness of the breach;

(b) the conduct of the firm or approved person after the breach;

(c) the previous regulatory record of the firm or approved person;

(d) guidance given by the FSA;

(e) action by the FSA in previous similar cases; and

(f) action taken by other regulatory authorities.

Whilst the chapter states that the list is not exhaustive and there may be other factors that are relevant, one potential problem area has already been identified in relation to the fourth factor – "guidance". During consultation, some commentators feared that "guidance" was being elevated to the status of something that a party cannot afford to ignore and which, if ignored, might render the firm or approved person automatically in breach. It now seems clear that where guidance on any particular topic exists and a firm or approved person has followed that guidance, then it cannot be in breach. If, however, the relevant guidance has not been followed, that of itself does not necessarily mean that the firm or approved person is necessarily in breach, the breach still has to be proved. In short, mere non-adherence to guidance given is not itself a breach.

Similarly, given that one of the factors in determining whether to take disciplinary action is the regulatory history of the firm or approved person, another issue which appears relevant is how and for how long the FSA will rely on a firm's previous regulatory history. For example, the Manual seems to suggest that no matter is ever "spent", but it might be sensible if after a length of time certain matters were no longer held against an organisation which had taken all appropriate steps to deal with the original matter complained of.

10.8.4   *When will action be taken against a firm and/or against an approved person?*

The Manual makes clear that the primary responsibility for ensuring compliance with a firm's regulatory obligations rest with the firm itself.   The FSA's main focus in considering whether disciplinary action is appropriate will be on the firm rather than on an approved person (ENF 11.5.1G).

However, it may not be appropriate in all cases to hold a firm responsible for actions of an approved person; for example, where the firm can demonstrate that it took all reasonable steps to prevent the breach.   In practice, it is unlikely that the question of whether a firm or approved person is responsible will be clear cut and it may be appropriate for the FSA to take action against both the firm and the approved person.   The example given in the Manual is where a firm may have breached the rule requiring it to take reasonable care to establish and maintain such systems and controls as are appropriate to its business and an approved person may have taken advantage of deficiencies to front run orders or misappropriate assets (ENF 11.5.2G).

In general, the FSA will only undertake disciplinary action against an approved person where evidence of personal culpability on the part of that approved person exists.   Personal culpability arises where the behaviour was deliberate or the approved person's standard of behaviour was below that which would be reasonable in the circumstances (ENF 11.5.3G).   Section 66(1) of the FSMA contains specific provisions listing when the FSA may take action against an approved person, namely (a) where it appears to the FSA that he is guilty of misconduct, and (b) if the FSA is satisfied in all circumstances that it is appropriate to take action against him.   In summary, a person is guilty of misconduct if, whilst an approved person, he has failed to comply with a statement of principle issued under Section 64 of the FSMA or he has been knowingly concerned in the contravention by the relevant firm of a requirement imposed on it (*see* Sections 64-67 of the FSMA).

The FSA has issued Statements of Principle (APER 2) (*see* Chapter 2) about the conduct it expects of approved persons and a Code of Practice for Approved Persons (APER 3 and 4) to help determine whether an approved person's conduct is compliant. In deciding whether to discipline an approved person, the FSA takes into account the responsibility of those exercising "significant influence functions" for the conduct of the firm and its employee (ENF 11.5.6G). Generally, however, the FSA will not discipline approved persons on the basis of vicarious liability (i.e. holding them responsible for the acts of others) provided appropriate delegation has taken place (*see* APER 4.6.13G and 4.6.14G). In particular, an approved person performing a significant influence function will not be disciplined simply because a regulatory failure has occurred in an area of business for which he is responsible. The FSA will consider that an approved person performing a significant influence function may have breached statements of Principles 5 to 7 only if his conduct was below the standard which would be reasonable in all the circumstances, having regard to the Statements of Principles for Approved Persons and the Code of Practice. In short, if an approved person has exercised due and reasonable care when assessing information and has reached a reasonable conclusion and acted on it, he is unlikely to be disciplined (ENF 11.5.6G).

10.8.5   *Discipline for breaches of Principles for Businesses*

The FSA's Principles for Businesses are a general statement of the fundamental obligations of firms under the FSA regulatory system. They derive their authority from the FSA's rule making powers at Section 138 of the FSMA and form part of the Conduct of Business Rules. A breach of a Principle will make a firm liable to disciplinary action. In determining whether a Principle has been broken, it is necessary to look at the standard of conduct required by the Principle in question (these vary depending on the Principle) but the onus is on the FSA to show the firm is at fault. In some cases it will not be necessary to look at the standard of conduct required because it may be appropriate to discipline a firm on the basis of the Principles alone, for example where there is no detailed rule which prohibits the behaviour, but that behaviour clearly contravenes a Principle (ENF 11.6.3G).

10.8.6 The standard of reasonable care

A number of rules require a firm to take reasonable care in relation to particular behaviour in, for example, organising or controlling a firm's affairs responsibly with adequate risk management systems. In considering whether a firm has taken "reasonable care" the FSA regards the following as particularly relevant:

(a) what information the firm knew at the time of the behaviour and what information it ought to have known in all the circumstances;

(b) what steps the firm took to comply with the rule and what steps they ought to have taken in all the circumstances;

(c) the standards of the regulatory system that applied at the time of the behaviour (ENF 11.7.2G).

Some types of breach by a firm or approved person may result not only in potential disciplinary action by the FSA, but other regulatory authorities both domestic and overseas. The FSA is developing operating arrangements with each of the relevant UK authorities concerning cases where more than one regulator has an interest to ensure a co-ordinated effective approach. Similarly, the FSA is contributing to a number of international initiatives to enhance effective enforcement where overseas authorities have an interest. The FSA will consider the circumstances of each case to decide whether it is appropriate for the FSA or another authority to take action (ENF 11.8.4G).

In considering if the FSA's Money Laundering Rules (set out in ML1-9) have been contravened, the FSA will have regard to whether a firm has followed the provisions in the Joint Money Laundering Steering Group's Guidance Notes for the Financial Sector (ENF 11.9.1G).

10.9 Public censures and public statements

This is dealt with in detail in ENF 12. There are four circumstances in which the FSA may publish a public censure or public statement under the FSMA:

(a) the FSA may issue a public censure on a firm pursuant to Section 205 where the firm has contravened a requirement imposed on it by or under the FSMA;

(b) the FSA may issue a public statement of misconduct on an approved person pursuant to Section 66 if it considers that he is guilty of misconduct;

(c) the FSA may issue a public statement pursuant to Section 123 where a person has engaged in market abuse; and

(d) the FSA may also issue a public statement under Section 91 of the FSMA where there has been a contravention of the Listing Rules.

Public censures or public statements of misconduct are used as alternatives to financial penalties where the FSA considers that formal disciplinary action is appropriate but has decided not to impose a financial penalty. The Manual makes clear that the FSA regards a decision to publish a public censure or public statement as a serious sanction and one which may have particular value in helping the FSA pursue its regulatory objectives by highlighting the requirements and standards of conduct expected of firms and approved persons and by promoting public awareness of the standards of behaviour expected of firms and approved persons (ENF 12.2.2G).

The criteria for determining whether it is appropriate to impose a public censure or public statement of misconduct are similar to those discussed below in relation to financial penalties. The starting point is that the FSA will consider all the relevant circumstances of the case. But in considering whether to impose a public statement rather than a financial penalty the factors listed at ENF 12.3.3G are relevant:

(a) whether a profit has been made as a result of the misconduct (or a loss avoided), in which case the FSA may favour a financial penalty to prevent anyone benefiting from the misconduct;

(b) if the misconduct is of a more serious nature or degree, this also favours the imposition of a financial penalty. Generally speaking, the more serious the misconduct, the more likely it is that the FSA will impose a financial penalty;

(c) a firm or approved person which has admitted misconduct and provided full and immediate co-operation to the FSA and taken steps to ensure that consumers are fully compensated for any losses is more likely to receive a public censure or statement of misconduct, rather than a financial penalty;

(d) where the firm or approved person has a poor disciplinary record or compliance history, it is likely the FSA will favour a financial penalty on the basis that it may be useful as a deterrent for future cases;

(e) the FSA's conduct in similar previous cases; the FSA will seek to achieve consistency on whether to impose a penalty or issue a public statement;

(f) if the firm or approved person has inadequate means to pay the level of financial penalty which their conduct would otherwise attract, this is said to be a factor in favour of a lower level of penalty or a public statement of misconduct. However, it would only be in exceptional cases that the FSA would be prepared to agree to impose a public statement rather than a financial penalty if a penalty would otherwise be the appropriate sanction, for example, verifiable evidence that an approved person would suffer serious financial hardship if a financial penalty was imposed; and verifiable evidence that the firm would be unable to meet other regulatory requirements, particularly financial resource requirements.

In summary, the FSA appears to view public censures and statements of misconduct as being at the lower end of the enforcement spectrum, used only in the case of relatively minor breaches or where for specific financial reasons a financial penalty is not appropriate.

10.10   Financial penalties

This is likely to be the most frequently used disciplinary method and is dealt with in detail in ENF 13. There are four circumstances in which the FSA may impose a financial penalty:

(a) on a firm where the FSA considers that the firm has contravened a requirement imposed on it by or under the FSMA (Section 206);

(b) on an approved person where the FSA considers that he is guilty of misconduct, in other words failure to comply with a Statement of Principle issued by the FSA under Section 64 or being knowingly concerned in a contravention by the firm of a requirement imposed under the FSMA (Section 66);

(c) on any person where the FSA is satisfied that the person is or has engaged in market abuse (Section 123 discussed separately); and

(d) on an issuer of listed securities or an applicant for listing where there has been a contravention of the Listing Rules under Section 91 of the FSMA.

The principal purpose of financial penalties is said to be the promotion of high standards of regulatory conduct by deterring firms and approved persons who have breached regulatory requirements from committing further contraventions, helping to deter other firms from so acting and by demonstrating generally to firms and approved persons the benefits of compliant behaviour (ENF 13.1.2G).

Sections 69 and 210 of the FSMA require the FSA to issue statements of policy about the imposition by it of financial penalties and the FSA is required to have regard to these statements of policy in deciding whether to exercise its powers under Sections 66 and 206 of the FSMA. The FSA's statements of policy, and guidance, are those set out at ENF 13 summarised below. The obvious problem with setting policies and guidance for such a wide subject is that it is impossible to legislate for all specific instances and yet general statements of policy, which these are, inevitably are vague and therefore fairly unhelpful in informing firms what specific level of financial penalty to expect.

However, the FSA recognises these difficulties and has indicated that because there will be few cases in which all the circumstances of the case are the same, it does not propose to adopt a tariff of penalties for different kinds of contravention, thereby leaving it free to maintain a flexible and proportionate policy (ENF 13.3.1G).

The FSMA itself provides, at Section 69, for approved persons and Section 210(2) for firms, the factors the FSA will consider in determining the amount of penalty:

(a) the seriousness of the misconduct in question in relation to the nature of the principle or requirement concerned;

(b) the extent to which that contravention was deliberate or reckless; and

(c) whether the "person" on whom the penalty is to be imposed is an individual.

The FSA has analysed these elements in greater detail and the various elements identified are expanded at ENF 13.3.3G summarised below.

10.10.1   Seriousness of misconduct

The FSA recognises the need for the financial penalty to be proportionate to the nature and seriousness of the contravention and believes the following factors may be relevant:

(a) seriousness of misconduct in relation to nature of Statement of Principle or requirement concerned;

(b) the duration and frequency of the contravention, when was the contravention identified by persons exercising significant influence functions at the firm;

(c) whether the contravention revealed serious or systemic weaknesses of the management systems or internal controls relating to all or part of a firm's business;

(d) the impact of the contravention on the orderliness of financial markets, including whether public confidence in those markets has been damaged;

(e) loss or risk of loss caused to consumers or other market users.

10.10.2   Extent to which contravention or misconduct was deliberate or reckless

The FSA may have regard to whether the firm or approved person's behaviour was intentional, that is that they intended or foresaw the consequences of their actions.   In determining whether a contravention was reckless, the FSA may have regard to, but are not limited to, whether the firm or approved person:

(a) has failed to comply with a firm's procedures;

(b) has taken decisions beyond its or his field of competence;

(c) has given no apparent consideration to the consequences of the conduct that constitutes the contravention.

Not surprisingly, if the FSA decides the conduct was deliberate or reckless it is more likely to impose a higher penalty on a firm than will otherwise be the case.

10.10.3   *Whether the "person" on whom the penalty is to be imposed is an individual and the size, financial resources etc. of firm or individual*

The FSA will also consider whether the person on whom the penalty is to be imposed is an individual and the size, financial resources and other circumstances of the firm or individual. The FSA may take into account whether there is verifiable evidence of hardship or financial difficulties if the firm or approved person were to pay the proposed level of penalty.

Although it is not surprising that size and financial resources will be taken into account in determining the level of a penalty, the Manual states that there is not a direct correlation between those factors and the level of penalty. Size may be relevant because the purpose of penalty is not to render a firm or approved person insolvent but also because the degree of seriousness of the contravention may be linked to the size of the firm. A systemic failure in a large firm might damage a larger number of consumers than would be the case in a small firm. It seems therefore that a breach in a large firm might attract a larger penalty because of its potential or actual wider impact, even though the same breach in a smaller firm may attract a smaller penalty. Size may also be relevant to the question of mitigation because a large firm with sophisticated systems might be expected to take more immediate or widespread corrective steps.

10.10.4   *Profits accrued, losses avoided*

The FSA may have regard to the amount of profits accrued or losses avoided as a result of a contravention and will impose a penalty which ensures that the firm does not benefit from the contravention as well as acting as an incentive to comply with the regulatory standards.

10.10.5   *Conduct following contravention*

The FSA may take into account the speed with which the firm or approved person brought the contravention (or failed to bring the contravention) to the FSA's attention and the degree of co-operation shown during the investigation – any remedial steps taken against the contravention identified, including identifying whether consumers suffered loss and compensating them, taking disciplinary action against staff involved and taking steps to ensure that a similar problem could not arise in the future.

10.10.6   *Disciplinary record and compliance history*

The previous disciplinary record and general compliance history may be taken into account. This will include whether the FSA or any previous regulator has taken previous formal disciplinary action or required the firm to take remedial action by a variation of permission and the Manual makes clear that penalties could be increased, for example if similar contraventions were made in the past. The Manual appears to have addressed some concerns raised in the consultation process regarding whether private warnings will be taken into account by confirming that, as regards penalties, they will not be, but *see* 10.8.2. The age of a particular matter will be taken into account although the Manual states a longstanding matter may still be relevant (presumably if it was very serious or similar to the contravention in question).

10.10.7   *Previous action by the FSA*

The FSA is seeking to ensure consistency and if it has taken disciplinary action in relation to a similar contravention, this will be a relevant factor in deciding a penalty; however this obviously runs counter to the statement that the FSA does not adopt a tariff system (which is restated) but the Manual suggests there may be other factors which could increase or decrease the seriousness of the contravention.

10.10.8   Action by other regulators

The final factor to be taken into account in assessing the appropriate level of penalty is action taken by other regulators, which may be relevant if it relates to the contravention in question. No doubt arguments may arise between firms and the FSA as to the correct tests for relevance. Regard will also be had to actions taken by the FSA's predecessor regulators regarding the general level of penalties.

The Manual makes clear that the factors listed are not exhaustive and all relevant circumstances of the case will be taken into consideration in assessing the appropriate level of penalty. The FSMA specifically provides that the FSA may not take account of expenses which it incurs or expects to incur in discharging its functions or determining its policy.

10.11   Financial penalties for late submissions of reports

Although the Manual deals at ENF 13.5 with the financial penalties for late submissions of reports, this is an entirely separate procedure designed to underline the importance the FSA attaches to the timely submission by firms of reports, because the information they contain is essential to the FSA's assessment of whether a firm is complying with the requirements and standards under the regulatory system and to the FSA's understanding of that firm's business. The FSA considers that in the majority of cases, it would be appropriate to limit the sanction imposed on a firm concerned to a financial penalty fixed by reference to the indicative scale of penalties set out in annex 1G to ENF 13; although there may be exceptional circumstances where the FSA decides to impose higher or lower penalties, as is appropriate. Where it decides to impose a financial penalty for the late submission of a report, the FSA uses the decision-making procedure and the warning notice and decision notice procedure described below. If that procedure includes a final notice being issued, the FSA will consider whether to publish information relating to that decision and is likely to do so, unless unfairness or prejudice will exist, by entering the details of the decision on the FSA Register.

10.12   Breaches of prudential requirements and financial penalties

Where a firm has breached a prudential requirement such as adequacy of financial resources, the FSA will consider all the relevant circumstances (including the factors in ENF 13.3.3G).

In deciding whether to impose a fine on a mutual, whilst the FSA will take account of the impact on the firm's customers, it may nevertheless impose a financial penalty because a significant proportion of a mutual's customers are shareholder members and to that extent their position involves an assumption of risk not assumed by customers of a firm incorporated as a company (ENF 13.6.2G).

10.13   Other enforcement measures

10.13.1   *Variation of Part IV permission on the FSA's own initiative*

ENF 3 explains that Sections 45, 46 and 47 of the FSMA permit the FSA in certain circumstances to vary or cancel a firm's Part IV permission (or to impose certain provisions upon that firm) or to vary a firm's permission when a person has acquired control over the firm; or, in support of an overseas regulator, to vary or cancel a firm's permission. ENF 3.2 specifies the limitations and requirements that may be imposed, including:

(a) removing a regulated activity from the firm's Part IV permission, varying the description of a regulated activity and varying a requirement imposed by Section 43 of the FSMA;

(b) adding new requirements into the variation of a permission as if it were a fresh application and also in support of the FSA's enforcement activities and its supervision activities as well as limitations on the disposal of, dealing with, or transferring of the assets of a firm.

Section 45 of the FSMA specifies grounds for varying or cancelling a permission. The Manual explains the general grounds for exercising the power to vary or cancel a permission, namely, where it appears to the FSA in respect of an activity for which permission has been granted that the firm is failing or is likely to fail to satisfy the threshold conditions required, or the firm has failed for a period of not less than 12 months to carry on the regulated activity in question, or it is desirable that the interests of consumers or potential consumers be protected (ENF 3.3). The FSA must ensure that firms continue to satisfy the threshold provisions for all of the regulated activities for which that firm has permission and the FSA may take such steps as it considers necessary to protect consumers.

Section 47(1) of the FSMA permits the FSA to exercise its "own-initiative" power to assist an overseas regulator in respect of any authorised person. The regulator must be of a kind prescribed in regulations made by the Treasury – Section 47(1) and ENF 3.3.3G. The Treasury is also enjoined to prescribe provisions for the exercise of the FSA's own-initiative power in respect of an overseas regulator. The FSA must in exercising its power consider whether or not it must comply with a Community Directive. If not, it may consider whether or not the overseas regulator would give corresponding assistance to a UK regulator, whether or not the breach concerns a law which has no close parallel in the UK, involves assertion of a jurisdiction not recognised in the UK or it is in the public interest to give the assistance sought and how serious the case is and how important it is to persons in the UK (Section 47(4), ENF 3.3.6G) *see* also Section 47(5) and ENF 3.3.7G.

ENF 3.5 sets out the FSA's policy on the exercise of its powers to vary or cancel a permission. It will consider its regulatory objective and its regulatory tools, the responsibilities of a firm's management to deal with concerns about it or how its business has or is being run and the principle that a restriction imposed should be proportionate to the objective to be achieved. A firm is primarily responsible for the conduct of its business in compliance with the law and the FSA may act or give instructions to enforce compliance or deal with the consequences of non-compliance where, for example, commercial business is conducted in a manner that is insufficiently controlled and gives rise to risks that are not covered by the FSA's rules, or new products or selling practices of the firm are not controlled by existing requirements, or a change in the firm's structure, controllers, activities or strategy creates uncertainty or unusual or exceptional risks. The FSA states that it envisages that most changes will be agreed with firms and the FSA will not have to use its powers. If the firm fails to comply or if the FSA cannot rely on that firm to act effectively, the FSA will consider using its powers under Section 45 of the FSMA, especially where the consequences of non-compliance could be serious and the firm appears unwilling or unable to comply or the imposition of a formal statutory requirement may assist the firm to take steps that would otherwise be difficult because of legal obligations owed to third parties (ENF 3.5.6G).

The FSA may vary a firm's permission where, for example, the firm appears to be failing or likely to fail to satisfy the threshold requirements relating to one or more of its regulated activities because its material and financial resources appear inadequate to support the scale or type of regulated activity it is carrying on, or where it is not a fit and proper person to carry on the regulated activity because it has not complied with high conduct standards, has not been managed competently and prudently or has not exercised due skill, care, and diligence in carrying on a regulated activity or it has materially breached a requirement imposed by the FSMA. Where the interests of consumers or potential consumers are at risk because the firm appears to have breached certain of the Principles established by the FSA, the FSA will vary that firm's permission (ENF 3.5.8G).

Under Section 53(2) of the FSMA, a variation may be determined to take effect either immediately, on a specified date or when the matter is no longer open to review. In the former two instances the FSA may make the determinations in a statement in the supervisory notice which it must give to the firm involved if it reasonably considers it necessary (considering the grounds for variation) for the variation to so take effect (ENF 3.5.10). Where information indicates that there are immediate serious concerns about the firm or its business or there are actions by the firm to be required or prohibited immediately, the FSA will consider exercising its own-initiative powers urgently. Urgent circumstances may, for example, arise in respect of information or evidence that indicates significant loss, risk of loss or other adverse effects for consumers (and their interests need protection), evidence that the firm's conduct has put it at risk of being used for the purposes of financial crime or being otherwise involved in such crime, that the firm has submitted to the FSA inaccurate or misleading information that raise serious concerns about the firm's ability to meet its regulatory obligations; and circumstances indicating serious problems within a firm or with a firm's controllers that call into question the firm's ability to meet the threshold conditions (ENF 3.5.12G).

In determining whether the own-initiative powers should be used, the FSA will consider factors such as the seriousness and extent of the loss, risk of loss or other adverse effect on consumers, the extent of risk to customer assets, the nature and extent of false or inaccurate information given, the seriousness of the suspected breach of the legislation or rules and the remedial steps needed, the financial resources of the firm, the risk of use of the firm for financial crime or laundering the proceeds of crime, the risk that the firm's conduct or business presents to the financial system or to confidence in that system, the firm's conduct and the impact that the use of the FSA's powers will have upon the firm's business and its customers (ENF 3.5.13G).

The Manual explains that the FSA's approach in respect of the support of overseas regulators differs according to whether or not European Community obligations apply. If a Community obligation applies, the FSA will exercise its power wherever an EEA Competent Authority requests it to do so and it is satisfied that the use of the power is appropriate to enforce the requirements arising from the relevant directives. In respect of "relevant overseas regulators" to whom the Community obligations do not apply, the FSA will consider whether grounds exist for it to exercise its own-initiative powers where the relevant authority's concerns are related to a UK firm. Where the regulatory provisions sought to be enforced extend significantly beyond the purposes of the UK provisions the FSA will not enforce the foreign provisions. The FSA will, however, not need to be precisely satisfied that the overseas provisions mirror the relevant UK provisions exactly or that precisely the same assistance would be provided to the UK if the situation were to be reversed. It would need to be confident that the foreign authorities in question would have the powers and willingness to provide broadly similar assistance to UK authorities. Assistance by the FSA may be dependent upon the willingness of the overseas regulator undertaking to make contributions to the costs of enforcement.

Section 49 allows the FSA, in exercising its powers to vary a permission, to have regard to any person appearing to it to be in a relevant relationship with a firm. Where it is dealing with a firm that is connected with an EEA firm it must consult the EEA firm's home state regulator.

10.13.2 *Intervention against incoming European Economic Area ("EEA") firms (ENF 4)*

EEA and Treaty firms have a right to carry on a regulated activity in the UK. The FSA has power to intervene against incoming firms and to impose limitations and requirements upon permitted firms. The FSA may intervene and impose any requirement on an incoming firm which it could impose if the firm's permission was a Part IV permission and the FSA was entitled to exercise its power to vary that permission.

Under Section 194(1) the FSA may intervene if it appears that an incoming firm has contravened or is likely to contravene a requirement imposed by the FSMA, where the firm has knowingly or recklessly given the FSA materially false or misleading information or the interests of actual or potential customers should be protected in relation to a regulated activity carried on by the firm. Section 194(3) applies to incoming investment firms and credit institutions exercising EEA rights to carry on Consumer Credit Act business and which are authorised by their Member home state regulators. This Section allows the FSA to intervene and it may do when the Director General of Fair Trading has informed the FSA that the firm, any past or present employee, agent or associate thereof or any controller or associate of a controller of the firm has offended against certain provisions of the Consumer Credit Act 1974. The FSA may also exercise its power in order to help an overseas regulator, including providing assistance where an overseas (EEA home state) regulator has requested such help in pursuance of a Community obligation or it has withdrawn an EEA firm's EEA authorisation.

Although the FSA's power of intervention and its own-initiative power are not identical in nature, the powers have enough in common for the FSA to be able to commit itself to taking a broadly similar approach to both kinds of powers (ENF 4.4.1G). The FSA states that it will seek and take account of the firm's home state regulator's views when considering action.

Under Section 197 of the FSMA, the FSA may impose a requirement upon an incoming firm by using the supervisory notice procedure described above. Additionally, Section 199 provides a procedure for intervention in respect of the contravention of a relevant requirement relating to an incoming EEA firm. Section 200 empowers the FSA to rescind or vary a requirement it imposed either on its own initiative or on the application of the person subject to the requirement.

10.13.3   Cancellation of Part IV permission (ENF 5)

The FSA may cancel a firm's Part IV permission either using its own-initiative powers or, at the request of a firm, under Section 44 FSMA. Once permission has been cancelled, authorisation of the firm will be withdrawn. Under Section 45(1) a firm's permission may be cancelled where it appears to the FSA that the firm is failing, or is likely to fail, to satisfy threshold provisions in respect of one or more or all regulated activities for which it has permission, or the firm has failed for at least 12 months to carry on a regulated activity to which the permission relates, or it is desirable to vary the permission to protect the interests of consumers or potential consumers. Where as a result of a variation of the firm's permission, it no longer actually carries on a permitted regulated activity the FSA may cancel its permission. The FSA may, at the request of or in assistance to an overseas regulator, cancel a permission.

When proposing to cancel a permission the Manual states that the FSA must proceed under Section 54 and must give to the firm concerned a warning notice, followed by a decision notice of cancellation. Cancellation may be considered when the FSA either has very serious concerns about a firm or the way its business is being conducted or where the firm's regulated activities have come to an end and it has not applied for cancellation. Examples given of circumstances that may lead to cancellation are situations where the firm's financial or material resources are inadequate to support the regulated activities, or where the firm is not a fit and proper person to carry on any regulated activity because:

(a) it has conducted business with a lack of integrity or has failed to comply with high standards;

(b) it has been managed incompetently or imprudently and has not exercised due skill, care and diligence;

(c) it has materially breached requirements imposed by or under the FSMA;

(d) it has knowingly or recklessly given the FSA materially false information so as to cast doubt on whether the firm is a fit and proper person or on the adequacy of its material or financial resources.

The Manual says that the FSA's own-initiative powers to vary and to cancel permission may be exercised on the same grounds. The FSA may vary the permission (by removing all regulated activities from the permission) in a way that has a similar effect to cancelling it. Statutory procedures for the two powers are different and may affect which approach the FSA decides to adopt. ENF 5.5.5G explains that whereas a variation may be imposed with either immediate effect or effect at a specified date, cancellation becomes effective only upon completion of the statutory procedure or referral to the Tribunal or appeal. The FSA may decide to vary prior to considering cancellation, especially where immediate action is required. Once a firm's permission has been cancelled the FSA must direct that that firm's authorisation be withdrawn so the FSA may rather decide to vary the firm's permission to remove all content therefrom but to retain the status of "permission" in order to enable the FSA to monitor the firm's activities or to use its enforcement powers. The FSA will consider cancelling a permission in support of an overseas regulator and will proceed in a similar manner to the procedure in respect of a variation.

10.13.4   Injunctions (ENF 6)

The FSA has statutory power to seek an injunction (or, in Scotland, an interdict) against any natural or legal person, whether or not that person is authorised, in the following circumstances:

(a) in connection with the contravention of a "relevant requirement" (Section 380 of the FSMA). This is defined as a requirement imposed by the FSMA or under another statute where the FSA has authority to prosecute;

(b) in a case of market abuse (Section 381); and

(c) in relation to certain insurance companies, at the request of a home state regulator of an incoming EEA firm (Section 198).

ENF 6 contains guidance on these powers and on how the FSA intends to exercise them.

The FSA's powers in the first two cases above are similar and are considered together. They can be exercised in the following situations:

(a) if it is reasonably likely that a "relevant requirement" will be contravened or that a person will engage in market abuse or it is reasonably likely that an existing contravention or market abuse will continue, the FSA can apply for an order to restrain the contravention or abuse;

(b) if a requirement has been contravened or a person has engaged in market abuse and steps can be taken to remedy or mitigate the effect of the contravention or abuse, the FSA can apply for an order that those steps be taken;

(c) if a requirement is being contravened or a person is knowingly concerned in the contravention, or if a person may be or may have been engaged in market abuse, the FSA can apply for an order to restrain the relevant person from disposing of, or otherwise dealing with, certain assets.

As an alternative to applying to court under Sections 380 or 381, the FSA may ask the court to exercise its inherent jurisdiction to grant a freezing order restraining a person from disposing of or otherwise dealing with assets. To succeed in an application for an asset-freezing injunction the FSA will have to show a good arguable case for granting the injunction.

The FSA may also request the court to exercise its inherent jurisdiction in cases where it has evidence showing that there is a reasonable likelihood that a person will contravene a requirement of the FSMA and that such contravention will result in the dissipation of assets belonging to investors. Unlike an application under Section 380(3) or 381(3) and (4) the FSA will not have to show that a contravention has already occurred or may have already occurred.

ENF 6.6 sets out the FSA's policy in relation to Sections 380 and 381 (injunctions and asset freezing-injunctions) and states that, before exercising its powers, the broad test the FSA will apply is whether an injunction will be an effective means of addressing its concerns. It will take into account all relevant circumstances including:

(a) the nature and seriousness of the contravention or misconduct;

(b) in cases of market abuse, the impact on the market and the extent and nature of losses likely to be imposed on other users of the market as a result;

(c) whether the conduct has ceased and consumers are adequately protected;

(d) whether there is a danger of assets being dissipated;

(e) the costs the FSA would incur in taking action compared to the benefits which would result;

(f) the person's disciplinary record and compliance history; and

(g) whether the exercise of its powers would disrupt the timetable of a takeover – if it would, the FSA will consult the Takeover Panel before taking any action.

The FSA will also consider whether it is appropriate to take any other action in addition to or instead of applying for an injunction (ENF 6.7). The FSA indicates that an injunction may be more appropriate than exercising its own initiative powers – the breach of an injunction would place a person in contempt of court.

Section 198 of the FSMA gives the FSA power to apply for an injunction at the request of a home state regulator of an incoming EEA insurance firm to prevent that firm disposing of, or otherwise dealing with, any of its assets. This power is intended to implement relevant European directives relating to general and long-term insurance and the home state regulator may only make a request in certain circumstances. The FSA states at ENF 6.8 that it will only consider applying for such an injunction when the EEA regulator has confirmed that the relevant requirements of the directives have been satisfied.

The prime consequence of breaching an injunction is that it would place a person in contempt of court and liable to imprisonment, a fine and/or to have his assets seized as a result. The FSA believes that it will generally be appropriate to publish details of all successful applications for injunctions to assist in consumer protection. However, where publication could damage market confidence or undermine market integrity in a way which could prejudice the interests of consumers it may decide not to publicise relevant details or at least to delay publication. The FSA will consult the Takeover Panel in relation to the timing of publication where it may affect the timetable or outcome of a bid.

10.13.5 *Withdrawal of approval of approved persons (ENF 7)*

The power under Section 63(1) to withdraw an approval granted under Section 59 is described in ENF 7.2 as helping to prevent an approved person from continuing to perform the controlled function to which the approval relates if that person is not a fit and proper person to perform that function. Section 61(2) sets out matters that the FSA may take into account in determining whether someone is fit and proper to perform the function to which the person's application for approval relates, having regard to matters such as the levels of competence and the qualifications and training possessed by the person involved or other persons undertaking the performance of functions on behalf of that person. Where the FSA proposes to withdraw its approval of an approved person it must give a warning notice to all interested parties. If it decides to withdraw approval it must give the interested parties a decision notice. Any interested party may refer the matter to the Tribunal.

The criterion used by the FSA is whether or not the approved person is fit and proper to perform the approved function. In making its decision, the FSA states its policy on withdrawal of approval is that it will consider all relevant factors, including qualifications, training and competence, the criteria contained in FIT (*"Fitness and Propriety Manual"*) Annex C (including honesty, integrity and reputation, competence and capability and financial soundness), the extent of any failure to comply with the "Principles for Approved Persons" or the knowing involvement in a contravention by a relevant firm of a requirement imposed by or under the FSMA on that firm as well as other factors indicating fitness (ENF 7.5). Withdrawal may be based on the cumulative effect of factors which, although insufficient individually, together show the person to be not fit and proper. The FSA says that it may take account of the particular nature of the controlled function that the approved person is performing within a firm and the characteristics of the nature and activities of the firm in the market in which it operates. The factors above are merely examples of the sort of factors that will be considered. The FSA may also use its investigative powers in circumstances that indicate that an individual is not a fit and proper person to be involved in the discharge of any function or an approved person is not fit and proper to perform a function or a person may be guilty of misconduct. In respect of misconduct, the FSA may withdraw approval and also take disciplinary action in terms of Section 66 of the FSMA. In respect of approved persons involved in regulated activities, the FSA may both withdraw approval and make a prohibition order against that person.

The Manual states at ENF 7.7.1G that a withdrawal of approval comes into effect on the date specified in the decision notice. However, where the matter is referred to the Tribunal no action may be taken until the reference or appeal has been finalised. Once the decision to withdraw approval is effective, the firm on whose application the approval was granted will be in a different position depending on whether it directly employs the person concerned or whether its contractor employs that person. The FSA will take enforcement action against a firm which continues to employ the person to perform a controlled function in terms of Section 59(1) which states that a firm must take reasonable care to ensure that a person does not perform a controlled function in respect of a regulated activity unless that person is approved to perform that function by the FSA. Where the person concerned is employed by a contractor of the firm, Section 59(2) sets out that the person must be approved. If the contractor is not approved, and if that contractor continues to employ the person to perform the controlled function, the firm itself will have breached Section 59(2) unless it has been reasonably careful not to let this happen. The FSA says that it will then take enforcement action. The FSA will give a copy of the decision notice to the firm and to the contractor. Once a final notice of withdrawal of approval has been issued, the FSA will ordinarily publicise it.

10.13.6   *Prohibition of individuals (ENF 8)*

The FSA has power under Section 56 of the FSMA to prohibit individuals who are not fit and proper from performing functions in connection with regulated activities. Its powers extend to all individuals and can be exercised on similar grounds to the withdrawal of approval from approved persons. Prohibition orders can be extremely broad – "regulated activities" has a wide interpretation and the orders can range from prohibiting a person from performing specific activities to prohibiting him from being employed by a particular type of firm. If the FSA proposes to make a prohibition order, it must first issue a warning notice and then a decision notice. Upon receipt of a decision notice, the individual concerned may refer the matter to the Tribunal. The FSA considers that a prohibition order is a more serious penalty than the withdrawal of appeal because a prohibition order will usually be much wider in scope. In most cases the FSA will consider whether the particular unfitness can be adequately dealt with by withdrawing approval or other disciplinary sanctions for example public censure or financial penalties or private warnings (ENF 8.4).

The FSA views this power as a protective and preventative measure. It will consider all relevant circumstances when deciding whether or not to make an order and the FSA's policy on making prohibition orders against approved persons is set out at ENF 8.5. The factors to be taken into account include:

(a) the general criteria for assessing fitness and propriety;

(b) if an approved person is involved, whether and to what extent the approved person has breached the Principles for Approved Persons or has been knowingly concerned in a firm's breach of its regulatory requirements;

(c) the length of time which has elapsed since the matters concerned;

(d) the particular controlled function performed by the approved person and the risk the individual poses to consumers and market confidence; and

(e) the individual's previous disciplinary record and compliance history.

The Manual considers separately at ENF 8.6-8.8 prohibition orders against individuals employed by firms who are not approved, prohibition orders against exempt persons and professional firms and other individuals.

The same factors will be generally taken into account in relation to approved persons (ENF 8.5) and those performing regulated activities under an exemption (ENF 8.7). The FSA recognises that the consequences of the prohibition order may be more serious for an individual than the withdrawal of approval for a particular controlled function. It therefore states that it will only make a prohibition order where the approved person presents a degree of risk to consumers or to confidence in the financial system that would not be sufficiently addressed by the withdrawal of his approval. Individuals may apply to the FSA to have a prohibition order varied or revoked; if the FSA refuses the application warning/decision procedure is used and an individual can refer the matter to the Tribunal.

The effects of a prohibition order are as follows:

(a) the FSA will maintain a public register of individuals subject to prohibition orders although an entry will not be made on this record until the decision to make an order is beyond review;

(b) the FSA will publicise its decision to make a prohibition order, again only once the decision is beyond review;

(i)   an individual who breaches a prohibition order may also be subject to further disciplinary action;

(ii) the performance of, or agreement to perform, an activity in breach of a prohibition order will be an offence and the individual will be liable to a fine not exceeding level 5 on the standard scale (currently £5,000). An individual will have a defence however if he can show that he took all reasonable precautions and exercised all due diligence to avoid committing the offence; and

(iii) in addition, authorised persons must take reasonable care to ensure that relevant functions are not performed by persons prohibited from doing so and private individuals may have a right of action against them if they breach this duty (e.g. by not searching the FSA's Register (*see* below)).

10.13.7   *Restitution and redress (ENF 9)*

The FSA has statutory power under Sections 382, 383 and 384 of the FSMA to seek redress for consumers and, in certain limited cases, market counterparties where:

(a) they have suffered loss as a result of a contravention of the FSMA or another statute under which the FSA has power to prosecute, or as a result of market abuse; or

(b) the person who committed the contravention or market abuse (or who was knowingly concerned in the contravention or required or encouraged the abuse) has made a profit as a result.

The FSA can do this by either applying to court for an order of restitution or by exercising its administrative powers to require restitution. These powers are dealt with at ENF 9. A person will have a defence against the exercise of these powers if he can show that he reasonably believed his behaviour did not involve a contravention of a relevant requirement or market abuse and that he took all reasonable precautions to avoid a contravention or abuse.

When considering whether to exercise its powers, the FSA will consider the circumstances of each case and whether redress might be obtained more efficiently and cost effectively by the persons concerned or by other means. In particular, the FSA will consider the factors set out at ENF 9.6.2G to 9.6.15G which include:

(a) whether it is possible to identify the persons suffering loss, the numbers suffering loss and the amount of loss and/or other adverse effects suffered;

(b) the costs which would be incurred by the FSA in securing redress and whether such costs are justified;

(c) the availability of redress through the relevant Ombudsman and Compensation Schemes, through other regulatory authorities or through separate civil action;

(d) the conduct of the persons who have suffered loss; and

(e) solvency of a firm or unauthorised person concerned.

Once the FSA has decided that it is appropriate to seek restitution, it must decide whether to exercise its own administrative powers or whether to apply to court. ENF 9.7 states that the FSA will first consider using its own administrative powers under Section 384 before considering court action. (When it does so it must issue appropriate warning notices and decision notices and the decision can be referred to the Tribunal.) However, it may apply to the court for an order of restitution under Section 382 or 383 in certain circumstances including those listed at ENF 9.7.3G:

(a) where it wishes to combine the application with other court action (e.g. an application for an injunction to prevent a breach of the FSMA or the dissipation of assets);

(b) where it wishes to bring related court proceedings against an unauthorised person based on the same facts; and

(c) where it suspects that its own administrative requirements will not be complied with.

The effect of seeking restitution is that:

(a) the relevant person will either be ordered by the court to pay an amount to the FSA which the FSA will then distribute as the court directs, or will be required by the FSA to pay an amount directly to the appropriate person(s) depending which power is exercised; and

(b) generally, all details of successful applications to court and/or the exercise of administrative powers will be published. However, where publication could damage market confidence or undermine market integrity in a way that would damage the interests of consumers, the FSA may choose not to publish the information. The FSA will consult the Takeover Panel if publication could affect the timetable or outcome of a bid.

10.13.8   *Insolvency proceedings (ENF 10)*

The FSA has various rights and powers in connection with insolvency proceedings which appear at ENF 10.5 including:

(a) the power to seek administration and compulsory winding up or bankruptcy orders from the court;

(b) the power to apply to court to challenge company moratoria, voluntary arrangements and to seek orders for debt avoidance;

(c) the right to be heard in relation to petitions by third parties for insolvency orders or to be involved in creditors' meetings; and

(d) the general right to be involved in the insolvency regimes affecting firms or individuals who carry on regulated activities.

ENF 10.6 explains which factors the FSA will take into account and provides guidance on when the rights and powers will be exercised.

Generally, the FSA intends to exercise its rights and powers in the pursuit of its regulatory objectives and, in particular, to:

(a) stop both authorised and unauthorised persons carrying on insolvent or unlawful investment business; and

(b) ensure the orderly realisation and distribution of their assets.

Before exercising its rights and powers, the FSA will keep in mind the general principle that recourse to insolvency regimes is a step to be taken for the benefit of creditors as a whole and that a court will have regard to the public interest when considering whether to wind up a body on the grounds that it is just and equitable to do so. The FSA will also keep in mind its other powers and the rights of consumers under the FSMA and other legislation.

The main areas of the FSA's guidance are as follows:

(a) ENF 10.6 sets out the FSA's proposed policy for seeking insolvency orders, administration or winding up orders, bankruptcy orders and, in Scotland, sequestration awards. The factors the FSA will take into account include:

  (i) the causes of the financial difficulties being experienced and whether it is possible to overcome them;

  (ii) the need to protect the claims and assets of consumers and the extent of likely redress to consumers; and

  (iii) whether financial crime is or may be involved;

(b) ENF 10.8 sets out the FSA's proposed policy on the use of its power to challenge voluntary arrangements. These will only be challenged in exceptional circumstances as the FSA acknowledges that such arrangements will have been approved in advance by a majority of creditors;

(c) ENF 10.9 explains the FSA's policy on seeking orders against debt avoidance and ENF 10.11 describes how the FSA proposes to exercise its right to be heard on petitions by third parties and to be involved in creditors' meetings. All relevant factors will be considered in each case including whether consumers' funds are involved and whether the FSA has relevant information which would not otherwise be drawn to the attention of those concerned.

10.13.9 Other miscellaneous matters – prosecution of criminal offences (ENF 15)

ENF 15 deals with the powers to prosecute criminal offences. Section 401 of the FSMA gives the regulator powers to prosecute a large number of offences which are listed at ENF 15.3. The regulator has power to prosecute criminal offences in England, Wales and Northern Ireland but not Scotland.

The FSA's general policy is to pursue through the criminal justice system all those cases where criminal prosecution is appropriate. The principles the FSA will apply when it decides whether a case is appropriate for criminal prosecution are those contained in the Code for Crown Prosecutors, which is outlined briefly at ENF 15.5 and a full copy of which is annexed to the chapter. Broadly speaking this is based on an evidential test and a public interest test. The FSA will consider whether there is sufficient evidence to provide a realistic prospect of conviction and will have regard to the seriousness of the offence and whether in all the circumstances criminal prosecution is in the public interest.

In cases where criminal proceedings have been or will be commenced, the FSA may also consider whether to take civil or regulatory action. This may include injunctions (ENF 6), restitution (ENF 9), own-initiative action (ENF 3), the withdrawal of approval or authorisation, the cancellation of permission (ENF 5 and 7) and the prohibition of individuals (ENF 8). These penalties and the circumstances in which the FSA will decide to take regulatory action are set out in more detail at ENF 15. The FSA may decide to issue a formal caution rather than to prosecute an offender. It will only do so if the conditions at ENF 15.6 are met. These include sufficient evidence giving realistic prospect of conviction, an admission and an understanding of the significance of the caution on the part of the offender.

Finally at ENF 15.7 the regulator sets out the factors it will take into consideration when deciding whether to "prosecute" for market abuse. This offence is intended to complement the existing criminal regime for insider dealing and misleading statements and practices.

10.13.10   Collective investment schemes (ENF 16)

The regulator's approach to enforcement in relation to authorised unit trust ("AUTs"), authorised open-ended investment companies ("ICVCs") and recognised schemes is outlined in ENF 16.

Under Sections 242 to 261 of the FSMA the regulator is given powers to revoke authorisation of an AUT, give directions to an AUT or to apply to court for the removal of a manager or trustee or the winding up of an AUT. The three powers and the circumstances in which they would be applied are listed separately at ENF 16.2.10G. The factors taken into consideration include the seriousness of the contravention, the consequences of the failure, whether false information was knowingly or recklessly given to the FSA, the conduct of the manager or trustee and other factors.

With regard to ICVCs, ENF 16.3 notes that regulations for setting up, running and regulating ICVCs are contained in the Open Ended Investment Companies Regulations 2001. The Regulations include FSA enforcement powers to revoke authorisation of an ICVC, give directions or apply to court to remove any director of an ICVC or its depository. These are additional powers to the FSA's normal disciplinary powers (ENF 12 and ENF 13).

At ENF 16.4 the FSA sets out its enforcement powers with regard to recognised schemes.

Finally at ENF 16 Annex 1G the FSA sets out a table of powers, procedures and circumstances in which these will be used, numbered according to the sections of the FSMA, in relation to AUTs and recognised schemes.

10.13.11   Disqualification of auditors and actuaries (ENF 17)

Under Section 345 of the FSMA the FSA is given power to disqualify auditors and actuaries for failure to comply with duties imposed on them under the FSMA or subordinate rules. This disqualification may be from acting for specific firms, schemes or investment companies or it may be a blanket disqualification for all such entities. At ENF 17.4 the FSA sets out which factors it will take into account when considering whether or not to disqualify an auditor or actuary. Under Section 249 of the FSMA if it appears to the FSA that an auditor has failed to comply with the duties imposed on him by trust scheme rules it may disqualify him from being the auditor of any AUT or ICVC.

The procedures for exercising the powers under Sections 345 and 249 are the same, namely those set out in Section 345, that is the warning and decision notice procedure. However, as the Treasury have not yet published the regulations referred to in Sections 342(6) and 343(6) of the FSMA the regulator acknowledges that its draft proposals may need to be changed.

When the Treasury have completed these regulations the FSA proposes to take the following into account when deciding whether to disqualify auditors and actuaries: the nature of the information and the effect of its non-disclosure; the seriousness of any breach of rules; and any action to remedy the non-disclosure. Some special points apply to breaches of trust scheme rules.

At ENF 17.5 and ENF 17.6 the FSA sets out how it will deal with requests to remove a disqualification and outlines the effect of a disqualification upon the parties concerned.

10.13.12   *Disapplication orders against members of the professions*

Sections 326 to 329 of the FSMA deal with the provision of financial services by professional firms. Exemptions from the general prohibitions contained in the FSMA are available to those professionals supervised by "designated professional bodies". At Section 329 the FSA is given powers to disapply those exemptions – effectively disqualifying the professionals from providing financial services – if it has concerns that the professionals are not "fit and proper persons" to carry on regulated activities.

ENF 18.2 to ENF 18.7 outlines the regulator's general approach to the exercise of these powers, the procedure for doing so and the effect of a disapplication order on the parties involved. How the FSA will approach applications from professionals to vary or revoke disapplications is also briefly dealt with.

Amongst the factors to be taken into account before making a disapplication order are the existence of any disciplinary action by a designated professional body, the risk to the clients of the party in question, the extent of the party's compliance with rules made under Section 332 of the FSMA and the consequences of a disapplication for the party involved. These are listed at ENF 18.4.

Similarly there is at ENF 18.5 a list of factors to be taken into account when varying or revoking a disapplication order. These include remedial steps taken, cessation of risk to clients or consumers and elapsed time since the order.

Breach of a disapplication order will amount to a contravention of the main sections of the FSMA as the party involved will no longer benefit from the "professionals" exemption. As such, the guilty party would be open to the criminal and civil enforcement procedures outlined above.

10.14 Statutory notices and the decision making process

10.14.1 *Statutory notice procedure and decision making*

Part XXVI of the FSMA provides the statutory basis for statutory notices, which consist of warning, decision, final and supervisory notices, as well as notices of discontinuance. Section 395 provides that the FSA must determine the procedure that it proposes to follow in relation to such statutory notices. It is the purpose of the Decision Making Manual to satisfy the requirement under Section 395 to give guidance on the FSA's decision-making and other procedures for giving statutory notices (it also gives guidance on the FSA's procedures for using its powers in relation to insolvency or injunctions and restitution offences). The principle made clear at Section 395(2) underpins the decision-making process, namely that a person involved in establishing the evidence cannot be the person who makes a decision in relation to that matter.

10.14.2 *Statutory notices*

Section 387 deals with warning notices which give the recipient details about the action that the FSA proposes to take and about the right to make representations. Section 388 deals with the decision notices. The decision notice gives the recipient details about action that the FSA has decided to take. Section 389 deals with notices of discontinuance and Section 390 with final notices. Section 395 deals with supervisory notices. A supervisory notice gives the recipient details of an action that the FSA has taken or proposes to take.

Decisions whether to give a statutory notice will be taken by a decision maker which will be either the Regulatory Decisions Committee (the "RDC") or FSA staff under executive procedures. DEC 4.1 lists the circumstances in which the RDC must have responsibility for the statutory notices. Not surprisingly, where the FSA proposes to take significant action to limit or affect regulated activity, restricting Part IV permission, imposing a financial penalty or public censure or making a restitution order against any person, then these matters can only be dealt with by the RDC. Those matters that are not specifically required to be taken by the RDC can be taken by the FSA under executive procedures.

10.14.3   *Warning notice and decision notice procedure*

The FSMA requires that when the FSA proposes to exercise its powers in certain circumstances it must use the warning notice and decision notice procedure. The circumstances in which the warning notice and decision notice procedure must be used are listed at DEC 2, Annex 1G, and are generally where the FSA proposes a significant step in relation to the firm's permission or taking disciplinary action, such as publishing a statement in respect of an authorised person or imposing a financial penalty.

Where the RDC has decided to issue a warning notice then, in accordance with Section 387 of the FSMA, the notice must:

(a) state the action which the FSA proposes;

(b) be in writing;

(c) give the FSA's reasons for the proposed action; and

(d) state whether Section 394 of the FSMA (access to FSA material) applies and if the section does apply describe its effect and state whether any secondary material exists to which the person must be allowed access under it.

A warning notice will also inform the person that he is entitled to make representations to the FSA and specify a reasonable period of time of at least 28 days from receiving a warning notice within which the person may give their representation. If appropriate it will also inform the recipient of his right to mediation in respect of the dispute. This is an important change to the disciplinary process and is dealt with at Appendix 1 to DEC and is discussed below. It may be that the representations made may persuade the FSA that no further action is required, in which case a notice of discontinuance will be served under Section 389. If, however, having considered the representations the FSA remains of the opinion that the action proposed in the warning notice is appropriate, a decision notice will then be issued.

Under Section 388 of the FSMA, decision notices must:

(a) be in writing;

(b) give the FSA's reasons for the decision;

(c) state whether Section 394 (access to FSA material) applies and if it does, state whether any secondary material exists to which the person must be allowed access; and

(d) state the right within 28 days of the decision notice to refer the matter to the Tribunal giving details of that procedure.

10.14.4   Final notices

Under Section 390 of the FSMA, the FSA must give a final notice to a person to whom it has given a decision notice either, if the matter is not referred to the Tribunal, within the 28-day period, or, if the matter is referred to the Tribunal, the FSA will give its final notice at the same time as it takes action in accordance with the directions from the Tribunal (or the court, if there has been an appeal on a point of law under Section 137).

10.14.5   Third party rights

Section 393 provides important additional procedural rights relating to third parties who are subject to the statutory notice procedure. Section 393 gives third parties referred to in notices the right to receive the notices and make representations about them if, in the FSA's opinion, that comment is prejudicial to the third party. This additional right (together with access to FSA material under Section 394) does not apply in all circumstances where a warning or decision notice may be given, but does apply in relation to the FSA's decisions to impose financial penalties and publicly censure under Section 205, or publish statements, in relation to disciplinary powers against an approved person under Section 66 and in relation to sanctions for market abuse. Generally it applies where warning or decision notices are given or where the FSA is exercising its own initiative power. A full list of the circumstances in which third party rights arise under Section 393 appears at DEC 2 Annex 1G.

10.14.6   Access to material

The circumstances in which the FSA must give access to certain material are the same as for third party rights and are listed at DEC 2 Annex 1G. If the right to give a recipient of a warning or decision notice access to FSA material arises under Section 394, the FSA must allow the person served with the warning or decision notice access to the material on which the FSA relied in taking the decision and any secondary material which in the opinion of the FSA might undermine that decision. A number of qualifications to this right arise under Sections 394(2) and 394(3), such as where the material relates to another person or would not be in the public interest or would be unfair, in which case the FSA must provide a written notice and under Section 394(3) explain the reasons for refusing to provide it.

10.14.7   Supervisory notice procedure

In certain circumstances the FSMA requires that the FSA issues supervisory notices. A full list of the relevant circumstances appears at DEC 3 Annex 1G and includes where the FSA is exercising its own initiative powers to vary a firms Part IV permission. In some respects, the procedure has similarities to the warning and decision notice procedure in that it is a two-stage process. In other respects, the procedure is materially different, for example in the fact that the rights to third parties under Section 393 and access to FSA material under Section 394 do not arise.

The first procedural step is the service of a "first" supervisory notice, following which the recipient may make representations, after which will be the "second" supervisory notice. If the FSA decides to issue a first supervisory notice, the notice must:

(a) give details of the actions;

(b) state when the actions take effect;

(c) state the reason;

(d) inform them of the right to refer the matter to the Tribunal, explaining procedure; and

(e) inform them of the right to make representations to the FSA. This is usually within 28 days.

Having considered any representations, if it decides to take no further action, the FSA will promptly communicate this to the person concerned. However, if it decides to proceed, it will issue a second supervisory notice, the content of which will depend on the action the FSA decides to take. If it decides to proceed with the action proposed in the first notice it must inform the person that he has a right to refer the matter to the Tribunal and describe the procedure. It may decide on taking different action from that originally proposed, in which case the second supervisory notice must be in the same form as the first supervisory notice.

10.15   The Regulatory Decisions Committee (the "RDC")

The provisions relating to the RDC were initially dealt with in the draft Enforcement Manual. Following consultations it was decided that a separate DEC Manual be produced and the final text DEC was published in May 2001. DEC 4.1.4G gives a list of the decisions which must be taken by the RDC. Decisions that are not taken by the RDC will be taken by the FSA under executive procedure. The RDC is appointed by the FSA Board to exercise regulatory powers on behalf of it. The RDC is answerable to the FSA Board. The RDC comprises a chairman, a deputy chairman and other members. A significant difference from some of the various bodies which it supersedes and which exercised control over regulatory organisations, is that it is not inside the FSA's management structure. It is designed to be as far as possible independent of the FSA's executive staff, its membership

461

being drawn from current and recently retired practitioners with financial services industry skills and other suitable individuals representing the public interest.

10.15.1   Procedures

Normally the RDC will meet as a full committee or panel, the size of which will depend upon the nature of the particular matter under consideration. However, except in urgent supervisory notice cases, the RDC will include its chairman or deputy chairman and at least two other members. Another of the significant differences between the RDC and bodies which have previously exercised disciplinary functions, is that it is going to be possible for parties to make representations directly to the RDC. Where a party has received a warning or first supervisory notice he will be notified of his right (within 28 days) to make representations. (A procedure exists for requesting an extension of time to the 28-day time limit in which case such request must be made within 14 days of receiving the notice in question.) Under Section 387(3) the RDC may extend the period of time for representations. Representations may be made in writing or orally, but if orally, the FSA must be notified at least five business days before the end of the period for representation specified in the notice that the party wishes to make oral representations. The notification should also specify the matters on which the person wishes to make oral representations and there should be a clear estimate of how much time will be required. The RDC will specify a time as soon as reasonably possible after receiving the notification for hearing the oral representations. The ability to make direct oral representations to the RDC is a new power and is likely to be heavily used. Not surprisingly, DEC 4.4.10 provides that the RDC may limit the type, length and content of any representations. (Those third parties who received a copy of the warning notice are also entitled to make representations to the RDC.)

Where decisions are to be made under the executive procedure, DEC 4.3 specifies the procedure that will apply to decision making by individual FSA staff members specifying the seniority and the manner in which the decision is taken.

10.15.2   *Settlement and mediation*

Appendix 1 to the Decision Making Manual explains the settlement procedure and mediation scheme for FSA disciplinary cases. The introduction of a mediation scheme is a significant step mirroring the trends in civil litigation and is likely to be extensively used.

10.15.3   *Settlement*

After receiving a warning notice, the person may discuss the proposed action with FSA staff on an informal basis and the warning notice will contain details of the person to contact for these purposes. These discussions will usually be on a without prejudice basis, that is neither party may subsequently rely on admissions or statements made in the context of the discussion. Before any settlement can be reached with FSA staff it has to be considered by the RDC, which may accept the proposed settlement by issuing a decision notice, or in appropriate cases by issuing a notice of discontinuance, or it may decline the proposed settlement.

10.15.4   *Mediation*

If it is not possible to reach a settlement in informal discussions, a person may elect to have the dispute mediated. Mediation is a confidential without prejudice dispute resolution process in which a neutral mediator tries to assist the parties to settle their differences. The mediator has no power to bind the parties or give a ruling. Again, the mediation will be on a without prejudice basis.

It is likely that mediations will take place following the issue of a warning notice, because at that stage the parties will, in appropriate cases, have access to the material that the FSA has relied on in deciding to commence the proceedings. DEC Appendix 1.4 provides the scope and details of the mediation scheme. Generally, it will be available in all disciplinary matters and market abuse cases except as provided at DEC 1.4.2G, which involves for example:

(a) allegations of criminal offences;

(b) cases involving allegations of unfitness or impropriety – dishonesty or lack of integrity;

(c) cases involving the exercise of the FSA's own initiative powers on variation of permission.

The FSA mediation scheme will be administered by an independent body, The Centre for Effective Dispute Resolution ("CEDR").

10.16　Hearings and appeals

10.16.1　Introduction

Section 132 of the FSMA establishes the Financial Services and Markets Tribunal (the "Tribunal"). This is an entirely new body, independent of the FSA, whose function is to hear references to it from those firms and individuals who wish to challenge the FSA's decisions (that is decision and supervisory notices which may have proposed imposing fines or public censure or otherwise altering authorisations/approval). Section 133 provides that any references to the Tribunal must be made before the end of 28 days from the date on which the decision notice or supervisory notice is given.

Section 133(a) provides that the FSA must not take the action specified in a decision or supervisory notice during the period in which the matter may be referred to the Tribunal and, if the matter has been referred, must not take any action until the reference, and any appeal, has been finally disposed of.

The conduct of proceedings before the Tribunal is determined by the Lord Chancellor who in July 2001 exercised his power under Section 132 to make detailed rules of procedure in relation to Tribunal hearings – the Financial Services and Markets Tribunal Rules 2001 S.I. 2001 No 2476 (the "Rules"). Tribunal hearings are not in the nature of an appeal from the RDC but are instead by way of a full re-hearing. Section 133(3) makes clear that the Tribunal may consider any evidence relating to the subject matter whether or not it was available to the RDC.

10.16.2　Composition of the Tribunal

Schedule 13 to the FSMA provides that the Lord Chancellor must appoint a panel of persons to act as Chairmen of the Tribunal who must be solicitors or barristers of at least seven years standing. The

Lord Chancellor then selects one of these to preside over the Tribunal – the President. The Lord Chancellor may also appoint a Deputy President (both President and Deputy President posts are only open to solicitors or barristers of 10 years standing).

In addition the Lord Chancellor must also appoint a panel of persons who appear to him to be qualified by experience or otherwise to deal with matters of the kind which may be referred to the Tribunal. When a reference is made to the Tribunal the persons who act as members are to be selected from the panel of Chairmen or the lay panel in accordance with arrangements made by the President, called standing arrangements. These provide for at least one member to be selected from the panel of Chairmen. In cases of special difficulty the Tribunal may appoint one or more experts to provide assistance (Schedule 13(7)(4)).

10.16.3   *The Tribunal's procedure*

The Rules provide that a "reference notice" must be filed by an applicant within 28 days of the day on which the decision notice or supervisory notice was given. The reference notice will state that it is a reference notice, the relevant names and addresses of the applicant and its representatives (together with an applicant's address for service in the UK) and will state the issues concerning the notice which the applicant wishes the Tribunal to consider. The Tribunal Secretary then informs all the parties of the service of a reference notice and, within 28 days of being so informed the FSA must file a "statement of case". The statement of case shall specify the statutory provisions providing for the referred action, the reasons for the action, shall set out the matters upon which the FSA relies to support the action and specify the date on which the statement of case was filed. The statement of case must be accompanied by the documents on which the FSA relies and "the further material which in the opinion of the [FSA] might undermine the decision to take that action". No later than 28 days after receiving the FSA's statement of case the applicant must file a written reply stating the grounds on which the applicant relies identifying all the matters in the statement of case which it disputes and the reason for disputing those matters and must specify the date on which the reply was filed. The reply must be accompanied by all the documents upon which the applicant relies. The Rules provide that following the reply there is secondary disclosure by the FSA of any further material which might be reasonably expected to assist the applicant's case as disclosed in the reply.

Rule 17 provides that generally all hearings shall be held in public however the Tribunal may direct that all or part of the hearing be in private – on the application of all parties or on the application of any party if the Tribunal is satisfied that a hearing in private is necessary. In deciding whether such a hearing is necessary the Tribunal has regard to the interests of morals, public order, national security or the protection of the private lives of the parties or any unfairness to the applicant or prejudice to the interests of consumers that might result from a hearing in public. In either case the Tribunal must be satisfied that a hearing in private would not prejudice the interests of justice. The fact that hearings will generally be in public may well dissuade some potential applicants who might otherwise think of challenging a decision notice or supervisory notice to reconsider whether they wish their concerns to be aired in public.

10.16.4   Evidence

Section 133(3) of the FSMA makes clear a point which had previously been debated, namely that the Tribunal has a complete and unfettered jurisdiction to consider all matters of fact whether or not available to the FSA when the RDC made the original decision from which the reference to the Tribunal has been made. There was originally some debate as to whether the Tribunal could interfere with findings of fact but the point is now beyond argument.

The Tribunal also has full powers by summons to require any person to attend to give evidence or produce documents which the Tribunal considers necessary. Failure to comply with such requirement is an offence punishable by a fine not exceeding the statutory maximum (currently £2,000). If someone alters, suppresses, conceals or destroys or refuses to produce a document for the purposes of the Tribunal, an offence is committed, punishable by an unlimited fine or in more serious cases imprisonment (evidence "may" be taken on oath or instead following a declaration of truth).

10.16.5   *Decisions of the Tribunal*

These may be by majority and the decision must state whether it was unanimous or by majority; the decision must be recorded in a document which contains reasons and must be communicated as soon as is reasonably practicable to each party and any authorised person concerned if not a party. A decision must be signed by the member of the panel of Chairmen dealing with the dispute. The decision will determine what (if any) the appropriate action is for the FSA to take in relation to the matter referred to it. The Tribunal does not itself implement any action (Section 133(4)). The Tribunal must remit the matter to the FSA with such directions (if any) as the Tribunal considers appropriate for giving effect to its determination. Important limitations exist in Section 133(6) and (7) to prevent the Tribunal seeking to impose a sanction which the FSA could not in the particular circumstances of that case have imposed.

10.16.6   *Appeals*

A party to a reference to the Tribunal may, with permission (either from the Tribunal or the Court of Appeal) appeal on a point of law arising from a decision to the Court of Appeal (or in Scotland the Court of Session). If the appeal is successful the court may remit the matter to the Tribunal for rehearing and determination or itself make a determination. Appeals from the Court of Appeal can only be made with the leave of the Court of Appeal or the House of Lords. Rules 23 – 25 deal with the mechanics of appeals from the tribunal.

10.16.7   *Costs*

There will usually be no order as to costs unless a party is found to have acted vexatiously, frivolously or unreasonably in which case the Tribunal can order payment by one part of such costs to the other. If the Tribunal considers that the FSA has acted unreasonably it may be ordered to pay the other party's costs (Schedule 13(13)).

Chapter 11

CONSUMER RELATIONS: COMPLAINTS AND COMPENSATION

Philip Mackay
Partner
Dundas & Wilson CS

11.1 Introduction

This Chapter explains the main elements of the Complaints Code and the compensation manual which together comprise Block 4 of the FSA Handbook ("Redress") and how they may be interpreted and work in practice. It does not deal with the rules as to funding of either the Financial Ombudsman Service (the "FOS") or the Financial Services Compensation Scheme.

11.2 Complaints

11.2.1 *Financial Services and Markets Act 2000 framework for consumer complaints and single Ombudsman Scheme*

Two of the objectives which the Financial Services Authority (the "FSA") has been given under Section 2 of the Financial Services and Markets Act 2000 (the "FSMA") relate to the protection of consumers and promotion of public awareness and understanding of the financial system. It is these two in particular that underlie both the formal arrangements in the FSA Handbook governing consumer complaints and compensation and their likely increased use after N2, as the FSA is proactive in its efforts to grow a more sophisticated consumer personal finance culture.[1] Firms and their advisers need to bear in mind these two objectives, as well as the FSA's recorded thinking in relation to their meaning, when interpreting the detailed rules and guidance in relation to complaints and compensation.

In spite of the enshrinement in the FSMA of the general principle that consumers should take responsibility for their decisions,[2] more and more of the FSA's work is concerned with protection and education of consumers. The FSA has highlighted fair post-sale treatment of customers as a key policy theme which will inform much of its future work and, it is probably also fair to conclude, its expectations of the standard of conduct of authorised firms and approved persons. Design and operation of internal complaints, handling procedures and firms' knowledge of rules and procedures of the Financial Ombudsman Service (as well as general co-operativeness with the FOS) will all be factors that will contribute to fair post-sale treatment of customers and, equally importantly, the FSA's perception of that fairness.

The adequacy and effective operation of a firm's internal complaints handling procedures will also be matters for the firm to take into account in its compliance with the rules and guidance governing senior management arrangements, systems and controls as well as Principles 3, 6 and 7.[3]

---

[1] The FSA initiative on comparative information tables on retail financial products which it plans to introduce in 2001 is central to this consumer awareness work. *See* FSA Consultative Paper 28 *Comparative Information for Financial Services* October 1999 and the FSA response paper thereon June 2000. The inevitable consequence of increased awareness, a growing rights culture, and consumer information initiatives taken in the course of the FSA's own highly publicised current reviews of the selling of personal pensions, FSAVCs and mortgage endowments will be more active consumers who are more familiar with and willing to use complaints and redress mechanisms, both legal and extra-legal.

[2] Section 5(2)(d) FSMA.

[3] Block 1 FSA Handbook.

Block 4 of the FSA Handbook "Redress" contains rules and guidance for firms in respect of the Compensation Code to be operated by the Financial Services Compensation Scheme established under Part XV of the FSMA (*see* Section 11.2.8.5), and the Complaints Code handling of complaints by authorised firms themselves and by the Ombudsman Scheme, established under Part XVI and Schedule 17 of the FSMA, the operator of which is now the FOS. The single Ombudsman Scheme will, from N2 onwards consolidate into one scheme what the FSA has described as a patch-work quilt of dispute-resolution bodies that is confusing to consumers.[4] Early in the lengthy consultation process that has gone into building the new Scheme, the FSA made clear that although revolutionary rather than evolutionary, unification of the eight existing schemes was preferable to their rationalisation in order to capture the necessary harmonisation, simplification and cost saving which would work to the benefit of consumers and industry.[5] Despite the intention to preserve sector specific departments within the unified scheme[6] the FSA and FOS have emphasised that the new single scheme is to be "more than the sum of its parts" and has stated the following objectives:

(a) to provide, as far as possible, a one-stop shop for dealing with disputes about financial services;

(b) to resolve disputes quickly and with minimum formality;

(c) to provide a prompt, user-friendly and unbureaucratic service;

(d) to take decisions which are consistent, fair and reasonable;

(e) to be cost-effective and efficient;

---

[4] FSA CP4 *Consumer Complaints*. These bodies are: the Banking Ombudsman, Building Societies Ombudsman, Investment Ombudsman, Insurance Ombudsman, Personal Insurance Arbitration Service, PIA Ombudsman Bureau, SFA Complaints Bureau and Arbitration Service, FSA Direct Regulation Unit and Independent Investigator.

[5] FSA CP4 December 1997 paragraph 39.

[6] Ibid paragraph 32.

(f) to be accessible to all groups in the community, including the vulnerable and the disadvantaged;

(g) to be regarded as good value by the industry;

(h) to be forward-looking, adaptable and flexible, making effective use of new technology;

(i) to be trusted and respected by both consumers, the industry and other interested parties.[7]

Dubbed "Son of Leviathan" by opposition Members of Parliament during the Commons Committee stage of debate on the FSMA,[8] a recent prediction of the sheer scale of the operation that will be the single Ombudsman Scheme put the estimated annual budget at £20 million, staff requirement at 350 – 400, number of individual Ombudsmen at 15 – 20, and number of firms subject to the Scheme's compulsory jurisdiction at 10,000.[9]

The rules and guidance constructing the Ombudsman Scheme set out in Section 138, Part XVI and Schedule 17 of the FSMA are considered in more detail below.

11.2.2 General rule-making power

Under the FSMA, the FSA has power to make rules governing internal complaints handling procedures under its general rule-making power contained in Section 138. This section allows the FSA to make:

"such rules applying to authorised persons

(a) with respect to the carrying on by them of regulated activities, or

(b) with respect to the carrying on by them of activities which are not regulated activities

---

7   Joint FSA and FOS CP33 November 1999, paragraph 1.21.

8   Howard Flight MP Introductory Comments on Clause 197 (The scheme and scheme operator). Standing Committee A, HC Hansard 30 November 1999.

9   Paragraph 1.17 Joint FSA and FOS CP33 November 1999.

as appear to it to be necessary or expedient for the purpose of protecting the interests of consumers."[10]

When considered together with the definition of "consumers", the general power is potentially wide-ranging.[11]

Breaches of these rules are actionable in damages at the suit of private persons[12] unless otherwise specified by the FSA and so careful attention must be paid to the actionability of such rules. In practice the risk of damages actions brought under Section 138 would be hard to sustain on the grounds of breach of internal complaints handling rules alone, as the normal ingredients of an action for breach of statutory duty would need to be present such as causation and loss but, if accompanied by other more material FSA rule breaches, then breaches of internal complaints handling rules will not be helpful to any defence mounted to a Section 138 action.

11.2.3 *Part XVI and Schedule 17 FSMA the Ombudsman Scheme*

This Part of the Act provides for the establishment and rules of operation of "a scheme under which certain disputes may be resolved quickly and with minimum formality by an independent

---

[10]   Section 138(a)and (b) FSMA.

[11]   Section 138 (7) FSMA defines "consumers" broadly to mean: persons who either: (a) use, or have used, or are or may be contemplating using, any of the services provided by authorised persons carrying on regulated activities or persons acting as appointed representatives; or (b) have rights or interests which are derived from, or are otherwise attributable to, the use of any such services by persons acting on their behalf or in a fiduciary capacity relating to them; or (c) have rights or interests which may be adversely affected by the use of any such services by persons acting on their behalf or in a fiduciary capacity in relation to them.

[12]   The meaning prescribed by HM Treasury in the current draft of the FSMA (Rights of Action) Regulations 2001 is: "any individual, except when acting in the course of carrying on a regulated activity; and any person who is not an individual, except when acting in the course of carrying on business of any kind" Regulation 3.

person".[13] The scheme is to be administered by an independent company, the scheme operator, established and overseen by the FSA. The FSA appointed the scheme operator's board in February 1999 and it is the scheme operator, rather than the FSA, that is responsible for the establishment of the Ombudsman Scheme itself, appointment of ombudsmen including a Chief Ombudsman,[14] making procedural rules (FSA approval required) governing the compulsory jurisdiction of the scheme,[15] making rules governing the terms of reference of, and procedure to be followed in the scheme's voluntary jurisdiction,[16] giving guidance as to any matter it considers appropriate,[17] and reporting annually to the FSA.[18] The Chief Ombudsman is also under a statutory duty to report annually to the FSA.[19]

The FSA has rule-making competence with respect to the compulsory jurisdiction including application of the compulsory jurisdiction[20] and certain procedural matters.[21]

The FSA also has power to make rules levying the industry to provide funding for the establishment of the Ombudsman Scheme and the operation of its compulsory jurisdiction,[22] as well as

---

[13]   Section 225(1) FSMA.

[14]   Paragraphs (4) and (5) Part II Schedule 17.

[15]   Paragraph (14) Part III Schedule 17.

[16]   Section 227 (3) and paragraphs (18) and (20).

[17]   Paragraph (8) Part II Schedule 17.

[18]   Paragraph (7) (1) (a) Part II Schedule 17.

[19]   Paragraph (7) (1) (b) Part II Schedule 17.

[20]   These rules are to be known as the "Compulsory Jurisdiction rules" and are made under Section 226(3).

[21]   Paragraph (13) Part III Schedule 17.

[22]   Section 234.

approval of the annual budget for the scheme operator, variation of which by the scheme operator must also be with the FSA's approval.[23]

With the scheme operator constituted by the FSA, mechanisms of its accountability (both financial and general), as well as rule-making competence, so closely linked to the FSA, one might query the degree to which it can be truly said to be "an independent person" within the meaning of Section 225(1). Indeed the pre-legislative scrutiny committee of both Houses of Parliament chaired by Lord Burns (the "Burns Committee") recommended that the Ombudsman Scheme be required to report annually to Parliament on the adequacy of its budget.[24] In response to this point the Government preferred that the Parliamentary Committee which would review the FSA's annual report to HM Treasury which is required be laid before Parliament[25] should also take a proactive interest in reviewing the annual report that the Ombudsman Scheme is to make to the FSA and indeed, other strands in the new complex web of regulatory accountability, such as reports of the Consumer and Practitioner Panels to the FSA.

The scheme operator and other persons exercising functions pursuant to the compulsory jurisdiction part of the Ombudsman Scheme enjoy the same immunity from liability in damages as does the FSA.[26] The existence of this immunity is a major reason why the issue of accountability received such close attention both within and without Parliament in the passage of the FSMA.

The Burns Committee also expressed concern that in order to be as effective and inclusive as possible it should not become over-legalistic although of course its procedures should be sufficiently fair and transparent to comply with Article 6 of the European

---

[23]   Paragraph (9) Part II.

[24]   Paragraph 291 *First Report Joint Committee on Financial Services and Markets,* May 1999, HC 328-II.

[25]   Paragraph (10) Schedule 1.

[26]   Paragraph (10) Schedule 17.

Convention on Human Rights. It also urged application of cost-benefit analysis by the FSA to rules to be made in relation to the FSA's rule-making and approval powers for compulsory jurisdiction rules *vis-à-vis* the Ombudsman Scheme with sensitivity, and in a way that takes full account of the objectives of the Scheme. Cost-benefit analysis is not to be applied by the FSA in the exercise of its levy powers to fund the Scheme under Section 234.[27]

11.2.4   *FSMA provisions as to scheme eligibility and awards*

The Burns Committee expressed the view that eligibility to bring a complaint to the Ombudsman Scheme be limited to individuals and that authorised firms be precluded from using the Scheme.[28] The Government took the view that while the scheme should not be used for dispute resolution between professional firms as a matter of course there could still be circumstances where small authorised firms, perhaps small family firms, were in an analogous position to individuals and therefore merited access to the Scheme. So the FSMA now provides that so far as the compulsory jurisdiction is concerned: "a complainant is eligible, in relation to the compulsory jurisdiction of the ombudsman scheme, if he falls within a class of persons specified in the rules as eligible..." and those rules may "include provisions for persons other than individuals to be eligible; but may not provide for authorised persons to be eligible except in specified circumstances or in relation to complaints of a specified kind".[29]

The eligibility rules made by FSA in respect of the compulsory jurisdiction are considered below in Section 11.2.7.8.

As for the grounds and finality of the Ombudsman's determination of a complaint to which the compulsory jurisdiction relates Section 228 provides simply that: "A complaint is to be determined by reference to what is, in the opinion of the Ombudsman, fair and reasonable in all the circumstances of the case".

---

[27]   Section 155 (9) (c).

[28]   Paragraph 296 *Burns Committee First Report* op.cit. at n 18.

[29]   Section (6) and (7) Section 226.

The determination of the complaint binds the respondent but is only binding and final on the complainant if he positively accepts by notifying the Ombudsman, if no acceptance or rejection is received by the due date then he is to be treated as having rejected the determination and the courts remain open to the complainant. The Ombudsman's determination under the compulsory jurisdiction may include a monetary award under the compulsory jurisdiction that he considers "fair compensation for loss or damage suffered by the complainant (including non-financial loss of specified kinds)" within the limits to be set by the FSA, and/or a direction that the respondent takes steps that the Ombudsman considers just and appropriate.[30] A monetary award is enforceable by the complainant in the courts. As for costs awards the scheme operator has power under the compulsory jurisdiction to make costs rules (subject to FSA approval) which enable the Ombudsman to award the costs incurred in determining a complaint, except that there are statutory safeguards in favour of complainants so that a respondent's costs can never be awarded against a complainant and the scheme operator's costs may only be awarded against a complainant if the complainant's conduct was improper, unreasonable or the complainant was responsible for an unreasonable delay.[31]

The Ombudsman also has powers to compel the production of information considered necessary to the determination of a complaint.[32]

11.2.5 *FSA's Rules and arrangements for complaints' handling and dispute resolution*

It is at the level of the FSA Handbook, however, that the way in which the enabling provisions in Part XVI of the FSMA have been employed to flesh out the new single Ombudsman Scheme is revealed. The FSA and the FOS have been involved in a lengthy process of public consultation to ensure that the process of integration of the very disparate and different eight existing

---

[30]   Section 229.

[31]   Section 230.

[32]   Sections 231, 232.

complaints and arbitration schemes into one Ombudsman Scheme was as coherent and comprehensible as possible.[33] These consultation papers are important and should be retained for it is arguable that a degree of formal legal status will attach to the FSA commentary which accompanies proposals for rules. This is because Section 155 (2) (b) FSMA obliges the FSA when consulting on proposed rules to provide, amongst other things, "an explanation of the purpose of the proposed rules". So, what is said by the FSA in explaining how it sees the rules operating can, at a later date, in perhaps an enforcement, supervision or in this particular instance, a complaints handling context, be used in argument by a firm or individual in support of its preferred interpretation of the rule in question.

The joint approach that the FSA and FOS have taken to consultation and exercise of their rule-making competences under the FSMA to construct a complaints handling system makes sense when viewed from the perspective of both users of the Scheme and of firms who are subject to internal complaints handling rules and need to understand the linkages between those rules and the Scheme rules. As far as possible the same requirements apply to the Voluntary and Compulsory Scheme jurisdictions. The rules that comprise the complaints component of Block 4 of the FSA Handbook are as follows and the main elements of each one are discussed in turn below:

---

[33]   FSA CP4 *Consumer Complaints* December 1997, Joint FSA and FOS CP33 *Consumer Complaints and Single Ombudsman Regime* November 1999, Joint FSA and FOS CP49 *Complaints Handling Arrangements* May 2000, published in final form in a Joint Policy Statement and feedback response to CP49 from FSA and FOS published in December 2000 and Joint FSA and FOS Consultation Paper 99 *Complaints-Handling Rules: the transitional arrangements and other amendments* June 2001. The rules were published in "final form" in the FSA's response to CP49, although they were subsequently amended in part by CP 99 to take account of pre/post N2 transitional arrangements.

(a) *complaints handling procedures for firms:* these must be established both by firms which are potentially subject to the compulsory jurisdiction and are also applied by the terms of reference of the voluntary jurisdiction to those firms which opt to submit to the voluntary jurisdiction;

(b) *jurisdiction rules:* these set out the scope of both the compulsory and voluntary jurisdictions;

(c) *complaints handling procedures of the Scheme Operator (the FOS):* comprises rules on procedures to be applied by the Scheme Operator, awards, costs, types of damage and loss in respect of which monetary compensation can be awarded as well as the maximum amount of such compensation;

(d) *standard terms (for participation in the voluntary jurisdiction):* these are the contractual terms pursuant to which firms participate in the voluntary jurisdiction.

11.2.6   *Complaints handling procedures for firms*

The rules and guidance contained in this section of the Handbook aim to achieve a consistent, industry wide approach to complaints handling irrespective of whether the subject matter of the complaint would fall within the compulsory or voluntary jurisdictions. They are addressed as much to individuals who might wish to refer a complaint to the Ombudsman Scheme as to firms subject to its two jurisdictions.   Reference must obviously be made to the FSA Handbook itself but some of the main areas dealt with in the rules and guidance contained in this Section include:

11.2.6.1   *The content and level of the obligation to maintain internal complaints handling procedures*

Firms are under an absolute obligation to "have in place and operate appropriate and effective internal complaints handling procedures (which must be written down) for handling any expression of dissatisfaction...whether justified or not, from or on behalf of an eligible complainant about that firm's provision of, or failure to provide, a financial services activity" (DISP 1.2.1R). There is no room for manoeuvre here, the obligation is total, unlike many of the obligations contained in higher level rules from the FSA this is not qualified by any "reasonableness" fetter. Although this may not seem significant at first reading, firms need to be aware that the word "effective" means just that and when the effectiveness of a firm's complaints handling system is judged on an *ex post facto* basis, for example in a disciplinary context, a risk arises that different criteria will apply than pertained at the time of establishment and operation. In guidance accompanying this rule the FSA indicates that a complaints handling system would provide for: receiving complaints, responding thereto, appropriate investigation of those complaints and notifying complainants of their right to go to the FOS where relevant. In judging the "appropriateness" of their schemes, firms should have regard to: the type of business undertaken by the firm, nature and complexity of complaints likely to be received, the likely number of complaints it may need to investigate, size and structure of their organisation. Interestingly, the FSA suggests and is going so far as to make available to firms the British Standards Institution ("BSI") standard on complaints management systems.[34]

While these criteria are, technically speaking, only regulatory guidance, firms would be well advised to employ those criteria in both the design and subsequent operational testing of their complaints handling systems.

11.2.6.2   What is a complaint?

Complaint is about as widely defined as it could possibly be for the purposes of DISP 1.2.1R to cover "any expression of dissatisfaction, whether oral or written, and whether justified or not." So, no matter how spurious, vexatious or just plain "off the wall" such an expression may appear at the time it is made to a firm it matters not and they must err on the side of caution and treat any expression of dissatisfaction as a complaint. As for devising an effective measure of what constitutes "dissatisfaction" firms would be well advised to take as generous and customer friendly an approach to this as possible. It should be viewed from the point of view of the customer and in as subjective a manner as possible and if a customer communicates in any way with a firm which so much as hints at

---

[34]   British Standard 8600:1999 *Complaints Management Systems – Guide to Design and Implementation* referred to specifically at paragraph G 1.2.5 Guidance in Chapter 1 Complaints Rules Section 4 FSA Handbook.

latent dissatisfaction then that should be either positively and proactively drawn out of that customer or his confirmation sought that he is not in fact making a complaint.

This will entail awareness at the level of every customer facing member of staff within the firm, not just those with specific complaints handling responsibilities. Indeed this need for firm wide awareness is reflected in DISP 1.2.15R which requires that "A firm must take reasonable steps to ensure that all relevant staff and appointed representatives are aware of the firm's internal complaint handling procedures and must endeavour to ensure that they act in accordance with them". The qualification of this obligation by the need to take "reasonable" steps towards awareness, and to endeavour to ensure that staff comply with internal procedures ensures that the firm does not carry absolute responsibility for the lack of compliance of individual staff which it could not reasonably have foreseen and prevented. However the complaint itself must be "investigated by an employee of sufficient competence who, where appropriate, was not directly involved in the matter which is the subject of the complaint" and "the person charged with responding to complaints to have the authority to settle complaints (including the offering of redress where appropriate) or to have ready access to someone who has the necessary authority" (DISP 1.2.13R). The Rules also require that any response to a complaint must address its subject matter and an offer of appropriate redress must accompany a complaint being upheld by a firm. Such redress can take a number of forms, including financial (which can include a reasonable rate of interest) and may involve a simple apology.[35]

11.2.6.3 *Linkage to senior management arrangements, systems and controls*

DISP 1.2.16R provides a layer of context specific detail which illustrates how the FSA has, throughout its Handbook, attempted to particularise compliance obligations in a way which firms' senior management will find most helpful in illustrating the meaning of the very generally phrased rules and guidance in Block 1 of the Handbook on senior management arrangements, systems, and

---

[35]   1.2.21G.

controls, as well as Principle 3 of the FSA's Principles for Business. DISP 1.2.16R provides that "A firm must put in place appropriate management controls and take reasonable steps to ensure that in complying with DISP 1.2.1R it handles complaints fairly, consistently and promptly and that it identifies and remedies any recurring or systemic problems, as well as any specific problem identified by a complaint".

11.2.6.4 *Time limits for resolution of complaints by firms*

Firms must acknowledge complaints within 48 hours of receipt. A firm has a maximum time period of eight weeks from the time it receives a complaint to resolve the complaint before it becomes eligible for reference to the Ombudsman Scheme (in the case of complaints that fall within the Scheme's jurisdictions) and within that maximum eight-week time period a firm has four weeks in which to either issue a final response or a holding response in the prescribed form. A "final response" is defined as either an acceptance of the complaint accompanied where appropriate by an offer of redress (financial or otherwise), an offer of redress that does not accept the complaint, or a reasoned rejection of the complaint. As an alternative to a final response the firm may issue a holding response providing an explanation of the delay in resolution of the complaint and indicating when it will be in contact again (which must be a time within the eight-week period (DISP 1.4.4R)).

Either within the eight-week time period or in accompaniment to the final response if earlier the firm must send the complainant details of the FOS (including FOS's own leaflet) and his right to refer his complaint to it within six months (DISP 1.4.7R). Those firms which operate a two tier branch and head office complaints handling system can, if the complainant delays for more than one week in progressing his complaint up to the head office tier, set that time off against the eight week total but the FSA warns firms in accompanying guidance that it expects to see easy access for customers to the second stage of any two-tier process.[36]

---

[36]   DISP 1.4.10R and DISP 1.4.11G.

11.2.6.5   *Basis of redress offered by firms*

DISP 1.2.14R directs firms that once they have decided that redress for a complaint is appropriate they should "aim to provide a complainant with fair compensation for any acts or omissions for which it was responsible". An offer of financial redress can include a reasonable rate of interest and firms should take into account guidance published by the FOS, the FSA or any of the predecessor schemes, so providing for an element of continuity.

11.2.6.6   *Time limits for referral of complaints to Ombudsman Scheme*

Other than in exceptional circumstances such as, FSA guidance suggests, incapacity or ignorance of the complainant of his right of reference, a complainant has six months from the date on which he was advised by the firm that he may refer his complaint to the FOS and within six years of the event giving rise to the complaint or, if outside that time limit then within three years of the date on which he became aware, or ought reasonably to have become aware, of his cause for complaint (DISP 2.3.1R).

11.2.6.7   *Record-keeping and reporting*

Authorised firms must make and retain adequate records of complaints falling within the jurisdiction (compulsory or voluntary) for a minimum of three years and must report to the FSA twice a year on a category-by-category basis statistics relating to receipt, completion and acceptance of complaints by the firm.[37] The FSA has explained the importance of this type of reporting and monitoring indicator to the operation of the risk assessment methodology behind its risk-related approach to supervision.[38] The FSA has indicated that it will aim to co-ordinate the times for submitting these reports with other reporting requirement time limits to which firms are subject and that it will also use the data to assist in the

---

[37]   For record-keeping and reporting requirements *see* the Rules and Guidance contained in Rule 1.5.

[38]   *A New Regulator for the New Millennium* January 2000 and Policy Report *Building the New regulator: Progress Report I* December 2000.

identification of specific consumer education initiatives and will consider whether, and if so how, to use the complaints data supplied in the FSA comparative information tables.[39]

11.2.6.8   FOS Jurisdiction rules

At and after N2 the compulsory jurisdiction of FOS will extend to all regulated activities as well as mortgage lending and unsecured lending by way of provision of overdrafts, loan accounts and credit cards and will also extend to the provision of ancillary banking services, but only where those activities are conducted by authorised firms.

The definition of ancillary banking services is wide and encompasses all services offered by a bank or building society, whether or not the service itself is a regulated activity. This will include general insurance business sold by banks and building societies as well as the operation of cash machines and safe deposit boxes; it also includes the provision of advice so that, for example, mortgage advice given by an authorised person will come within the scope of FOS' jurisdiction even though mortgage advice itself will not be regulated by the FSA.

It was pointed out during the course of consultation as well as during the passage of the FSMA, that the inability of the compulsory jurisdiction to reach beyond authorised firms will lead to an unlevel playing field in respect of lenders that do not need to be authorised to conduct activities which, while not themselves regulated activities are nevertheless within the scope of the compulsory jurisdiction as they are carried out by authorised firms.[40] For that reason, as well as in the general interest of furthering the FSA's statutory objective of consumer protection by maximising the Ombudsman Scheme's coverage, the voluntary jurisdiction will, at and after N2, be open to unauthorised mortgage lenders until such time as they transfer to

---

[39]   Paragraph 1.83 Joint FSA and FOS CP49 *Complaints Handling Arrangements*.

[40]   Evidence of the Banking Ombudsman to the Burns Committee, who gave the example of credit cards and personal loans, extracted at paragraph 288 *First Report Joint Committee on Financial Services and Markets*, May 1999 HC 328-II.

the compulsory jurisdiction.[41] It will also be open to unauthorised firms whose activities are covered by an existing scheme and who wish to maintain a redress mechanism for consumers.

It is highly likely as financial consumers become increasingly aware that firms not subject to the compulsory jurisdiction will see membership of the Voluntary Scheme as a quality mark conferring competitive advantage.

11.2.6.9   *Who is eligible to complain?*

Private individuals, businesses with a group annual turnover of less than £1 million, registered charities with annual income of less than £1 million,[42] and trustees of a trust with net asset value of less than £1 million are all within the classes of persons eligible to refer a complaint to the FOS to the extent that they are not classified as either an intermediate customer or a market counterparty in relation to the firm against which the complaint lies. They must therefore be classified as a private customer in relation to that firm in order to be eligible to use the service.[43]

11.2.6.10   *Territorial scope of scheme*

The scope of the scheme extends to complaints about activities of firms conducted in or from the UK including activities of firms which are incoming EEA firms, incoming Treaty firms and UCITs qualifiers which qualify for automatic authorisation under the FSMA.[44] The residence or base of the complainant is irrelevant to eligibility of the complaint. Guidance provides some limit on the

---

[41]   At the time of writing this is expected to be near the end of 2001 when such mortgage lenders will require authorisation.

[42]   FSA's research shows that 98 per cent of registered charities will qualify for access to the Scheme on this basis.

[43]   DISP 2.4.3R. For customer classification rules *see* Chapter 4 *Conduct of Business Rules* Section 2 FSA Handbook.

[44]   Schedules 3, 4 and 5 FSMA.

territorial scope of the compulsory jurisdiction of the scheme insofar as it does not extend to complaints concerning business conducted by branches of UK firms outside the UK.[45]

In order to increase consumer confidence in cross-border retail financial services business within the EU the Commission has, along with a wide range of substantive legal and regulatory matters, identified the development of effective, out of court redress procedures for cross-border business as a priority within its "Financial Services Action Plan".[46]

This blueprint for action urged the Commission and other EU institutions to take a wide range of internal market enhancing measures and initiatives, one of them being to "consider the development of a union-wide complaints network (including the use of an Ombudsman for financial services)".[47] Progress continues to be made on this and the Commission highlighted in its third progress report on the Financial Services Action Plan the setting up, in October 2000, of a network of national bodies dealing with consumer complaints to co-operate in providing assistance in cases of cross-border problems which will develop along the lines recommended by the Commission in its recommendation on the principles applicable to the bodies responsible for out-of-court settlement of consumer disputes.[48] The early work of this network has included the development of a Memorandum of Understanding as a necessary basis for effective inter-scheme co-operation.

11.2.6.11   Complaint handling procedures of the FOS

The rules and guidance that comprise Chapter 3 of the Complaints Rules have the difficult task of achieving a balance between a speedy, informal and effective resolution mechanism that avoids legalism and a set of procedures that is fair, transparent and compliant with

---

[45]   2.7.3G.

[46]   May 1999 Implementing the Framework for Financial Services COM (1999) 232.

[47]   Ibid page 10.

[48]   Recommendation 98/257/CE.

the European Court of Human rights. Introductory guidance indicates the parameters for the achievement of that balance:

> "The Ombudsman will attempt to resolve complaints at the earliest possible stage and by whatever means appear to be most appropriate, including mediation or investigation. ...In deciding if there should be a hearing and, if so, whether it should be in public or private, the Ombudsman will have regard to the provisions of the European Convention on Human Rights."[49]

They deal with both the procedures for investigation and consideration of complaints by the Ombudsman along with the substantive bases for determination and making awards and costs awards. Important features include:

11.2.6.12   *Procedural stages of determination*

There are a variety of procedural safeguards for both complainant and respondent firms to make representations and request a hearing before any final determination is made.[50]

The rules permit the Ombudsman to terminate a complaint early without proceeding to a full determination without considering its merits on one of some 17 different grounds. These grounds range from the frivolous or vexatious nature of the complaint, through to where the Ombudsman "is satisfied that the complaint relates to a transaction which the firm in question has reviewed in accordance with the regulatory standards for the review, unless he is of the opinion that the standards did not address the particular circumstances of the case".[51] This provides some demarcation between any regulatorily ordained administrative review and redress procedure, such as the current pensions and FSAVC reviews, and the Ombudsman Scheme. The Ombudsman Scheme is not wholly inaccessible however to those dissatisfied with the outcome

---

[49]   DISP 3.2.10G and 3.2.14G.

[50]   DISP 3.2.5R, 3.2.7R, 3.2.11R, 3.2.12R and 3.2.13R.

[51]   DISP 3.3.1R(2) and (5) respectively.

of such reviews as the accompanying guidance provides that a complaint about the result of the review can be referred to the Ombudsman if it is alleged that the standards of any published regulatory guidance at the time have not been followed.[52]

Where the complaint is an eligible one and there is a reasonable prospect of resolution by mediation then the Ombudsman may attempt to negotiate a settlement.[53]

The rules as to the admissibility and form of evidence that may be heard by the Ombudsman aim to achieve maximum flexibility so that he has power to direct the issues on which evidence is required, the extent to which it should be written or oral and the way in which it should be presented to him. He may exclude evidence that would be admissible in court and court rules on inadmissibility do not apply.[54]

After the gathering and assessment of evidence, the stages through which the Ombudsman's determination will progress are as follows:

(a) once a complaint has been determined a signed written and reasoned statement of the determination will be given to both complainant and firm;

(b) the complainant's written acceptance or rejection by the due date of the determination will be invited;

(c) positive acceptance by the complainant within the specified time limit binds both the complainant and the firm finally;

(d) rejection of the determination or non-notification within the time limit by the complainant releases the respondent firm from any binding effect that the determination might otherwise have had;

(e) the respondent firm must be notified of the complainant's response (or lack thereof).[55]

---

[52]   DISP 3.3.4G.

[53]   DISP 3.2.9R.

[54]   DISP 3.5R.

[55]   DISP 3.8.3R.

11.2.6.13 Relationship between the courts and the Ombudsman

The Ombudsman may dismiss a complaint if either he is satisfied that the subject matter of the complaint has been the subject of court proceedings where there has been a decision on the merits, or is the subject of current court proceedings, or considers that it would be more suitable for the matter to be dealt with by a court, arbitration or another complaints scheme.[56]

One of the factors that the Ombudsman may take into account in making the latter assessment is, guidance suggests, where there is a conflict of evidence underlying the complaint whether its fair resolution could be achieved only through examination of the evidence by the courts.[57]

11.2.6.14 Referral of complaint to another body for determination

With the consent of the complainant the Ombudsman may redirect the complaint to another complaints scheme where he considers it could be more suitably determined.[58]

11.2.6.15 Basis of determination

The criteria with reference to which complaints are to be determined is as broadly phrased as possible and fuses the lodestars of the common law and equity when it calls upon the Ombudsman to determine complaints "by reference to what is, in his opinion, fair and reasonable in all the circumstances of the case".[59]

The rules do however provide some structure and content to the Ombudsman's assessment of fairness and reasonableness insofar as they state that he will "take into account the relevant law,

---

[56] DISP 3.3.1R (8), (9) and (10).

[57] DISP 3.3.5G.

[58] DISP 3.4.1R.

[59] DISP 3.8.1R (1).

regulations, regulators' rules and guidance and standards, relevant codes of practice and, where appropriate, what he considers to have been industry practice at the relevant time".[60]

There will therefore be a large body of legal and extra-legal material both substantive and procedural which can help the Ombudsman arrive at a determination and so firms may well wish to take account of these criteria in constructing their written and oral (where a hearing is held) submissions to the Ombudsman. The commitment for the Ombudsman to take into account material from such a wide range of sources, coupled with the duty to give reasons with its determinations will leave disgruntled respondent firms (on whom an unfavourable determination is binding and final) with the possibility in appropriate cases of an action for judicial review.

The Review of Banking Services in the UK recommended a more proactive standard setting role for the Ombudsman Scheme. It wished to see the rules specify that the Ombudsman should draw up consumer guidelines, after due consultation with interested parties including the Office of Fair Trading (the "OFT"), and that these guidelines should then be used to determine whether a banking supplier's actions are "fair and reasonable".[61] However in its subsequent response to this recommendation the FSA, after pointing out the broad range of hard and soft legal and regulatory material that the Ombudsman would be taking into account in making his determinations, replied that "making the Ombudsman a front-line standard setter could change the nature of the FOS from an organisation set up to resolve deadlocked consumer disputes to a regulator in its own right. It could introduce 'conduct of business' regulations for banking without the accountability and cost benefit analysis checks required of the FSA".[62]

---

[60]   DISP 3.8.1R (2).

[61]   Paragraph 4.112 *Review of Banking Services in the UK chaired by Cruickshank* (the "Cruickshank Report") (March 2000).

[62]   Paragraph 4.6 *Response by the FSA to the Cruickshank Report on Competition in UK Banking* (August 2000).

11.2.6.16   *Awards*

Where the Ombudsman decides to make a money award then the rules provide that "in addition to (or instead of) awarding compensation for financial loss, he may award compensation for pain and suffering, or damage to reputation, or distress or inconvenience,"[63] irrespective of whether or not a court would award compensation for such types of loss. The FOS was asked to provide further guidance in relation to what might constitute the latter two heads of loss and has undertaken to provide such guidance.[64] By way of example of reputational damage FOS singled out wrongly "bouncing" a customer's cheque. Assessment of financial loss can take into account consequential or prospective loss as well as actual loss and the maximum money award which can be made is £100,000.[65]

11.2.6.17   *Costs*

Despite the statutory power for the Ombudsman to award costs in a complainant's favour[66] guidance makes clear that it is not anticipated that such awards will be at all common since complainants are not expected to have any need for professional advisers to bring complaints before the Ombudsman.[67]

11.2.7   *Standard terms (for participation in the voluntary jurisdiction)*

These rules have been promulgated by the FOS as scheme operator and are the contractual terms which apply to firms which participate in the voluntary jurisdiction ("VJ participants").

---

[63]   DISP 3.9.2R.

[64]   Paragraph 4.50 FSA and FOS Response statement to CP49 (December 2000).

[65]   DISP 3.9.3G and 3.9.5R respectively.

[66]   Reflected in DISP 3.9.10R.

[67]   DISP 3.9.11G.

11.2.7.1   Scope and jurisdiction

The same rules as apply to delimit the scope of the compulsory jurisdiction (discussed in Section 11.2.7.8) are imported into the voluntary jurisdiction except, obviously for those rules which delimit the activities falling within the compulsory jurisdiction.

11.2.7.2   Complaint handling procedures for firms participating within the voluntary jurisdiction and awards

Again, the same rules and guidance that are applied by firms subject to the compulsory jurisdiction to firms' internal complaints handling procedures are imported into the voluntary jurisdiction.[68] Money awards may also be made in favour of the complainant where a complaint has been resolved in his favour under the voluntary jurisdiction.[69] Such an award can be made in respect of the same kind of loss or damage as may be compensated within the compulsory jurisdiction.

11.2.7.3   Exclusion of liability

The same immunity from liability in damages that is enjoyed under the FSMA[70] by the FOS, its staff and officers in relation to exercise of is functions under the compulsory jurisdiction is extended to their acts and omissions in the discharge of functions in connection with the voluntary jurisdiction.[71]

11.2.7.4   Withdrawal from voluntary jurisdiction

Voluntary jurisdiction participants may not unilaterally and immediately withdraw their participation without first setting out its written proposals to the FOS as to how it intends to notify its existing customers of its intention to withdraw from the voluntary jurisdiction and how it proposes to handle those complaints made

---

[68]   DISP 4.2.2R.

[69]   DISP 4.2.8R and DISP 4.2.9G.

[70]   Paragraph (10) Schedule 17 respectively.

[71]   DISP 4.27R.

against it prior to its withdrawal from the voluntary jurisdiction. It must then await formal approval of its withdrawal which must not take effect for at least six months from the date of such approval.[72]

11.2.7.5 *Compensation*

Consumers of financial services will, after commencement of the FSMA, continue to enjoy any rights to obtain redress that may arise under the general law and may also be able to bring an action in damages in respect of any of the contraventions of FSA requirements in respect of which the FSMA confers a right of action for breach of statutory duty on "private persons" and provides for the specification of certain circumstances in which non-private persons too may bring such action.[73] The difficulties faced by individuals in bringing and sustaining individual damages claims are, despite the recent changes to the administration of civil justice, still considerable which is why the FSA's right to take action against authorised persons to require restitution in favour of those who have suffered loss as a result of such persons' contravention of regulatory requirements[74] and it's right to apply to the High Court for restitution orders in such cases,[75] may prove of more assistance to more consumers in practice than their own individual rights of recovery in damages.

However the greatest assistance in respect of consumer losses in the past has come from the statutory safety net of the various compensation schemes operating across different sectors of the financial industry and it is the eligibility and entitlement to recover compensation under the new single Statutory Compensation Scheme set up by the FSMA to which the remainder of this Chapter

---

[72]   DISP 4.2.12R.

[73]   Sections 20(3), 71(2) and (3), 150 (3) and (5), 202 (2) and 241 FSMA. The Draft Financial Services and Markets Act 2000 (Rights of Action) Regulations 2001 specify the circumstances in which such action may be taken.

[74]   Section 384 FSMA.

[75]   Section 382 FSMA.

is devoted. The operation of these schemes has not given rise to quite extensive litigation. This has been so in particular with regard to both claim eligibility[76] and also finding a fair basis for firms' funding of such mutually based co-insurance of each others' liabilities of these schemes.[77]

11.2.7.6 *Transitional Arrangements for pre-N2 complaints*

Transitional Arrangements for the treatment of complaints which had been made or which could have been made to one of the former Ombudsman Schemes prior to N2 are contained in the Treasury's draft Order, the FSMA (Transitional Provisions) (Ombudsman Scheme and Complaints Scheme) Order 2001 (the "Draft Order"),[78] and corresponding amendments to the FOS rules.[79] The basic Scheme, as currently drafted, is that as of N2 the FOS will automatically inherit all pre-N2 complaints. The treatment of such complaints depends on whether they are categorised as "relevant existing complaints", that is, partly-completed complaints made to the former Schemes before N2, or "relevant new complaints", that is, complaints which are made to the FOS after N2 but which relate to pre-N2 business in respect of which the firm concerned was covered by a former Scheme. Relevant existing complaints are to be dealt

---

[76]   *Deposit Protection Board v. Dalia and Another* (HL) [1994] 2 All ER, *R v. Investors Compensation Scheme Ltd. ex parte Bowden and others* [1995] 3 All ER.

[77]   *Securities and Investments Board and Others v. Financial Intermediaries, Managers and Brokers Regulatory Association Ltd.* [1992] Ch. 268.

[78]   SI 2001 No. 2326.

[79]   The "final" FOS rules are contained in FSA/FOS Joint Policy Statement issued in December 2000 entitled *Complaints Handling Arrangements – Response on CP94*. The proposed amendments in respect of such transitional arrangements are contained in FSA/FOS Consultation Paper 99, entitled *Complaints-handling Rules: transitional arrangements and other arrangements.*

with largely under the rules of the relevant former Scheme,[80] with a few exceptions, while relevant new complaints are to be largely subject to the new rules, again with some exceptions.

11.3   The FSMA framework for Compensation Scheme

11.3.1   Scope

Part XV of the FSMA sets out the legislative basis for the new industry-wide single compensation scheme, the Financial Services Compensation Scheme, which replaces the five statutory compensation schemes that have been operating in the financial services sector: the Building Societies Investor Protection Scheme, the Deposit-Protection Scheme, the Friendly Societies Protection Scheme, the Investors Compensation Scheme and the Policyholders Protection Board. The FSA is charged by the Act with the duty of making rules "to establish a scheme for compensating persons in cases where relevant persons are unable, or are likely to be unable, to satisfy claims against them".[81]

To that end the FSA is further charged with the establishment of a corporate body referred to in this Part of the Act as the "scheme manager" and the maintenance of overall regulatory oversight of the scheme manager on a continuing basis to ensure that it is at all times capable of exercising the functions conferred on it by Part XV of the FSMA.[82] The core functions are:

(a)   the assessment and payment of compensation to claimants in respect of claims made in connection with regulated activities carried on (either with or without permission) by authorised persons or appointed representatives;[83] and

---

[80]   Including the relevant rules as to eligibility, dismissal of complaints without considering the merits, criteria to be applied to determine the complaint and the determinations, directions and awards that can be made.

[81]   Section 213(1).

[82]   Sections 212(1) and (2).

[83]   Section 213(3) (a).

(b) to impose levies on authorised persons or classes thereof for the purpose of financing the compensation scheme.[84]

The FSA has responsibility for appointment and removal from office of the chairman (in his case the responsibility is shared with HM Treasury) and members of the board but the terms of their appointment must be such as to secure their operational independence from the FSA.[85] The same immunity from liability in damages enjoyed by the FSA, the Ombudsman Scheme and their respective staff and officers is also extended to the scheme manager for acts and omissions done in the discharge of their functions under this Part of the FSMA Act.[86] Whether or not the scheme manager's board should have a specifically representative nature was the subject of some discussion at the committee stage of the FSMA where Opposition members pressed an amendment that would require at least three directors of the scheme manager to also be directors of authorised persons which they argued was an essential check on "how the industry's money was spent" within what was described as "yet another cost centre" within the new regulatory system.[87] However the Economic Secretary to HM Treasury made clear in response to the amendment that the board of the scheme manager was not supposed to represent any particular interest groups and so the appointment process remained open and free from quotas designed to secure any forms of representative. The scheme manager must report annually to the FSA on the discharge of its statutory functions.

Funding difficulties that have dogged the Investors Compensation Scheme in the past due to the widely different exposures and claims records of the different sectors of the industry that funded the

---

84   Section 213(3) (b).

85   Section 212.

86   Section 222.

87   HC Hansard 30 November 1999, Howard Flight M.P. in Standing Committee A consideration of Financial Services and Markets Bill.

scheme and the FSMA provides a basis for both the FSA and the new Scheme itself to recognise and reflect that factor in its levying of contributions on the industry after N2:

> "In making any provision [to impose levies on authorised persons or any class thereof to recover the cost of establishing the scheme] the [FSA] must take into account the desirability of ensuring that the amount of the levies imposed on a particular class of authorised person reflects, so far as practicable, the amount of the claims made, or likely to be made in respect of that class of person."[88]

This differentiated, risk related approach to funding is carried over in the conferment of FSA's wide rule-making competence so that the costs of running, as opposed to just establishing the Compensation Scheme will not fall disproportionately onto those whose activities have given rise to fewer claims. The non-exhaustive list of examples of matters which the Compensation Scheme Rules may provide for, given by FSMA include: the establishment of different funds for meeting different kinds of claim, the imposition of different levies in different cases, limiting the levy payable by a person in a specified period or for repayment of a levy in whole or in part.[89] Other important areas within rule-making competence are eligibility of claimants, maximum amounts of claim payable, circumstances in which a judgment will be made by the scheme manager that the authorised person or is likely to be unable to meet any claims against him. The FSMA also envisages that the territorial scope of the Scheme may be limited by the Scheme Rules and, specifically that certain categories of inwardly passporting firms may elect to participate in the Scheme in relation to some or all of the activities being conducted in the UK.[90]

---

88   Section 213(5).

89   Section 214 (1).

90   Section 214 (4) and (5).

If a claim has been paid by the Compensation Scheme in respect of the rights and liabilities of a relevant person in the event of that relevant person's insolvency, the FSMA provides that the Compensation Scheme may make provision for the scheme manager to enjoy a right to claim against that relevant person in place of the claimant.[91] Where the relevant person is insolvent however that right of recovery will not exceed such right (if any) as the claimant would have had against the relevant person.[92]

The FSMA makes special provision for compensation by the Compensation Scheme in relation to Insurers in financial difficulty[93] and, broadly, allows the Compensation Scheme to secure continuity

---

[91]   Section 215 (1) (b).

[92]   Section 215 (2).

[93]   The concept of financial difficulty is addressed slightly differently in each case (i.e. long-term and general insurance) and in both cases is introduced in the definition of "relevant insurer". In the context of long-term insurance, the Compensation Scheme will be able to make provisions under the relevant section of FSMA (Section 216) where the relevant insurer is "unable, or likely to be unable, to satisfy claims made against [it]" (Section 216(2)(b)). The same mechanism is used in the context of general insurance, except that the definition of "relevant insurer" refers to insurers "in financial difficulties" (Section 217 (2) (b)). The Financial Services Compensation Scheme Draft Rules (*see* Section 11.3.2 below) (the "Rules") outline the definition of "financial difficulties" which broadly covers situations where: (a) a company is in provisional liquidation; or (b) where it has been proved for the winding up of the relevant person under the Insolvency Act 1986 (or for the voluntary winding up of the relevant person where the Insolvency (Northern Ireland) Order 1989 is applicable) (unless in either case the petition is made for the purpose of reconstructing the relevant person or for amalgamating with another insurance company); or (c) an application has been made for the sanctioning of a compromise or arrangement between the relevant person and its creditors (Rule 3.5.2).

of insurance for policyholders, or policyholders of a specified class, in the context of both long-term and general insurance.[94]

In the context of long-term insurance, the Scheme may provide for the Scheme Manager to take such measures as appear to the Scheme Manager to be appropriate:

(a) for securing or facilitating the transfer of a relevant long-term insurer's business so far as it consists of the carrying out of contracts of long-term insurance, or any part of that business, to another authorised person;[95] and

(b) for securing the issue by another authorised person to the policyholders concerned of policies in substitution for their existing policies.[96]

The Scheme may also provide for the Scheme Manager to make payments to the policyholders concerned during any period in which he is making arrangements for securing continuity of their insurance.[97]

The powers of the Scheme Manager are similar in the context of general insurance. The Scheme Manager has the power to make interim payments in respect of eligible policyholders of a relevant insurer and to indemnify any person making payments to eligible

---

[94] Sections 216 and 217. Chapter 3 of the Rules sets out in general terms the conditions that must be satisfied before the Scheme Manager can make an offer of compensation, secure continuity of insurance cover, or provide assistance for an insurer to enable it to continue insurance business. The actual payment and calculation of compensation is dealt with by Chapters 11 and 12 respectively of the Rules.

[95] Section 216 (3) (a).

[96] Section 216 (3) (b).

[97] Section 216 (4) (a) and (b).

policyholders of a relevant insurer.[98] The Scheme may also provide for the FSA to have power to give such assistance to the Scheme Manager as it considers appropriate.[99]

The Scheme Manager also has a general power under the FSMA to require a relevant person to provide specified information or documents as the case may be.[100] The production of any documents held subject to a lien will not affect such lien.[101]

11.3.2   *Financial Services Compensation Scheme Rules*

At the time of writing, the Financial Services Compensation Scheme Rules were still in draft form (the "Rules"). The Rules have been made in accordance with the specific duty set out in Section 213(1) of the FSMA to establish the Compensation Scheme by such rules and may be divided into five broad headings:[102]

---

[98]   Section 217 (6).

[99]   Section 217 (5) (a).

[100]   Section 219.

[101]   Section 219(7).

[102]   These headings are taken from and based upon the executive summary to Consultation Paper 58 headed *Financial Services Compensation Scheme Draft Rules* at page 3.

(a) the powers and accountability of the Scheme Manager;[103]

(b) the conditions to be met before compensation can be offered;

(c) the criteria for assessing how much compensation should be paid;

(d) how the Scheme Manager may levy contributions to meet the costs of paying compensation; and

(e) EEA firms' participation in the Scheme.

Sections (a) and (b) above are dealt with in this Chapter.

11.3.2.1   Conditions to be met before compensation can be offered

The following criteria must be satisfied in order to be offered compensation[104] (the words in italics are terms defined in the Rules):

---

[103]   Under Section 212 (1) FSMA, the FSA must establish a body corporate to be the Scheme Manager. Financial Services Compensation Scheme Limited, a company limited by guarantee, has been incorporated on 3 March 2000 for this purpose. Chapter 2 of the Rules sets out the powers (and restrictions on them) of the Scheme Manager. Chapter 2 also describes briefly the relationship between the Scheme Manager and the FSA. Chapter 2 of the Rules also requires the Scheme Manager to make and publish an annual report to the FSA on the discharge of its functions and on the operation of the Scheme covering each financial year (COMP 2.6.1R of the Rules). The Scheme Manager must also make a regular three-monthly report to the FSA within one month of the period reported on, and must give details of the exercise by the Scheme Manager of its powers of management and such other information as the FSA may request from time to time (COMP 2.7.1R of the Rules).

[104]   *See* Table COMP 1.5(1)G of the Rules. The Scheme Manager is required to take reasonable steps to inform potential claimants how they can make a claim for compensation as soon as possible after the Scheme Manager has become satisfied that a relevant person is unable or likely to be unable to meet claims against the relevant person in relation to regulated activities that constitute Scheme business (COMP 2.11.1R of the Rules).

(a) the claimant must be an *eligible claimant*;

(b) the claimant must have a *protected claim*;

(c) the claimant must be claiming against a *relevant person*;

(d) the *relevant person* must be *in default*.

In addition, the Scheme Manager will ordinarily[105] require the claimant to assign his legal rights in the claim to the Scheme Manager and the claim must be brought within a set time (normally within six years from the date of the claim). The component parts of the above are addressed below in turn.

11.3.2.1.1   Eligible claimant

Broadly, all private customers other than large companies or large partnerships (as each is defined in the Rules) will be eligible claimants whatever type of claim they have.[106] Certain other categories of customer as they are classed and defined in the Rules, for example Intermediate Customers and Market Counterparties, will be more restricted in the types of claim which they may bring and certain customers with a connection to the defaulting firm and companies within the same group will not be eligible to claim compensation.[107]

---

[105] The guidance to COMP 7.2.1G states that the FSA anticipates that the Scheme Manager will make an offer of compensation conditional on the assignment of rights to it by a claimant. Chapter 7 of the Rules deals with assignment of rights.

[106] COMP 4.3.3G. The mechanics for working out whether a person is an eligible person is set out in COMP 4.3.1R and COMP 4.3.2R of the Rules.

[107] Table COMP 4.3(1)R sets out a list of potentially ineligible claimants. Persons falling within the table will however be able to claim compensation in respect of a liability subject to compulsory insurance (this is defined in the Rules and includes, for example, insurance required under Part VI of the Road Traffic Act 1988).

11.3.2.1.2   Protected claim

The types of claim which a claimant may bring are divided into three general headings in the Rules[108] and are in respect of the civil liabilities owed in respect of the claim by a relevant person:

(a) a claim for a protected deposit;

(b) a claim for a protected contract of insurance;

(c) a claim relating to protected investment business.

Protected deposits[109] include:

(a) credit balances, denominated in any currency, resulting from funds left in an account;

(b) any debt evidenced by a certificate issued by a credit institution;[110] or

(c) any share in a building society which is not of a capital nature. Certain deposits are excluded however, for example building society deferred shares, secured deposits and any deposit made without disclosing the depositor's identity.[111]

Protected contracts of insurance includes contracts of insurance issued by a relevant person through an establishment in the UK, the EEA or the Channel Islands or the Isle of Man (or a contract of insurance issued by an EEA firm through an establishment in an

---

[108]   Rule 5.3.1.

[109]   "Deposit" itself is a defined term in the Rules and means a sum of money paid on terms: (a) under which it will be repaid with or without interest and either on demand or at an agreed date; and (b) which are not referable to the provision of property or services or the giving of security. Mortgage loan accounts for example would be excluded from the definition.

[110]   Defined in the Rules as "an undertaking whose business is to receive deposits or other payable funds from the public and to grant credits for its own account, as defined in Article 1 of the First Banking Coordination Directive".

[111]   These and further exclusions are set out at COMP 5.4.4R of the Rules.

EEA state) which relates to a protected risk or commitment.[112] Certain contracts of insurance are excluded, for example contracts of insurance relating to aircraft, ships and goods in transport, contracts of reinsurance and contracts of insurance written at Lloyds.[113]

Protected investment business includes designated investment business[114] carried on by the following: certain authorised persons; a branch of a UK firm carried on elsewhere in the EEA; an EEA firm carrying on home state regulated activity from a branch in the UK which has elected to participate in the Compensation Scheme; or an appointed representative.

11.3.2.1.3 *Relevant person*

The Rules define a "relevant person" as a person who was at the time the act or omission giving rise to the claim took place:

(a) an authorised person;[115]

(b) a UK branch of an EEA firm carrying on home state regulated activity;[116] or

(c) an appointed representative of (a) or (b).[117]

---

112   COMP 5.5.1R of the Rules.

113   COMP 5.5.2R of the Rules.

114   "Designated investment business" is defined as: (a) a regulated activity in relation to a designated investment; and (b) an ancillary activity in relation to a designated investment.

115   "Authorised person" does not include in this context an EEA firm carrying on home state regulated activity (within the meaning of the Rules) from a branch in the UK under the provisions of the Second Banking Co-ordination Directive or the Investment Services Directive.

116   Under the provisions of the Second Banking Co-ordination Directive or the Investment Services Directive.

117   COMP 6.3.1R of the Rules.

11.3.2.1.4   *In default*

A relevant person will be in default when he is in the opinion of the Scheme Manager either unable or likely to be unable to satisfy protected claims against him.[118] Ordinarily,[119] the Scheme Manager will determine a relevant person to be in default if one or more of the following circumstances arise in relation to that person:

(a) the passing of a resolution for a creditors' voluntary winding up;

(b) a determination of insolvency by the relevant person's home state regulator;

(c) the appointment of a liquidator or administrator, or provisional liquidator or interim manager;

(d) the making of an order for the winding up, administration or bankruptcy of that person (as the case may be);

(e) the approval of a company or individual voluntary arrangement (whichever is applicable to the relevant person);

(f) the Scheme Manager is satisfied that the relevant person cannot be contacted at his last place of business and that all reasonable steps have been taken to establish a forwarding or current address but without success;

(g) the claim is in respect of protected investment business and there is no evidence that the relevant person will be able to meet claims made against it.

---

[118]   COMP 6.4.1R of the Rules.

[119]   Under COMP 6.4.5R of the Rules, where the protected claim arises out of activity relating to the Second Banking Co-ordination Directive or the Investment Services Directive, the FSA is to determine whether the relevant person is in default, unless a judicial authority has made an earlier ruling which had the effect of suspending the ability of eligible claimants to bring claims against the relevant person (in which case the relevant person will automatically be in default in terms of the Rules).

The Scheme Manager is obliged to give the relevant person notice that the relevant person is in default if the relevant person is, or appears to be, carrying on business or if the relevant person was at the time of default a sole trader or a partnership. The notice is to set out the reasons for the Scheme Manager's opinion.

The Rules allow the relevant person to make representations at a hearing (which may be in public) and the Scheme Manager must take account of any decision reached at the hearing.[120]

11.3.2.2   *The criteria for assessing how compensation should be paid*

The amount of compensation which will be received and its method of calculation will depend on the whether the claim is a protected deposit claim, a protected contract of insurance claim or a protected investment business claim.[121]

There is a limit on the amount which the Scheme Manager can pay, depending on the type of claim. The limits are as follows:[122]

---

[120]   COMP 6.4.10R of the Rules. Nothing further is said however in the Rules as to how the hearing is to be conducted or what weight the Scheme Manager must place on the findings of the hearing.

[121]   *See* paragraph 11.3.2 above of this Chapter.

[122]   The table is based on Table COMP 10.3(1)R of the Rules.

Type of claim	Level of cover	Maximum payment
Protected deposits	100 per cent of first £2,000 of claim; and 90 per cent of next £33,000 of claim.	£31,700
Protected insurance contracts when the contract is a general insurance contract	Where the claim is in respect of a liability subject to compulsory liability insurance:[123] 100 per cent of the value of the claim.	Unlimited
	In all other cases: 100 per cent of the first £2,000 of a valid claim; and 90 per cent of the remainder.	Unlimited
Protected insurance contracts when the contract is a long-term insurance contract	At least 90 per cent of the value of the policy (including future benefits declared before the date of default).	Unlimited
Protected investment business	100 per cent of the first £30,000 of the claim; and 90 per cent of the next £20,000 of the claim.	£48,000

The Scheme Manager will ordinarily pay compensation for protected contracts of insurance only in circumstances where the Scheme Manager is unable to secure continuity of insurance or decides not to take measures to safeguard policyholders.[124] Those measures may

---

[123]   *See* footnote 103 above.

[124]   COMP 10.3.3G. This is particularly dealt with at COMP 3.4 and 3.5 of the Rules.

include, for example, securing or facilitating the transfer of an insurance business to another insurer or securing the issue of policies in substitution for the claimants' existing policies.[125]

The Scheme Manager may also pay interest on any compensation sum paid out under Chapter 11 of the Rules where the Scheme Manager considers it would be appropriate.[126] Interest must be paid at a rate no higher than the base rate of a clearing bank in the UK during the period to which the interest relates.[127] Any interest paid is not to be taken into account when applying the limits on the compensation sum available (*see* table above).[128]

Chapter 12 of the Rules sets out how (and from when) a claim will be quantified and will broadly be the sum of the claimant's protected claims against the relevant person in default, less the amount of any liability which the relevant person may set off against any of those claims.[129] Where the claimant is a trustee and some of the beneficiaries of the trust are persons who would not be eligible claimants if they had a claim themselves, the Scheme Manager must adjust the amount of the overall net claim to eliminate that part of the claim which in the Scheme Manager's view is a claim for those beneficiaries.[130]

---

[125]   COMP 3.4.3R and 3.5.1 of the Rules.

[126]   COMP 11.3.7R of the Rules.

[127]   COMP 11.3.8R of the Rules.

[128]   COMP 11.3.9R of the Rules. The guidance at COMP 11.3.10G of the Rules gives the following example by way of illustration: if A has a protected investment business claim of £50,000, the Scheme Manager can pay A £48,000 by way of compensation. If the Scheme Manager decides that interest is payable, and the interest totals £5,000, the interest will be paid to A in full, along with the £48,000. It is not aggregated to A's claim to make a claim for £55,000 (on which £48,000 would be the maximum sum that the Scheme Manager could pay).

[129]   COMP 12.4.1R of the Rules.

[130]   COMP 12.4.2R of the Rules.

GLOSSARY

APER	Statements of Principle and Code of Practice for Approved Persons
AUTH	Authorisation Manual
AUTIF	Association of Unit Trusts and Investment Firms
BSC	Building Societies Commission
CF	Controlled Function
CIS	Collective Investment Scheme
COB	Conduct of Business Sourcebook
CP	Consultation Paper (as issued by FSA)
EEA	European Economic Area
ENF	Enforcement Manual
FESCO	Forum of European Securities Commission
FIT	Fitness and Propriety Manual
FS Act	Financial Services Act 1986
FSA	Financial Services Authority
FSMA	Financial Services and Markets Act 2000
IMRO	Investment Management Regulatory Organisation
IOSCO	International Organisation of Securities Commissions
IPC	Inter-professional Conduct

ISD	Investment Services Directive
JMLSG	Joint Money Laundering Steering Group
LCC	London Code of Conduct
MAR	Market Conduct Manual
MLRO	Money Laundering Reporting Officer
N2	The date on which the FSA acquires its full powers under the FSMA, fixed for midnight on 30 November 2001
NMPT	Non-market price transaction
PIA	Personal Investment Authority
RAO	Financial Services and Markets Act 2000 (Regulated Activities) Order 2001
RIE	Recognised Investment Exchange
RPB	Recognised Professional Body
SIB	Securities and Investments Board
SFA	Securities and Futures Authority
SRO	Self Regulatory Organisation
SUP	Supervision Manual
SYSC	Senior Management Arrangements, Systems and Controls
TAP	Training Advisory Panel
TC	Training and Competence Sourcebook
UCITS	Undertakings for Collective Investment in Transferable Securities

INDEX

NB: All references are to chapter number followed by paragraph number, e.g. 7.11.3 refers to Chapter 7, paragraph 11.3